WOMEN ON THE MARGINS

Women on the Margins

THREE SEVENTEENTH–CENTURY LIVES

Natalie Zemon DAVIS

HARVARD UNIVERSITY PRESS

Cambridge, Massachusetts

London, England

1995

Second printing, 1995

Library of Congress Cataloging-in-Publication Data
Davis, Natalie Zemon, 1928–
Women on the margins: three seventeenth-century lives /
Natalie Zemon Davis.
p.   cm.
Includes bibliographical references and index.
ISBN 0–674–95520–X (alk. paper)
1. Women—Biography.   2. Biography—17th century.   3. Glueckel, of
Hameln, 1646–1724.   4. Marie de l'Incarnation, mère, 1599–1672.
5. Merian, Maria Sibylla, 1647–1717.   6. Jewish women—Germany—
Biography.   7. Women merchants—Germany—Biography.   8. Women
missionaries—Québec (Province)—Biography.   9. Protestant women—
Surinam—Biography.   I. Title.
CT3233.D38 1995
920.72′09′032—dc20
95–17094

TO THE MEMORY OF

Rosalie Colie
(1924–1972)

AND

Michel de Certeau
(1925–1986)

CONTENTS

WOMEN ON THE MARGINS

PROLOGUE

Place: Thoughtland

Time: October 1994, Heshvan 5755

Persons: Four women past sixty. Three of them stand near a well-thumbed manuscript, sometimes addressing each other, sometimes musing to themselves. The fourth listens for a time from the shadows.

Marie de l'Incarnation: I've read it. I'm scandalized. Imagine her enclosing me in a book with such godless women.

Glikl bas Judah Leib: What do you mean? God, may he and his name be praised, was always in my heart and on my lips. You can't understand a word I wrote.

Marie de l'Incarnation: I could have learned Yiddish if Our Lord had wanted me to. I learned Huron, didn't I? I read what she said about how you cared about money. You Jews are as hardhearted as the Huguenots. I thank my Beloved Spouse that he called me to the Savages far from Europe.

Glikl bas Judah Leib: I read what she said about how you left your son before he was set in life. Never in all my trials and sorrows would I have neglected my children. I don't belong in a book with such a mother. And why should she put me together with non-Jews at all?

Maria Sibylla Merian: I am completely out of place here. These women were not lovers of nature. They had no eyes for God's small creatures and their beauty. They didn't read the kind of books I did or talk to the kind of people I did. This is not my setting.

Marie de l'Incarnation: Listen to Mistress Proud and Haughty. But what can you expect from a woman who even began to doubt the adorable Incarnate Word? To think we are back-to-back in the same pages. I wouldn't have minded if she had put me with those who have tried to spread the universal kingdom of God.

Glikl bas Judah Leib: I wouldn't have minded if the author had just written about me and my stories for her Jewish children and grandchildren.

Maria Sibylla Merian: I don't object to being in a book with Jews and Catholics. In fact, I was pleased to discover that the learned Salomon Perez wrote a poem for the edition of my Suriname book that came out after I died. But I don't belong in a book about "women." I should be together with the students and painters of nature, with scholars of insects and plants.

Natalie Zemon Davis (stepping forward from the shadows): I'm the author. Let me explain.

The Other Three Women: You have a lot of explaining to do.

NZD: Glikl bas Judah Leib, you told stories in your memoirs about non-Jews as well as Jews. Mistress Merian, you mixed studies of butterflies with those of other insects. I put you together to learn from your similarities and differences. In my day it is sometimes said that women of the past resemble one another, especially if they live in the same kind of place. I wanted to show where you were alike and where you were not, in how you talked about yourselves and what you did. Where you were different from the men in your world and where you were the same—

Maria Sibylla Merian: That's better kept a secret.

NZD: To show how each of you wrote about relations with people outside your world.

Glikl bas Judah Leib: That's better kept a secret.

NZD: I chose you because you were all city women, the daughters of merchants and artisans—of commoners—in France and in the German states.

Glikl bas Judah Leib: You know perfectly well that among the children of Israel, however illustrious our families, we do not talk about commoners and nobles.

NZD: I wanted to have a Jew, a Catholic, and a Protestant so I could see what difference religion made in women's lives, what doors it opened for you and what doors it closed, what words and actions it allowed you to choose.

Marie de l'Incarnation: Choose? Choosing religion means becoming a nun—

Maria Sibylla Merian:—or joining a community of the repentant—

Marie de l'Incarnation: But worshiping God is a matter of truth and absolute obligation.

Glikl bas Judah Leib: With that last remark of the Catholic, because of our sins, I have to agree.

NZD: Mother Marie, the *Chronicles* of your Ursulines are full of women's struggles. I wanted to find out whether you three women had struggles with gender hierarchies.

The Other Three Women (indignantly): *Gender* hierarchies? What are gender hierarchies?

NZD: Look what happened, Mistress Merian, when you went to Suriname to observe its insects. If you'd been a man, some important person would have paid your way. You had to borrow the money to do it.

Maria Sibylla Merian: Yes, and I paid back every cent.

NZD: Glikl bas Judah Leib, you wrote of your husband Haim ben Joseph as a "shepherd" and he called you "my child."

Glikl bas Judah Leib: "Gliklikhen," "min Gliklikhen." What other words to use for a couple as dear to each other as we were?

NZD: Why did you always call your sons "rabbi," but never give your daughters any special title?

Glikl bas Judah Leib: That is the question of a wicked daughter at the Passover Seder.

NZD: But I didn't portray you three as merely long-suffering. I also showed how women in your position made the best of it. I asked what advantages you had by being on the margins.

Glikl bas Judah Leib: Margins are where I read comments in my Yiddish books.

Marie de l'Incarnation: In my Christian books.

Maria Sibylla Merian: River margins are the dwelling place of frogs.

NZD (desperately): You *found* things on margins. You were all adventurous. You each tried to do something no one had ever done before. I wondered what the sources and the costs of adventure were—for Europeans and for non-Europeans—in the seventeenth century.

Marie de l'Incarnation: The Lord did not summon me to "adventures."

Maria Sibylla Merian: It sounds to me, historian Davis, as though *you're* the one who wanted adventures.

NZD (after a pause): Yes, it was an adventure following you three to so many different climes. And I wanted to write of your hopes for paradise on earth, for remade worlds, since I have had those hopes, too. At least you all must admit that you loved to describe your world. Glikl and Marie, how you loved to write! And Maria Sibylla, how you loved to look and paint!

The Other Three Women: Well . . . maybe, maybe . . .

NZD: Give me another chance. Read it again.

Arguing with God

IN THE LAST DECADE of the seventeenth century—the year 5451 by the Jewish reckoning—a Jewish merchant woman of Hamburg wrote down a story for her many children. It told of a father bird who lived with his three fledglings along a seashore. One day a fierce storm came up, sending huge waves over the sands. "If we cannot get to the other side at once we are lost," said the bird, and took the first fledgling into his claws and started over the sea. Halfway across, the parent said to his son, "What troubles I have to stand from you! And now I'm risking my life-strength for you. When I am old, will you also do good to me and support me?" The little bird replied, "My dear beloved father, just take me across the water. I will do for you in your old age all that you want of me." Whereupon the parent dropped the birdling into the sea and said, "So should be done with a liar like you."

The parent bird flew back for the second fledgling and halfway across said to it the same words. The little bird promised to do for him all the good in the world. Again the father dropped his young into the sea, saying, "You, too, are a liar." Carrying the third birdling across the water, he asked the same question. The little bird answered, "Father, dear father, all that you say is true, that you have had troubles and grief because of me. I am duty bound to repay you, if it is possible; but I cannot promise for certain. This, however, I can promise: when one day I have young children of my own, I will do for them as you have done for me."

At this, the father said, "You speak aright and are also clever. I will let you live and will take you across the water."[1]

Glikl's story of the un-Learlike bird was not an immediate message to her offspring. Though some of her twelve living children were still fledglings when she wrote—they ranged in age from two to twenty-eight—she did not intend them to read or hear her narrative right away. Rather, the bird story was one of the opening tales in a carefully constructed Yiddish autobiography, which she would complete over the years and pass on to her children at her death. For the time being, as she strove to order the hopes, joys, and disappointments of her life, she was addressing herself as much as she was addressing her children. The resulting book, mingling Glikl's tales with Glikl's account of her vicissitudes, is remarkable. Not only is it a rich source for the social and cultural history of Ashkenaz and of seventeenth-century Europe; it is also an autobiography of unusual literary structure and religious resonance.

Michel de Certeau has given us much guidance on the unfolding of early modern spirituality in the course of autobiographical composition. Spiritual discoveries are made through dialogue. Pierre Favre, a Jesuit of the generation of Ignatius Loyola, reviewed his life when he was in his early forties, looking for signs of God's graces and recording his prayers and meditations in churches across Europe. The dialogue in his *Memorial* is between the "I" of himself and the "you" of his soul, the self imploring the reluctant soul to receive God's love. In her *Libro de la vida*, the Carmelite Teresa of Avila created two dialogues. One is between the ecstatic self who loves God to distraction and the authorial self who keeps the life on track by ordered writing. The other is between the learned men who have commanded her to write the book and who will judge it and the female readers who will understand it with a special love. In the autobiography of the Ursuline prioress Jeanne des Anges (1605–1665), it is precisely the lack of dialogue which, according to de Certeau, sets a limit to spiritual advancement. As she describes her demonic possession and her cure, she puts on mask after mask, studying how to please all around her: her sister Ursulines, her demons, her Jesuit exorcisers, and the Ursuline authority who ordered her to write her book. There is no internal I and you, no *je* and *tu*, in the account, but only "I" and "me."[2]

Storytelling did not come up in Michel de Certeau's discussion of these three figures—these Catholics recounted only their visions and dreams, not traditional tales—but he did analyze the power of stories in his *Practice of Everyday Life*. Stories set up a special space for themselves with their "once upon a time." They are an economical instrument for making a point, for striking a blow, "for taking advantage of an occasion . . . by taking it by surprise." The storyteller can move into the way others remember the past and change it merely by introducing an unexpected detail into a familiar account. Everything depends on the skill of the teller, on how she or he takes the stories from the "collective treasury of legends or everyday conversation" and puts them into play.[3]

In this chapter I would like to explore the thematic structures in the autobiography of the woman known in published works since the end of the nineteenth century as "Glückel von Hameln" or "Gluckel of Hameln," the life events she thought worth describing, celebrating, or complaining about, and the surprises of her storytelling. We will listen for her dialogues, for the inner contention around which her life swirled, and for her account of why things happened to her and others as they did. We will see how Christians figured in the recital of this woman so identified with the religion that Teresa of Avila's grandfather and father abandoned many years before. How did Glikl locate herself and her people in a world where Christians thought Jews should be on margins or in ghettos or excluded altogether? And what cultural resources were available to a Jewish woman in seventeenth-century Europe—resources that she could bend to her own use, that would supply the notes with which she could find her own voice?[4]

But first, some facts about Glikl, starting with her name. "Glückel von Hameln" was assigned to her in 1896 by the editor of the first published edition of the Yiddish memoirs, a good German-sounding first name and a last name with an aristocratic "von" that evoked her husband, Haim, born in the town of Hameln. But it was "Glikl" that circulated in the Yiddish accents around her and in the written name in the seventeenth century,[5] whereas a woman's signature in the Jewish mode associated her not with her husband but with her father. (This was also the case in seventeenth-century France, where the woman's last name was taken from her father and her marital status was indicated by the notary's added phrase "wife of so-and-so" or "widow of so-and-so." In Germany in the late seventeenth century, Christian women increasingly took their husband's name upon marriage, adding their maiden name under certain circumstances: *"geboren Merian."*)

So Glikl's daughters signed in Hebrew characters "Esther bas reb Haim," "Miriam bas reb Haim" ("Esther daughter of our teacher Haim," "Miriam daughter of our teacher Haim"), sometimes adding "Segal" to stress their father's origins in the house of Levi. If signing in a non-Hebrew script, a Jewish woman added one of the surnames her father had assumed for Christian recordkeepers and Jewish tax collectors: Glikl's married daughters wrote "Goldschmidt" for the Christian notaries in France (as we can see in the picture given in this book), whereas Glikl's sons in Germany used sometimes "Hamel" and sometimes "Goldschmidt."[6] Meanwhile, Jewish scribes might designate a woman's status through her husband, as Glikl was in the Jewish community tax book after Haim Hamel died: "Almone Glikl," "the widow Glikl" (but not "widow Glikl Hamel"). When she herself died in France, the civil records identified her as "Guelic, widow of Cerf Levy" (Levy was her second husband), but the Jewish memorial book named her more traditionally by her father, as it did men as well: "Glik, the daughter of Judah Joseph of blessed memory from Hamburg."[7]

Jewish names slipped and slid about in the seventeenth and early eighteenth centuries much more than Christian names, rather to the enjoyment of their referents. I will call Glikl by the Jewish name that she is most likely to have used herself: Glikl bas Judah Leib, Glikl daughter of Judah Leib, the name she chose among her father's names to give to her son born after his death.[8]

Glikl was born in Hamburg in late 1646 or in 1647, one of the six children born to Judah Joseph, also known as Leib, a trader and notable of the German-Jewish community, and to the businesswoman Beila, daughter of Nathan Melrich of nearby Altona.[9] At mid-century the Free and Hanseatic City of Hamburg was a thriving cosmopolitan port of more than 60,000 people, a commercial center and financial market with connections to Spain, Russia, London, and the New World.[10] The Jews had been part of this expansion. In 1612 the Hamburg Senate had signed an agreement with the small community of Portuguese Jews (or Sephardim, as Glikl usually called them), many of them prosperous international bankers and merchants; the agreement allowed them to reside and trade in the city as aliens or "protected Jews" in return for an annual payment.[11] By the 1660s they numbered about 600 people and were trying to turn their informal prayer houses into a synagogue. When Queen Christina of Sweden visited Hamburg in 1667, she and her entourage stayed for more than a month in the fine house of her Jewish bankers, Abraham and Isaac Teixeira, not far from Saint Michael's Church.[12]

Not all Hamburg residents welcomed these developments. The Lutheran clergy fumed to the Senate about its tolerant policies toward the Jews. "In their synagogue there are loud murmurs and cries . . . They practice their own Sabbath not ours . . . They keep Christian manservants and maidservants in their employ . . .

Their rabbis dispute without fear against our Messiah."[13] The Senate, concerned to sustain the city's economic expansion, did what it could to keep the great bankers in the city, though in 1674 the Sephardim were ordered to close their synagogue. Their numbers began to dwindle, and in 1697, when the Senate demanded a high fee from the Portuguese Jews and reduced their distinctive status, Teixeira and others left for Amsterdam.

The German Jewish community then became the center of Jewish life in Hamburg—the *hochdeutsche Juden,* as the Senate called them.[14] Back in the 1630s and 1640s, a few dozen families of German Jews (among them Glikl's father) had filtered into the city without official permission, trading in gold and jewels, lending money, handcrafting small items, and preserving their insecure status by informal tax payments to the government. Whereas most of the Sephardim lived in the Old City, the Ashkenazim clustered to the west in the New City, not far from the Miller's Gate.[15]

This location was convenient for the German Jews, and not merely because it symbolized the possibility of a quick getaway. It shortened their walk a few miles west to the city of Altona, where Jews enjoyed official "protected" status under the tolerant eye of the counts of Holstein-Schauenburg and (after 1640) of the kings of Denmark. It was to Altona that the German Jews repaired when the Hamburg Senate, goaded by the Lutheran clergy and complaints from the Bürgerschaft (the town Assembly), expelled them in 1650.

In the next years, German Jews slipped into Hamburg to trade, braving attacks from soldiers and sailors as they passed through the Miller's Gate and risking arrest if they had not paid an escort fee. After the Swedish invasion of Altona in 1657, the Senate allowed the *hochdeutsche Juden* to reside in Hamburg once again, though they were not to scandalize Christians by practicing their religion in any way within its walls. To attend synagogue and bury their dead, the German Jews were supposed to go to Altona, and their community organization—their Jüdische Gemeinde— was based in Altona as well.[16]

By the last decade of the century, the population and prosperity of the German Jews had multiplied. If they could still arouse suspicion and violence among Hamburg journeymen and prompt theologians' outrage about, say, the blatant "superstition" of their Sabbath lamps, kept alight for twenty-four hours so as not to violate the Lord's command, they now had supporters from beyond the Senate: people who saw them as potential converts to Christianity or as valuable contributors to the economy. In 1697, when the Senate offered the *hochdeutsche Juden* a contract to regularize their status in return for a fee higher than that demanded of the Portuguese Jews, they agreed to pay. Finally, in 1710, they were allowed to have a Gemeinde of their own in Hamburg.[17]

Glikl's childhood in the 1650s was thus spent during the years of uneasy Jewish movement between Hamburg and Altona. She recalled that her father had been the first German Jew to get permission to resettle in Hamburg after the Swedish invasion, but as a parnas (elder of the Gemeinde) he had to cross back to Altona for community business and prayer whenever the risk of conducting illegal services in Hamburg was too great.[18]

Glikl's girlhood was brief. Before she turned twelve, she was betrothed to Haim, only a few years older, the son of the trader Joseph ben Baruch Daniel Samuel ha-Levi (or Segal), known also as Joseph Goldschmidt and Joseph Hamel, of the small town of Hameln.[19] She was wed to him two years later. This early age of marriage was much in contrast with that of the Christian women in Hamburg and elsewhere in western Europe, who rarely took their vows before they were eighteen, but it was not uncommon among better-off Jews in central and eastern Europe.[20] Among other uses, it guaranteed a Jewish marriage to the parents' liking and promoted the *mitzvot*—the command and the good deed—of progeny. And why wait when parents were endowing the young with credit connections and liquid capital rather than landed property or a craftsman's shop? Furthermore, the newlyweds could be shepherded through the first period of marriage by the Jewish custom of *kest*, or boarding, provided for in the marriage contract.

After a year with Haim's family in Hameln and a year with Glikl's family in Hamburg, the couple established themselves on their own with two servants in a rented house—all a Jew was permitted to have—in the Ashkenazic section of the New City not far from the Elbe.[21] Over the next three decades they brought fourteen children into the world, one dying in infancy, another dying near the age of three, the other six boys and six girls living long enough to marry and, in all but one case, to have children of their own.[22] For seventeenth-century Europe, where a third to a half of those born died before they were ten, this is a remarkable record for getting children to the other side of the sea, even in the case of a well-off family where the mother wet-nursed her own children.[23]

Meanwhile, Haim traded in gold, silver, pearls, jewels, and money, arranging sales from Moscow and Danzig to Copenhagen, Amsterdam, and London. The fairs of Leipzig and Frankfurt am Main he attended regularly, while usually employing other German Jews as agents or partners to travel elsewhere. Glikl participated in all the business decisions ("he sought no advice from anyone, having talked over everything with me"), drew up the partnership contracts, and helped with the books and the local pledges. The couple started out young and "without great wealth," said Glikl, but eventually could draw on much credit in Hamburg and elsewhere. Haim was becoming one of the most prosperous of Hamburg's Ashkenazim.[24]

Then, one evening in January 1689, Haim fell on a sharp stone as he was on his way to the non-Jewish quarter of Hamburg for a business appointment. A few days later he was dead, and Glikl was left a widow with eight children still at home to raise, dower, and marry. In the next years, she carried on the Jewish strategy of marrying some of her children close to home and some of them in distant cities. Before Haim's death, two sons had been married in Hamburg, a daughter in Hannover, and the oldest daughter, Zipporah, in Amsterdam. Glikl's matchmaking placed Esther in Metz, and other children in Berlin, Copenhagen, Bamberg, and Baiersdorf, with only daughter Freudchen settling for a time in Hamburg.[25]

What were the reasons for such a policy? In part, it resulted from the fact that there were insufficient Ashkenazim of the proper status to go around in any single locality, even when one took advantage of the Jewish law permitting first cousins to marry (as did Haim and Glikl for one of their daughters). More important, the wide dispersal of one's kin was an economic advantage and a safety measure. One never knew when the wheel of fortune might turn: in 1674 and 1697 demands to expel the German Jews were voiced again in Hamburg, though they were thwarted by the Senate and other economically minded segments of the Hamburg citizenry; in 1670 the Jews had been let into Berlin to reside, but in 1669–1670 they had been expelled from Vienna and were able to return only at the end of the decade. The wedding of Glikl's son Moses to the daughter of Samson Baiersdorf, court Jew to the Margrave of Bayreuth, was held up for a year when a new counselor to the Margrave tried to destroy Samson.[26] "Another Haman," said Glikl of Samson's enemy, referring to the wicked counselor who, in the Book of Esther, threatened to kill the Jews.

As for the family business, Haim had felt no need to name executors or guardians ("My wife knows about everything," he said on his deathbed),[27] and the widowed Glikl assumed the responsibility herself. After an initial and profitable auction to pay off her husband's debts, she survived pressure from creditors both on her and her son Mordecai. Ultimately she developed sufficient business activities to be able to marshal immediately 20,000 reichstaler in notes on the Hamburg Exchange from Jews and Christians alike—a rating well below that of the great bankers, but quite substantial nonetheless.[28] She set up a shop in Hamburg for manufacturing stockings and sold them near and far; she bought pearls from every Jew in town, sorted them, and sold them by size to appropriate buyers; she imported wares from Holland and traded them in her store along with local goods; she attended the fairs of Braunschweig, Leipzig, and other towns; she lent money and honored bills of exchange across Europe. Unlike Haim, she did not have partners or agents outside the family: one of her elder sons, Nathan or Mordecai, would accompany her to fairs (a respectable woman could not travel alone),[29] while a son might be sent, say, to Frankfurt am Main to sell goods on her account. Even more than Haim, she never let a moment for trade be lost. Her many trips for negotiating marriages or weddings brought their profits: precious stones sold at Amsterdam after Esther's wedding, a fair at Naumburg fitted in after a betrothal agreement in Bayreuth, children's dowry money lent out at interest until it had to be paid.

Was she unusual as a businesswoman? Among the German Jews, it was expected that women would work. Glikl's maternal grandmother Mattie bas Jacob and her own mother Beila provided excellent models (described by Glikl in her *Life*, so that they might serve as models for the next generation as well). Widowed by the plague of 1638 and robbed (her husband's bags of jewels and golden chains were stolen by neighbors), Mattie started again in Altona with small loans and pledges. When this was not enough to support herself and her last daughter, Beila, the two of them began to make lace from gold and silver thread. So satisfied were the Hamburg traders with their work that Beila took in apprentice girls and taught them the same skills.[30] Glikl describes other resourceful matrons besides Mattie, including Esther, "a pious, honorable woman who . . . always went to the fairs," and the widow of Baruch of Berlin, "who still remained fully in business" and to whose son the widowed Glikl married her daughter Hendele. The Jewish widow carrying on her husband's trade can be found in many other families as well.[31]

Christian women, too, made small-scale loans and went into goldspinning and stockingmaking.[32] Where Glikl seems different from Christian women in Germany is in the scope of her trade and credit operations. She was no "court Jew": Esther Schulhoff, wife of Judah Berlin, alias Jost Liebmann, worked openly with her husband in providing jewels to the court of Prussia and continued to do so after his death; on the whole, though, raising loans for princes and provisioning their armies remained in the hands of men.[33] But Glikl's transactions did take her into long-range commerce and involved significant sums of money, which she exchanged in person on the Hamburg Börse. (Possibly she had a companion with her at the Börse; the Jewish Gemeinde of Worms recommended that women not go to the marketplace without another Jew.)[34]

Christian women in Germany ordinarily stayed within the city walls, playing a major role in retail trade. If they were carrying on credit operations in Hamburg, they seem to have gone infrequently to the Börse themselves; at least, pictorial conventions in seventeenth-century Hamburg scarcely ever represent them there.[35] In the late seventeenth century, some Christian widows in Hamburg did attend to their husbands' firms until their sons were old enough to take over, but those inheriting a business as extensive as Haim's would often leave its management to a male relative or agent while they devoted themselves to household or religious activities appropriate to a woman of affluence. For the German Jews, traveling around to fairs did not detract from a woman's reputation, especially when she made as much money as Glikl did. If anything, it brought additional marriage proposals.

For more than a decade Glikl turned down all such offers of marriage. Then, in 1699, when she was in her early fifties, she accepted a match with the widower Hirsch Levy, a wealthy financier and Jewish leader of Metz, just within the border of the kingdom of France. The next year, keeping her betrothal a secret so as to avoid paying to the Hamburg government the large exit fee required of departing Jews, she sold all her stock and paid all outstanding debts. Her fellow Jews in the Altona Gemeinde realized what was happening and assessed her an exit tax, but she left it unpaid as well.[36] Together with her last unmarried child, Miriam, Glikl departed from her birthplace forever.

The city on the Moselle in which she arrived in 1700 had only about 22,000 persons within its walls and was more limited in its economic and religious range than Hamburg. As a frontier town,

Metz had a military garrison and was a locus of French royal administration, with its own *parlement* (high court) and mint. Its population kept busy provisioning Louis XIV's troops, producing craft products, and redistributing grain from the region around Metz. Whereas Lutheran Hamburg permitted—albeit not always very willingly—some Catholics, Jews, and Dutch Calvinists to reside on its streets, Catholic Metz was experiencing the effects of the revocation of the Edict of Nantes. Some 3,000 Reformed Protestants—bankers, lawyers, goldsmiths, apothecaries, booksellers, and their families—had left the city rather than convert to the Mass.[37]

But the Jews were still there. They were allowed to live and worship openly and were a more important presence numerically in the population of Metz than in Hamburg. In the 1560s, a decade after Henri II had wrested Metz from imperial control and installed the first royal institutions there, a few German-Jewish families had been authorized to reside in the city and engage in moneylending. Hirsch Levy's ancestors arrived not long afterward. By 1657, when Louis XIV made his entry into Metz and visited the synagogue "in pomp and circumstance," the privileges of the growing Jewish community had been confirmed by every king since Henri III. In 1699, when Glikl was negotiating her marriage contract with Hirsch Levy—or Cerf ("deer") Levy, as he was known to notaries and officials in the French world of Metz—some 1,200 German Jews, 5 percent of the city's inhabitants apart from the garrison, were crowded into the Saint Ferroy quarter along the Moselle.[38]

Their privileges and presence did not, of course, go unchallenged. Officers took worried note when a Jew dared to build a house rather than just rent one. Mercers and clothiers complained when Jewish traders moved into goods threatening their commercial rights. Young Joseph Cahen disappeared in 1701 in the course of collecting debts from the butchers, whereupon a trial ensued in which his widow accused two butchers of robbery and murder and the butchers accused the Jewish community of "persecuting two innocent Christian families."[39]

It was even worse when the Jews themselves were accused of violence. In 1669 a ritual-murder charge had been leveled by some Catholic peasants against one Raphaël Levy (not related to Hirsch), and he had been burned by decree of the *Parlement* of Metz even though the child's body had been found in the woods, partly eaten by animals, not far from where he had been lost. Other arrests ensued, and the cry went up to expel the Jews from the city, until Louis XIV intervened and peremptorily put a stop to it. In Glikl's day, the Jews of Metz were still fasting on the twenty-fifth of Tevet, the anniversary of the burning of their innocent martyr Raphaël Levy. At the house of Glikl's daughter Esther and her husband, Moses Schwabe, they surely recalled those troubled times: during Levy's trial, Moses' grandfather Meyer had been accused of reenacting Christ's crucifixion in his house one Good Friday. A ritual-murder charge would be raised again, though not prosecuted, during Glikl's years in Metz.[40]

The argument for the Jews' usefulness was made by the royal intendant Marc Antoine Turgot in 1699: they provided the city and especially the frontier troops with much-needed grain and horses. They constituted "a kind of republic and neutral nation," able to travel easily and inexpensively, acquire accurate price information, and move merchandise across borders because of their connections with fellow Jews.[41] During the threatened famine of 1698, Cerf Levy and Abraham Schwabe (the latter was the father-in-law of Glikl's daughter Esther) brought 6,000 sacks of German grain to Metz, losing money on the deal but gaining the goodwill of the royal and municipal authorities. Apart from this, the Jews were bankers, making big loans to officers and seigneurs and petty loans to butchers and peasants; and dealers in gold, jewelry, currency (including illegally debased currency), and secondhand goods.[42] Among the Jewish women, no Glikl seems to emerge from the business contracts (and perhaps some of the wealthiest wives were withdrawing, like their Christian counterparts, from extensive commerce), but numerous Jewish matrons made small loans to peasant families and to Christians in Metz.[43]

Into this circle of banking families and the splendidly appointed household of Hirsch/Cerf Levy came Glikl bas Judah Leib with her "straightforward German ways."[44] It took her some time to get used to so many servants and a cook who made decisions without consulting her mistress. The memory of Hirsch's first wife was still bright for his seven children—he had buried her only the year before the wedding—and they let Glikl know that they preferred their mother's lavishness to their stepmother's economies. But she became interested in their lives (at least three of them were already married) and especially in the nearby household of Esther and Moses, who after ten years had finally been blessed with a child who did not die young. She often chatted with Esther's mother-in-law, the wealthy and influential Jachet bas Elias (known as Agathe in French), with whom she had exchanged quarrelsome letters in Yiddish a decade before when they had been negotiating the children's marriage.[45]

Then, after a mere year and a half, Hirsch Levy went bankrupt. He was honest and trustworthy in his enormous business, said Glikl, but his creditors devoured him. The Jewish Gemeinde thought there had been some "disorder" in Levy's affairs, but blamed the fall especially on the greed of Christians who had lent to him at exorbitant interest. Throughout 1702 notaries were busy drawing up contracts whereby Jewish and Christian creditors consolidated their claims against Hirsch, and finally there was a settlement in which they received about half of what they were owed.[46]

Instead of living in opulence and independence, Glikl bas Judah Leib and Hirsch ben Isaac had to be helped by their children. Perhaps Glikl resumed some trading, for she became known in Metz as "extremely skillful in the commerce of precious stones."[47] At least her daughter Miriam was able to make a reasonably good marriage within the Jewish commercial circles.[48] Hirsch was reduced to giving business advice to his son Samuel, urging him to be satisfied with his house in Metz and his role as rabbi of Alsace and not take on in addition the mint of the duke of Lorraine, outside France. Samuel ignored him, and Hirsch's premonition was borne out: Louis XIV, concerned about currency being brought in and out of France for profit and egged on by Jewish competitors in Metz, forbade Samuel Levy and his partners to reenter the kingdom unless they broke with the Lorraine mint.[49]

Samuel ben Hirsch stayed in Lorraine, and his father died brokenhearted in 1712, leaving Glikl less than a third of her marriage portion. As she neared seventy, Glikl finally moved in with her daughter Esther and her son-in-law Moses Schwabe (or Moses Krumbach, as Glikl called him, using his Yiddish name). From there she saw her daughter Miriam give birth to a son Haim (the name reborn again), her grandson Elias marry well, and her stepson Samuel build a house like a "palace" in Lunéville in Lorraine. And there she died at seventy-eight in 1724, on Rosh Hashanah (New Year's) 5485 by the Jewish reckoning.[50]

Glikl began to write the book of her life "with an aching heart" after the death of her husband Haim, "to help me against the melancholy thoughts [*malekuleshe gedanken*] which came . . . during many sleepless nights."[51] Was composing her memoirs a strange activity for her to undertake? From our vantage point it may seem so, for hers is the first autobiography from a Jewish woman that we know of from the past. But Glikl never described herself as doing something odd or new, and, indeed, recent scholarship is showing that autobiographies—full or in fragment— were composed by early modern Jews more often than has previously been believed. In Italy, the learned rabbi Leon Modena of Venice and the physician Abraham ben Hananiah Yagel left accounts of themselves in Hebrew; in Alsace the trader and teacher Asher Halevi wrote his *Book of Remembrances;* in Prague, one Samuel ben Jishaq Tausk penned his *Scroll,* known as *Megillat Samuel,* in Yiddish, recording his sufferings and those of the Prague Jews in 1704. Other autobiographies were to come out of the Altona milieu in the eighteenth century as well.[52]

Like many Christian autobiographies, Jewish life histories

were given a frame of family interest, recording something of past generations and elaborating on the present so that children would know where they came from and be guided in how to live. The Venetian rabbi Leon Modena wrote his Hebrew *Life* for his "sons . . . and their descendants, and for [his] students, who are called sons." Glikl bas Judah Leib directly addresses her "dear children," her "beloved children," several times in her manuscript: "My dear children, I write so that if today or tomorrow your dear children or grandchildren come and do not know about their family, I have recorded here briefly who their people are." One copy of the autobiography that has come down over the centuries was made by her son Moses Hamel, rabbi of Baiersdorf.[53]

But there are some interesting contrasts between the sources of Christian and Jewish autobiography that help us understand Glikl's mixing of genres—that is, her blend of memoir and story. Christian life history was often a spinoff from an account book and/or from a record of births, marriages, and deaths penned into a book of hours, Bible, religious calendar, or other devotional text. Thus, Hamburg men in Glikl's day were writing down family news, Communion days, and business actions in Christian calendars, conveniently printed with blank columns to leave them ample space.[54]

Jewish merchants certainly kept account books and travel ledgers. Recorded in Hebrew characters, this writing must have encouraged the sense of a protected space in which Jews could pass around family and personal secrets.[55] But Jewish life history was fostered especially by the centuries-old "ethical will," an exposition of moral lessons and personal wisdom passed on to one's children along with instructions for one's burial and the disposition of one's goods. These were texts that had some circulation and reputation. In her manuscript, Glikl speaks of the will of her sister's mother-in-law, "the pious Pessele, [who] had no equal in the world with the exception of our Mothers—Sarah, Rebecca, Rachel, and Leah . . . It is a wonder to read the testament that she made, may she rest in peace. I cannot write of it, but anyone who wishes to read it can still find it with her children; they would surely not have thrown it away." She also quotes at length from the ethical will of the learned rabbi Abraham Halevi Horowitz, left for his children and then published in Prague in 1615.[56]

When the autobiography took over from the will, the impulse to moralizing still remained strong: one could make the life itself exemplary; one could add religious poetry and lament, as did Asher Halevi in his Hebrew memoirs; one could tell stories, as did Glikl.

There is a confessional strain in both Jewish and Christian autobiography, but it operates quite differently within the two traditions. For the Christians, the major model was still Augustinian confession with a definitive conversion. We see it in the widely read Latin autobiography of Anna Maria van Schurman, *Eukleria*, published in 1673 in Altona. The *Eukleria* tells how Schurman renounced worldly fame and the scholarship in languages and secular literature that she had begun in her native Utrecht and how she embraced a life of humility and religious fellowship with the Labadist sectaries, just then inhabiting Altona. (They were changing their money with the Jews; Glikl and Anna Maria may have passed each other on the street.)[57] A variation on the model is the *Leben* of the Pietist visionary Johanna Eleonora von Merlau Petersen, published in 1719 when she was seventy-five (she was almost an exact contemporary of Glikl's). It describes not a single conversion experience but rather a set of tests, all of which she passed with God's help, from her motherless childhood in Frankfurt to her marriage with a Pietist preacher in 1680. Her autobiography then expands into a description of God's revelations to her over the years, including her 1664 dream of the future conversion of the Jews and heathen.[58]

With Jewish confessional autobiography of the seventeenth century, the model is not a personal trajectory but the history of Yahweh's chosen people, the individual life repeating and recombining the rhythm of Torah, sinning, and the sufferings of exile.[59] When a Marrano or crypto-Jew is telling the story of his return to open Judaism, the larger narrative goes beyond personal conversion to the lengthening or the shortening of the Jews' Exile.[60] For others, suffering often triggers the autobiographical act: the journal of Josel of Rosheim tells of the cruelties committed against his family and other Jews in the first half of the sixteenth century and his role as rescuer in different German cities; Abraham Yagel's *Valley of Vision* tells of his father's death and his own wrongful imprisonment for debt in Mantua.[61] But suffering and sinning are linked. "This day I remember my sins," writes Abraham Halevi Horowitz in his testament amid admonitions to serve the Lord with ears, eyes, and feet; "I used to stumble in matters of intoxication." The sin of gambling crops up in Leon Modena's autobiography from beginning to end, following tragic death and disappointment, undercutting his service to the Torah, and demonstrating the frailty of human expectations.[62]

Glikl bas Judah Leib's autobiography fits within this general Jewish frame, as we will see, but has original features connected with her gender and her learning. As a master of Hebrew, Latin, Italian, and Judeo-Italian, Rabbi Leon had access to the whole range of Jewish scholarship and male religious action: he prayed at the synagogue, taught, and preached; he lived by the law, the Halakhah—or, at least, by most of it; the list of his published books, commentaries, translations, and poems takes up two pages of his memoirs.[63] Among the German Jews of the Hamburg/Altona community, there were men of considerable learning, too: the merchant Moses ben Leib, to whose son Glikl married her daughter Freudchen, had studied with one of the greatest Talmudists of the day and continued to read the Talmud, quite indifferent (as were other Hamburg Jews) to the Senate's prohibition of it.[64] By the last decade of the century, the esteemed Zevi Hirsch Ashkenazi was giving rabbinical teaching in Altona and being solicited by other Jewish communities across Europe for his judgment on, say, whether a golem could be counted in order to make up a minyan—that is, the male religious quorum needed for services. (Zevi Hirsch said no.)[65]

Glikl bas Judah Leib respected such learning and sent two of her sons who "studied well" to Talmudic schools in Poland and

Frankfurt.[66] But her own culture was of another kind, characteristic of the most bookish of the Ashkenazic merchant women. She had attended Cheder, the Jewish primary school: "my father educated his children, son and daughters both, in things heavenly and worldly."[67] In subsequent years, she had acquired numerous books in Yiddish—that is, in what she called "Taytsh" and what some Jewish contemporaries referred to as "the language of the Ashkenaz."[68] This literature, always written in Hebrew characters, comprised several genres.[69] There were ethical tracts and manuals, such as the *Brantshpigl* (Burning Mirror) by Moses ben Henoch Altschuler (1596), and the *Lev Tov* of Isaac ben Eliakum (Prague, 1620), both of them much reprinted after their initial appearance and recommended by Glikl to her children. Indeed, one such morality tract had been written by a woman—the *Meineket Rivkah* of Rebecca bas Meir Tiktiner, published posthumously in the early seventeenth century and known even to Christian Hebraists.[70]

There were Yiddish books on the religious and household duties of women, such as *Ayn Schoyn Fraun Buchlayn* (Krakow, 1577; Basel, 1602). There were women's books of prayers, such as Rabbi Izmuns' *Korbonets*, a paraphrase of Hebrew prayers for the holidays (Krakow, 1577), and especially the more intimate *tkhines*, to which we will return below. There were Bible translations in prose and verse, and the immensely popular *Tse'enah u-re'enah*, put together by Jacob ben Isaac Ashkenazi around the turn of the seventeenth century and sometimes illustrated with woodcuts of Bible stories. Each portion of the Pentateuch, the Prophets, and other parts of Scripture read in synagogue through the year was discussed with commentaries drawn from the Talmud and midrashic and medieval sources.[71] There were books of proverbs in Yiddish, like *Der kleyn Brantshpigl*, printed in Hamburg in 1698, and numerous books of fables and stories, such as the *Mayse Bukh*, in print by 1602 (as you can see in the illustration) if not before. There were historical accounts and news of Jewish persecution. Indeed, the story of the 1669 ritual-murder charge in Metz was recorded in "Taytsh so that everyone . . . can read it," and was thus available in manuscript to Glikl when she moved to the town on the Moselle thirty years later.[72]

What united this Yiddish production besides its language was its presumed audience of unlearned folk and especially of women. Jacob ben Isaac Ashkenazi called himself "the writer for all pious women" and proclaimed on the title page of his *Tse'enah u-re-'enah*, "Go forth, O ye daughters of Zion and behold." The book became known as "the women's Torah." Moses ben Henoch said he was composing the *Brantshpigl* in Yiddish "for women and for men who are like women in not being able to learn much."[73] And the books were printed in a special typeface, different from the square type used for the text of the Bible and the semi-cursive type used for Hebrew commentary. It was known as "Vayber Taytsh" ("women's Taytsh") and was based on the cursive Hebrew hand that women like Glikl were taught for their business contracts, marriage agreements, and correspondence. The Taytsh typeface is analogous to the French "civility typeface," which was based on French handwriting and used in the mid-sixteenth century for story collections and educational tracts in the vernacular. In France, the civility typeface was thought of as "popular," aimed at a broad lay audience, whereas in Jewish culture, with Hebrew viewed as the men's language, the typeface used for Yiddish was construed as women's type. Many men read and wrote in Yiddish, too, but the convention remained that they were using the language of women.[74]

Could Glikl read the Hebrew language—the *Loshn-koydesh* (Holy Tongue)—as well? Her Yiddish text is mixed with Hebrew words, as Yiddish always is: in the bird story, for example, "troubles," "life-strength," and "liar" are among the words from Hebrew. Her mode of expression has struck some specialists as full of Hebrew rhythms. Hadn't she heard them in sermons, where Hebrew quotations from the Bible and the sages were interspersed with Yiddish "so that women, children, and others who do not understand Hebrew may listen and learn"?[75]

Her knowledge of that language in its written form may have increased as she acquired more time free from business. While still in Hamburg she had had the Hebrew ethical will of Abraham Horowitz, the *Yesh Nochalin,* "read aloud to her in Taytsh." Perhaps her reader was the "worthy teacher" she and Haim had employed to instruct the younger children, or the special tutor she hired for her studious son Joseph after Haim's death.[76] Later, in Metz, she could sit in the women's gallery at the synagogue every day. She also had the chance to converse with her learned stepson Rabbi Samuel and his wife, who knew enough Hebrew and Aramaic to make a copy of treatises of the Talmud, and with the students supported at the houses of her stepdaughter Hendele and of her in-law Jachet bas Elias. And now in Metz, Glikl says she "has written out" *(oysgishryben)* an important tale "from the Holy Tongue into Taytsh." If by "written out" she means a kind of translating, then her knowledge took a leap in the last twenty years of her life.[77]

But *oysgishryben* can mean simply "copying," and Chava Turniansky has amassed impressive evidence that Glikl's knowledge of Hebrew writings came to her orally or through the copious world of Yiddish publication.[78] Whatever her sources, Glikl bas Judah Leib's citations were drawn from many parts of Scripture and of the Talmud. Though no one would have praised her (as Leon Modena did his aunt Fioretta) as "very wise in Torah and Talmud" or have found in her the talmudic mastery of the sixteenth-century Rebecca bas Meir Tiktiner, her memorial notice in Metz did call her *melumedet* ("a learned woman") in matters of proper conduct and ethics. This was a rare compliment, for in hundreds of notices I have examined, the Jewish women of Metz were remembered ordinarily by their community for their piety, rectitude, or charity and in only a few instances for being "wisehearted," or "devoted to study," or "reading every day the entire Book of Psalms and its commentary."[79]

Beyond her familiar Yiddish and a possible struggle with a few Hebrew texts, it is very likely that Glikl read some High-German publications in their own Gothic print. She does not satisfy our twentieth-century curiosity on this point, for like her Jewish contemporaries, she uses the word "Taytsh" for her mother tongue and also for German spoken with its separate forms and written in its own alphabet.[80] (In contrast, Christian contemporaries stressed the difference. "Their *Teutschen* is very *undeutsch*," grumbled Christoph Helwig in translating the Yiddish tales of the *Mayse Bukh* into German, "and not understandable." "You'll see the contrasts between *Juden-Teutsch* and *wahren Teutsch*— true German," said Johann Christoph Wagenseil to the reader of his 1699 book on Yiddish, "between *Juden-Teutsch* and our *Teutsch*.")[81]

The evidence for Glikl's reading some German is of two kinds. First, she says of Charlemagne that he "was a mighty emperor, as one can find written about in all the *Taytshe bukher*."[82] She then goes on to recount a tale of Charlemagne and Empress Irene of Constantinople that was not part of the medieval corpus of Jewish legends about Charlemagne, which mostly concerned his relations with the Jews.[83] Rather, she follows quite closely an account written in Greek in the early ninth century which soon found its way into Latin manuscripts; it was printed in various versions in Latin for the first time at the hands of a Jesuit and a Dominican and other learned men in the late sixteenth and early seventeenth centuries, and was incorporated into the German "universal histories" that came off the presses of towns like Nuremberg and Hamburg in the seventeenth century.[84] It is thus plausible that Glikl's *Taytshe bukher* were German books, and that she read the tale of Empress Irene in some popular history, bought, say, at a bookstall in Hamburg or when Haim was at the Leipzig fair. Her Yiddish telling contains not one word taken from the Hebrew.[85]

Second, her economic activities and travels put her in touch with the world that spoke and wrote in German. She did business with both Jews and non-Jews, in Hamburg before Haim died, at the Leipzig fair, and elsewhere afterward. With non-Jews, at the very least this meant negotiating, drawing up, and signing contracts in German. She talked and exchanged news and stories with Jews and non-Jews. If her autobiography captures many moments of conversation with Jewish women and men, it also provides a glimpse of talk with non-Jews while she was traveling with Haim. Returning to Hamburg overland from Wittmund in Friesland, they had a young and "worthy" corporal in the service of General Buditz traveling in their coach for protection and chatting with them the whole trip. On the way they stopped at a village inn about eight miles from Hannover:

> At night we sat around the fire and our innkeeper and other peasants sat by the fire, too, and smoked tobacco. The conversation skipped from one place to another and one person to another. Then a peasant got caught up talking about the duke of Hannover and said, "My lord has sent 12,000 men to Holland." My husband—may the memory of the righteous be a blessing—was very happy when he heard we were on the soil of Hannover, for the Lüneburg dukes kept their lands clean and no soldier was allowed to harm even a chicken.[86]

From such conversations it could be but a short step to reading the newspapers that had been coming off the Hamburg presses since the early seventeenth century. Glikl (and Haim, while he was still alive) got information about the Muscovy trade and the English market from merchants' reports and from letters. But twice a week the *Relations-Courier* brought news with recent datelines from all over Europe and beyond about wars, ships thought lost that had been found at the Cape of Good Hope, political disturbances in England, the movement of the Swedish fleet, and more.[87] If Glikl makes no reference to such reading in her autobiography, she does say to her children there that one found "wise men of the nations of the world" (a standard phrase for non-Jews) who had written "quite beautifully" on moral subjects like stinginess and charity. The formula she adds—"because of our many sins" (that is, they have written things that we might well have written)—makes it all the more likely that she is speaking of something she had read in German.[88]

At that time French was finding its way into the polite phrases and salutations of the Hamburg patriciate, and was not unknown among the Hamburg Jewish community. Glikl's father had a step-daughter by his first marriage "who knew French like water." The family folklore about her told how she had one day saved Judah Leib from being cheated by his debtors as they plotted against him in French. Glikl, who knew individual words of that language, was to regret her general ignorance only in 1700, when she arrived in Louis XIV's Metz and found she could not exchange compliments with some of the Jewish population. Presumably she learned more French late in life, but on the whole her culture was deeply rooted in Yiddish, with some porous areas for Hebrew and for German.[89]

In a broad sense, the character of Glikl's culture was analogous to that of the best-educated Lutheran women in Hamburg during her own day. Women of great erudition, such as the linguist Anna Maria van Schurman or the Greek specialist Anne Dacier, are not found in seventeenth-century Hamburg; salons and literary women emerged there only in the course of the Enlightenment of the eighteenth century. The women in prosperous and Senate families among Glikl's contemporaries were nourished primarily by religious and ethical reading and practical manuals in German. To be sure, they read their Bible directly in Luther's translation rather than through the mediation of a *Tse'enah u-re'enah*. But they were interested in story collections and news accounts, so much so that in 1695 Christian fathers and husbands in Hamburg were allegedly forbidding their daughters and wives to read newspapers, which were seen as spurs to reckless curiosity and vain conversation.[90]

They did not, however, forbid them participation in Hamburg's amateur musical life or attendance at Hamburg's Opera, already in a permanent opera house in 1678 and attracting composers and librettists from near and far. Some Jewish women shared that taste: the French-speaking stepdaughter of Judah Leib played the clavier and there were enough Jewish women going to the Opera to incite the Altona/Hamburg Gemeinde to repeated prohibition. Although Glikl much appreciated the dance performances and the drums at a daughter's wedding in Cleve, it was not music and song but the oral story and the written word that were at the center of her mental world.[91]

When Glikl read, she does not say. She describes her husband Haim as never missing the Torah study for the day, no matter how busy he was running about town buying and selling gold.[92] Such regular observance was what the Halakhah demanded of a man: his individual and communal prayers were fixed around the day's activities and the movement of the liturgical calendar.

Women were expected to observe all the Jewish holidays and the food prohibitions of *kashruth,* but they were exempt from the daily requirements of Torah study and prayers at fixed times. The Jewish law prescribed only three unalterable duties especially for a woman: the avoidance of her husband during menstruation, and her bath of purification at its end; the separating out, blessing, and burning of a small portion of dough when baking bread, in memory of the ancient temple tithes; and the lighting of the Sabbath candles just before sundown on Friday and on the eve of festivals.[93] In other respects, the woman's personal religious performance was "not bound by time" but done where and when she wished. Needy scholars might be summoned to her table for Sabbath meals or when a member of the family was ill, but could be invited other times as well. The woman could send food to poor Jews every Sabbath, as did Hirsch Levy's first wife and daughter Hendele, or intermittently as she wished. She could decide never to eat bread baked by Christians, or fast every Monday and Thursday, or live by some other rule.[94] Torah bindings could be embroidered for a son's circumcision cloth, to be ready as a gift for the Holy Scroll a few years later when the son first visited the synagogue. (Two such bindings can be seen in the illustrations.) As her schedule permitted, fringes could be made for the men's prayer shawls and candles molded to light the synagogue.[95]

Especially important to Glikl's piety were the *tkhines* prayers in Yiddish, published in booklets for the woman's individual devotion and recited according to the rhythm of the Jewish holy days, but also the rhythm of her own life, body, and family affairs, from birth, pregnancy, and travels to death.[96]

Perhaps Glikl's reading was, like the *tkhines,* not "bound by time." Perhaps she began to read more regularly during the sleepless nights of her widowhood. At any rate, this was when she began to write her book, as we have heard her saying to her children. As we will see, its composition allowed her not merely to weave a thickly textured life history full of telling anecdote, but also eventually to resolve in her mind the tension between the old generation and the young. Further, the combination of personal and story narratives helped her to struggle with the moral significance of disappointment and sorrow and to take on an independent religious voice, different from a rabbi's, but different from "Vayber Taytsh" as well.

Glikl arranged her life narrative in seven books, like the seven decades that limited every human life.[97] This plan she announced early and held to over the three decades during which she wrote the manuscript—strong testimony to the seriousness of her writer's vision. The first four books and the opening sections of the fifth book seem to have been drafted consecutively in the months or year of mourning after Haim's death in 1689. The rest of Book 5 seems to have been drafted during the decade of the 1690s but given final form after her second marriage.[98] The sixth book was written in 1702 or shortly afterward, during the initial shock of Hirsch Levy's bankruptcy in Metz, and the seventh composed in 1715, a significant year in her second widowhood, with a final paragraph from 1719.[99]

Without Glikl's original manuscript, we can speculate about her practice of revising only from internal evidence in the text copied by her son Moses and in a second family copy with variants, now lost but used by the 1896 editor. The picture is inconsistent. Though she added a memorial formula to the name of a son who had died since the first draft, she did not change the formula "may she live" after her mother's name, despite the fact that Beila bas Nathan had died well before the autobiography was finished.[100] Though she softened the account of a fight in the 1660s between Haim and a business partner by inserting a comment about how graciously the partner received her in Berlin thirty years later, a story twice promised about another troublesome partner was never told. Episodes that she had "forgotten" to place in their precise chronological order at first writing stayed where they were in the version handed on to her children; contradictions in dating—say, between the date she gave for her birth and the age she gave at her second marriage—remained unresolved.[101]

Nonetheless, whether at first writing or through revision, she paid great attention to the important ordering—that is, to the literary and psychological ordering: to telling stories and anecdotes "in the right time and place."[102] After an initial book of moral tales and religious injunctions, the autobiography is shaped by life cycle events, a practice found in Christian women's autobiographies as well.[103] Book 2 moves from Glikl's birth to the birth and circumcision of her first son; along the way, she tells of the past of her family and of Haim's. Book 5 moves from the death of Haim ben Joseph through the ten years of her first widowhood, and includes the adventures of her children. To each book she gave a mood, and for each she sought a divine response. Book 4 ends ominously, anticipating her husband's death: "Every morning came new sorrows, of which I shall write in my fifth book, which is, unhappily, a book of lamentation to Zion, a book of bitter woe . . . The Lord make us rejoice even as he has afflicted us. And may he have mercy on my orphans. Amen, and Amen." And her seventh book, which recounts the downfall of her second husband, Hirsch Levy, and what happened afterward, opens: "Now will I, with God's help, begin my seventh book, which will be partly of sorrow and partly of joy. Following human nature, such is the way of the world . . . May God grant that no further sorrows befall my dear children and that in my old age I may only hear and see joy and their prosperity."[104]

Glikl's joys and sorrows cluster around life—that is, staying alive to one's appointed time—and around wealth and honor. Against the happy movement of births, marriages, and grandchildren are placed deaths out of season. The first one was that of her third child, Mattie, whom the Lord took away in the girl's third year. "A more beautiful and clever child was nowhere to be seen. Not only did we love her, but everyone who saw her and heard her speak, took pleasure in her . . . Our portion was heartache and great distress. My husband and I mourned indescribably." The last child to whom she bade good-bye was Zanvil, who died in 1702 in his early twenties when his wife was pregnant with their first child: "God have mercy, that so worthy a young man should have to chew the black earth! . . . The deep sorrow and heartache this was to me, only God knows, may he be praised. To lose so beloved a son, of such tender years. What am I to do or say to grieve more?"[105]

But there is a greater grieving—namely, the one over the untimely loss that dominates the autobiography: the death of Haim ben Joseph when Glikl was forty-three and he only a little older, after thirty years of marriage. It is there in anticipation, when she describes their first young household, away from their parents: "If God had not struck us such a severe blow and so soon taken the crown of my head, I do not think there would have been a more loving and fortunate couple than we in the whole world." It is there when she recounts the death of her parents-in-law in their eighties: "If God had only permitted my husband and me to live together to such a fine old age."[106] "To lose such a husband," she writes after describing his end, "I who had been so appreciated by him . . ." He had left her money and wealth enough, but it was no help against her "great loneliness." "When my husband (may the memory of the righteous be a blessing) was alive, we had worries now and again . . . [But] my beloved friend would allay all my troubles and comfort me so that somehow they passed easily . . . Who is now my comforter?" And with some bitterness, she calls him the lucky one who died first: "He had the privilege to depart from this sinful world in riches and honor, and suffer no trials through his children . . . But I was left desolate, in pain, sorrow and sighing, with my married and unmarried children . . . I shall not forget him all the days of my life. He is engraved in my heart."[107]

Riches were defined by Glikl primarily in terms of the reichstaler, a German coin of cash and especially of account: the reichstaler in a dowry given to a daughter or son; the reichstaler that a father, future in-law, or former business partner was worth. "My sister Hendele—may she rest in peace—received 1,800 reichstaler as her dowry, a very large sum in those days and one that no one had until then given in Hamburg. It was the most important match in all Ashkenaz, and the whole world wondered at the large dowry." The Jewish men in Hamburg/Altona at the time of Glikl's father are ranked in wealth by reichstaler (Haim Fürst 10,000; her father 8,000; others 6,000; some 3,000; some only 500); Elias Gompertz of Cleve, whose son married Glikl's oldest daughter, is "very rich, worth 100,000 reichstaler or more"; her grandson and his new bride in Metz put together in gifts and dowries "some 30,000 reichstaler. May God grant them luck and blessings."[108]

Sometimes household splendor served as Glikl's sign of wealth (Reb Elias Gompertz's house was "really like the dwelling of a king, furnished like the mansion of a ruler"),[109] but most consistently it was money, for which she as a businesswoman had an excellent memory. And what better marker for a Jew to use when one's house was ordinarily leased not owned, substantial landed property was not available, and, in the case of a family like Glikl's in Hamburg, most of one's sale goods were carried around in pockets, pouches, and small sacks? And what could be simpler than a monetary sum, as a means of circulating news rapidly about the marriage market and credit possibilities across Europe's German-Jewish communities?

Wealth was not, to be sure, an absolute value like life. For Glikl a Jew who chose death rather than convert to Christianity "sanctified the Holy Name," but holy martyrdom was not to be sought by Jews as it was by the heroes of Catholic spirituality.[110]

About wealth she had reservations: "Who knows if it is good to live in great riches . . . and spend our time in this transient world in nothing but pleasure?" Glikl asks this even in Book 1[111] and, as we shall see, reflects on the question almost as often as she talks about reichstaler. Though she can say admiringly of her uncle, who died at thirty-nine, "Had he lived he would have become immensely rich; in his hands, you should pardon the expression, dung turned to gold,"[112] she still disapproves of those with much wealth who never felt they had enough. Of them it was said, "No person dies who has gotten even half his wishes." It seems to her that in her father's day, people were content with their portion. Her children must remember Job's admission: "Naked were we born and naked must we depart."[113]

Honor in its most general form was often coupled with riches: Model Ries and his wife, Pessele, in-laws of Glikl's sister, "died in Berlin in wealth and honor" (in *"oysher un koved"*); "my mother married off her daughters in *oysher un koved*." "With Haim's death my *oysher un koved* departed," Glikl wrote in the wave of grief that followed her husband's loss, though she later saw herself as regaining both.[114] Honor was also a quality that inhered in a person by itself, measured by the esteem, the *Aestimatio*, which one enjoyed in different circles. For Jews it was especially connected with one's honesty and uprightness in business; Haim hoped for partners who were *erlikher, redlikher*. Like Christian merchants, Glikl feared business failure for its shame as well as for its cost.[115]

Honor was demonstrated through marks of respect accorded at the dining table and in hospitality, as when Glikl and Haim were received by a relative in Emden during the holidays of the Jewish New Year "with all the honor in the world." Glikl's mother, Beila, by then widowed, married off her last daughter in Hamburg: "not one of the leaders of the Gemeinde was absent from the wedding; they all came to do her honor." Glikl went to Furth for marriage negotiations for her youngest son, Moses: "I cannot describe what *koved* was extended to us there. All the principal men of the community and their wives came to our inn and wanted to take us by force to their houses."[116] For men, honor resided also in being chosen as an officer in the Gemeinde and as a representative of the Jews to the Christian authorities. A rabbi of great learning was showered with appreciative invitations from different communities. Death, too, brought its signs of respect: Glikl's grandmother Mattie was buried "with much honor" *"mit grusin koved"*).[117]

Glikl's attentiveness to honor stands in contrast to the shady status attributed to Jews in much Christian writing in the seventeenth century and to the limited sense of honor that Christians imagined Jews to possess. Shakespeare's Shylock has only a raw sense of injury against his debtor Antonio: "he hath disgraced me, and hindered me half a million: scorned my nation, thwarted my bargains, cooled my friends, heated mine enemies."[118] Glikl assesses much finer interactions, and so sure is she of the quality of Jewish honor that she almost always uses the Hebrew-derived noun *koved* rather than the German-derived *er* (from *Ehre*), even doing so in those few cases where her cast of characters is made up entirely of non-Jews. Thus, in her story of Croesus and Solon, the king asks the philosopher if he is not fortunate in all his *oysher un koved*, his "wealth and honor"; and Solon answers that the king will be fortunate only if he dies, as did a recent citizen of Athens, in *Aestimatio* and with *oysher* and *koved*.[119]

If Glikl's word use suggests a likeness between Jewish and non-Jewish sensibilities, she never forgets the asymmetric relations between her people and "the nations of the world." ("The nations of the world" is one of her phrases for gentiles, along with "non-Jews" and "the uncircumcised"; she never puts Christ into her text by using the word "Christians.")[120] In her account of her joys and sorrows, gentiles have a different explanatory status from Jews. Christian respect is, to be sure, a source of satisfaction and of income. Wasn't her own trade and that of Haim based on Jewish and gentile credit both? About one of the old-time businesswomen in Altona, Glikl observes, "The noble ladies of Holstein were very keen on her"; and Elias Ballin of Hamburg, whose daughter married her son Nathan, she describes as "an honorable man [*erlikher man*], very well regarded by Jews and non-Jews."[121] And if one becomes keeper of the mint for the duke of Lorraine, as did Hirsch Levy's son Samuel, then one is glad at least while one basks in the "favor" of His Highness.[122]

On one occasion—that of the wedding of Zipporah bas Haim to the son of Reb Elias in Cleve—Glikl describes Christians who brought honor to her and her family. Prince Maurits of Nassau and his courtiers and the young Prince Frederick of Brandenburg attended the ceremony. The bride was without equal; Prince Frederick was charmed by five-year-old Mordecai, whom Glikl and Haim had dressed with care; the courtiers were pleased with the delicacies, fine wines, and masked dancers provided by Reb Elias. "For a hundred years no Jew had had such high honor"— and here Glikl uses the word *koved*.[123]

But this is the only case of Christian *koved* toward Jews in the autobiography. The seventeenth-century Jew could not count on such relations. The protection of Christian councils and princes could never be taken for granted, even with the Hamburg Senate, which was willing "to look through its fingers" when the German Jews held services in private houses.[124] Glikl points to situations that were particularly bad (for example, Helmstedt was "a university town and hence a bad place"—that is, bad for Jews), or particularly good (God rewarded the king of Denmark, because "he was a merciful, just, and pious monarch and the Jews lived well under him").[125] But the boundary conditions to which she always returns are those of an anti-Semitic world.

We can see this in three blood-stained episodes centered around Jewish-Christian interactions, each of which Glikl uses to show how Jews must live under the constraints of Exile. Ten years into her marriage, when Glikl and Haim were in their twenties, their young business agent Mordecai was murdered on the short and usually safe road between Hannover and Hildesheim. As Glikl tells it, it was done by a poacher, who demanded money for a drink. When Mordecai laughed, the poacher responded, "You Jewish carcass, what are you thinking about so long? Yes or no?" and shot him in the head. She and Haim were deeply upset by the news: Mordecai had been a member of their household and a trustworthy business partner. "May God avenge his blood along with the rest of the holy and pious martyrs."[126]

Yet Glikl also reports that Mordecai died instantly, that there were no witnesses, and that the killer was never found. The scene with the anti-Semitic poacher is her imagined rendering of the episode. If a Jew died of violence on the road, who else but a non-Jew was to blame?[127]

A few years later, it was a matter of Jewish thieves. Two Hamburg traders stole diamonds from their host in Norway, threw the stones into the sea when they were pursued, and finally confessed their crime under torture. One Jew multiplied his evil deeds by converting to Christianity to escape being hanged. The other, from a family well known to Glikl, atoned for his sin by remaining steadfast. In such a case a Jew must "sanctify the name of the Lord." And in this case one sees where the excessive desire for money can lead. Glikl places the Jewish thieves at the opening of Book 4, in which the family business endeavor is the major theme; after the hanging of the stalwart Jew, she moves to reflections, taken from Hillel and other sages, on the limits that must be placed on riches and on the importance of alms.[128]

The third episode is recounted in Book 5, a *groyse mayse* ("big story") about two missing Jewish moneychangers who were discovered to have been murdered by a Christian from a good burgher family of Hamburg.[129] The heroine of the tale is a certain Rebecca, who identified the murderer from various clues and rumors and then, unable to sleep one Sabbath night, saw the suspect leaving Hamburg with his wife and a large box. (Here Glikl tells a story within a story, comparing Rebecca to the king of Spain, who, kept awake by the Lord, caught sight of some plotters leaving a child's body in a Jewish yard and thus averted a false charge of ritual murder.)[130] Against the advice of her husband not to stir up trouble in Hamburg "where [the Jews] dare not utter a word," Rebecca pressed the case before the authorities, tricked the murderer's maidservant into confessing and telling her where one corpse was buried, and encouraged her fellow Jews not to fear the consequences of rightful accusation. Meanwhile, a crowd of several thousand artisans and sailors gathered, ready to fall on the Jews if the body was not dug up in the Christian house. Ultimately both corpses were found, and the murderer confessed and was executed amid the murmur of popular threats against the Jews. "The children of Israel were in dire peril that day, for much wickedness was roused against them . . . but God in His great mercy for us sinful humans proved that 'in the land of their enemies, I will not cast them away [Lev. 26:44]' . . . and the Jews got off without harm."[131]

Like the murdered Mordecai, the slain Jewish moneychangers warn Glikl's descendants of the perennial hazards of Jewish life. Rebecca shows that one need not accept the shedding of innocent blood without a murmur. Glikl's placement of the *mayse* adds to its overtones. Rebecca denounced the Hamburg slayer in 1687; Glikl writes of it in Book 5, well after Haim's death in 1689, saying it happened "about this time."[132] Rebecca's tenacious efforts to avenge the Jews are thus reported amid the widowed Glikl's unflagging efforts to sustain her "orphans" against unnamed Jewish and Christian threats. She and Rebecca are mothers worthy of the biblical Matriarchs, Sarah, Rebecca, Rachel, and Leah.

Glikl's treatment of Christians in her autobiography can be summed up by the word "margins": the Christians are on the margins of her Jewish center, encircling the Jews with their institutions and worldly control. Jews have interactions with Christians across the border—interactions that ranged from violent to sociable.[133] Jews have diplomatic relations with Christians, carried on by a *shtadlan* such as Hirsch Levy.[134] They also have contractual relations—debts to Christians that Glikl honors as seriously as she does to Jews; and they pay wages to Christians such as Glikl's *shabes-froy*, her "Sabbath woman," who does errands for her on that day of rest.[135]

More intimate relations between Jews and non-Jews are imagined in Book 2, in a Joblike tale that Glikl includes to show why one should trust in the Lord. A Jewish version of a story found in several world traditions (Placidas, or The Man Who Never Swore an Oath), it tells of a pious Talmudist, imprisoned for debt through no fault of his own, and his wife, who was tricked and kidnapped by a sea captain as she washed clothes near the shore.[136] After his release, the husband took his two sons on a boat bound for the East Indies, hoping to find his wife, but he was shipwrecked and washed up alone in a land of "savages" *(vilde leyt)*. Saved by the local princess from being eaten, the Talmudist lived with her in a cave and she bore him a "savage son." In despair at all he had lost, he thought of suicide: "What if with the passage of time these wild unthinking brutes should eat his flesh and crush his bones, and he would not be buried among good Jews?"

A heavenly voice dissuaded him from putting an end to himself, led him to a treasure, and counseled his escape in an approaching ship, bound for Antioch. As he boarded the vessel, his *vilde* wife called to him to take her with him, "but he mocked at her and said, 'What have I to do with wild animals? I already have a better wife than you.'" "When she heard him say that he would return to her no more, anger arose within her. She took the little savage boy by his feet and, tearing him in two, threw one half into the ship and in her rage began to devour the other half. The wise Talmudist sailed away."

Settled on a new island with his treasure and chosen as the native people's duke, the Talmudist was finally reunited with his long-lost wife and sons when their boats happened to dock at his shore and identities were established by the solution of riddles. It turned out that the sea captain also had two wives, a housewife with children back on shore and his kidnapped Jewish one, "very delicate and intelligent," who managed the affairs on board ship for him. But he had never lain with the Talmudist's wife. She had told him that she would sleep only with a man who could equal her former husband by solving a riddle he had taught her. She would kill herself (another threatened suicide!) rather than lie with him under any other circumstance, for "it is not right for a peasant lout to ride a king's horse."[137]

Since the sea captain had not touched the Jewish wife, the

Talmudist spared his life, merely confiscating his wealth as punishment. Some of the sailors who heard these wonders converted to Judaism, and a Jewish community *(kehilah)* thereafter flourished on the duke's island.

Glikl added many motifs to the traditional tale of the Man Who Never Swore an Oath, such as the savage-princess interlude, the riddle tests, and the Jewish dukedom.[138] The savage-princess episode could have been suggested to her by European travel accounts, in which ill-fated love between European and non-European became a main theme. Jean Mocquet, a French voyager to the Caribbean in the early seventeenth century, heard a similar story about an English sea pilot there. Shipwrecked in the Caribbean, the pilot was saved by an Amerindian woman, who took care of him through two to three years of wandering in northern lands and had a child with him. Meeting English fishing boats, the pilot refused to take his companion on board with him, out of shame and "because she was a savage." Whereupon the Amerindian woman, forsaken and enraged, tore their child in half, threw one half toward him, and carried off the other "in mourning and sorrow." Glikl may well have heard or read this story, Mocquet's book having been published in an illustrated German translation in 1688 in Lüneburg, a town not far from Hamburg.[139]

Glikl could also have woven parts of the savage interlude from Jewish travel literature. There was the story of the ninth-century Eldad, shipwrecked among eaters of human flesh in Ethiopia.[140] There was the story of the shipwrecked Jewish man saved by and married to a she-demon, who then killed him with a kiss when he preferred to return to his first wife and children.[141] (Glikl's Talmudist was luckier.) Glikl's Jewish duke may have been an echo of the Marrano Joseph Nasi, duke of Naxos from 1566 to 1579 through the favor of the Turkish sultan—and Naxos is on the way to Antioch, the destination of the Talmudist's second boat. There was finally a long-distance traveler in Glikl's own family in 1712, when her son-in-law Mordecai Hamburger, also known as Moses Marcus the Elder, sailed to India to trade in diamonds in Pondicherry and Madras. This was some twenty-two years after she penned Book 2 with its tale of the pious Talmudist. Or could Mordecai's voyage have inspired some later additions?[142]

Whatever the sources for her tale, Glikl's additions intensify relations across the border between Jewish and non-Jewish, and the intimate ones lead to no good. In the episode on the "savage" shore, Jewish is equated with "civilized." Glikl also reminisces in Book 2 about how she and her mother, both nursing infants, became confused one dark night about whose child was whose, and it threatened to turn into an affair needing the judgment of King Solomon. But only the *vilde* princess tears her son in two. (This was at a time when, on the one hand, Jews were among the new owners of sugar plantations and of African and Indian slaves in Suriname[143] and, on the other, Christian travel literature was noting similarities between Jewish customs and those of the "savage" New World peoples, and Christian theologians were claiming, with the partial assent of Menasseh ben Israel himself, that the Amerindians were the descendants of the Lost Tribes of Israel.)[144] The learned Jewish husband and his gentle and intelligent wife are contrasted by Glikl with the rather stupid Christian skipper and his wife back home, who was suitable only for housework. Christians are not merely on Jewish margins in this tale; they are below the Jews. The reconciliation at its end—the Christians converted to Judaism and living under the rule of a wise Talmudist duke and his joyous family—is a fantasy of inversion, a happy ending to the sufferings of Exile.

Christians figure in Glikl's autobiography, but she devoted no pages to their strange religious customs or beliefs. In contrast, certain of her Christian contemporaries had much to say about the practices of the Jews on their margins or under their jurisdiction. In 1644 the Hamburg pastor Johann Müller had published his *Judaismus oder Jüdenthumb*, fifteen hundred pages on Jewish belief, religious comportment, and life, intended to show the Jews' "blindness and stubbornness" and the need for their conversion to Christianity. To that end, in the last decades of the century the Hebraist Esdras Edzardi was instructing Christian missionaries in rabbinical studies out of his house in Glikl's Hamburg.[145] Meanwhile, in Frankfurt am Main, the Pietist clergyman Johann Jacob Schudt was collecting materials for his *Jüdische Merckwürdigkeiten* (Jewish Curiosities). When its final fat volume appeared in 1718, it included a story about Glikl's son-in-law Mordecai Hamburger and his wife Freudchen in London: how in 1706 Mordecai had challenged the Ashkenazic rabbi on a divorce letter for a bankrupt merchant, how he had been excommunicated, and how his wife had been denied the right to have her new daughter named in the synagogue. Whereupon Mordecai had founded a synagogue of his own. The account, on the whole favorable to Mordecai, was intended to show that the German Jews conducted themselves as if there were no Christian magistrates to control them.[146]

Among the "curiosities" in Schudt's first volume was the method used by the Jews of Hamburg/Altona for getting around the ancient prohibition against carrying even a prayer book or a prayer shawl on the Sabbath outside the domestic space of one's own dwelling. Actually it was also forbidden to walk more than a certain distance from one's town and to cook for Sabbath meals during a festival that immediately preceded the Sabbath. A set of actions and objects, known in the Talmud and afterward as *eruvin*, allowed one to suspend these prohibitions. *Eruv* means "mixture" in Hebrew. Wires and "gates" were set up between people's houses and the synagogue; bread was taken to the synagogue and prayer houses and placed in the houses of neighbors in the same courtyard, where, say, water had to be carried on the Sabbath. Bread and prepared food were set aside before the festival preceding a Sabbath, so cooking could continue into forbidden hours.

These were symbolic instruments that enabled the community to mix the forbidden public space (the space under the jurisdiction of the many, *Reshut-Ha-rabbim*) with private space (the space under the jurisdiction of the single person, *Reshut-Ha'yahid*), to mix the activities of ordinary time with the time of festival. In an area like Hamburg/Altona, much of the space redefined by a gate and enclosed as *Reshut-Ha'yahid* so as to permit Jews to carry things through it on the Sabbath belonged to Christians. For example, the records of the Gemeinde list payment to a Mennonite brewer whose property was crossed by an *eruv*. In terms of both space and time, the dispensation granted by the *eruvin* allowed one to move through a mixed world still centered as a Jew.[147]

The *eruv* suggests the processes of thought and feeling that allow Glikl with her mixed culture to center Jews in her narrative and even to speak, in her diasporic world, of "my little nest" "in our dear Hamburg."[148] The Christian world sets conditions for the Jewish world, and occasionally Christians intervene directly in Jewish life, as in the *koved* at a wedding and in the slaying of a member of the household. In her seven books, they are more often on the periphery. The family deaths she mourns the most have little to do with the Christian/Jewish border; they are a result of illnesses, epidemics, or accidents that could happen to anyone in her day and that she interprets within a Jewish religious frame. The discord she focuses on most in her text concerns her fellow Jews, starting with her father's struggles with the other leaders of the Altona Gemeinde and ending with fisticuffs in the synagogue at Metz.

For centuries news of such local strife had circulated throughout Europe's Jewish communities in manuscript, as the opinion or "response" of one or another rabbi was sought by the different factions. Once the printing press appeared on the scene, these reports were often published in Hebrew, prepared by learned men but discussed by everyone. Glikl's autobiography is pervaded by such "Jewish news," and she gives her woman's response to it: "In my father's day, there were angry quarrels in the Gemeinde, and as is the way of the world, each person belonged to a different party." Then most of the synagogue officers died. "Thus God— may he be praised—settled the disputes among the parnasim."[149]

The quarrels in which she herself was an actor concerned marriage negotiations (disputes about the size of a dowry or even the suitability of a prospective spouse, which then softened into the harmonies of a wedding) and business relations. When a Viennese court Jew, Samuel Oppenheimer, was imprisoned and temporarily defaulted on his large debts to Glikl's son Nathan, she blamed not intriguers in the imperial government but the Oppenheimers: "In all their lives they cannot repay us for the frights, troubles, and worries we suffered through them."[150]

For Glikl Jews lived in a world where they could suddenly go from rich to poor and perhaps, with God's help, be rich again. Business trouble from Christians was to be expected, and inspired her to description only in special circumstances, as in Louis XIV's actions against the Jewish minters of Lorraine. Trouble from Jews provided her with some of her best stories. Thus, she relates at length how Judah Berlin withheld 1,500 reichstaler from her husband during their partnership and then, despite all the good they had done the young man, refused to return their merchandise when Haim politely dissolved the contract. Partisanship was intense in their respective Jewish communities, and Glikl had to admit that Haim's reluctance to compromise did not help. The case almost came before a gentile court (this would have been a shocking departure from solidarity), but finally a Jewish court ruled against Haim in Judah's favor. At least Haim recouped his losses in other sales—"the dear Lord saw our innocence," comments Glikl—and Judah and Haim finally lived in peace.[151] Other false partners and agents are described with more indignation. "The real Herod of my whole family," she says of one (presumably drawing on Herod I's bad reputation in the Talmud as a destroyer of Jewish institutions and slayer of Jewish leaders).[152] And of another: "a puffed-up, fat, overstuffed, arrogant, wicked man."[153]

If Glikl could say she was "beside herself" at such losses of reichstaler—"we were still young people . . . and with a house full of children"[154]—it was as nothing compared to the sorrows brought by her son Leib when she was a widow. Married and with a big shop in Berlin, the inexperienced and good-natured

Leib allowed himself (or so the mother tells it) to be robbed by assistants and in-laws, to lose money in poor bargains and in credit to Poles, and finally to sink so deeply into debt that he was threatened with arrest. His brothers and especially Glikl kept bailing him out with reichstaler, but it also cost Glikl much in the way of fainting, "trembling and anxiety as though of death," and bitter tears. Ultimately, she set Leib up in Hamburg selling for her, and under her watchful eye, he began to enjoy good credit again. When he died at twenty-seven several years later, she could write that though he had caused her much misery, his death was a heavy blow. Recalling David and Absalom, she forgave him completely. Besides, "he was the best *mentsh* in the world and studied well and had a Jewish heart for the sufferings of the poor."[155]

Clearly, with Leib, there was much more at stake for Glikl than reichstaler, and this takes us back to the bird story near the opening of her autobiography. If the telling of her life is a balancing of joys and sorrows (with sorrows often the heavier), her narrative is pulled forward by the question of what the generations owe each other. The bird story argues that the arrow moves ahead in time, the old loving and caring for the young even while, like Glikl, they complain about how hard it is to do so and how inconsiderate present-day children are in their demands. Glikl compares the joy with which she and Haim received a modest present from his parents ("a small jug worth about twenty reichstaler, but as precious as if worth a hundred") with the reactions of the young nowadays, "who want to take away everything from their parents without asking whether they are in a position to give that much."[156] But God has arranged that the old take care of the young, and this arrangement is practical, for "if children had the same trouble with their parents as their parents with them, they would soon tire." In the next world, too, parents can continue to care for their progeny. As she says about Haim's father,

"What a holy man he was! May his merits benefit us. And may he solicit God to send us no further sorrows; and that we may not sin or come to shame."[157]

But then Glikl herself moderates the message of the bird story and redirects the arrow in time. Early in Book 2, she recounts how her father took care of his mother-in-law, Mattie. Right after their marriage, Glikl's father and mother invited Mattie to live with them, which she did for seventeen years, continuing from their house her business of petty loans, "my father . . . treat[ing] her with the all the honor in the world, as if she was his own mother," placing her at the head of the table and bringing her gifts from every fair. Mattie died blessing and praising him before the whole family.[158] The care of the young for the old can also extend beyond the grave, as when Haim ben Joseph hired ten rabbis to pray and study Talmud in his house for a year after his father's death.[159]

The two models of links between the generations continue to vie with each other in the autobiography until the issue is joined for Glikl after Haim's death. In Book 4 she presents a portrait of a widow who avoids troubling her children: a portrait of her own mother, widowed at the same age as Glikl was to be, still alive as Glikl wrote, refusing all matches, supporting herself on what had been left her, living respectably in a little house with her maid, enjoying her children and grandchildren.[160] For ten years, this was the path Glikl followed, albeit with much greater business activity, turning down marriage offers with "the most distinguished men in the whole of Ashkenaz," offers that would have brought fortune to her and her offspring. She had even thought of going to live and serve God in the Holy Land once she had married off her last child.[161]

Her choice of widowhood was based on more than piety and seemliness, however, and on more than loyalty to Haim. In Book 5, she says that none of her kinfolk came to see her or offered to help her after her first thirty days of mourning. Nor did any of the people whom she and Haim had helped come to the aid of her newly orphaned sons when they were in need of business credit.[162] She concludes from this that one can depend on no one but God, and advises her children accordingly through a frightening story, which goes back to Jewish sources but whose somber ending may be her own addition or creation.

A king wanted to teach his naive son about how to prove true friendship. He instructed him to kill a calf, put it in a sack, and tell his steward, his secretary, and his valet that in the course of a drunken argument he had killed the royal chamberlain. From each he would ask help in burying the body so that the king would not punish him. The prince did as his father directed, and was refused help by his steward and his secretary, who said they would have nothing to do with a drunkard and murderer and would rather leave his service than obey. The valet answered that he was obliged to serve the prince as his master, but, fearing the king, he would only stand guard to see if anyone was coming while the prince buried the body; and this was done.

The next day, the three men told the king of the murder, thinking that he would slay his son and reward them as good servants. When confronted, the prince said that he had merely slaughtered a calf for sacrifice and, having done it improperly, had buried it as ritually impure. With the calf unearthed and the servants shamed, the prince admitted to the king that, among the three, he had found only half a friend. The king then advised his son to slay the steward and the secretary in order to make a full friend of the valet:

> "Should I slay so many for the sake of one?" asked the prince.
> "If a wise man is held captive under a thousand fools," the king answered, "and there is no other way to let him escape from them, I advise that the thousand fools be slain for the sake of saving the one wise man."

So the two men were slain, the valet became the prince's friend for life, and the prince agreed that a friend cannot be relied on until he is proved.[163]

This power test—which requires connivance in treason and

murder, begins with a lie, and ends, like the bird story, with two deaths (three, if we count the calf)—is not one that Glikl bas Judah Leib recommends putting into practice. Rather, it prepares for her self-description as a fiercely independent widow, relying only on God. In those days there was a popular image of the disloyal widow, embodied in an oft-told Yiddish tale (found in other European languages as well) which Glikl does not cite but surely knew. Weeping by her husband's fresh grave, a widow is seduced by a gallows guard who is keeping watch over several corpses. When one of the corpses is stolen, she offers her husband's body as a replacement so that her lover will not get into trouble. The *Mayse Bukh* version of the story opens: "The proverb says, women are weak-minded and can easily be persuaded."[164] Glikl's picture of herself as self-sustaining and steadfast effaces the competing image of the faithless widow.

The calf story also anticipates her self-judgment in Book 6: her decision to remarry had been a wrongful reliance on others. As she neared fifty-four, she explains to her children, she began to have new worries:

> All kinds of unpleasant things and troubles befell me through my children, and it always cost me much money. But it is not necessary to write of it; they are all my dear children and I forgive them, both those who cost me much and those who cost me nothing in the decline of my financial position.
>
> I still had a big business to manage, my credit was large with Jews and non-Jews both, and it all gave me nothing but grief. In the heat of summer and the rain and snow of winter I went to the fairs. Every day I went to market; even in winter I stood in my stall. And since little was left of what I once possessed, I was morose and tried only to sustain my honor so as not, God forbid, to become the charge of my children and not, God forbid, to live off the table of my friends. It would be worse to be with my children than strangers, in case, God forbid, through me my children sinned [by refusing to honor and take care of her?]. Day after day this would be worse than death for me.

The Börse (banking center) and weighing station of Hamburg, 1680

The Jewish quarter of Metz in 1696

*The piety of
Jewish women*

Lighting the Sabbath candles

Scalding the dishes to make them kosher
for Passover

Torah binders, embroidered by women for the circumcision of sons

Torah binder for Joseph ben Ari Leib, 1677

Torah binder for Mordecai Halberstadt, 1711

CREATING JEWISH SPACE: An *eruv* holder in the shape of a Star of David, placed in the synagogue with matzoh in it, to allow carrying on the Sabbath (Alsace, 1770). The bread *eruvin* in seventeenth-century Hamburg may have had a similar shape.

Jewish writing

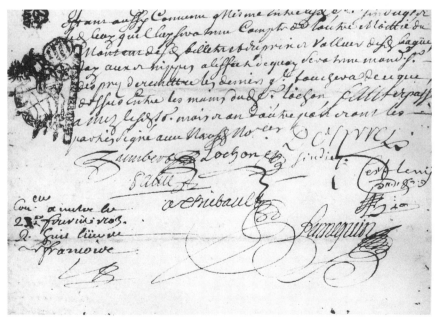

Signatures in French and Hebrew of Cerf (Hirsch) Levy, 1702

Memorial notice for Glikl bas Judah Leib, 1724

Signatures in French and Hebrew of Glikl's daughter Esther Goldschmidt, son-in-law Moses Schwabe, and granddaughter Anne (Hendele) on marriage contract, 1734

Yiddish books, with both cursive and semicursive type on their title pages

❧

Mayse Bukh (1602)

Tse'enah u-re'enah (1647–1648)

The opening paragraphs of the autobiography of Glikl bas
Judah Leib, in the copy made by her son Moses Hamel

Waare afbeeldinge van **Sabetha Sebi** den genaemden
herfteller des Joodfchen Rijcks.
rij pourtrait de **Sabbathai Sevi** qui fe dict Restaura:
teur du Roijaume de Juda & Ifrael.

Portrait of Sabbatai Zevi, who turned out not to be the messiah

Glikl also feared that as she became less able to endure the strain of fairs and to check on all her bales and goods, her business might founder and she "might, God forbid, become bankrupt and my creditors take a loss through me, thus shaming me, my children, and my pious husband, who lay under the sod."[165]

At this juncture, letters came from her son-in-law Moses and daughter Esther in Metz advising marriage with Hirsch Levy, "a widower, an outstanding Jew, a scholar, very rich, and maintaining a fine household." Glikl agreed to the match, made an advantageous arrangement for her own dowry and for the support of her last unmarried child, Miriam, and began to dream that Hirsch Levy's business connections might benefit her other children as well. "Unfortunately, God, may his name be praised, laughed at my thoughts and plans and had already long decided on my doom and affliction to punish me for my sins *in relying on people* [emphasis added]. I should not have thought of marrying again, for I could not hope to meet another Haim Hamel." Instead, "I fell into the hands of [Hirsch Levy] and had to live the very shame against which I had hoped to protect myself."[166]

Hirsch Levy's fall, as she tells it, was terrible. At one point, he even went into hiding, sergeants came to the house—"full of more gold and silver than I had seen in any wealthy man's house in all of Ashkenaz."—and sealed everything as they made an inventory, and Glikl and her maid had almost nothing to eat. Ultimately Hirsch settled with his creditors as best he could, grateful not to be imprisoned. Glikl was able to protect the moneys that belonged to her son Nathan and her daughter Miriam, but had to give up hope for much of her marriage portion. She was, she tells us (using a comparison that goes back to the Lord's words to Moses on Mount Sinai), "like the eagle who took his children on his wing, saying, 'It is better that I be shot at and not my children.' "[167]

Then, after the disasters which open Book 7, Glikl stops being a parent bird. Hirsch dies, leaving her "in misery and woe." When the husband of one of her stepdaughters forces her to vacate Hirsch's house, Glikl moves into a little room up a flight of twenty-two steps, cooking for herself with the aid of a single servant.[168] After three years, she "can no longer hold out" against the invitation of her daughter Esther and her son-in-law Moses Schwabe, now a parnas and "the wealthiest man" in the Jewish community of Metz. In 1715 she moves into their house.[169] There she lives with the honor that her father accorded her grandmother Mattie years before: she is "given the best of every dish," and dainties are saved for her if she stays past noon at the synagogue. Now she writes about Hirsch Levy with some forgiveness: he was a clever and able businessman, "loved and respected in prosperity," risking his life for the community which he served for so many years. As for her daughter Esther, never has Glikl seen a house run with such generosity and openness. "May the Almighty enable her to continue thus till her hundredth year—in health and tranquillity, in wealth and honor."[170]

Though the book does not end here, Glikl—now that she is willing to take her place at Esther's table and be cared for—gives a new agency to the children who will one day read her words. She has discovered that her personal life can have a resting point on a safe shore.

Up to now we have seen rather little reference to sin in Glikl's writing, and what there is has been much outweighed by the troubling quest for worldly wealth and honor. Stories about birds and calf burials may advance one's understanding of human solidarity and the relation of young to old, but what contribution do they make to religious sensibility? And what of the pious Talmudist? His happy ending seems to depend as much on the human solution of riddles as on trust in God's help.

But Glikl brings much more to bear upon her life than this. In the first place, God is repeatedly invoked in her autobiography, and not just in the closing of each book or in formulaic ejaculatory phrases, but in short *tkhines* prayers and in recollections of earlier prayers. "My husband—may the memory of the saintly be a blessing—stood weeping in one corner of the room and I in the other, imploring God's mercy," she says of the time one of their children was thought seriously ill, positioning herself and Haim in corners as rabbinical commentary had positioned Rebecca and Isaac when they were begging the Lord that Rebecca should conceive.[171]

In the second place, Glikl refers to herself often as a sinner and ordinarily uses her sins, in traditional Jewish fashion, to account for the worst blows of the Lord. This explanation for human suffering was being challenged in her day by the dualism of the Lurianic Kabbalah, which attributed evil in human life to the action of an eternal demonic power—the "Anti-Adam of Belial"—and not just to human sins.[172] Glikl had access to Kabbalah only in the watered-down version of Horowitz's *Yesh Nochalin*, but she had certainly read about spirit possession in her *Mayse Bukh* and about demons in her *Brantshpigl*, not to mention what her mother and grandmother would have told her. In her autobiography, she advises her children that giving alms during life will protect the soul at death against the "troop of angels (or demons) of destruction, the *malakhe habbalah*—God forbid— who are in the air between heaven and earth." (She does not mention the amulets widely used to ward off evil spirits, but her repeated "God forbid" is both a plea to the Lord and a deflection of the *malakhe habbalah*.)[173] Still, this familiar host of demons was no match for the Lord's power, as was the new Anti-Adam of Belial. Glikl held to the older view that "everything comes from the Lord," and her usual formulation was that "if we are sometimes punished, it is because of our own misdeeds." Haim Hamel was taken away "because of my sins"; "as it is said, because of the wicked, the saint is taken away." "My sins are too heavy to bear . . . Every day, every hour, every minute—full of sins."[174]

What were the sins of Glikl bas Judah Leib? Leon Modena confessed outright to at least one specific sin—that is, gambling. Glikl is less direct, but what emerges in the course of the *Life* is an impatience like that of Job as he argues with his three friends:

bitter complaining about what has happened to her, inordinate railing against her lot. Indeed, Glikl's identification with him may have begun with Job's wife, who (as Ilana Pardes has shown) opens the process of complaint with the words, "Dost thou still retain thine integrity? Curse God and die."[175]

Glikl says that her sorrow at Mattie's death was so great, "I was terrified that I had sinned against the Almighty God." Concerning her worries about her pregnancies and her children's illnesses she says, "Every two years I had a child, and I had much distress, as is the order of things, when there is a house full of children, God protect them. I often thought no one had such a heavy burden as I, and had as much vexation as I through children. But I, foolish one, did not know how well things were with me when 'my children were like young olive trees about my table.' " (Glikl's young olive trees come from Psalm 128.) Temporary business losses generate the same response, and then anxiety about its excess: "I fell very ill because of my worry," she recalls about a year when 11,000 reichstaler slipped out of their hands, "but to the world at large I put down my condition to my pregnancy. Yet a fire burned within me." Such sorrow and lamenting were a waste not only of health and life, but also of piety: "we . . . cannot rightly serve the Almighty with a grief-stricken body. The holy Shekhinah cannot dwell in a mournful body." (The Shekhinah is defined in the Talmud as the presence or dwelling of God in the created universe. In popular Jewish lore and in kabbalistic perception, the Shekhinah is personified and gendered as a female, seeking to unite herself with the Lord as his bride. Here Glikl carries the image further by imagining the Shekhinah dwelling in the individual person.)[176]

Glikl knows that others are not like her. When her mother was young, she and Grandmother Mattie had "at times not more than a crust of bread all day. Still they put up with it and trusted God—may he be praised—not to forsake them, and my mother has the same trust today. I wish I had such a nature; God does not bestow the same things on everyone."[177] And Haim, though he could mourn the death of a child as much as she, had greater strength and detachment for suffering losses in wealth and honor: "All his days he sought no position as leader in the community; on the contrary he refused it, laughing at people when he saw what store they set by these things. [For him, prayer and devotion were more important.] . . . When I often, in my human weakness, would let myself go and be impatient, he would laugh at me and say, 'You are foolish. I trust in God and set little store by people's words.' "[178] As long as Haim was alive, he could tease her and especially comfort her (she recalls that "Only comfort my Glik-likhen" were his last words to her mother),[179] but when he was gone, whom could she complain to and who could set her straight?

Thus, Glikl's autobiography is not only a life and moral teaching shaped for her children and not only a writing begun to distract her from melancholy. It is also a lament to the Lord, who is in some sense her reader; it lays out her grievances once again, while at the same time exploring the meaning of suffering and seeking to find a way to accept what God sends. Sometimes she turns to the simple moral recompense that Eliphaz defends to Job (Job 4–5) and echoes it: "So will God be mindful of the good person and protect him from all evil."[180] Sometimes she turns to Job's final resolution—that we cannot understand God's mysterious ways, but can only affirm and fear his power. Or, as Glikl puts it: "The evil and their children live in prosperity and riches, while things go badly for the righteous godfearing people and their children. And so we are wont to ask ourselves, how can it be that God the Almighty is a righteous judge? But I think this is vanity, for the deeds of the Almighty—may he be praised— are impossible to conceive or fathom."[181]

In this struggle for patience and meaning—a struggle that is *not ever wholly won*—storytelling was Glikl's most effective weapon. It gave her a way to "argue with God," a Jewish tradition going back through the rabbis to Jacob (Genesis 28).[182] It provided her with the dialogue at the center of spirituality and with the surprising blows and turns that are the powers of storytelling.

There are twelve full stories in Glikl's seven books, and several more brief summaries of or allusions to tales. Some of them are her variants on stories published in Vayber Taytsh collections: the much reprinted *Mayse Bukh*, the *Brantshpigl*, and others.[183] If Alexander of Macedon came into her repertory from medieval Jewish sources that went back to the Talmud,[184] Solon and Croesus she must have read about in some collection deriving from Herodotus, either in German or translated into Yiddish.[185] And as we have seen, Glikl's account of Charlemagne and Empress Irene of Constantinople came almost certainly from "German books."[186]

Nor were such "German books" difficult to find, for there was considerable interest in stories old and new and in storytelling modes among Glikl's Christian contemporaries. *Reynard the Fox* had German editions in Hamburg throughout the seventeenth century, to cite but one example of a traditional tale. Meanwhile, Eberhard Werner Happel, writer and newspaper editor of Hamburg, gave a story form to recent and curious events from all over the globe and, drawing upon the most up-to-date travel literature, published *Der insulanische Mandorell* (1682), adventure tales that took his brave hero from islands in the East Indies to the Caribbean.[187] By the time Glikl got to Metz, the *Fables* of La Fontaine had seen many printings, Charles Perrault had begun to publish his collection of French tales of Mother Goose, and the Comtesse d'Aulnoy was bringing out her fairy tales.[188] In short, Glikl's delight in stories was not exclusively Jewish and certainly not "archaic," but was an appetite shared across religious lines and renewed by seventeenth-century events and concerns.

Like any good storyteller, Glikl crafted her tales according to her own tastes and needs. In the account of the pious Talmudist she not only added the savage-princess episode and the riddle tests, but also subtracted the opening characteristic of the Jewish versions. In the latter, the story was linked to the Second Commandment, which prohibits taking the Lord's name in vain: the husband fell into debt and was imprisoned because he followed his father's deathbed counsel never to take an oath.[189] In contrast,

Glikl's studious hero gets into trouble when he is brought into court for debt, and his friends will not stand surety for him—a predicament reminiscent of Glikl's own feeling of abandonment by her relatives in the early months of her widowhood, and of her resentment at a Hamburg merchant who refused to honor the bills of exchange of her fatherless sons.[190] As for Glikl's story of the father bird and his fledglings, talking birds were used in Jewish fables, and her account draws from existing tale types; but her cast of characters and turns of plot may come largely from her own invention.[191]

The stories are placed among the episodes of her life to intensify mood, to deepen interest ("Here is a pleasant story," "Hir bey izt ayn hipsh mayse," says Glikl to introduce one that turns out to be quite sorrowful),[192] and to provide moral and religious commentary on what has just happened or is about to happen. The tales fall into two rough categories: those that illustrate why one should rise above all concern for wealth and pride in reputation, and those that illustrate how one should bear suffering. In fact, their narratives are sometimes so troublesome, so full of surprises and reversals, that they raise as many questions as they answer. Nor does the simple telling of a story end all conflict about the matter in the subsequent narrative of Glikl's life.

For example, a story early in Book 1 tells of how Alexander the Great visited wise men in a faraway land, who lived in nakedness and simplicity without riches or envy. He could neither threaten them with destruction nor beguile them with gifts, and so he said proudly, "Ask of me what you will and I shall give it to you." They answered with one voice, "My lord king, give us eternal life." "If I could give you that," the king responded, "I would give it to myself." The wise men then asked him to ponder how much he had exerted himself in destroying so many peoples and lands and how short a time there was to keep what he had won. To what purpose was it all?

"The king did not know what to answer, but he said to them, 'I found the world thus and thus I must leave it. A king's heart cannot be without the movement of war.' "[193]

Alexander is not completely transformed by the wise men's

arguments. And Glikl's heart is not transformed either, but remains torn. In later books she agonizes about worldly losses *and* tells stories proving that wealth and power are transitory: how Solon rebuked prideful Croesus that a man should not boast of his good fortune till he knows how his life will end; how Alexander of Macedon learned that the human eye is insatiable in its desire for riches but that at death a small grave will suffice.[194]

Her tales about accepting suffering with love of God are extreme and positioned to test her own responses sharply. One such test comes after Glikl reports how, in the course of a visit to Hannover, her young daughter Zipporah was suspected of having plague, placed by the local Gemeinde under the care of two old Polish Jews, and sent to live with Christian peasants. This is the episode that led Glikl and Haim to stand weeping in the corners of the room, begging God for mercy. Zipporah returned healthy and merry, and, thanking God, Glikl goes on to tell of the downfall of Irene, Empress of the East. Sought by Charlemagne in marriage so that their two empires might be united in friendship, Irene was dethroned by the wicked lord Nicephoros and tricked into revealing to him the location of all her treasure. After his coronation, Nicephoros treacherously banished her from Constantinople to the Isle of Lesbos, where, "in great grief," she died a year later. "To see what happened to so high an empress and with what patience she bore it all is to learn that everyone should accept with patience the troubles sent by God, may his name be praised."[195]

Glikl had taken her account from a version of an early ninth-century Byzantine chronicle by Theophanes,[196] from which she erased a few excessively Christian references (such as the ones to Judas' betraying our Lord and to Irene's interest in nunneries) and any mention of Irene's earlier political mischief (such as Irene's blinding her son Constantine VI in a quarrel about imperial control). Theophanes' Irene, like Glikl's, blamed her ruin on her sins, but Glikl's empress went on to quote from the Old Testament Job: "The Lord giveth, the Lord taketh away, the Lord's name be praised."[197] Even with these modifications, the faraway empress makes a strange model for Glikl ("I would have given half my own life so my children could be healthy," says the Jewish mother in Hamburg),[198] and Irene's patience does not silence Glikl's subsequent complaints.

The tale following little Mattie's death a few years after Zipporah's recovery is even more unsettling. Glikl recalls her enormous sorrow, as we have heard, and goes on to apply Psalm 31:12 to herself: "At last I was bound to forget my beloved child, as is the decree of God, 'I am forgotten as a dead one out of mind.' " The story of the third-century sage Johanan ben Nappaha, embroidered by Glikl from a source going back to the Talmud,[199] then demonstrates how a devout man accepts loss. Of Johanan's ten sons, all had died but a three-year-old (Glikl makes him about the same age as her Mattie). One day the little boy, curious about the big wash-kettle on the fire, fell into the boiling water. The father tried to snatch him out, but all that came was a finger of the child's hand. Reb Johanan banged his head against the wall and cried to his students, "Mourn my suffering star." "And from that time he carried hanging from his neck the child's bone as a remembrance. Whenever a strange scholar came to see him, he would show him in all tranquillity this little bone—just as though he were showing his son."[200] Glikl is remembering Mattie in her book against the decree of God, as Reb Johanan remembered his son in his bone. Although she admits she mourned too much and insists that one must accept what God sends, the tale suggests again that the argument with him is not wholly quieted.

My last example, from Book 6, is the most complex. A story of polygamy, incest, and violence recast from the biblical tale of David and Absalom (2 Samuel 13–18), it is placed in the midst of Glikl's description of her betrothal negotiations with Hirsch Levy. She says she has a double goal in this *mayse,* which she "knows for certain to be true and really happened": she will show that she is not the only person to whom misfortunes come, and she will also show that God helps those who suffer. "May it happen to me as it did to this pious king."[201]

There once was a king named Jedidiah ("Friend of God"),[202] who lived in the Arab lands with his many wives and children. Of these children his favorite was Abadon ("Destruction"), whom he always let have his own way, "and from this much evil came about." Another son, Emunis, fell sick with love for his beautiful sister Danila, by trickery got the king to send her to his chamber, and then had his way with her. When Abadon heard of the shame, he vowed revenge, especially since his father had not punished Emunis; he had his brother slain as he sat at table after the hunt. Enraged at Abadon, the king banished and disinherited him, whereupon the favorite son besieged the father's capital, seized it, and raped his father's wives. A battle ensued during which King Jedidiah admitted his own sins and asked his men to spare Abadon's life. "Putting their trust in God and their own just cause," the king's soldiers won the day and slew Abadon. The king returned to his throne, pardoning all his enemies, "reigning for the rest of his life in safety, peace, and honor," and seeing his son Friedlieb ("Beloved Peace") succeed him before he died.

Glikl's final commentary is that "God's punishment is slow but sure": Emunis and Abadon lose their lives, and the king suffers hardship. "If the king had not had so repentant a heart and God had not kept special watch over him, who knows what further ill might have befallen him? . . . We humans cannot know when God will punish or when he will do good. He slays and he heals, may his name be praised."[203]

Jedidiah and his wives and children certainly provide an ominous transition to the ill-fated second marriage of Glikl bas Judah Leib. Glikl used King David briefly as a model in two other places—once in praising the equanimity with which he accepted the death of his first child by Bathsheba (2 Samuel 12:19–23), and once in likening her forgiveness of her son Leib to David's pardoning of Absalom.[204] But the tumults that break out around "King Jedidiah" are much more violent and transgressive, even if the story does finally end in the peaceful dynastic succession of Friedlieb.[205] What can Glikl's children have thought of their mother's wish, "May it happen to me as it did to this pious king"?

Like the Book of Job, Glikl's storied life is full of "unresolved tension,"[206] and one suspects that she herself wanted her tales to provoke questioning among her readers—provoke them to go beyond her own brief commentary to wonderment and debate.

If so, then Glikl would be using her stories as the rabbis had long used exempla and parables—or *meshalim*, as the Jews called them—to illustrate their teaching and preaching. Though a few rabbis voiced opposition to this mixing of the sacred and the profane and even feared that the *mashal* would tempt listeners into false ideas, most of them in Glikl's day defended the exemplum as a device honored since the time of Solomon.[207] (Here the rabbinical repertory, extending even to legends, went beyond the contemporary Lutheran and Catholic prescription that parables and "moral paintings" for sermons be drawn only from true or historical events.)[208] From her seat in the women's balcony, Glikl would have understood the rabbi's sermons, delivered as they were in both Yiddish and Hebrew. She may well have picked up from them her willingness to make moral use both of tales like the one about Jedidiah, which she "knew to be true," and of those about Alexander the Great, which "she did not write as truth" and which might be "heathenish fable[s]."[209]

This brings us to the status of Glikl's religious voice in her autobiography. It is not a rabbinical voice, and she more than once disqualified herself from any claim to such a voice. (In the midst of a long description of a quarrel between two learned rabbis for a position at Metz, she comments with some irony, "It does not belong to a lowly unpretentious woman to write between great mountains.")[210] Perhaps she received some inspiration from the *firzogerin* in her Altona synagogue, the woman who led the prayers and songs in the women's balcony during the service; indeed, perhaps she was herself a *firzogerin* for a time in Metz. But Glikl's is not the ordinary voice of the Vayber Taytsh: the *tkhines* prayers of the seventeenth and eighteenth centuries may have gone so far as to image women studying Torah in Paradise, but they brought consolation for suffering rather than prompting questions about it.[211] Nor was the impressive Yiddish morality book by the sixteenth-century Rebecca bas Meir Tiktiner a sufficient model for Glikl, for it lacked a personal thread of life history.[212] In her "melancholy" and restiveness, Glikl used the Vayber Taytsh collections for different ends, placing the stories, the *mayse*, next to the discrete and prickly memories of her life. The Jewish oral practice—"that reminds me of a story"—is here raised to an elaborate art, one that does not bring tranquil closure. Through this unusual literary structure,[213] Glikl bas Judah Leib wrote the book of morals, spiritual inquiry, and religious reflection which, in rabbinical eyes, she had neither the learning nor the standing to do.

To be sure, Glikl's debates with the Lord would hardly have seemed dangerous to an age reacting to the audacity of Baruch/Benedict de Spinoza and to deists like Juan/Daniel de Prado, who had spent a year among the Sephardim of Hamburg during Glikl's youth.[214] Her queries about suffering always stayed within a Jewish and biblical frame and were addressed to a listening God. But we should not underestimate the range of what God had to hear from her. About the last hours of Haim Hamel, she recounted that she had said to him, " 'My heart, may I take hold of you? For I have been unclean.' And he said to me, 'God forbid, my child. It will not be long until you go to your bath.' But, alas, he did not live till then." Her autobiography allowed her both to show how rigorously Haim lived up to the Jewish law, and to lay out the cost to her of the constraints of ritual purity.[215]

Glikl's autobiography also allowed her to speak of Messianic hope. Her first book ends with a prayer that "God—may he be praised—should not desert us, nor all Israel, but bring us consolation soon and send us our Messiah, our righteous redeemer soon, in our time." She also recounted to her children with what joy the Jews of Hamburg had greeted the news of the proclaimed Messiah Sabbatai Zevi in 1665, about the time Mattie was born. The Portuguese and German Jews alike had danced and rejoiced and had embarked on acts of penance, prayers, and giving away of property as preparation for redemption. Glikl's father-in-law sent barrels of linen and dried foods to Hamburg, ready for a boat for the Holy Land, and kept them in Glikl's house long after the news had reached them that Sabbatai Zevi had converted to Islam. The Messiah had not yet arrived ("for two or three years your people Israel sat on the birthing stool, but nothing came forth save wind"), and the barrels were unpacked.[216]

Looking back on these momentous events more than two decades later, Glikl says that the delay in the Messiah's coming could have been due to human sin, "the envy and groundless hatred among us."[217] Perhaps it was this disappointment, when she was a young mother of twenty, that set her off on her long engagement with the issues of sin and suffering and also contributed to her framing her life so often in terms of loss: the lost Messiah, the lost Mattie, the lost Haim. And when we read her tale of the pious Talmudist ruling his island paradise of Jews and converts to Judaism, can we glimpse a muted expression of her youthful hope?

At the end of her seventh book, Glikl returns again to last things, which this time have dangerous portents. Safely now in Esther's household, Glikl recounts a tragedy that occurred in the Metz synagogue one Sabbath feast day in the spring of 1715. A great and mysterious rumbling was heard, and the women in the upper gallery, fearing that the synagogue was falling, began to run out, trampling each other and killing several women in the panic. Glikl in the lower women's gallery fell on her way out and was in terror for her pregnant daughter Esther, who subsequently miscarried. Especially she was devastated by the death of the innocent young women. How could such a thing happen? Addressing the Old Testament Mother, Glikl ponders the strange noise, which some heard and some did not, and a strange vision of six tall veiled women, seen by some in the upper gallery just before the panic.[218]

She decides that such punishment was called forth by what had happened in the synagogue during the Rejoicing of the Law festival the autumn before. The women had begun to quarrel with one another, pulling off their head coverings, and the men had begun to fight among themselves before the Scrolls of the Law, while the rabbi vainly shouted threats of excommunication.[219] Glikl does not mention that her stepdaughter Hendele/Anne Levy had been one of the culprits.[220] Nor does she record for her children the other disordering events of her last years: the bankruptcies and prosecutions of Hirsch Levy's son Samuel and Moses Schwabe's brother Reuben,[221] and, most terrible, the conversion of her London grandson Moses to the Church of England on the first of January 1723, only a few years after his father Mordecai had returned "with immense riches" from India. It may have been hard for Glikl's daughter Freudchen to shield her from such a blow, since Moses announced to the world in an English publication his reasons for believing that the Messiah had already come and the efforts of his horrified parents to get him to change his mind.[222]

The last entry in Glikl's seventh book is dated 1719. It records a vision by a woman, probably Glikl herself, as she washes dishes one evening along the banks of the Moselle River.[223] The night sky opens strangely and grows light as day; sparks (kabbalistic sparks?) fly across the heavens, and then abruptly all is dark. "May God grant that this be for the good," says Glikl bas Judah Leib, and ends her autobiography.

MARIE DE L'INCARNATION

───────────── ✦ ─────────────

New Worlds

IN THE SUMMER OF 1654, an Ursuline sister in Québec mailed her son in Paris a relation of her life and the Lord's conduct toward her. Among much else, she reminded him of what had happened when she had first taken the veil in the town of Tours some twenty-three years before. Everyone but her confessor had pressed her not to leave her son, who was then only eleven. Since she was a widow, the boy would be alone in the world and God would punish her. She herself had been torn in two. She felt her "natural love" for him and her obligations to him, "but the interior voice that followed me everywhere said, 'Hurry, it's time; it's not good for you to be in the world any longer.' Putting my son in the arms of God and the holy Virgin, I left him, and my aged father also, who wept in lamentation."[1]

Once installed in the Ursuline house, she had endured another trial. Her son's schoolmates had come to the convent door, taunting him that he was going to be "abandoned and despised" and goading him to get his mother back. They had set up a hue and cry at the gate, and her son's voice had pierced her heart: "Give me back my mother, I want my mother." He had poked his head through the Communion grill during Mass and shouted, "Hé, give me back my mother!" He had begged to see her in front of the visitors' parlor, and she had been sent to console him and give him little gifts. "He left walking backward, his eyes fixed on the dormitory windows to see if I was there. He walked that way till the convent was out of sight."

She discussed the matter (her verb is *traiter*) humbly and lovingly with Our Lord, whose holy will she had followed in abandoning her son, and over and over again asked his compassion for the poor lad. "One day, while I was walking up the novitiate stairs, Jesus assured me by interior words that he would take care of my son and consoled me so sweetly that all my affliction turned to peace and certitude."[2]

The mother was Marie Guyart, named Marie de l'Incarnation in religion, one of the two women who founded the first Ursuline convent and school for girls in North America. Her son was Claude Martin, who in 1654 was in his thirteenth year as a monk in the Benedictine congregation of Saint Maur. He had begged her to provide him an account of her interior life and of the grace and favors the Lord had bestowed upon her. "Ordered" to do so by her confessor, she sent the notebooks from Québec, insisting in return that Claude keep them secret.[3] Instead, in 1677, five years after she died in Canada, he published them in Paris, slightly revised and with many additions of his own and from her other writings, under the title *La Vie de la venerable Mere Marie de l'Incarnation*.

Marie Guyart's life has in it some of the same motifs as that of Glikl bas Judah Leib—the struggle against melancholy, the fear of abandoning or being abandoned by the younger generation, and the assertion of self against what life has meted out—but they are played out quite differently with Catholic instruments. Whereas Glikl did no more than dream of a move to Palestine, Marie fought her way to Canada, far from the France of Richelieu, Mazarin, Colbert, and their kings. Whereas Glikl was never in a position to tell outsiders what they should believe, Marie spent years insisting on Christian truth to peoples into whose lands her countrymen had intruded. Mother Marie's model for relating to outsiders was also different from that of the understandably vigilant Glikl bas Judah Leib. The two women resemble each other in one regard: they illustrate the significance of writing and language for self-discovery, moral exploration and, in Marie's case, the discovery of others. And like Glikl, Marie de l'Incarnation was a *femme forte,* a classical and biblical image used both by the literary feminists of seventeenth-century France and by the religious: "a *femme forte* such as Solomon depicted," her Ursuline sisters said of her after she died.[4]

Marie Guyart was born in 1599 in Tours, a textile town of almost 20,000 inhabitants and the judicial and ecclesiastical center of its region. The memory of the Wars of Religion was still vivid there when Marie was growing up. Old-timers could recall how the Protestants had for a few months in 1562 been masters of the city and cleansed all the churches of their statues and relics. If the Huguenots were now a small group living in uneasy legality under the recently promulgated Edict of Nantes, the ardent Catholics of Tours felt the need to deepen and expand their faith more strongly than ever. The Wars of Religion had also brought the king to Tours: from 1585 to 1594, with the Catholic League in control of Paris, the city on the Loire had been the provisional capital of France. Now the king and his *Parlement* were back in Paris, but Tours still had an important group of royal financiers living within its expanded walls.[5]

Marie Guyart came from a modest family. Though her son boasted in the *Life* of his maternal grandmother's connections to a Touraine family ennobled in royal service, Marie's father was at best only a "merchant baker," and it was a step up when he arranged to marry one daughter to a schoolteacher, another to a busy wagoner, and Marie to a silkmaker—a member of the city's most important industry. When Marie was a girl, Jesus had visited and kissed her in a dream, and as a teenager she had thought wistfully of the local Benedictine nunnery of Beaumont, where one of her mother's distant kin was abbess. In fact, that ancient and noble convent would have been unlikely to receive a baker's daughter as a novice, even if her parents had agreed to a religious vocation.[6]

Marie dutifully married the silkmaker Claude Martin when she was seventeen. She then put aside the "vain" reading of her youth to concentrate on books of piety and the Psalms in French, and surprised all her neighbors, if not her obliging husband, by going to church every day. At least her acts of devotion did not interfere with her care for her husband's silkworkers and other tasks around the shop. At eighteen she became a mother; at nineteen she was left a widow with her infant son, Claude.

Even before her husband's death, a shadow had fallen on the marriage—an unspecified threat to Martin's goods and a false accusation made against him by a woman of Tours. (Marie and her son refer mysteriously to "disgrace," "afflictions occasioned by her husband, although innocently and without design," and "persecutions.") After his death, there were lawsuits; Marie lost the silk shop and most or all of the inheritance she and her son had been left beyond her guaranteed dower. Proposals for remarriage came nonetheless, but after some hesitation in each case, Marie turned them down. "Though I loved your father very much," she said to Claude later, "and was at first sensitive to his loss, still, seeing that I was free, my soul melted in thankfulness that I no longer had anyone but God in my heart, and could use my solitude to think of him and raise you to be his servant."[7]

For a time she lived "in retreat" in a little room on the top floor of her father's house, supporting herself by embroidery and dressing "ridiculously" so that men would know she was not available for courtship. Claude she entrusted to a wet nurse—a custom more characteristic of wealthy Christian families than of mere artisans during her day, but perhaps Marie had lost her milk during her afflictions. After his return near the age of two, she moved with him to the busy household of her sister Claude Guyart and her brother-in-law Paul Buisson, which was soon enlarged by their son and daughter Marie. Buisson was a successful merchant wagoner, transporting commercial goods to different parts of the kingdom and artillery for the royal army. For the next decade Marie Guyart lived, as she put it, "amid the racket of merchants," spending days in the stables where the bales were stored and discharged, surrounded by porters, wagoners, carters, and fifty or sixty horses. Her duties might be anything from grooming the horses and making meals for the family and their many servants to keeping the books, advising Buisson and writing his letters, and running the entire business when her brother-in-law and sister were away in their country house. "God gave me talent for business," Marie Guyart admitted, and in fact the Buisson affairs prospered with her help.[8]

Privately, for Marie those years were filled with surprising mystical experience, the development of mental prayer, works of charity, and severe bodily mortification. On the vigil of the Feast of the Incarnation, 1620, as she went about her activities on the streets of Tours, she suddenly saw with her inner eye for the first time all the sins and imperfections of her entire life and felt herself plunged in the blood of the forgiving Christ. When she came to herself, she was in front of the chapel of the Feuillants, a penitential religious order that had arrived in Tours only a few months before. She entered and, indifferent to a woman eavesdropping nearby, tearfully poured out her sins to one of the Fathers. The astonished Feuillant told her to come back the next day and tell him all over again. So she acquired what she had never known existed: a Director for her soul. Up to that time she had confessed only in the routine question-and-answer of her parish priest.[9]

To the historian, the episode is paradigmatic of the Catholic reform that was stirring up diverse milieus in Tours: the order of the Feuillants, recently split off in its own austere rule from the Cistercians; Dom François de Saint Bernard taking seriously a young widowed mother and artisan who had simply come in off the street; the book she soon found herself reading, François de Sales's *Introduction à la vie dévote* (1609), written initially to instruct lay women who wanted to cultivate a religious life in the world.[10]

It was under the guidance of her Feuillant Director—first Dom François, then Dom Raymond de Saint Bernard—that she found the words to speak not only of her sins but of her visions. It was her Director who advised her to let Christ lead her soul and then tell him of it afterward. It was he who allowed her to discipline her flesh by means of nettles, chains, harsh clothing, and a bed of boards, and approved further ways of humiliating herself in everyday life. It was he who refused her request to nail to the cathedral door her signed account of all the sins she had ever committed, so that the whole world could walk upon her with contempt.[11] Indeed, it was he who encouraged Marie to make writing a central part of her religious experience, sending her into a world of literate culture that a Catholic tradeswoman would not ordinarily enter very far: Marie's sister Claude could read and write, yet when she died in the 1640s her family possessions included religious paintings but not a single book.[12]

Guyart's development in those years, from age twenty to thirty, can be summed up in the words "communication" and "mortification": in these actions the willful self was thought to be dislodged and reduced. Amid the bustle of the wagoner's household, she read in the French vernacular the life of Teresa of Avila, who had just been canonized a saint; the Scriptures in the Louvain Catholic edition (she lingered over the Song of Songs); and the mystical works attributed to Saint Dionysus the Areopagite, recommended by her Director. Not all reading set her on the right path. The books on mental (that is, internal or silent) prayer prescribed systematic meditation—a "method," with "preparations, preludes, divisions, and points"; these techniques were supposed to prevent the soul from falling into false illuminations and rebelliousness, but they just gave Marie violent headaches. At this point Dom Raymond forbade her to continue such human effort to reach God and told her simply to abandon her soul passively to the divine Spirit. He did not fear that as a weak-willed woman she would be deceived by the devil.[13]

Dom Raymond's advice worked. God made her speak to Christ "in a language beyond the power of the natural creature," and then her Beloved visited her directly, printing the divine Word on her soul. "No books, no study," she said, "can teach these divine ways of speaking."[14] Such communication might occur suddenly during Mass at the Feuillants, as she looked at the seraphim sculpted on the altar, when the meanings of the Trinity, its unity and distinctions, were revealed to her in wordless clarity; or as she prayed before the sacred Host, when God made her see that he was like a great sea that would suffer no impurity.[15] On this sea she could ride with safety when the Buisson business took her into the depths of a Huguenot shop or thrust her among the "noisy crude servants" in the stables.[16] God might also visit her as she went about her affairs—in the cellar, in the streets—or between waking and sleeping, when through the force of union between her soul and the "adorable" Word Incarnate she would feel her heart ravished from her body and united with his, two hearts in one.[17]

Throughout she wrote. The general confession of her sins was only the start. When the violence of her feelings for the sacred Incarnate Word could not be borne, she retired to her room for her pen. "Ah, you are a sweet love. You stop our eyes, you steal our sense." "Words of fire," her son said later when he found them among her papers. She wrote also for her Director, putting her visions and her inner dispositions on paper, trying to find a language as best she could. "How painful it is not to be able to speak of things of the spirit as they are, to talk only in stutters, to search for similes." And when the preacher seemed to her to falter in his sermons, with stale comparisons of the Lord to lions or lambs, she returned to her desk and wrote her own celebration of him: "ineffable, all . . . my all."[18]

The hand that wrote was also the hand that raised the flagellant's nettles to her body. She struck herself till she bled, then put haircloth to the wounds to intensify the pain. During the day, she wore chains and a hairshirt beneath her garments; at night, she slept on a plank with haircloth next to her flesh. No one must see her penance ("otherwise they would think I was crazy"), so when she felt the inspiration, she would slip away to cellars, grain attics, and stables for her flagellation. If it was night, she might sleep there fitfully on a bale or board (where her son Claude was at the time, she did not say; nor did he). All this she undertook in order to be worthy of Christ's love: "I treated my body like a slave," "like a dead person"; "because I was a great sinner, I hated my body." And the Word Incarnate responded, helping her raise her arm on cold winter nights, renewing her strength and determination through the Sacred Host, which she was permitted, as an exceptional grace, to take at the Feuillants' almost every day. The greater her mortification of the flesh, the greater her inner union with God. "I was insatiable."[19]

Amid these satisfactions, there were times of doubt. When she was around twenty-five, "the devil put the thought in my head that I was crazy to suffer so much, that there were many people in Christendom who kept God's commands and would be saved without so much trouble." And why should she be so subject to her Director? What harm was there in following her own will? "What good is all this?" she burst out one day before a startled serving girl. And then thoughts about her son filled her imagination. She loved him very much, so she said later; but was she wrong to prepare his future through her poverty? Certainly her relatives told her she was letting him down. Would God one day hold her to account for living as if her son had no needs?[20]

Worst of all was when she feared she was "a hypocrite, deceiving [her] Director, telling him stories and imagined things as true." Had she truly been united with the Incarnate Word? Had some trap of the devil or her imagination supplied her vision of the Trinity? In such a mood, she redoubled her mortifications without effect; her inner life darkened, and it was all she could do not to snap at those who rebuked her.[21]

Here Marie Guyart was facing the central doubt of all the mystics of her day, and she was all the more vulnerable since her internal prayer was improvised and inspired, rather than guided by a Jesuit or even a Salesian "method."[22] (Indeed, in Guyart's day, worries about believability and "hypocrisy" beset people in very different predicaments—spiritual, social, political, and scientific.)[23] Perhaps the pages of Saint Teresa's *Life* on coping with fear of hypocrisy and the devil gave her some consolation. Finally, God turned Marie's doubts to "smoke": passivity would still the tricky imagination and leave the soul open for divine impression. Magnifying his mercies, he renewed her design to live "in perfection."[24]

In many ways, in her late twenties Marie Guyart was already living "in perfection"—that is, as a religious in the world. Her Director had long since permitted her to take the vow of permanent chastity, which François de Sales recommended to widows as the highest ornament. The vows of poverty and obedience followed soon after, played out in the Buisson household, where she took as little money from her sister as she could and obeyed her sister and brother-in-law instantly without a murmur, no matter what she was doing.[25] Fearing for her health, Dom Raymond finally ordered her to moderate her acts of penance. Henceforth, a prickly straw mattress for six months, boards for the other six; flagellation with nettles could continue, but no more haircloth.[26]

Humility could be cultivated also in acts of charity: she cared for the sick servants no matter how foul-smelling their wounds; she sought the stench of death at the Tours charnel house for victims of the plague; she gave sustenance to a prisoner at the Palais de Justice whom she believed innocent.[27] She even took on a pastoral role toward the Buisson wagoners and stablemen, getting them to admit their faults and failings while she presided over their dinner table, lecturing them on God and his commandments, rousing them if they had gone to bed without saying their prayers. One Huguenot among them she converted to the Mother Church. Looking back on this teaching later, Marie used some of the same language about the workers as she did about the Amerindian men of Québec: "I reduced them to what I wanted"; "I reprimanded them frankly, so that these poor people were subject [soumis] to me like children."[28]

Some pious lay people in Marie Guyart's day were able to maintain this balance between spirituality and the world. Such a one was Jean de Bernières of Caen, in Normandy, who several years hence would enter her life in an important and comical way. A royal financial officer, he had nonetheless "banisht the World from his heart" and created (in the words of his much reprinted posthumous book) an "Interior Conformity" with Jesus

Christ.[29] Such equilibrium fell apart under the force of Marie's mystical fervor. She found it increasingly difficult to listen to the business affairs around her; sometimes her brother-in-law, knowing her mind was elsewhere, would tease her, asking her opinion on what had just been said. She was now thirty and yearned only for full union with God; her heart jumped every time she passed the Ursuline house, a sign that he wanted her there.[30]

She had tried to prepare the way for the separation from her son: "For ten years I treated him with denial, not permitting him to hug me or myself to hug him, so that he would not be attached to me when Our Lord ordered me to leave him." (We learn from Claude that she never spanked him either, and so her plan did not work.) In fact, detachment did not come easily for either of them. Claude, sensing from the pitying looks and whispered voices around him that something untoward was about to happen, fell into "a deep melancholy" (so he described his mood years later) and ran away to Paris. For three days Marie feared he had been drowned or abducted: "Our Lord sent me a heavy cross, the most painful in all my life." Was this a sign that he wanted her to stay in the world? Or rather God's test of her resolve, as her Director thought? When Claude was finally brought back to Tours, she decided it was the latter, and that leaving her eleven-year-old son, whom she "loved with a great love," was a sacrifice to which God summoned her.[31]

Indeed, the act of abandonment, from which all her relatives tried to dissuade her, was for her a form of spiritual heroism. Entering the nunnery must not be too easy. Her sister and brother-in-law finally agreed to take care of her son; Claude Guyart established a small pension for Claude Martin in recognition of all his mother had done for their household and their business. For the rest, Marie put her son into the hands of God and the Virgin.[32]

Marie Guyart's experience was not unique in a period when innovative Catholic reformers thought that chaste widows were as capable as virgins of attaining the highest spirituality. The story of Jeanne-Françoise Frémyot, widow of the baron de Chantal, was circulating in Salesian circles and beyond, and Marie Guyart surely heard it.[33] Inspired by her Director, François de Sales, Frémyot had left France for Annecy in 1610 to found with him the Order of the Visitation. She took her unmarried daughter with her to the convent, but left her fourteen-year-old son in the hands of her father in Dijon. On the day of her departure, her son begged her not to leave her life in the world; he then lay down on the doorsill, saying that if he could not keep her, then she'd have to step over his body to go. Frémyot stepped over her son, knelt for her father's blessing, and departed. The son's theatrical gesture was perhaps borrowed from his schoolboy's Plutarch; the mother and grandfather cast it in terms of Abraham's sacrificing Isaac.[34]

According to Claude Martin's description of the January day in 1631 when his mother departed, the scene was less dramatic. Marie finally revealed to him her "great secret": that she had long been planning to be a religious when he was old enough to do without her. She hoped he would approve, and would realize what an honor it was to be called by God to serve him. "But I won't see you any more," is all that Claude remembers saying to her. She promised that he would see her, since the Ursuline house was right in the neighborhood. Despite her compassion for her son, she kept a cheerful face and a sure step till she reached the convent door, where she threw herself at the feet of the Reverend Mother.[35] Of Claude's tears and his efforts to get her back, we have already heard.

The Ursulines were another feature of the Catholic reform in Tours, having arrived in the city on the Loire only in 1622. In the early decades of the Company of Saint Ursula, after its founding in Italy in the mid-sixteenth century, there would have been no convent. Angela Merici had established a company of sisters to live without walls in the world, bound only by promises rather than formal vows; in their own neighborhoods they would teach the girls and tend the sick. The first Ursuline efforts in France in the 1590s and at the turn of the seventeenth century—at L'Isle-sur-Sorgue and Aix-en-Provence, for example—still had this open character, even though the women had begun living in communities. By the early seventeenth century the experiment had foundered on the rocks of hierarchical reform of the Council of Trent, which demanded that all women's orders be fully enclosed, and on the complaints of the parents of Ursulines that they did not want their daughters so free in the world. Some of the sisters, too, wished for a life more devoted to prayer and inner communion. When the Ursuline house in Paris was opened in 1610–1612, the Company was called a Congregation, the religious were bound by the vows of chastity, obedience, and poverty (and later a fourth vow to teach), and strict enclosure was the rule. Enclosure would be the case for the house at Tours and the many other houses founded in France in the next years.[36]

Still, the Ursulines maintained some of Merici's initial ideals. Women of different social backgrounds were accepted into the order: daughters from the families of provincial nobles and royal officers took their vows along with the daughters of merchants and prosperous tradesmen. Marie Guyart, who had no savings, was permitted to enter the congregation at Tours without even a dowry at the same time as young Marie de Savonnières, daughter of a seigneurial family of Anjou. Later Guyart would recall Savonnières' belief that what mattered in the convent was not birth but only virtue: "Religion makes all its subjects equal."[37] What was especially important, from behind their grill the Ursulines kept their connection with the world through their teaching of girls, most of their pupils going back to lay life to marry. At the same time, the sisters encouraged one another's spirituality through preaching, correspondence, and the competition and pressures of conventual life.[38]

Enclosure was no barrier against the devil, however. In the early years of the century a priestly vision had already warned of a combat between the angels and the demons over the Ursuline order and the souls it was protecting. And now, in 1632–1634, in the convent of Loudun not far from Tours, the battle over sexual desire and sacrality was raging: numerous Ursulines were possessed by devils, denying God and vomiting the sacrament, and their golden-tongued priest Urbain Grandier was found to be the sorcerer behind it all.[39] News of the possessions led to Marie's only face-to-face contact with the evil spirit that she reported in her whole life of visions. One night in the dormitory, after she had prayed aloud for her afflicted sisters, the devil presented himself "to her imagination" in horrible human form, stuck out his long tongue in mockery, and howled. After she crossed herself, he left, only to return a few nights later as an evil spirit, paralyzing her as he slipped into her bones, marrow, and nerves. At last a good spirit rose within her and freed her. Marie characteristically cast herself as acting against the Evil One not just for herself but for the whole convent.[40]

If the devil no longer bothered Marie by his direct presence, he did send her temptations. On the one hand, she sank with bliss into the sweet concentration of the convent, replacing her acts of bodily mortification by the quieter discipline of the Ursuline rule and living in simplicity and obedience with novices half her age. She asked to be called Marie de l'Incarnation, since it was as the Word Incarnate that she had most often thought of Christ—an image beloved in the Berullian mysticism of her day, but also particular to her word-centered union with God.[41] On the other hand, her son's behavior made her worry again whether she had been right to leave him: first came his shouting outside the convent, and then his behavior at the Jesuit school at Rennes, where after a good start he refused to study, fell in with bad company, and was sent back to her sister.[42]

Even worse were the torments the world could not see. Filthy thoughts and desires that she had cast off years before returned; she resented her Mother Superior and found solitude unbearable. Most devastating, she feared once again that she was a hypocrite. The Lord sent her a new vision of the Trinity, but the devil made her think that what went on within her was "only make-believe and deception." At her lowest she blasphemed, saying to herself that it was "a great folly to believe there was a God and that all the things said about him were chimeras and imaginings, like those of Paganism."[43]

She struggled against these thoughts through conversations with her dear Love (as her son said later, "perfection consists not in not having temptations but in conquering them"), yet she got no help from the Ursuline confessor. Unlike Dom Raymond, who had left Tours, this new priest disapproved of her style of passive inner prayer, saying it led her to "illusions." He laughed at her reports of visions and special graces from the Lord, and asked her whether she was expecting to do miracles one of these days.[44] Somehow her Spouse got her through to her day of profession in January 1633—her son, still suspended from school at Rennes, was present for her vows—and her life took a turn for the better. As she lay prostrate in her cell after the service, she felt Christ lift all her crosses and heard him say that henceforth, like the seraphim of Isaiah (Isaiah 6:2–7), she would forever fly in his presence.[45]

Then the Jesuits, now arrived in Tours, began to preach at the convent, and she received permission from her Mother Superior to speak of her inner life to Father Georges de La Haye. Luckily for her, he and his circle were part of a Jesuit minority open to the passive or freely moving mysticism practiced by Marie de l'Incarnation (as contrasted with the formally directed exercises of their founder, Loyola).[46] Father La Haye also ordered her to resume writing, an activity that seems to have dried up after she fell into despair. She drew up two accounts: all the graces given her by God from her childhood, and, lest she seem a hypocrite, all her sins. (It is because La Haye saved these manuscripts that we know so much about her time of temptation, including her doubts about God.) La Haye reassured her that God's spirit had always been her guide, and also promised to supervise the future education of her son. "From then on, the direction of my inner life has always been in the hands of the Reverend Fathers of the Company of Jesus."[47]

The other novelty in her life was that she began to teach,

appointed instructor of Christian doctrine to the twenty or thirty sisters in the Novitiate. Her own education had advanced not long after she entered the convent: as she sang and recited the service in Latin, a language she had never studied, the Lord gave her a direct understanding of its meaning in French. (The Ursuline founder, Angela Merici, had had this experience of learning "infused" directly by God, and other Ursulines in Marie's day were able to do without Jesuit colleges and Sorbonne theology lectures by a similar divine shortcut.)[48] Now, in 1635, as she was training young women who would one day be instructors in the Ursuline schools, she read her Scriptures and even worked over the Catechisms of Trent and Cardinal Bellarmin; but her greatest insight into biblical meanings and metaphors came, so she said, not while studying but while praying, enlightened by the Holy Ghost.[49]

Write it down, her Jesuit Director told her, and so she produced her first pedagogic compositions: an explanation of the faith and an exposition of the Song of Songs. Twice a week, loosening the ordinary discipline that she placed on her tongue, she lectured on spiritual things in a torrent of words, "astonished at the quantity of scriptural passages that just came to her mind à propos." Her natural talent and zeal took her beyond herself, said her son: "one would not have known that it was a woman speaking." Enraptured as she taught her pupils to pray, she did not notice that they came to kiss her feet.[50]

But already, Marie was to claim, an apostolic fire burned in her heart to bring knowledge of Jesus Christ to the many poor souls in need of it in faraway lands. As with the earlier discoveries in her life, it began with a vision. One night "in a dream" (en songe), it seemed to her she was walking hand in hand with a laywoman into a vast silent landscape of precipitous mountains, valleys, and fog. Above the mist rose a small marble church, on whose roof sat the Virgin with Jesus. The Virgin talked to the child, and Marie understood that it was about her and that land. Then the Virgin smiled radiantly and kissed her three times as the laywoman watched.[51]

Her Jesuit Director identified the land as "Canada," a country which up till then she had never heard of as such, "thinking it just a word used to scare children" (like our "bogeyman"). The Lord confirmed her Director's identification one day when she was praying, and told her, "You must go there and make a house for Jesus and Mary." Now she began to read the printed *Relations* that the Jesuits were sending back each year from the missions of New France, and yearned to convert the "savages" of that distant clime—"an extraordinary enterprise," she knew, "apparently far removed from a person of my condition" (sometimes she added "and of my sex"). "My body was in our monastery, but my spirit was tied to that of Jesus and could not be enclosed ... I walked in spirit in those great vastitudes, accompanying those working for the Gospel."[52]

The truth was that an enclosed Ursuline convent in Tours was too small a world for the religious energy of Marie Guyart and for her daring. For the spiritual heroes of the Catholic Reformation, these traits were best expressed in the quest for martyrdom. Martyrdom was not a passive affair, a mere acceptance of meritorious suffering and death, as in the sanctification of the Lord's name approved by Glikl bas Judah Leib. Martyrdom was a prize one sought, a mobilizer for audacious action, a priming of that flesh already disciplined by nettles, an enflaming of the heart—the seat of bravery—already fueled by union with the heart of Christ.[53] Canada's terrors made it a splendid place to follow Christ's footsteps, especially for women: Father Le Jeune called for virtuous women to come there to instruct "the savage girls," but added that they "would have to surmount the fear natural to their sex." So much the better for Mother Marie de l'Incarnation. As she wrote to Dom Raymond de Saint Bernard in 1635, "I visualize the travail, both on the sea and in the country; I visualize what it is to live with Barbarians, the danger of dying there of hunger or cold, the many occasions when one might be seized ... and I find no change at all in the disposition of my spirit."[54]

The enclosed Ursuline convent in Tours was also too restricted for what we might call the "universalizing" impulse in Marie Guyart de l'Incarnation. For this woman who had never left the Touraine region and had only occasionally ventured outside the walls of her city, who seems never to have read any travel literature except for a life of François de Xavier (Jesuit missionary to Asia and Japan)[55] and the *Jesuit Relations*, the Christ who had shed his blood for all people, the Christ who would one day return as king of all the nations, bore her in spirit to every corner of the inhabited world:

> I saw, in inner certainty, demons triumphing over those poor souls, ravishing them from the domain of Jesus Christ, our divine master and sovereign, who had ransomed them with his precious blood . . . I could not bear it. I embraced all these poor souls, I held them in my breast, I presented them to the Eternal Father, saying to him that it was time he did justice in favor of my Spouse, that he knew well that he had promised him all the nations for his inheritance . . . "Oh, Father, why are you so tardy? It's a long time since my Beloved shed his blood!"
>   . . . And the Holy Spirit, which possessed me, led me to say to the Eternal Father, ". . . I am learned enough [*assez savante*] to teach of [Christ] to all the nations. Give me a voice powerful enough to be heard at the ends of the earth, to say that my divine Spouse is worthy of reigning and being loved by all hearts . . ." And in my excitement and my longing, without searching for them, but impelled by the Holy Spirit, I produced for the Eternal Father the passages from the Apocalypse that spoke of this divine king of all the nations.[56]

The plea of Marie de l'Incarnation draws from the tradition of the early fifteenth-century miracle worker Vincent Ferrer, who preached the conversion of the Jews and the spreading of the Gospel to all peoples by special "evangelical men" as the signs of the Last Days. Marie's contemporary, Vincent de Paul, was exhorting the missionaries to rural France and to Madagascar in similar apocalyptic terms, although he softened the certainties of Ferrer's prophecy into mere speculation about whether God was allowing his Church to be transferred from declining Europe to faraway lands.[57] In the mid-sixteenth century Guillaume Postel, expanding on a medieval dream of "universal peace," had called for a world monarchy under "a Prince of the people"—namely, the French king—who would see to it that the Gospel was received everywhere. All peoples had the potential for reason, and the divine plan was that they should one day live under one God, with one government and a single language. Though Postel had read something of the New World, his focus was on the Jews and the Moslems of Turkey and the Arab lands.[58]

The French king played no role in Marie's visions, and her arguments came from the Psalms, Saint Paul, and Revelation,[59] not from Postel's learned tracts. Ultimately her extension of eschatological hopes to the New World would rest on some French political space there, guaranteed by firearms. What is striking about her initial stance is its sentimental force, its expression of empathy with "reasoning souls" everywhere, not just among the Jews, Moslems, and other non-Christians of Japan, China, and India but among the "savages" of the vastitudes of Canada.[60]

Four years passed between Marie's first reading the *Jesuit Relations* and her boarding the boat for Canada. She talked often with the Lord, who sustained his "great design" for her. She corresponded with Father Le Jeune and other Jesuits in New France, who very much wanted some female religious to instruct the "unclothed" Huron women. She got the whole convent praying for the distant souls in need and found another Mother eager to cross the ocean with her.[61]

As always, there were obstacles. Her excessive fervor raised doubts for a moment in her Jesuit confessor and her Mother Superior. Could such "impetuosity" be a sign of God's call? More devastating were the doubts of Dom Raymond de Saint Bernard. Her Director from her pre-Ursuline days was himself contemplating a mission to Canada, but found something "presumptuous in her pretending with so much ardor to an enterprise so elevated above persons of her sex." "What?" she exclaimed in one of her numerous letters to him in Paris. "You're leaving, my dear Father, without us?" Later when his vocation had flagged, she promised that once God started her on her way, she would pull him along so strongly that part of his habit would tear off if he resisted.[62] Above all, there was the financial issue. Who would pay for a women's convent in Québec? Isaac de Razilly, a naval officer from a noble family of Touraine, was building a French colony in Acadia in the 1630s, but rather than funding a women's house in New France, he sent two Franco-Micmac girls to the convents back in Tours. When Marie de l'Incarnation was urging her sisters to pray for the conversion of the "savages," a young novice with a Micmac mother was already among the Ursulines.[63]

At last the laywoman from Marie's vision appeared, in the form of Madeleine de La Peltrie, born Cochon de Chauvigny, daughter and joint heir of a fiscal officer of Alençon and his noble wife, and widow of the seigneur de La Peltrie, whose noble stock went back several centuries. As Marie de l'Incarnation and Claude Martin told about her later, Madeleine was in many ways a slightly younger twin to Marie—a lay twin to Marie's religious. Married at nineteen to Charles Gruel, delivered of a daughter who died almost immediately, and widowed when Gruel was killed fighting the Protestant rebels at La Rochelle, La Peltrie felt free at age twenty-five to follow the religious yearnings of her girlhood. Like the widowed Marie Guyart, she engaged in acts of charity, especially bringing prostitutes into her house to keep them from sin. Like Marie, she received a message from the Lord while she prayed—a message telling her he wanted her to go to Canada. And like Marie, she was enflamed at reading Father Le Jeune's *Relations*. Critically ill, she took a vow to go to Canada, build a church there to Saint Joseph, and "employ her life and goods in the service of the savage girls." Instantly, her fever abated and she began to recover.[64]

Much was at stake in Madeleine de La Peltrie's vow to go to Canada: her large dower, the substantial properties she would inherit, the noble progeny she could produce. Pressured by her widowed father to take a second husband, she used a stratagem faithful to the Baroque literature of her age—a feigned marriage—to play for time and protect her goods till she could found the convent. (This kind of masking Marie de l'Incarnation did not mind.) The pretend spouse was none other than the Interior Christian Jean de Bernières of Caën, who was, on the exterior, a high financial officer like her father. Bernières asked for and was given her hand, and then, when Madeleine's father suddenly died in 1637, Bernières sustained the pretend marriage against family efforts to disqualify his future "wife" from managing her inheritance.[65]

By January 1639 La Peltrie and Bernières were assembling in the chambers of Louis XIII's councillor François Fouquet, along with several Jesuits and members of the royally chartered Company of New France. The Company agreed to provide the land and Madame de La Peltrie to put up the money for an Ursuline house and church in Québec and to provision a ship for the spring crossing.[66] By February the "married couple" were on their way to Tours so that Madeleine could meet Marie and plan their apostolic enterprise.

The two women had learned of each other a few months before, when one of the Paris Jesuits told Madeleine of Marie's Canadian hopes and Marie wrote Madeleine one of her impassioned letters. "My heart is in yours, and the two together are only one with the heart of Jesus amid those large and infinite spaces where we embrace all the little Savage girls." When Marie saw her face to face, the union was confirmed. Spiritual adventure could take the baker's daughter and the noblewoman, separated by birth and wealth, and make them feel, in Marie's words, that they had "only one will." Chosen to go with Marie as her Ursuline companion was the nobly born Marie de Savonnières (she immediately changed her religious name from Marie de Saint Bernard to Marie de Saint Joseph, to thank the Virgin's husband for intervening on her behalf); chosen as Madeleine's personal attendant was Charlotte Barré, a young commoner who hoped one day to be a nun.[67]

The Ursulines welcomed these events with a *Te deum*, but others in Tours reacted to them with less joy. Learning that her sister was about to leave for Canada, Claude Guyart did everything she could to prevent the departure, bringing a notary to the convent and revoking her pension to Claude Martin before Marie's eyes, berating her for abandoning her son once again, and sending news of Marie's plans to him. Now almost twenty years of age and a philosophy student at Orléans, he confronted his mother at an inn when she passed through Orléans with her party, heading for Paris. Marie told him that she had already given him to God as his father, and that if he obeyed and feared God and trusted his Providence, he would lack nothing. "I am going to Canada, it's true, and it is by God's command that I leave you for a second time. I could have no greater honor than to be chosen to carry out so great a design. If you love me, you will rejoice and share this honor." As Claude recalled it later, he went back to his room, burned the letter of revocation of his pension, and resolved to sacrifice his mother to God.[68]

In her final weeks at Paris—Marie's first visit there—the Ursuline met the Duchesse d'Aiguillon and the Comtesse de Brienne (the former a niece of Richelieu's and both of them patrons of women's religious action) and was received with her companions by the queen, Anne of Austria, at the château of Saint Germain-en-Laye.[69] Here was Marie Guyart's look at the courtly mixture of *politesse* and *dévotion* that she would remember with some reservations when she got to Canada.

On May 4, 1639, Marie Guyart de l'Incarnation set sail from Dieppe with Madeleine de La Peltrie, Marie de Saint Joseph, Cécile de Sainte Croix from the Ursuline house at Dieppe, and Charlotte Barré. Also on board the *Saint-Joseph* were three sisters from the order of the Hospitalers in Dieppe and their servant, on their way to establish a hospital at Québec, and two Jesuit fathers. "When I put my foot on the boat," said Marie, "it seemed to me I was entering Paradise, for I was taking the first step to risk my life for the love of him who gave it to me." She kept writing about their departure till their ship was at the end of the English Channel, throwing her letters to the fishermen to take back to France to mail.[70]

Marie kissed the soil when she got to Canada, finding the landscape like her dream but not so foggy. The colony in the Saint Lawrence valley at which the Ursulines arrived in August 1639 was made up of only a few hundred French people—religious, fur traders, administrators, soldiers, artisans, farmers, servants—whose numbers would grow to only a few thousand during Marie's life there in the next three decades.[71] The grandiose royal charter of the Company of New France assigned to its hundred Catholic associates governance and feudal dominion over all the lands from Florida to Newfoundland. In fact, apart from settlements in Acadie, which were constantly harassed by the English, the French were concentrated along the Saint Lawrence. Québec and Trois-Rivières had their forts and buildings when Marie arrived, and in 1642 construction began on the island of Montréal, subsidized from across the ocean by the Society of Gentlemen and Ladies for the Conversion of the Savages of New France. Over the next thirty years, little French settlements would increase around these towns and spread down the river from Québec to the port and trading post of Tadoussac. By the 1660s Colbert was filling summer boats with unmarried women from the Charité of Paris and other orphan hospitals, and Marie de l'Incarnation could note that they found husbands among the French *habitants* within a few weeks.[72]

The shape of religious and political authority changed along with these changes in population. At the beginning of the colony in the 1640s, Québec was the spiritual kingdom of the religious, and more specifically of the Jesuits. Only a few secular priests lived along the Saint Lawrence, two or three of them saying low Mass for the Ursulines and the Québec Hospital. The Jesuits did all the preaching, organized the public ceremonial life, gave the veil to new religious, and served as "vicars" to an invented "parish" of French settlers and converted indigenous peoples, whose boundaries were improvised for Rogations Day processions in the spring. Supervisory ecclesiastical authority was far away—in

Rome or with the Archbishop of Rouen—and Marie Guyart de l'Incarnation liked it that way. "There's talk of giving a bishop to Canada," she wrote her son in 1646. "My feeling is that God does not yet want a bishop in Canada. This land is not worked enough yet [*pas encore assez fait*], and our reverend Fathers, having planted Christianity, need to cultivate it somewhat longer without anyone's being able to oppose their plans."[73]

By Christmas 1650 the "parish" had a new church, Our Lady of Québec, constructed from profits from the fur trade. By Christmas 1659 Bishop François de Laval de Montigny was presiding there over the midnight Mass sung by the Jesuits, having been confirmed in office that summer at the Hospital before one hundred Algonquins and Hurons. Québec was not yet a French diocese on its own—that would happen only in 1674, two years after Marie's death—but with Laval's installation, a new set of institutions linked Marie's "Paradise" to European structures of power and conflict.[74]

On the whole, Guyart now thought a bishop a good idea. The Jesuits, she wrote her son, were splendid confessors, but Canada was currently producing cases of conscience that required a bishop's force. A pious bishop could defend those who had come to New France on an apostolic mission against those who had come merely for beaver pelts or land. If Monseigneur Laval stepped out of line, the Ursulines usually found a way to get around him: in 1660, when he ordered the Mother Superior to open all Ursuline letters destined for France, she simply broke the seals but did not read the contents.[75]

A similar redistribution of power occurred in political institutions. To begin with, the Hundred Associates of the Company of New France chose the governor of Canada and distributed from France the seigneuries and trading privileges along the Saint Lawrence. Then, in 1645, as political conflicts in France were escalating toward the Fronde, the Company turned over control of the fur trade to the Communauté des Habitants—that is, the male French householders residing in Canada. Now local people could protect their trade monopoly against independent merchants who struck private deals with the Amerindians at Tadoussac, and balance off the years with many beaver pelts against those with few. In 1647 the governor set up an advisory council in Québec, which included the Jesuit superior and men elected from the towns. Now they could fight among themselves about whether eau-de-vie and wine should be sold to the native peoples.[76]

In the early 1660s these decentralized institutions were dismantled as the young Louis XIV and his minister, Colbert, reordered France and its dreamed-of empire. The Company of New France and the Communauté des Habitants were swept away, and economic control over Canada was vested in a royally directed and for the most part royally owned West India Company. A royally appointed governor and intendant brought the king's policies to the Saint Lawrence, and the French settlers on the governor's council were no longer elected but chosen by the governor and the bishop. "The king is now master of this land," Marie de l'Incarnation wrote her son, in a letter sent on the autumn boat of 1663.[77]

The indigenous peoples would have made a different judgment. The busy woodlands into which the French had penetrated comprised Algonquian-speaking peoples (the Micmacs far to the east, the Abenaki south of the Saint Lawrence, and the Montagnais and the Algonquins to the north) and speakers of Iroquoian languages—that is, the Iroquois, based in the Finger Lakes region, and the Hurons, Petuns, and Neutrals above Lake Huron and Lake Erie.[78] They traveled extensively through the waterways and forests of the whole region, and if Hurons and Iroquois referred to the French governor as Onontio—that is, "Great Mountain," after the early governor Huault de Montmagny—there is no sign that they took him or his faraway chief for master of their land.[79]

The Algonquins, Montagnais, and other speakers of Algonquian languages were mostly hunting-and-gathering peoples and moved their camps often. The Hurons and Iroquois and other speakers of Iroquoian languages engaged in digging-stick agriculture, along with gathering, fishing, and hunting. The men opened the fields for cultivation, but the women were the farmers, growing maize, beans, squash, and in some places tobacco. (We can see women farming as pictured by the Jesuits in the illustrations reproduced here.) The women were in all cases the gatherers, picking fruits and other edible food and bringing in the firewood. When agricultural villages changed their base, as they did every few years, it was sometimes in fear of enemies, but usually because the women had declared the fields infertile and the suitable wood exhausted for miles around. The men were in charge of hunting and fishing, although the active women accompanied their husbands or fathers on these expeditions when not held back by farming or other cabin tasks. Along the way, the women were expected to do much of the carrying.

Responsibility for the arts and crafts was similarly divided. Men made weapons and tools of stone, wood, bone, and sometimes bits of copper, carved the pipes and calumets, built the lodges and cabins, and constructed frames for canoes and snowshoes. Women were in charge of anything that had to do with sewing, stringing and weaving, preparing thread and laces by hand-spinning and winding, stringing snowshoes, and making baskets, birchbark kettles, nets, and rush mats. Women were also the potters and the creators of decorative objects constructed of porcupine quills, shells, beads, moosehair, and birchbark.[80] Once the men had made a kill during the hunt, the animal was the charge of the women, who dragged the carcass to the camp, skinned and prepared the hide, softened and greased the furs, and made garments, pouches, and moccasins. As for the meals, the women took care of them, pounding the corn into flour, roasting and smoking the meat, and cooking much of the food in a single kettle.

This division of labor looked very lopsided to the French men who first reported it, presumably contrasting it with European agriculture, where men were usually at the plough and women at the hoe or garden, and with European carrying and carting, where men did at least as much as the women. "The women work incomparably more than the men," Jacques Cartier had said of the Iroquoian-speaking people he had met along the Saint Lawrence back in 1536. In 1616, among the Abenakis, the Jesuit Biard put it more harshly: "[The men] have no other servants, slaves, or artisans but the women; these poor creatures suffer all the miseries and hardships." Gabriel Sagard of the order of the Recollets made a similar observation about the Hurons among whom he lived in 1623 ("the women do all the servile tasks, work[ing] ordinarily harder than the men"), but concluded cheerfully that "they are neither forced nor constrained to do it."[81]

For Marie de l'Incarnation, in contrast, the women's heavy work was simply a given, a fact determining when young women and girls could come to the convent for instruction: "in the summer," she wrote her son in 1646, "the children can't leave their mothers, or the mothers their children, for they use them to help in their fields of Indian corn and in softening beaver skins."[82] What else would Marie Guyart expect? Hadn't she done everything from grooming horses to keeping accounts in the wagoner's household? Hadn't she kept her hands busy in the Tours convent making altarpieces and ornaments? Wasn't she now back to altar painting once again,[83] not to mention cooking, carrying slops, and lugging logs in the Ursuline house in the Québec woods? Years later, she saw the division of labor as part of the "freedom" of the "savage life," which made the Amerindians prefer it to French ways. The men smoked while the women did their cabin tasks; the women and girls paddled canoes just like the men. That was what they were used to, what they thought "natural."[84]

There was one thing the Hurons, Algonquins, and Iroquois did not find natural, however. New illnesses had come to Canada in the body fluids of the English, French, and Dutch—influenza, measles, and especially smallpox—and were taking their toll on the vulnerable Amerindian populations the way bubonic and pneumonic plague had been decimating European populations in epidemic waves since the mid-fourteenth century (its most recent hit at Tours had been in 1631, and in the wake of a novice's death at the Ursulines the sisters removed temporarily to a country house lent them by Claude Guyart).[85] As early as the mid-1630s smallpox contagion had appeared in trading posts and in the villages where the Jesuits tried to convert; it spread along the Saint Lawrence valley in 1639, entering the Ursuline house only months after the convent opened and taking four Algonquin girls. Epidemic returned to smite Hurons and Iroquois in 1646–1647 and again in 1654. The Amerindians responded variously to these disasters: by denouncing the Black Robes as sorcerers, who brought disease in their baptism, holy images, crosses, and refined sugar (an "error" on the part of the "savages," said Marie, who traced the epidemics, as she would in France, not to hidden carriers but to God's decision);[86] by intensifying shamanic action and curative dances and feasts; by seeking Christian spells and consolation. Whatever these methods accomplished, the toll was high. The indigenous populations were reduced by mid-century to perhaps one-half their previous size, some of them never to return to their pre-1630s numbers.[87]

Even with their lower population, the Amerindian communities sustained and expanded their activities of exchange, warfare, and diplomacy. Friendly tribes had long exchanged mats with each other, as well as ornamented baskets, wampum beads, copper beads, pelts, corn, and tobacco, their trade range extending 400 miles or more up waterways and across hunting ranges. The French presence added European textiles, items of clothing, and glass beads to the Amerindian circuit and especially iron hatchets, copper and brass kettles, and other metal tools, while multiplying a hundredfold the movement of beaver pelts out of the forests, through the women's hands, and into wooden boats bound for Europe. Montagnais and Algonquins both served as intermediaries in this exchange, but until 1650 the Hurons were the major middlemen between the interior Amerindian peoples and the French. Not without opposition, however. The Iroquois nations, even while supplying the Dutch with pelts, attacked the Hurons and tried to blockade their fur-laden canoes as they came down the Ottawa River and the Saint Lawrence for the summer *traite*.[88]

Marie de l'Incarnation commented rather little on the fur trade, except to disapprove of sailors and merchants who gave the indigenous peoples eau-de-vie and so turned them to folly. Insofar as she envisaged a good French colony in the 1650s and afterward, it was based on farming, fishing, and saltworks, not on the merchants' quest for riches through fur.[89] About the Iroquois, she had much to say, and during the early years it was mostly bad. Allies of the heretical Dutch, opponents of the Hurons, Algonquins, and Montagnais, a menace to Jesuits and French settlers, the Iroquois peoples were inspired by the devil. "They are at the moment [she was writing her son in 1644] the greatest hindrance to God's glory in this land, except for my own evildoing."[90]

In fact, the events she was hearing about from her Huron, Algonquin, and Jesuit informants were part of a long-term elaboration of Amerindian political institutions and practices, to which European newcomers and their firearms were adding new challenge. Beyond the local councils in a village long-house, beyond periodic assemblies of chiefs in the allied kinship groups that made up a "tribe," two federations had emerged over the previous hundred and fifty years, in each case creating "one people" out of previously separate or even warring groups. One was the Huron League, or League of the Ouendats, as they termed themselves (people of "the land apart"), made up of the Attignaouantan (Bears) and the Attigneenongnahac, who called each other "brother" and "sister" when they met at councils, and of two other tribes. The other federation was the Iroquois League of Five Nations, three elder "brothers" and two younger "brothers." Whereas Marie de l'Incarnation always lumped the League of the Ouendats together as "Hurons," the Iroquois she knew as a confederation, often sorting out its members as separate actors: the Mohawks, the Oneidas, the Onondagas, the Cayugas, and the Senecas, to give their names in English. These federations enlarged the terrains of amity in the Amerindian world and led to a flowering of male oratory in treaty making and the wooing of allies. Marie could not hear these speeches from her convent yard, but read them in the Jesuit manuscripts, copying over for her son the eloquent words of the Mohawk Kiotseaeton at the Iroquois peace initiative of 1645.[91]

Much of the time, however, there was war or fear of war, with its distinctive Amerindian aftermath: the seizure of male prisoners, who were either adopted into the captors' tribe to replace slain warriors or kept alive as slaves or tortured to death and eaten; and the seizure of female prisoners, who were sometimes made servants but most often taken as wives. The quarrel between the Iroquois, on the one hand, and the Hurons, with their allies the Algonquins, Montagnais, and French, on the other, was in part about fur, about the desire of the Mohawks and other Iroquois to become the purveyor of furs to French and Dutch alike. It was even more about honor and power—old struggles for power and new ones—and replenishment. As Marie saw it in 1652, when the Iroquois slew the French governor of Trois-Rivières: "Now they'll imagine they're the Masters of all of New France." Rather, the Iroquois talked of being moved to war to avenge the killing of their ancestors and relatives and to replace them with new kin.[92]

For a time the Iroquois were the winners. In 1650, armed with the arquebuses that the Dutch had been willing to trade them for furs, the Iroquois destroyed and burned the villages of the League of the Ouendats. The Hurons, upon whom the Jesuits had concentrated so much of their missionary effort, had to flee from their "land apart" near Lake Huron. Their trading empire and their League were destroyed, and the refugees established themselves in dispersed settlements in Québec or went to live as adopted kin—either captured or as voluntary migrants—with the Iroquois themselves.[93] In 1652, when the Mohawks and the Senecas joined forces against the French, Father Ragueneau thought the devil was doing his work on both sides of the Atlantic: Old France was being torn to pieces by its children (in the Fronde), and New France was likewise in danger of destruction.[94] Meanwhile, in December 1650, the Ursuline convent had been ravaged by an accidental fire, and some Ursulines in France thought their Québec sisters should come back home.

But the situation began to change in the 1650s. Marie's convent was rebuilt with miraculous speed, the Virgin being present in interior union with Marie the whole time she and the sisters hastened about their work.[95] French *coureurs de bois* took off through the woods for distant locales, their sacks loaded with gifts and French goods, to acquire the beaver pelts so loved for European hats.[96] The Jesuit missionaries went on seeking souls to convert and—surprise of surprises—were invited in 1653–1654 by the Onondagas and Senecas (themselves in part inspired by adopted Huron Christians in their midst) to come live among them and instruct them. The Iroquois ambassadors even visited the Ursuline convent (so Marie de l'Incarnation wrote to her son in 1654), and were astonished to hear the Amerindian girls sing so well in the French manner, "for the Savages love song, and they made a return with a song in their own mode, not so measured a style as ours."[97]

Harmony did not reign immediately: trouble with the Iroquois resumed, and the Onondagas turned against the Black Robes in their midst. "Our Convent has been turned into a fort," Marie wrote Claude Martin in 1660, and for months she kept her ears cocked all night lest it be time to get the ammunition to the soldiers guarding their buildings. The bishop now believed "either one must exterminate [the Iroquois], or all the Christians and the Christianity of Canada would perish." Marie was still praying that God would turn the Iroquois toward heaven.[98]

Several years later, the new royal administration put in place in Canada by Louis XIV and Colbert changed the military situation in France's favor. In the early fall of 1666, a commander seasoned from capturing Cayenne from the Dutch in Guiana led 1,000 French soldiers and settlers and 100 Hurons and Algonquins to burn all the villages of the Mohawks. "No one would have believed how well built and magnificently decorated were their long-houses," wrote Marie de l'Incarnation. How many fine cabinets they had! how many kettles! While the Mohawks watched from the mountains, the French troops also set fire to the women's unharvested fields and seized their ample stores of corn and beans, "enough to feed all of Canada for two years." A *Te deum* was sung, Mass was said, and a cross was planted with the arms of France. During those very hours, Marie heard that some soldiers en route to the Iroquois lands had seen a great opening in the sky filled with flames and plaintive voices—"perhaps Demons enraged at the depopulation of a country where they had been such great Masters for so long."[99]

The following summer, the Mohawks and Oneidas came to Québec with gifts, made peace, and asked for Black Robes to come and instruct them. "A miracle," Marie wrote to an Ursuline in France in 1668—"a miracle" that the Iroquois Nations, once "so ferocious and cruel, today . . . live with us as if we were one people."[100]

Much changed in Canada during the thirty-two years after Marie de l'Incarnation set off for Paradise. First there was the time of the dominance of the Huron League and their allies, of the imagined kingdom of the Jesuit religious, and of decentralized settler institutions. Then there was the decade of the dominance of the League of the Iroquois—for the French, a decade of disorder and shifting fears and hopes. Finally there were the 1660s, with strong royal institutions, with a bishop making his rulings where Jesuits had once held sway, with new French settlers taking their places in fields and parishes, and the Iroquois aware that the Onontio in France and the Onontio in Québec could join forces successfully against them. How did Marie de l'Incarnation's hope to clasp the "savage girls" to her breast fare over the decades? And what did she learn from those to whom she had come to teach that Christ was the king of all people?

Always ready for the tests of adventure, the Jesuits had numerous settings for conversion.[101] Québec was their center, with a residence, chapel, school, and ultimately a seminary. Beyond this, there were "permanent" missions to relatively stable populations: at Sillery, only a few miles from Québec, where the Jesuits had persuaded some Christian families among the Montagnais and the Algonquins to begin tilling the soil and where (in Marie's words) "God is served *comme il faut*";[102] at Sainte-Marie, a residence constructed by the Fathers in the Huron country; at five other Huron villages, whose names were changed, say, from Teanaustaië to Saint-Joseph and from Taenhatentaron to Saint-Ignace;[103] and at Sainte Marie de Gannentaa on the shores of Lake Onondaga. There in 1656 Father Chaumonot told the Iroquois in their own tongue:

> For the Faith, we have departed from our country; for the Faith, we have abandoned our relatives and our friends; for the Faith, we have crossed the Ocean; for the Faith, we have left behind the great ships of the French to set off on your small canoes; for the Faith, we have relinquished our fine houses to live in your bark cabins; for the Faith, we have deprived ourselves of our natural nourishment and the delicious foods that we could have enjoyed in France to eat your boiled meal and your other victuals, which the animals of our country would hardly touch.[104]

There were also the "flying missions," as the Jesuits called them. Out of Trois-Rivières Father Buteux went north in 1651 through weeks of snowshoeing and canoeing to the summer gathering places of the Montagnais Attikamegue, and was delighted to find Christians using small sticks, bark, and caribou skin as mnemonic devices to recall their sins when he came. (He was killed by Iroquois on the same trail the following year.)[105] In 1665–1667 Father Allouez began his travels among the Ottawas and other nations around Lake Superior, struggling against their "imaginary deities" of sun, moon, and lake and against their *jongleurs,* who practiced (so he claimed) dog sacrifice to calm storms and to banish the new diseases ravaging their villages.[106]

In contrast, the little band of Ursulines, living under the rule of enclosure, set up their buildings on the Québec promontory high above the Saint Lawrence and did not move about. Their walls were not of stone as they had been in Europe, but of cedar wood, like a low stockade, and their large yard, with its birchbark cabins and great trees, invited much more assembling and activity of outsiders than at Tours.[107] By the time of the convent fire in 1650, the number of sisters had gone from four to fourteen, plus

Madame de La Peltrie; by 1669 it was up to twenty-two.[108] As the first Mother Superior, Marie de l'Incarnation had drawn up a constitution for the house with the advice of the Jesuit Provincial; it had won the assent of Ursulines both from Paris and from Tours—a delicate task, requiring diplomatic skills worthy of the elder and younger "brothers" of the Iroquois League.[109] Except for three weeks after the fire of 1650 and a few nights in 1660 when there was threat of a serious Iroquois attack, the Ursulines never went beyond the bounds of their wooden fence. (Indeed, in the 1660 episode Marie and three sisters stayed behind to feed the soldier guards.)[110]

The native peoples had to come to them, whether on their own initiative, on their parents', or brought by the Jesuits. The most important early arrivals were Algonquins, Montagnais, and Hurons, the last coming in increasing numbers after the destruction of their nation by the Iroquois. Abenakis from the east and Nipissings and Attikamegues from the north were sometimes seen in the convent yard and parlor. By the late 1660s even Iroquois women were sending their daughters to the *"saintes filles,"* as the Amerindians called the sisters.[111] From the start the Ursulines had to study the American languages, learning them from Father Le Jeune and from their own pupils and visitors, and then teaching them to each other. Marie de Savonnières de Saint Joseph specialized in Huron; Marie de l'Incarnation specialized first in Algonquin and Montagnais, learned the Iroquoian Huron around 1650, and by the late 1660s was speaking and teaching Iroquois itself.[112]

For the girls—that is, for the *"filles sauvages"* and the daughters of French colonists—the Ursulines set up a school (still existing today). Around twenty to fifty pupils lived at the convent in the early days, most of them Amerindians ranging in age from five to seventeen. By 1669 the boarders numbered around twenty-five each year. A higher percentage of them were now French, but it was still "a seminary filled with French and Savage girls . . . We have Savage girls of four Nations."[113] Marie talked about the Amerindians as "being given to us" ("Marie Madeleine Abatenau was given to us at only six, still covered with smallpox"),[114] but their parents might pull them out at any time, for the hunting season or for the harvest (if they were from a people that practiced agriculture) or to take them home to marry. Around this core was a large group of Amerindian girls and women who came and went, listening to instruction in the convent as they wished, and after prayers getting a meal of peas, cornmeal mush, and plums.[115]

The Ursulines' first act was to wash the Amerindian girls and then give them French undergarments and a tunic:

> When they are given to us, they are as naked as a worm, and one must wash them from head to foot because of the grease that their parents have smeared all over their bodies. And no matter how diligently one does it or how often one changes their clothes, it takes a long time before one can get rid of the vermin caused by the abundance of their grease. One sister spends part of each day at this. It is an office each of us seeks with eagerness. Whoever wins it esteems herself rich with a happy fate; whoever is denied it considers herself unworthy and remains in a state of humility.[116]

The Ursuline classes centered on the elements of Christian belief, prayer, religious song, and sacred practices and on learning to speak French. At least some of the boarders were taught to read and write in French, and eventually—once the Ursulines themselves had mastered the Amerindian languages—to write in their mother tongues.[117] (A letter written in Huron by one of them can be seen in the illustrations.) Lessons were given in the Algonquian and Iroquoian languages and in French, for the "seminarians" (as Marie de l'Incarnation liked to call them) were expected to take the message back to their nations and to begin talking of the Christian God already to kinfolk who came to see them at the convent.[118] The pupils who delighted the Iroquois captains in 1654 were singing a French melody, but their hymns were in Huron and Algonquin as well as French.[119] In addition, the girls were taught European ways of embroidering and painting. The older pupils would already have learned artistic techniques from their mothers, and in all likelihood their Amerindian tastes and styles had some effect on the decorative work they did at Marie's side for the chapel and the parish church.[120]

Apart from the crowds of girls and women living in or periodically visiting the convent, there were also many Amerindian men who appeared at the Ursuline grill and in the guest parlor for instruction, for the cornmeal sagamite available from the convent kitchen at any time of day, or simply out of curiosity.[121] "I see generous and brave captains on their knees at my feet," Marie de l'Incarnation wrote in 1640, "begging me to have them pray to God before they eat. They join their hands like children and say all that I wish."[122] "The Hurons who come down here are almost all the time in our parlor," she reported six years later about captains who were in Québec for the fur trade and negotiations with the Iroquois. "Mother Marie de Saint Joseph has the mission of instructing them . . . One Huron . . . is so scrupulous in his obedience [to her] that he will do nothing unless she orders it."[123] Sometimes when the press of people was too great, the two Maries instructed both men and women in the birchbark cabins or out in the open in the convent yard.[124]

Sustained throughout the teaching, the visiting, and the charitable meals was the liturgical life of the convent. The sisters sang the office and the Jesuits preached in their church at Lent and other important feast days, but it was much the better in Marie's eyes when Christian Amerindians were part of the ceremony. Baptisms of converts were held at the Ursuline chapel (Marie de l'Incarnation served as godmother to an Algonquin teenager who had got his start with Father Le Jeune),[125] and religious processions for the major feast days always had the Ursuline house as one of their stations. Algonquins and Hurons from Sillery and other Amerindians marched in bands, the men and women separate, preceded and followed by crosses and banners and by French artisans, officers, and Jesuits. For Corpus Christi 1648, the Ursulines dressed their youthful French servant Benjamin as an angel, and sent him off with a box for the sacred Host, along with two Amerindian boys carrying candles.[126] In the summer of 1646, when little Charity Negaskoumat died at the convent of a lung infection, the body of the young Algonquin was borne to the French cemetery with two French pupils and two Amerindian pupils holding the ends of her shroud. Marie de l'Incarnation mourned her in a letter to Claude Martin: though only five and a half, Charity had sung the Psalms along with the Ursulines in choir and had learned to respond perfectly to her catechism.[127]

Marie's teaching was the heart of her apostolic work; she described it as a source of joy even when she had times of spiritual suffering and agonies of unworthiness. "Everything concerning the study of languages and the instruction of the Savages . . . has been so delectable to me that I have almost sinned in loving it too much."[128] In fact, her first lessons in Algonquin had been difficult. She was so out of the habit of such study and the language was so unlike French that she felt "as though stones were rolling around in my head." She talked about it with her Chaste Spouse, the Word Incarnate, and in no time at all she could understand and speak Algonquin easily. "My study became a prayer, rendering the language no longer barbaric to me, but sweet."[129]

For Marie's teaching style in Canada, we have no independent witness. "I would like to make my heart go out through my tongue to tell my dear Neophytes how the love of God feels," she wrote to a religious back in Tours.[130] Of her two pedagogic compositions from her French days—the lyrical and image-laden *Retraites* and the dry *Ecole sainte*[131]—the former surely provided her a better start toward describing to her Amerindian listeners a world in which a triune God, a devil, and guardian angels replaced their well-stocked repertory of Manitous and oki spirits. Sometimes she would simply express to them her personal thoughts about God and then invite them to do the same while she listened.[132]

Finally, in 1661–1668, she began to write in the Amerindian tongues. In Algonquin, she composed catechisms, prayers, dictionaries, and a "big book of sacred history and holy things"; in

Iroquoian, a Huron catechism and an Iroquois dictionary and catechism. Although catechisms, prayer books, and dictionaries were also being prepared by enterprising Jesuits in these same years, Marie de l'Incarnation's *Sacred History* seems to have been a first. And since in the woodlands certain subjects and ways of speaking were special to the women, linguistic and pedagogic books authored by a woman were, by Marie's own reckoning, a "treasure."[133]

Meanwhile her writing in her mother tongue continued at a pitch that is difficult to imagine amid all her other tasks (she was elected superior three times for six-year stints, and had other offices in the intervening years). Once the ships had arrived from France in midsummer, Marie began her letters to her son and relatives, to her sister Ursulines and other French religious, and to friends and potential donors to the mission in Canada. Along with spiritual reflection and advice, she sent them news of what she had seen, of what she had heard from the many Amerindians and French who came to "visit and consult her" in the parlor, and of what she had read in advance copies of the annual *Jesuit Relations*.[134] Indeed, she wrote for the *Relations* herself, as Fathers Vimont, Lalemant, and other Jesuit superiors solicited her reports on events concerning the Ursulines and native peoples in their circle, while the Jesuit François Du Creux in Paris asked her for material for his growing *Historia Canadensis*.[135] And, of course, there was the spiritual autobiography sought by Dom Claude Martin and finally sent to him in 1654. When the boats lifted anchor for France in early autumn, Marie's hand ached from so much writing.[136]

Let us now consider this body of writing for what it can tell us about the relation of Marie de l'Incarnation to herself, to her son and his world back in France, and to the diverse peoples and tongues of the New World. Her manuscripts in Amerindian languages are all lost, alas, though we can get some inkling of their structure from Jesuit analogues; but a substantial part of her composition in French has come down to us.[137]

The French writing, Marie claimed, was unstudied, not planned in overall structure and revised, as in Glikl bas Judah Leib's seven books. That this was the case when Marie's pen was hastening across the page in summer correspondence is not surprising.[138] But she even said it was the case for the hundred or so leaves of the spiritual autobiography made for Claude Martin, where there was no need to hurry: "Don't think," she told her son, "that these notebooks I send you have been thought through ahead of time in order to observe some order, as one finds in well-digested works ... When I took up my pen to begin this, I did not know a word I was going to say, but the spirit of Grace that leads me made me write as it wished ... And besides, I always wrote with many interruptions and diversions because of our domestic affairs."[139] In fact, she had given both her confessor and Claude an outline of the autobiography the year before, saying that "it came back to my mind continually." Still, it may be that the actual putting of words on paper was carried on in a state of inspired creative flow. The manuscript, when it reached Claude Martin, had scarcely a cross-out or erasure anywhere.[140]

What did vary were Marie's expectations about her audience and about how public her writing would become. When she wrote for the *Jesuit Relations* or composed obituaries for the Ursuline sisters who had died at the house in Québec, she knew she was going right into print in France, with or without her name as author.[141] Her letters with news and spiritual advice and consolation she would expect to be circulated, say, among the Ursuline houses in France or in the networks around certain pious laypersons with whom she corresponded. Her manuscripts in Algonquian and Iroquoian languages were produced for the teaching needs of her sister Ursulines, though Marie may have hoped that they would serve a few of her literate converts directly. Her most intimate confession, the autobiography of 1654, was intended for the edification of her son alone—and if he died without burning it, then only for the eyes of her niece, Marie Buisson, now an Ursuline at Tours.[142]

The self-discovery in Marie's autobiographical texts proceeded by means of multiple dialogues. Like Glikl bas Judah Leib, she had inner debates about her parenting, but Glikl's were all established by herself, while Marie's were also pressed on her by her son's letters. Both women intended God as a listener and reader, but Glikl's Lord did not answer her directly; he responded only through biblical quotations, whereas Marie's Incarnate Word and Spouse gave her repeated personal commentary.

Glikl bas Judah Leib's distress about her inability to accept suffering with equanimity persisted throughout her *Life*, whereas the core of Marie de l'Incarnation's unease and self-doubt changed from one side of the Atlantic to the other. Before the voyage, Marie's Old World torment centered, as we have seen, around hypocrisy: Am I lying about my graces and desires?

In the New World, the dialogue of doubt and affliction concerned the question of power and Marie's unworthiness for authority. She had reached the status of *assistante* to the Mother Superior in her last years at Tours, but without disquiet.[143] Some months after her arrival in Québec, she fell into a spiritual "abyss," lasting seven or eight years and hidden to all but her Jesuit Director. As she reported it, this "crucifixion" had nothing to do with her association with the Amerindian women, which she always described as a source of rejoicing. Nor did the native captains praying at her feet, in a posture recently taught them by the Jesuits, raise any conscious doubts. Rather, she agonized over her relation to Madeleine de La Peltrie and her Ursuline sisters at the convent, where she was now Mother Superior. She felt low, deserving only of their contempt. She felt alone, tempted to bitterness toward them, and believed that they, too, were tempted into repugnance for her. At her most despairing, she saw herself on the brink of hell, ready to plunge into the flames "to give displeasure to God."[144]

In fact, things were not going smoothly at the nunnery: Madame de La Peltrie left for two years with much of her furniture to try to live more closely with Amerindian groups at Montréal and Tadoussac; Marie de Saint Joseph found Marie's constitutional reforms trying; and a "mysterious" letter in odd handwriting suddenly arrived from Trois-Rivières urging the Mother Superior to be sweeter and more charitable to those around her.[145] (So we learn that Marie sometimes appeared sharp and peremptory to others.) God and her Jesuit Directors kept her from jumping into the flames, and the final resolution was given by the Virgin Mary, to whom she recounted her suffering on the feast day of the Assumption, 1647. Instantly she felt her aversion toward her sisters change into cordial love. Her power over them she redefined as service, and more specifically as a service in which only the Incarnate Word and not her personal will was at stake.[146]

Peace flooded back into Marie's soul, but it was not lit by the visions and divine revelations of her Old World days. God had told her that in Canada she must live "a common life," strictly according to the Rule like everyone else, with no extraordinary graces to interrupt the work of conversion. Her Jesuit confessor supported God's view. Holy union with the Incarnate Word was now achieved "without ravishment and ecstasy," by everyday prayer, mortification, obedience, sacrament, and especially by the divine communication "at the center of her soul." Thus, her writing had even more value in her New World spirituality than in her Old: not only did it stretch to encompass the subjects of the Canadian woodlands, but also it was now the privileged vehicle for the words that God made her say.[147]

Nothing shows better how much Marie cared about her writing than her actions and feelings during the fire that destroyed the convent on that cold December night in 1650. She rushed to save what was most important for the convent's affairs. With the flames around her, she felt a great liberty of spirit and great tranquillity as she saw the nothingness of all things. She threw the convent papers out the window to safety. Then she looked at the manuscript of the first version of her spiritual autobiography. She hesitated for a moment, touched it, and then, led by her unerring sense of sacrifice, calmly left it to burn.[148]

The rewritten spiritual autobiography and the sequence of letters between Marie Guyart and Claude Martin constituted an act of forgiveness, Marie of herself and Claude of his mother for the abandonment. Through an ocean of words, mother and son came to terms with each other. A critical transformation in their relationship occurred in 1641, when Marie heard that her son had taken a religious vocation and at age twenty-one had been received as a novice with the Benedictines of Saint Maur. The year before, she had been reproaching him for letting the fleet leave for Canada without a letter for his mother and for failing to be accepted by the Jesuits. Now he had fulfilled the dedication she had made of him at his birth: "You have gained much in losing me, and my abandonment has been useful to you. And I likewise, having left in you what was most dear and unique to me in the world. Having voluntarily lost you, I have found myself with you in the bosom of this kind God through the holy calling that you and I have both followed."[149]

Claude now enjoyed playing on the double meanings of "mother" when he wrote, and Marie enjoyed signing herself as both his mother and his sister. Ever apart, they wished each other growth in holiness, life in Christ, and the crown of martyrdom ("If I heard such a thing of you, my dear son, what joy I would receive," she wrote in 1650, after describing how her Algonquin godson Joseph Onaharé was burned alive as a Christian).[150] Meanwhile she instructed him liberally in the practice of the spiritual life, adjusting her tone over the years as he became a priest, prior of several houses, and assistant to the Superior General of the order, and finally as he began to send her his own religious publications.[151] When he complained in 1649 that he had no direct news of how she looked, she lifted her veil for the servant who would bring him her letter in France.[152] When he asked her for her "secrets"—that is, the successive states of her inner life— she finally complied, and included her feelings about him and her marriage to his father as part of the story.

As for Claude, he wrote his mother his news, asked her questions about herself, and sought her advice.[153] He seems to have been quite forthcoming about his own "secrets," telling her of his long bout with heterosexual desire, which began in 1652 with an involuntary ejaculation in the presence of a young woman seeking religious counsel and which did not end until ten years later when, in imitation of Saint Benedict, he rolled in the nettles and left in their sting. "It's not possible," Marie had calmly observed, "to live a long while in spiritual life without passing through such trials."[154]

After she died, he took her over, incorporating himself into the life of "this excellent Mother" through publication. Her letter eliciting his promise that no one but him or her niece would ever see her autobiography he put in the preface to his 1677 *Vie*, revealing to readers both her humility in not wanting to spread her graces before the world and his laudable breach of faith in publishing them. He tracked down a copy of her general confession to her Jesuit Director in 1633 ("I'd been looking for it for more than twenty years," he said), interviewed Ursuline sisters and others who had known her, and drew from thirty years of correspondence and his own memory to create an "Addition" to each chapter, duly identified and often longer than what Marie had written herself. "There is not one Author to this work; there are two," he told his readers. "Both are necessary to its completion."[155]

The two voices in the published volume sometimes reinforce each other and sometimes pull against each other. For example, Marie never spoke explicitly about sexual desire. She referred generally to the "crosses" of marriage and to her belief that God had placed her in that estate only to bring her son into the world and to be tested by the loss of her husband's goods. Yet as an Ursuline novice at Tours, she said she had had to struggle against "horrible filth" *(saletez horribles)* and worldly desires that she did not know she had or thought she had shed years before.[156] A reader might assume that sexual desire had been one of the many targets of Marie Guyart's chains and hairshirt.

Claude, however, was sure that his mother's love of chastity had been unremitting: she had wanted to join a nunnery as a girl "and had an extreme aversion to the laws of [the married] state. Though she faithfully rendered the duties of marriage because God wished it, she never on her part asked that they be rendered to her." The sexual act had made no impression on her, neither in heart nor in soul, and the very memory of it had vanished. For the reader who might wonder how her son could know all this, Claude added: "so she attested one day to a woman Religious of Québec, with whom she was talking familiarly and they happened to take up her married state."[157]

In their expectations for what women could accomplish, mother saw somewhat farther than son. Both expressed some doubts about women's qualifications for publishing and even writing on theology. Devotional literature and spiritual guides, like the *Spiritual Letters* of Jeanne de Chantal and *The Way of Perfection* of Teresa of Avila and like Marie's own spiritual manuscripts and letters, were one thing; theological expositions were another. Marie's God-given understanding of biblical texts and doctrine, received through visions or in prayer, she used freely for her teaching, but she said in the *Relation* of 1654 that she had never drawn a book from it, "the sight of my unworthiness and the lowness [*bassesse*] of my sex having kept me from it." Dom Claude added that "reflecting on her sex . . . made her ashamed to speak of Holy Scripture."[158]

It turned out that the shame did not go very deep. Marie de l'Incarnation had actually compiled a text to help her teach the novices at Tours, a concise explanation of the Creed, Commandments, and sacraments, without elaborate reasoning or citations from the church Fathers, but with appropriate Bible quotes. Claude published it several years after the *Vie*, admitting that readers might be surprised that "a simple religious, who had not studied humane letters, who had read scarcely any books, who had had no communication with learned men except for what was necessary for the direction of her soul, could be heard speaking as a theologian." God had given her "the key" to Christian mysteries, though Claude hastened to say that he had published the *Ecole sainte* not for the learned but for simple folk.[159]

In the last decade of her life, Marie composed a much more ambitious theological work in her "big book" of sacred history and holy things in Algonquin. "I am learned enough to make Christ known to all the Nations," she had affirmed in the *Relation* of 1654, and in the "sweet language" of the Amerindians she finally dared write the theology for which she felt unqualified in the language of the French.

Claude never read the *Sacred History*, but he did hear a sweeping claim in his mother's apostolic plea, "I am learned enough . . ." After the chapter in the *Vie* where Marie de l'Incarnation spoke so vehemently to God the Father, her son went on to set limits to that claim in his Addition about women as preachers and missionaries:

> I know women have never been permitted to take on publicly the office of Preacher in the church; beyond the several places where Saint Paul forbids it in his Epistles, natural modesty does not permit them to expose their face to the public view of all kinds of people. Nor are they any less forbidden to exercise the function of Missionary and carry the Gospel to infidel lands, both because of the weakness of their sex and the accidents that can happen to them, and because of the common view that with their simplicity, women would be more likely to discredit the religion they were preaching than to add to it the weight of their authority. Besides that, women are not capable of receiving the impress of the Priesthood, which is indispensable for this ministry.[160]

Saint Thecla had never preached to the Africans in the desert, Claude Martin went on, evoking an ancient figure in Saint Paul's circle. He pointed out—like the good seventeenth-century Maurist scholar that he was, separating the true from the false in Christian history—that all Thecla's sermons had been shown to be fabrications. Similarly, in a 1676 examination of Saint Ursula and her 11,000 virgins, he softened the Amazonian warriors celebrated in current Ursuline historiography: How could Ursula have organized a women's army out of "so many delicate girls from houses of the highest quality"?[161] Nonetheless, he concluded in his mother's *Life:* "[In Canada] Marie de l'Incarnation . . . fulfilled evangelical functions insofar as it was permitted to one of her sex and condition. If one cannot give her the name of Apostle, still one can give her that of an Apostolic woman [*femme Apostolique*]. And if she did not do externally all that Missionaries have done, one may still wonder whether . . . she does not now have the recompense and crown [for that role] in heaven."[162]

As an "Apostolic woman," Marie de l'Incarnation's perceptions expanded as she wrote about the people she had come to instruct and save. But there was one direction in which she did not go. In all the hundreds of pages of her writing on the indigenous peoples of North America, Marie de l'Incarnation never provided the *systematic* description of their beliefs, ceremonies, and ways of life that one can find throughout the *Jesuit Relations,* among the Jesuits' narratives of conversion, apostasy, war, and diplomacy: Pierre Biard's report of the "character, dress, dwellings, and food" of the Abenakis in 1616; Paul Le Jeune's chapter "On the Belief, Superstitions, and Errors of the Montagnais" of 1634; Paul Ragueneau's account entitled "Opinion of the Hurons Regarding Diseases" in 1647–1648; Jean de Quen's portrait "Of the Character and Customs of the Iroquois" in 1656–1657, to give only a few examples.[163] Systematic description provided advice for future missionaries and stimulated donations from readers in whose "souls was aroused pity for the wretchedness and blindness of these poor tribes." It also allowed the Jesuits to use the New World to criticize the Old, as when "the wonderful patience" of the Amerindians reflected unfavorably on the quarrelsomeness in French households, and Amerindians' communal sharing of their goods and food put to shame the beggary and increasingly punitive poor-hospitals of Christian France.[164]

In Marie de l'Incarnation, there was little or no independent ethnographic impulse. She gave fascinating bits of detail incidental to her narrative purposes—on the greased bodies of the girls;

the foods that satisfied Algonquins at convent banquets; the treatment of the elderly left behind during the hunting season; the divining and healing drum relinquished by the captain of the Montagnais Attikamegues when he converted; the custom of "resuscitating" a dead man by giving his name to another, who took the deceased's place in the family; the belief of the Ottawa women that the parhelia seen in the sky above Manitoulin Island were the wives of the Sun[165]—but the first and only time she provided a full picture of what the Amerindians wore was in answer to a precise question from her son, written in 1644, five years after her arrival. Her one systematic account of the beliefs of indigenous peoples about gods and the afterlife was also in answer to a questionnaire sent to her by her son, and she composed it only in 1670, after three decades in Canada.[166]

Marie de l'Incarnation was deeply interested not in the *difference* between the Amerindians and the French but in their *similarity*. It lay in one thing, for her the most important thing of all: their capacity for Christianity. Marie liked the kinds of Christians her girls and women became, the quickness with which they learned, their ways of imitating the sisters ("elles se forment sur nous"), their fervor, their docility—all admirable traits that European Christians would do well to have. Of the earliest Huron, Algonquin, and Montagnais seminarians in 1640, she said: "They are so attentive to what they are taught that . . . if I wanted to go over the catechism with them from morning till night, they would submit to it voluntarily. I am overcome with astonishment; I have never seen girls in France so ardent to be instructed and to pray God as they."[167] And several months later: "The girls sing with us in the choir, and we teach them what we wish, and they adapt themselves so well to it [*elles sont si souples*]; I've never seen in French girls the disposition that I remark here." Toward the end of her life, when Iroquois were among the seminarians, she was still enthusiastic: "they are the delight of our hearts."[168]

Male converts pleased her as well. Of a young hunter just baptized, she said, "I questioned him at length about the mysteries of our holy religion and was enchanted . . . to see that he had more knowledge [*connoissance*] of them than thousands of Christians who pass for learned. So we named him Augustin."[169]

Was she exaggerating? her son Claude began to wonder.

> You ask [she writes him in 1644] if the savages are really so perfect as I've been telling you. In regard to manners [*moeurs*], they don't have the French *politesse*, I mean for making compliments and for acting in French ways. We have not tried to teach them this, but only the commandments of God and the Church, all the points of our faith, all the prayers . . . and the other religious actions. A savage confesses just as well as a religious, as naive as possible ["naive" is here a positive term], making a case of the smallest of things. And when they have fallen, they do public penance with great humility.[170]

To the Mother Superior of the Ursuline convent at Tours, she makes a similar comparison: "We have here Savage *dévots* and *dévotes*, as you have polite ones [*polis*] in France. The difference is that the former are not so subtle and refined as some of yours, but they have the candor of a child, which shows that they are souls newly regenerated and washed in the Blood of Jesus Christ. When I listen to the good Charles Montagnez, Pigarouich, Noel Negabamat, and Trigalin, I wouldn't leave the place to hear the best preacher in Europe."[171] An Assumption Day procession of the French and some 600 Amerindians brought Marie to tears in 1650: "I have never seen in France a procession where there was so much order and devotion."[172] The "fervor" of the converts reminded her of the Christians of the early Church.[173]

Much of the time, Marie conveyed the words—or claimed to convey the words—of the converts, in whose conversation she "took a singular pleasure." In her many portraits of individual women and men, Christianity brought to the Amerindians some of the same consolations it brought to her: freedom from intense care for things of the world, and the ability to accept whatever the future held. Etienne Pigarouich, formerly an important shaman among the Algonquins, said to Marie: "I don't live for the animals [that I hunt] as I used to do, nor for beaver pelts. I live for God. Now when I go hunt, I say, 'Great Captain Jesus, lead me. Even if thou stoppest the animals and they do not appear before me, I will always believe in thee. If thou wantest me to die of hunger, I am content. Dispose of me, thou, who disposest of everything.' "[174] A convert with the baptismal name of Louise came to the Ursuline grill for further instruction on the Sacrament and said:

> God does me many graces. Before [I was a Christian] the death of my children afflicted me so that I could scarcely console myself. Now my spirit is so convinced of the wisdom and goodness of God that even if he took them all away, I would not be sad. I think to myself, "If a long life were necessary for my child to make his salvation better, then God would not have refused it to him. He who knows all saw that perhaps my child would cease to believe in him and commit sins that would lead him to Hell." I say to God, "Dispose of me and dispose of my children, too. No matter how thou testest me, I will not stop believing in thee . . . I want what thou wantest." And I say to my children when I see them dying, "Go, my child, go to heaven to him who has made everything. And when you are there, pray to him that I may come there, too."

And indeed, since Louise had been baptized, the Lord had been taking her children, one after another.[175]

Other women converts, as they appear in Marie's writings, resemble her in the education that religion has brought them and in their subsequent activism. Young Khionrea the Huron, baptized Thérèse, learns at the convent to speak French and Algonquin and to read and write, and begins preaching to Huron visitors when she is only fourteen. She starts back to her village to marry and to instruct her people in Christianity, but is captured by the Iroquois and married to one of their warriors. Ten years later, in 1653, she is found to be the mistress of her Iroquois longhouse and leading its several families in Christian prayer.[176] The Montagnais Angélique, a woman of sixty, makes her way across rocks and forests in the February snows, to go north to the At-tikamegues, sustaining their faith and prayers, "playing the office of Apostle ... God knows with what affection I will embrace her when I see her."[177]

A middle-aged Nipissing widow, Geneviève, carries her hus-band's corpse hundreds of miles, through wood and river, to give him a Christian burial. She comes to the Ursulines in 1664, hun-gry for instruction in the holy mysteries since there are no Black Robes among her people. She begins to pray in words of fire, tries out an iron belt and other instruments of penance, weeps ecstatically during Good Friday service as God impresses in her his love for humankind, learns to look inside herself for signs of grace and corruption, and then goes off to prevent her brother from exchanging furs for eau-de-vie and to preach to the women of her nation with marvelous fervor. Geneviève appears an Al-gonquian-speaking version of the widowed Marie Guyart her-self.[178]

So much for the converts who came into the Ursuline yard. What of the many people in the woodlands hostile to Christian-ity? Every once in a while one of them emerges as an individual in Marie's letters, reworked by her from some observer's account. Thus, she tells how a Huron woman, "one of the oldest and most notable of that nation," spoke against the Jesuits at a village assembly:

> It's the Black Robes who are making us die by their spells. Listen to me, I will prove it by reasons that you will recognize as true. They set themselves up in a village where everyone is feeling fine; no sooner are they there but everyone dies except for three or four people. They move to another place, and the same thing happens. They visit cabins in other villages, and only those where they have not entered are exempt from death and illness. Don't you see that when they move their lips in what they call prayer, spells are coming out of their mouths? It's the same when they read their books. They have big pieces of wood in their cabins ["guns," explains Marie to her correspondent] by which they

make noise and send their magic everywhere. If they are not promptly put to death, they will end up ruining the country, and no one will be left, young or old.

"When she stopped speaking, everyone agreed that this was true," Marie concluded. And indeed, "it seemed true . . . , for wherever the [Jesuit] Fathers went, God permitted death to accompany them so as to render more pure the faith of those who converted."[179]

In all of Marie de l'Incarnation's letters, this is the moment when she most effectively put herself into the mind of an anti-Christian Amerindian, one who she thought was "inspired by demons." With Marie's interest in voice, it is surely no accident that her subject was a woman speaking eloquently, and, indeed, a woman overlooked in Father Lalemant's *Relation* of that year.[180] Ordinarily, so long as the Iroquois were enemies of Christians and French, Marie cast them as "barbarians," mocking, tormenting, and killing Christian captives.[181]

But even "barbarians" turned out to have the same full capacity for Christianity as anyone else, and once the Iroquois began to convert, Marie described them in terms of enthusiastic likeness. The shift began as early as the visits of the Iroquois ambassadors and an Onondaga *capitainesse* to the convent during the peace negotiations of 1655. The *capitainesse,* a chief's wife, impressed Marie because, like other women notables among the Iroquois, she could influence decisions at local councils and name ambassadors. More important, the *capitainesse* was so charmed by the young Huron Marie Aouentohons, who made a Christian speech to the company and sang hymns in Huron, French, and Latin, that she promised to send her own daughter to the convent.[182] When Iroquois girls were finally baptized, Marie de l'Incarnation praised their "taste for the mysteries of the Faith," but reserved her greatest joy for the activities of a preaching woman: "A good Iroquois woman, converted not long ago, has been so zealous of our holy Mysteries, which she possesses in perfection, that she goes everywhere in her village to instruct the old and young and attract them to the faith. She has been very much persecuted by her nation, but remains victorious despite Hell and its agents."[183]

How much did these Amerindians have to remake themselves as Christians to satisfy the standards of Marie de l'Incarnation? How much "civilizing" did she require? Though we have seen her telling her French correspondents that the Ursulines were not teaching *politesse* to the adult Indians, the young seminarians were degreased, given French garments, and taught the language, manners, craft, and musical skills of European women. This is what the Jesuits had encouraged, especially in the 1650s, for Huron girls who were now living far from their burned villages, so that they could marry French men. This is what the administrators of New France encouraged, especially in the 1660s, when Louis XIV's governor wanted "savages to become little by little *un peuple poli.*" This is what even a few Iroquois mothers asked for, eager to find out how long it would take the Ursulines to raise their daughters *à la Françoise.*[184]

Looking back from 1668 over twenty-nine years of teaching, Marie de l'Incarnation noted that she and her sisters had "Frenchified a number of Savage girls"—about seven or eight—who had gone on to good marriages with French husbands.[185] But to her that was neither a likely outcome nor the most desirable outcome. "For a hundred who have passed through our hands, we have civilized scarcely one." Most women came into the yard for conversation or instruction and left again as they wished. Most girls stayed in the convent for limited periods of time. Not only might they be withdrawn by their parents for chores or hunting, but they became despondent within the enclosure of the convent: "We find docility and wit [*esprit*] in [the girls]; but when one least expects it, they climb over our walls and run in the woods with their parents, where they find more pleasure than in all the attractions of our French houses . . . Besides, the Savages love their children extraordinarily, and when [the parents] know they are sad, they'll do everything possible to have them back."[186]

Almost all the Ursuline seminarians had returned to the "liberty" of their woodland life, "although as very good Christians" ("quoi que très-bonnes Chrétiennes").[187] On the whole, Marie preferred this future for them to a French marriage.[188] As early as 1642 she had described approvingly the Christian resourcefulness of three youthful Algonquins—Anne-Marie Uthirdchich, Agnès Chabvekveche, and Louise Aretevir—who were helping their mothers prepare furs during the hunt. As they wrote Marie, one of them was organizing public prayers, the second deciding what hymns to sing, and the third urging a community examination of conscience.[189] It was on women like them, and on the Huron Thérèses, the Montagnais Angéliques, and the Algonquin Genevièves and their male counterparts, that Marie de l'Incarnation rested her main hope for a Christian woodland.[190]

That Christian woodland would, in Marie's view, be somewhat different from one presided over by Manitous and okis. The Amerindian economic life and the division of labor and authority could continue as before. Only for a moment did she echo the early Jesuit notion that, once Christianized, the Algonquian-speaking peoples should become sedentary.[191] After the early 1640s Marie seems to have assumed that Christianity could be sustained by peoples on the move, led by Jesuits who traveled with them or by some of the converts themselves. She also appears indifferent to whether Christian loyalty had to bring with it a redefinition of tribal identity or a reshaping of the brotherly bonds of Indian federation.

What Marie required of a Christian was two things. First, a break with all non-Christian religious practice, shamanic action or consultation, dream interpretation and prescription, and ritual feasts and dances intended to placate okis and Manitous. If the Amerindians had, independent of the Europeans, the "beautiful knowledge" of a Virgin who gave birth to a world-savior Messou (as the Montagnais named him), all their "ridiculous fables" about how Messou had preserved the world by means of a muskrat would have to be put aside.[192] Her second requirement was a commitment to Christian marriage. This meant a break with Amerindian standards that encouraged premarital intercourse to find the right spouse, that permitted in some communities extramarital intercourse for both spouses, and that allowed divorce and re-marriage and sometimes polygamy. Marie may not have worried much about the sexual control of her female converts. She and Marie de Saint Joseph had found it easy to persuade the seminarians that their guardian angel would leave them if they went around almost naked: "the women of this America, although Savages, are shamefaced and decent," she said more than once about how they clothed their bodies.[193] Temptations outside marriage for the men she took more seriously. Hadn't the eloquent Etienne Pigarouich succumbed to a maddening passion for an Onontchataronon woman, left his Algonquin wife and community, and slipped back into his shamanic ways?[194]

But the rock-bottom requisite for Marie de l'Incarnation was that Christian be married to Christian. If one of the betrothed was not a convert, better to put promises to marry aside. For a Christian with a spouse who stubbornly refused to convert, even Amerindian divorce might be invoked. Thus, Marie described the predicament of the Montagnais Charles Meiachkouat, "a Savage Christian Apostle," as he preached through the villages: "This generous Christian has the most wicked and insupportable of pagan wives. He suffers her mischief and fury with patience and does not want to leave her yet in order to try to convert her and save the soul of their little girl; for it is the custom of the country that when married people separate, the wife takes the children."[195] Other times it was the Christian wife trying to convert her husband or, failing that, deciding to leave him. The stakes were high for Marie de l'Incarnation. Through the woodlands family and the long-house or cabin wife, the Amerindians could be—with or without *politesse*—"very good Christians."

Marie de l'Incarnation had come to Canada to bring its reasoning souls to faith in the King of all the nations. She died blessing the "Savage Seminarians" around her bed, preferring them over the French pensionnaires, and whispering in her final agony, "Everything is for the Savages."[196] Along the way, she had imagined an extravagant similarity between her inner life and spiritual capacities and those of Amerindian converts, in this one regard almost effacing the boundary between "savage" and "European." The pattern of likeness is found whether her letters to France were intended to stimulate money, prayers, or simple curiosity, whether they were expected to circulate widely or be read by one set of eyes. While accepting the Christian French presence in the New World, this perception at least unsettles the assumption that among Christians the French need always be dominant.

Only in 1663, when Marie had to admit that after twenty-four years no Amerindian had sought to stay at the convent as a professed Ursuline, was there a significant limit to her universalizing: "We have tested the savage girls," she wrote an Ursuline back in France. "They cannot survive in enclosure. Their nature is strongly melancholic, and being restrained in their customary freedom to go where they want increases their melancholy."[197] Of course, Marie herself had been provoked to melancholy by French enclosure in Tours and had revived only in her vocation for Canada and in the wider space of the Québec convent yard. And she died several years before the Mohawk convert Katharine Tekakwitha developed at Sault Saint Louis a distinctive form of communal ascetic life for women without enclosure.[198] If she reported meeting no fully developed mystics among the Amerindian Christians, it is also true that her own mystical action had changed its course in the New World, reinscribed in the busyness of everyday life. She seems to have believed that the Amerindian women, too, however hardworking, could still have divine communication at the center of their souls.

In the extravagance of its sense of likeness, Marie de l'Incarnation's universalizing was not a view commonly held in the American woodlands. The expectations of the male religious for Amerindian spirituality were more tempered, their perception of difference and its consequences more acute. The Jesuits seem to have started with a gloomier sense of the obstacles placed by "savage" life in the way of Christian reconstitution. "I could not say that I have seen one act of true moral virtue in a Savage," Paul Le Jeune said after his first winter with the Montagnais. "They have nothing but their own pleasure and satisfaction in view. Add to this the fear of being blamed and the glory of appearing to be good hunters, and you have all that moves them in their transactions."[199] "From the standpoint of human prudence," Jérome Lalemant wrote after his first stint with the Hurons, "I can scarcely believe that there is any place in the world more difficult to subject to the Laws of Jesus Christ." This is "above all because I do not believe there is any people on earth freer than they, and less able to allow the constraint of their wills by any authority whatsoever—so much so that the fathers have no power over their children, or the captains over their subjects, or the laws of the country over any of them, except in so far as each is pleased to submit to them."[200]

Marie must have heard such views as well as read them in the *Relations,* for she was in frequent communication with Le Jeune and Lalemant on administrative matters, and both men served as her spiritual Director. Yet she made no such somber generalizations, stressing rather the natural "sweetness" and "docility" of the Amerindian women. "Savage birth renders men naturally inconstant," she said in her most negative characterization of the savage nature, but it was remediable by the "miracle" of baptism, as evidenced by the Christian loyalty of Huron captives among the Iroquois.[201] (She may have savored this argument, since in Europe "inconstancy" was supposed to be a female trait par excellence.) She who had never spanked her son, Claude, never recommended the spanking of Amerindian children, as did the Jesuits; she who had followed her own religious path in the household of her husband and brother-in-law never insisted that Amerindian wives should have the supreme duty of obeying their husbands. And as for the "liberty" of "savage life," she defined it (as we have seen) not in terms of authority structures but in terms of the freedom to move in the woods, and saw it as an obstacle not to the laws of Christian conduct but to an Ursuline vocation.

In contrast to Marie's ever exuberant retellings of Amerindian conversions, Jesuit accounts blended enthusiasm with suspicion. Hurons portrayed by Brébeuf and Lalemant in the 1630s were having recourse to Christian prayers and baptism only in hopes of immediate material benefits, like recovery from an illness, rain, ample crops, or victory at the sacred gambling game of "dish."[202] An Onondaga overheard by Father Allouez in 1664 was urging a fellow Iroquois to be baptized simply so as to prolong his life.[203]

At least, the Montagnais Charles Meiachkouat knew better than that. In Paul Le Jeune's account, he pleaded with a sick man, "Do not think that the water of Baptism is poured out to heal thy body: it is to purify thy soul and to give thee a life that cannot die."[204] Meiachkouat's conversion had begun with a vision, which Le Jeune came to believe had been sent by Christ himself: a man dressed like the Black Robes appeared to him in the woods and told him to forsake his old ways, do as the Jesuits did, and then instruct his people. Le Jeune devoted many pages to Meiachkouat's spiritual achievements: his abandonment of "superstitions" about respecting the bones of beavers he had killed at the hunt; his willingness, after a moment of anger, to forgive and pray for one who had spoken ill of him; his ruminating over some point of doctrine he had been taught.[205] But even here, in this best of cases, there was a moment of distance between Jesuit and convert: "He had it so much in his mind to imitate our way of doing things that he asked if we would be willing to receive him among us; for he would like to leave his wife, since she was not pressing for her baptism. 'The voice that I heard,' he said, 'exhorted me to imitate you. I don't care to be married. I will give my little girl to the Ursulines and stay with you.' This proposal made us laugh."[206]

Similarly, Jérome Lalemant thought there were times when Christian converts had gone too far. This was certainly his reaction to Father de Quen's report of events among the Montagnais in 1646. On the one hand, Lalemant liked what he heard about the piety of an old woman, "strangely above the common in her devotions." She memorized long prayers on first or second hearing and taught them to others, and even better, retired to pray on her own: "her heart speaks a language that no one has taught her." On the other hand, Lalemant was shocked at the "indiscreet zeal" and "arrogance" of the Montagnais during their long winter months of hunting in the forests. In the absence of their Black Robe, one of the men served as priest and celebrated Mass, an elderly woman set herself up as confessor for those of her sex, and other unsuitable practices were instituted as sacred mysteries. Learning this in the spring at Tadoussac, Father de Quen rebuked them until the Montagnais priest admitted that "the devil had led him astray." When the Jesuit departed, he gave them a black memory stick "to remind them of the horror they must have for their innovations and their former superstitions."[207]

Let us speculate on the sources of Marie's extravagant universalizing—that is, on the way her New World life seemed to confirm so strongly her sense of inner likeness to, rather than of difference from, the Christian "savages." It was certainly nourished by the character of her contact with other cultures. She was not saturated with the scholarly literature from Aristotle to Acosta on the nature of the "barbarian," or with French historical theory on the relations between climate, geographic terrain, bodily humors, and customs. Such references never figure in her writing, and from what we can reconstruct of the Ursuline library in Québec, such books were not on the convent's shelves.[208] Moreover, she had seen little of the world. From Tours to Québec she had made only a brief detour, and in Canada she did not visit Amerindian villages as did the Jesuits.

But the contrast between her and the Fathers is not a matter of their having more "knowledge" than she did. Rather, it is the setting for learning, exchanging, and observing that made the difference, and the character of the alliance between "knower" and "known." The Jesuits set themselves up in their own cabins as soon as they could in Amerindian settlements. They moved back and forth between their own male space for living and prayer and the Amerindian space of men and women ruled by the Manitou and/or Christ. In an act resembling Amerindian adoption, they were given Algonquian or Iroquoian names by their hosts—Le Jeune was Echom among the Hurons and Lalemant was Achiendassé—and these names were often assigned to their successors, just as the Amerindians "revived" or remade a captain's name by giving it to his successor.[209] But when they returned to Québec and to France (both Le Jeune and Lalemant went back to France for a time),[210] the Jesuits simply shed these kinlike ties. This back-and-forth movement between the two worlds sustained mental distance for the Jesuits; it allowed them to become involved in village life and quarrels, while never forgetting their outsider status. The tensions brought on by this role-playing they expressed and resolved from time to time through writing their *Relations*.

Marie de l'Incarnation's world had much less doubleness. For her, there was no Indian adoptive alliance or shifting of name from French to Amerindian. The Amerindians addressed all the Ursulines as *sainte fille*, or called them "my mother" (*Ningue* in Algonquin, possibly also one of the respectful terms of address to a woman of the woodlands), or used a version of their convent name: "Marie Joseph" for Marie de Saint Joseph and perhaps "Marie Incarnation" for Mother Marie.[211] Everything went on in the same enclosure. This was Ursuline turf—Marie de l'Incarnation's salon—and yet with its birchbark cabins, big cauldrons full of Amerindian food, and multiple languages, it was a hybrid space rather than a transplantation of European order. Marie's intimate knowledge of the Montagnais, Algonquins, Hurons, and Iroquois was drawn from what went on in convent dormitories, schoolrooms, chapel, and yard, and especially from conversations with girls and women. They spoke often in an Amerindian tongue, engaging in leisurely conversations in close quarters, which could well have given Marie de l'Incarnation the impression that she was listening to women whose inner states were like her own.

Other features of her life may also have closed the gap. Her own learning had come rather like that of her converts, in a modest classroom or sent by God himself; their seeming to understand holy mysteries as easily as did French doctors of theology would seem less unexpected to her than to the Jesuits. Then, too, Marie de l'Incarnation was a mystic, for whom simplicity and fervor were valued qualities, essential for inner grace. To one who had reached ecstatically for words to describe union with God, the Amerindian love of metaphor need not be just an aid to the rhetoric of diplomacy (so it was praised by the Jesuits), but could also be a path to knowledge of the divine. Not surprisingly, then, Marie brought to her writing about the converts some of the same appreciative enthusiasm she bestowed on her obituary portraits of Marie de Saint Joseph, Madame de La Peltrie, and other members of the house.[212] In the inner landscape of spirituality, she saw them as one people.

Do we have here a sensibility shared by the other Ursuline and Hospitaler *femmes fortes* of Marie's generation? Father Vimont thought as much, remarking on the women's devotion to the Amerindians, even though the Hurons and Algonquins were "dressed in rags" and ignorant of "even the elementary principles of civility": "The love constantly felt by the Hospital Nuns for the sick and the poor, and by the Ursulines for the pupils of their Seminary and for the Savage women—in whom they see but Jesus Christ alone, without any of the attraction that pleases the senses—is an inclination in which I expect perseverance only from Jesus Christ himself. Their sex does not possess such constancy, but like Saint Paul, [women] can do everything when sustained and fortified by God."[213] The few letters left to us from Marie de Saint Joseph and Madame de La Peltrie express unalloyed warmth toward the youthful Amerindian converts at the Ursulines: "[The girls] take unutterable pleasure in being instructed on the adorable mystery of communion . . . They conceptualize this lovable truth beyond their ages."[214] The Christian converts, young women and old, who emerge from the seventeenth-century reports and *Annales* of the Québec Hospitalers were also spiritual heroines, though the sisters resorted to phrases such as "no savage tendencies" and "showing no savage humor" much more consistently than Marie.[215]

But simply being a woman did not mean that connection with

Amerindians was central in one's spiritual life, even in the generation of the *femmes fortes*. The religious style that young Catherine de Saint Augustin brought over to Québec from Cherbourg took her in other directions, as we learn from her journal. Hospitaler in Québec from 1648 to 1668, she was consumed by her struggles with the demons imprisoned in her body, who might come out of an aching tooth in the middle of a Jesuit sermon to contradict everything the preacher said. She was blessed by visions, which were often guided from Paradise by the "martyred" Father Brébeuf, but they concerned the fate of the blessed and the damned in France, in Japan, anywhere. To be sure, during her term as head nurse, she begged the Lord that "no one who died at the Hospital would be outside of God's grace"—a prayer that included Amerindians—but the religious energies she described in her journal were directed toward French settlers: a possessed woman, whom she helped; a man concealing his sorcery and witches' Sabbaths; people complaining about the new bishop of Québec.[216]

At the end of the century appear women who distanced themselves spiritually much farther from the Amerindians. Marie Morin's 1695 history of the Montréal hospital, at which she had been a sister for the previous thirty-three years, scarcely mentioned them except to record the Iroquois threat and the appreciation felt by "savage" patients for Judith Moreau de Brésoles, the first superior of the house. (They named her "the sun that shines," since she gave life to the sick.) Morin's subject was the Christian virtues of her sister religious, all of them of European or settler origin, rather than "the salvation of perhaps a million Savages," which had attracted the hospital foundress from France decades before.[217] In 1740, a hundred years after Marie de l'Incarnation began joyfully receiving her first seminarians, a Québec Hospitaler dismissed the Amerindians as *"vilains Messieurs."* "There are some fervent Christians among them, even saints," she wrote, "but the greatest number of them listen to the mysteries preached to them as if they were just stories that made no impression on them."[218]

ÆTAT. SUÆ. XXXX.

LA MERE MARIE DE L'INCARNATION,
Premiere Superieure des Ursulines de la nouvelle
france decedée a Quebec en odeur de Sainteté le
dernier jour d'avril 1672. ageé de 72 ans 6 mois 13 j.ˢ

Marie Guyart de l'Incarnation at the age when she left France
for Québec, a portrait possibly done from life

LE CHEMIN
DE PERFECTION
Composé par Saincte Terese de IESVS,
Fondatrice des Carmes & Carmelines
Dechaussez, pour ses Religieuses à leur
instante priere.

Nouuellement traduit d'Espagnol en François,
par le R. P. F. E. D. S. B.

A PARIS,
Chez SEBASTIEN HVRE', ruë
S. Iacques, au Cœur-bon.

M. DC. XXXVI.
Auec Approbation.

Favorite reading of Marie Guyart: Saint Teresa in French

The Ursuline convent of Québec before the fire of 1650, as painted with archival guidance in the nineteenth century

Amerindian women tending the crops with a digging stick and hunting for birds' eggs

Wampum belts, strung by women for male diplomacy

✦

Right: Huron, from the Christian community of Wendake (Lorette), eighteenth century

Below: Huron, commemorating the Four Nations of the Huron, a belt said to have been given to Samuel Champlain in 1611

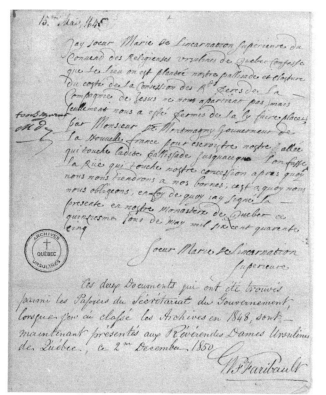

Attestation of the convent boundary by Marie de
l'Incarnation, 1645

*Ursuline writing,
Amerindian
writing*

✧

Thank-you note to a French donor, written in Huron and French on birchbark
from Amerindian seminarians of the Ursulines, 1676.

A son edits his mother's writing

✷

precieuse.

50. Estant donc arrivée en ce Pays le voyant, je le
reconnu estre celuy que N. Seigneur m'avoit mon[stré]
Il y avoit 6 ans les fidés montagnes, ou vastitudes
La situation et la forme qui estoit encore marqué[e]
mon Esprit, come à l'heure mesme, le mé[s]toit la mesme
Chose a la viie, Excepté que Je ny voiois pas tant de
Brunes, ce qui renouuela beaucoup la ferueur de
Vocationer une Fente, par un abandon de tout me[s]me
mesme Pour tout Souffrir, Et faire ce que N[ost]re
Voudroit de moy, en ce nouuel Establissement, [en g]e-
res de vie, quil ny failloit embrasser entierement,
feroit de Celuy de nos monasteres de france, [De]
moins Pas moins regulier dans Sa façon et m[a]

De vie, Pauure et Inegale des Labord nous som[m]e[s]
cames par la Closturee de gros piux de Cédres au-
Lieu de murailles auer ttt Licence de donner entré
aux filles Et femes Sauuages Seminaristes Et externes
et aux filles francoises, toutes aux fins de L'Ino-
truction. N[ost]re Logement estoit Si Petit qu'en une cham-
Bre d'enuiron 16 Pieds en care estoit n[ost]re Choeur n[ost]re
Parloir dortoir Refectoir Et Dans une Aue La Classe
pour Les francoises et Sauuages et Pour n[ost]re Cuisine
Nous fismes faire un Appentif Pour La Chapelle
Et Sacristie exterieure. La Saleté des filles Sauuages —
qui n'estoint Point encore faites à La Propreté des tra-
cois nous faisoit quelquefois trouuer un Soulier en n[ost]re
Pot et Journellement des Cheueux et des Charbons, ce qui
ne nous donnoit [illegible] aucun desgoust. Les Perso[n]ées
qui nous Visittoint a qui Par recreation nous raconti-
[illegible] comprendre coment nous Pouuions

CHAPITRE III.

I. Comparaison du Canada avec le grand païs qui luy avoit été montré en vision. II. Pauvreté de vie & richeffe de regularité dans fon nouvel établiffement. III. Patience admirable à fupporter les faletez des filles Sauvages. IV. De fa perfeverance dans l'amour pour les Sauvages. V. Et du vœu qu'elle a fait de fe confommer à leur fervice VI. Incommoditez des Religieufes dans leur commencement. VII. Le Monaftere eft bâti. VIII. Les Religieufes ayant été prifes de diverfes Congregations s'uniffent en une, & conviennent des reglemens qu'elles doivent garder.

I. **A**Prés que je fus arrivée en ce païs, & que j'eus fait reflexion fur tout ce que j'y voyois, je reconnus que c'étoit celuy que Nôtre Seigneur m'avoit montré il y avoit fix ans : ces grandes montagnes, ces vaftes forefts, ces païs immenfes, la fituation & la forme des lieux qui fe prefentoient à ma veuë, étoient les mémes que j'avois veus, & qui étoient encore auffi prefens dans mon efprit qu'à l'heure méme, excepté que je n'y voiois pas tant de brunes. Cela renouvella beaucoup la ferveur de ma vocation, & me donna une pente à m'abandonner toute moy-méme pour tout fouffrir, & pour tout faire ce que Nôtre Seigneur voudroit de moy dans ce nouvel établiffement entierement different de nos

II. Monafteres de France, pour la maniere de vie pauvre & frugale où il fe falloit reduire, mais non pour les pratiques & les obfervances de la Religion, qui, graces à Nôtre Seigneur, y étoient gardées dans leur plus grande pureté. Nous commençâmes par la clôture que nous fîmes faire de gros pieux de cedres au lieu de murailles, avec la licence neanmoins de donner entrée aux filles & aux femmes Sauvages, tant Seminariftes qu'externes, & aux filles Françoifes qui voudroient venir à l'inftruction. Nôtre logement étoit fi petit qu'en une chambre d'environ feize pieds en carré étoient nôtre Chœur, nôtre parloir, nôtre dortoir, nôtre refectoir; & dans une autre, la claffe pour les Françoifes & les Sauvages; & pour la Chappelle, la Sacriftie exterieure, & la cuifine nous fîmes faire une gallerie en forme d'appenti. La falleté des

III. filles Sauvages qui n'étoient pas encore faites à la propreté des Françoifes nous faifoit quelque fois trouver un foulier dans nôtre pot, & tous les jours des cheveux, des charbons & de femblables ordures,

The arrival in Canada as published in the *Vie* by Claude Martin

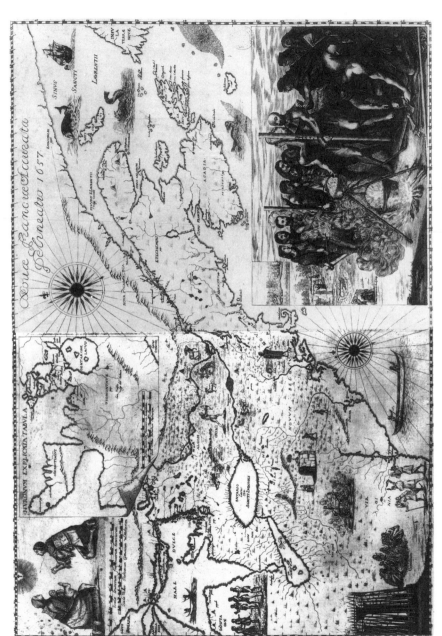

New France and the Amerindian world in a Jesuit map of 1657

What stories would the Amerindian converts have told about the Europeans? Let us take a few of Marie de l'Incarnation's most admired Christians, such as the Hurons Thérèse Khionrea and Marie Aouentohons, the Algonquin Anne Marie Uthirdchich and her companions on the hunt, and the Nipissing Geneviève, and imagine how they would have regarded Marie's claims about them and their Christianity. Surely they would not have come to the encounter with Marie de l'Incarnation believing that likeness and human alliance were expanded by religious conversion. The Amerindians were temperate in their knowledge claims on matters of belief. When the Jesuits challenged them about their high divinities—say, on how Yoscaha, the first creator, could possibly have a grandmother Aataentsic—they would answer that it was difficult to get firm evidence about such things. Some people claimed to have acquired this information during a dream-visit to the other world, but others simply observed that "about a thing so far distant nothing sure can be known."[219] Likewise, they were politely tolerant of religious tales and customs different from their own, so long as they did not suspect witchcraft. As some Hurons said to Father Brébeuf, "Each country has its own ways of doing things."[220]

Differing nations and communities were connected as "one people" not by a shared religious belief or spiritual capacity, but by processes of incorporation: the adoption of male captives as sons and brothers; the marriage to women captives; and the commingling of the bones of the dead from different nations during the periodic reburial known as the Feast of the Dead, a ceremony described by the Jesuits as "their strongest witness to friendship and alliance."[221] The diplomatic kinship established among nations in the Huron and Iroquois leagues ("brothers," "sisters") was the closest analogue of the spiritual kinship established among individuals in Christian baptism.

With this mental frame, Khionrea, Uthirdchich, and the other women converts would not readily have assumed an inner likeness between the French and themselves. The young seminarians imitated the religious gestures of the Ursulines, and some Huron women used a woodlands metaphor to say how much they hoped to learn from the example of the Ursulines and Hospital sisters: "They know the path to heaven . . . Our eyes are not yet good enough." But welcoming instruction need not rest on a belief in likeness. The Huron women, accounting for the "love" they felt for some unknown women in France, spoke not of similarities but of gift relations. The French women had sent them gifts and they felt an obligation in return.[222] The enthusiastic sentimentality of Marie de l'Incarnation may have missed the mark from the Amerindian point of view.

The Huron, Algonquin, and Iroquois women would surely have described their conversion to Christianity in a somewhat different fashion from Marie. Where the Ursuline mother saw almost a complete break with indigenous religion, the Amerindian women could well have seen links. Where the Ursuline mother claimed full consolation and tranquillity as the fruits of baptism, the Amerindian women could have reported strains.

A good case in point is the relation between the Amerindian dream and the Christian vision. For the Hurons and Iroquois, the importance of dreams was connected to their belief that the soul was "divisible." One of the divisions was the desiring soul, which especially spoke to one in dreams: "this is what my heart tells me; this is what my appetite desires" *(ondayee ikaton onennoncouat)*. Sometimes the desiring soul was counseled by a familiar *oki* or spirit, who told the soul what it needed or wanted—its *ondinoc*, its secret desire. There were strong grounds, then, for Amerindians to take their dreams very seriously. They described and interpreted them to one another, and then acted on them with intensity and determination.[223]

By the time she wrote her dictionaries, Marie de l'Incarnation must have had to deal with the divisible Indian soul, but in her letters she spoke only of the belief of the people of America in the immortality of the soul, "which served much in their conversion." Their conviction that they "must obey their dreams" she found utterly superstitious, incompatible with Christianity, and quite incomparable to the dream vision of Mary and Jesus that God had sent her and that she had obeyed to come to Canada.[224]

Her converts must have felt otherwise. They would have heard about visions like that of a Huron woman of Angoutenc, who, walking one night with her daughter, met the moon deity (an avatar of Aataentsic) in the form of a beautiful woman with a daughter of her own. Told by the moon that she must dress henceforth in red and be given presents, the woman returned to her long-house, fell ill, and then dreamed further orders for the feast that would heal her. Wearing the moon's fiery red, she was cured at the ceremonies that followed.[225]

Such experiences prepared the way for visions from other gods. Thus, a Huron woman, "a very good Christian of wholly innocent life," received divine word in advance of the Canadian earthquake of February 1663. During the night of February 3, while everyone slept around her, she heard a voice saying distinctly, "In two days marvelous and astonishing things will happen." Collecting wood the next day with her sister, she heard the same voice predicting an earthquake on the morrow between five and six in the afternoon. Trembling, she took the news back to her long-house. According to Marie's account and that of the Hospital sisters, she was not taken seriously but was suspected of following her "dreams" or trying to play the role of a shamanic "prophetess." The earthquake came the next afternoon, between five and six. At the Hospital, Catherine de Saint Augustin immediately began having visions, including one of Saint Michael, who informed her that the people of Canada were being punished for their impiety, their impurity, and their lack of charity.[226]

The uses of dreams must have varied for different converts. Surely the habit of self-examination required by dream interpretation nourished the remarkable confessional skills of the converts, noted both by Marie de l'Incarnation and the Jesuits. Some converts may have been relieved to lay down the anxiety of precise dream fulfillment in favor of the more diffuse fear of sin.

Others may simply have carried along into their Christianity certain of the practices and ecstasies of dream visions, just as some European villagers sent their souls out at night to battle witches or visit the dead. Such a religious mixture, undermined in Europe by the Inquisition and witchcraft prosecutions, was easier to sustain in the woodlands and winters of northeastern America.[227]

Evidence for mixture surfaces in the French reports. The Algonquin Louise, whom we have already heard talking to Marie de l'Incarnation about her willingness to accept the death of her children, made her own choices as she cared for and buried her daughters. On the one hand, she reportedly sent away two non-Christian Algonquin women who urged her to take her nine-year-old from the Québec Hospital into the woods and let her be cured by shamanic drumming and blowing. (Or did Louise accede to this alternative? The Hospital sisters said that the daughter "having received some relief at the Hospital," her mother took her into the woods on a journey, where she died.) On the other hand, when her older daughter Ursule fell ill, she cared for her in a cabin next to the Hospital door, decorating it as an oratory both with Christian objects and, *"à la sauvage,"* with embroidered robes of beaver and moose. The Hospitalers and priests tolerated this mixture of customs as "indifferent" (that is, not important one way or the other), but Louise's interment of Ursule was unacceptable. The mother "had her daughter buried with all the solemnity possible to a Savage, and put in her grave all that she had most precious in the way of Beaver, Wampum, and other items of which they make account." The Jesuits had been inveighing against these grave gifts which, together with community gifts "to dry the tears" of the bereaved kin, replaced the European property system of inheritance and bequest. How could Louise bury such goods with her daughter, the Hospitalers wanted to know, when she herself was so "poor"? The Algonquin went ahead with her ceremony, reminding the sisters that they had buried a religious two years before in her beautiful robe and in all honor. God did not forbid what she was doing, she was sure. "I wish to honor the dead."[228]

Such episodes suggest that the converts of Marie de l'Incarnation sustained or required a religious sensibility much more hybrid than she knew or allowed.[229] On one point, however, they all might have agreed: the importance of women's speaking on sacred things. There is an interesting parallel between Europe and America in regard to voice. Just as political eloquence in France was primarily the domain of learned men, so political eloquence in the American woodlands—around the male village council fire, at tribal assemblies, at the treaty meetings of the Huron and Iroquois leagues—was primarily the domain of men. About crops, food distribution, and the fate of prisoners, Amerindian women made the decisions. Especially among the Iroquois, women had a role in naming successors to chieftains and ambassadors. Women strung the mnemonic wampum belts taken on embassies. (Two such belts can be seen in the illustrations.) But the eloquent arguments, imaginative metaphors, and dramatic gestures that won the approving, deep-throated "Haaa, Haaa," of the listeners came from the men. When the Mohawk chief Kiotseaeton wanted to persuade the Hurons to take part in a peace treaty, he presented a wampum necklace "to urge the Hurons to hasten forth to speak. Let them not be bashful like women."[230] The old woman described by Marie as denouncing the Jesuits at a Huron assembly was all the more dramatic because she was unusual.

As priestly power in France was in the hands of men, so the healing power of shamans among Iroquoian- and Algonquian-speaking peoples was primarily in the hands of men. Women had roles in dances and rituals to placate the oki spirits or drive evil spirits out from the sick; they surely dispensed the herbal remedies known to be part of the lore of later Amerindian women; presumably some of them played a religious role in the menstrual cabins of the Iroquois, Huron, and Montagnais communities. Perhaps it was beliefs about menstrual defilement that ordinarily barred women from handling the sacred shamanic objects and rattle used in spirit cures by the master shaman, as similar beliefs in Europe kept women away from the Communion table during their periods.[231] In any case, soothsaying was the one shamanic function in which women were welcome in the seventeenth century, as with the old woman of Teanaostaiaë village in the Huron country, who saw events in distant battles with the Iroquois by looking into fires.[232]

As women in Europe, like Marie, expanded their religious voice through the Catholic Reformation orders (or through the radical Protestant sects that we will look at in the next chapter), so it may be that women in the American woodlands were expanding their voice in religious culture while the men were expanding their political oratory. Conceivably, the role of Amerindian women in dream analysis and in soothsaying was not a timeless one, but a response to political changes that began in the fifteenth century and were intensified by the arrival of Europeans. Then the women converts that people Marie's letters, the Hospital records, and the Jesuit *Relations*—women praying, preaching, and teaching—would be an energetic Christian variant on a process also at work in the religion of the okis and the Manitou.

Khionrea, Aouentohons, Uthirdchich, and Geneviève left no portrait of Marie de l'Incarnation as she did of them. They may have seen her in part as she wanted to see herself, like Mary, the mother of Jesus, with her cloak spread from her arms to protect the people in her care. They may have seen her in part like Aataentsic, the mother of Yoscaha: sometimes kindly, sometimes angry and ready to play a dirty trick on humans.[233] But as lovers of language, knowing and fervent in their speech, Marie de l'Incarnation's "words of fire" would have won praise from them all: Haaa, Haaa.

On the other side of the Atlantic, Marie de l'Incarnation's style of writing was greeted by its most devoted reader with a few reservations. Claude Martin admired his "excellent Mother" in myriad ways. Her life had in it singular adventures, heroic virtues, exemplary holiness, and the highest understanding of mystical ways. About her gift for speaking, we have heard him marvel. In his prefaces to her books, he went on to praise the "inner sweetness" *(onction intérieure)* of her writing and its clarity and sincerity. Rather than a politic style full of disguises and vanity, her fashion of expressing herself was *"honnête."* "God is always the principle and rule of her civility."[234]

And yet, despite the fact that Marie's writing embodied a form of those supreme seventeenth-century French virtues of *honnêteté* and civility, he thought it needed an editor's firm hand before it could be published in Paris. "As for her style," Claude Martin said in his preface to the *Vie,* "I admit that it is not one of the most polished [*des plus polis*] and that it does not approach the delicacy of the works of today, when pleasantness of words and discourse arouses the mind to reading by a sweet violence."[235] When she quoted the Bible (he went on in another preface) she used an outmoded translation, and she preferred quotations from the Roman catechism of 1588 despite its *"rudesse."* For his editions, Martin used modern translations or made his own, so as to make "a newer and more intelligible style. If the work does not have all the pleasantness and *politesse* that one would wish, at least it will not seem wholly shocking."[236]

So, very much in the literary spirit of his day, Claude went through his mother's *Relation* changing certain words, adding phrases of his own, and omitting some of hers as he prepared to publish it as part of the *Vie.*[237] (You can see an example of one page in the illustrations.) We can follow his editorial hand by comparing his printed version with an early and independently verifiable manuscript copy of the 1654 text that Marie had sent him.[238] Three concerns guided Claude Martin's pen. The first was to make sure that Marie de l'Incarnation was always on safe ground in regard to doctrine and obedience to the Church. He was not worried about a Jansenist temptation for Marie: despite her ties of friendship with the sisters at Port-Royal, she had taken seriously his advice not to become involved in the debates about frequent Communion and other Jansenist topics.[239] But as a distinguished Benedictine of Saint Maur, author of several widely read devotional manuals, and organizer of the Maurist edition of Augustine, Dom Claude Martin was going to make sure that his mother's formulations were irreproachable.[240] When Marie remembers how as a child she had heard that "holy water erased venial sins," Claude adds "provided one uses it with devotion." The Incarnate Word, "great God, equal to his Father," becomes with Claude "consubstantial with and equal to his Father"; "conforming to the faith of the Church" becomes "conforming to the Church and the sentiment of the Doctors."[241]

Claude Martin's second concern was that Marie de l'Incarnation appear a trustworthy mystic. Here she had to be defended against serious critics of mysticism, such as the Jansenist Pierre Nicole and Louis XIV's Bishop Bossuet. Some charged that mysticism in general was a dubious spiritual enterprise, others that Marie's specific path to it—the passivity of mental prayer—led "to illusions and chimeras, which have reality only in the imagination of a few pious women and feeble minds." That is not true, said Claude in rejoinder, for several great men have also expressed themselves in the language of mysticism.[242]

He stressed the reliability and precision of his mother's divine communications. Where Marie repeatedly "experiences" things (expérimenter), or where her soul "tends" toward something (tendre)—favorite terms in the mystical vocabulary—Claude will usually prefer something less impetuous: "I saw clearly," "had an experience," "had an inclination," "felt itself carried toward."[243] In the course of mental prayer, Marie hears a reproach from God "in interior words"; Claude adds "by interior words, but very distinct."[244]

The "ravished" heart of Marie's *Relation* is merely "taken" in the printed text, one of several instances where Claude lowers the temperature of his mother's expressiveness and her experiments with language about the self. "C'est mon moi" ("he is my me"), Marie says of an embrace between her soul and the Person of the Word. Claude draws the line: "Il est comme un autre moi-même" ("he is like another myself").[245] Describing the paradise in which the soul enjoys direct communication with God, Marie speaks of a "melting love from which are born jubilations full of torrents of tears." Claude leaves it at "joys and tears."[246]

Claude Martin's third editorial concern is the most interesting from the vantage point of Marie's Canadian years: his desire to rid her language of elements offending late seventeenth-century French *politesse*. On the whole, his targets were words that were too popular or local and situations where the civility boundary was at stake. So Marie's *"hantise"* (a "ridiculous, vulgar" word to literary purists of the time, rather like our "hanging around" or "hanging out") becomes *"conversation"* for Claude, in her reminiscence of how as a girl she withdrew from young people of her age. Marie's *"tracas"* or "bother and bustle" of everyday affairs is lengthened by Claude into "l'embarras des soins domestiques" ("the confusion of domestic cares"), as she talks of her life in the wagoner's household. Hadn't one of France's judges of language recently said that the word *tracasser* "smelled of the village"?[247] The street-fair metaphor that Marie uses to suggest how the lower or sensitive part of the soul in its corruption tries sneakily to imitate the higher part so as to participate in its blessings —"faire les singes," or mimic like a carnival monkey— Claude flattens out into "corrupted nature, which at every moment and in diverse fashions would like to make the senses and the sensitive faculties enter into commerce [with the divine spirit] or at least into imitation of the spirit [the higher part of the soul]."[248]

In writing about her own body, Marie sometimes went too far for her son's taste, or for the taste of the readers he hoped for beyond her sister religious. Enough to say that in her twenties she thought herself a great sinner; he cuts "I had a mortal hatred for my body." Enough to say that in Tours her soul made her go to the plague hospital to get a whiff of the infected corpses; he cuts "it made me take care of stinking wounds and compelled me to get close enough to smell them." An episode during her years of self-doubt in Québec he leaves out entirely: fearing that the imperfections of her nature and spirit were rooted in her blood, she bled herself so amply that if God had not come to her aid, her health would have been seriously impaired.[249]

As for the Amerindians, Claude widened the space between them and his mother in a few places, changing Marie's "accustomed" *(accoutumées)* to "tamed" *(apprivoisées):* "when [the girls] were a little accustomed to us, we degreased them for several days" became "when the girls were a little tamed." Where Marie writes, "the dirtiness of the savage girls, who had not yet been made over into the cleanliness of the French, led us sometimes to find a shoe in our cooking pot, and every day hair and coals, which did not disgust us at all," Claude adds after "coals" (to make things absolutely clear): "and other filth."[250]

Claude explained the difference between himself and Marie primarily as a difference in epoch: his mother was old-fashioned. This is a commonplace about the French language in Canada, one that inappropriately archaizes it. It is true that Marie de l'Incarnation was reading little of the literature produced according to the criteria of the court, Academy, and salons of mid-seventeenth-century France. The books that crossed the ocean to her convent were religious texts, such as the life and letters of Jeanne de Chantal.[251] Nor were she and her sister religious part of the audience when Corneille's *Le Cid* and *Héraclius* were performed in 1651–1652 before the Governor of Québec.[252]

But this does not mean that her expression and sensibility were static, caught in amber in 1639 when she left for Paradise. Rather they changed (as they must have for the Jesuits as well) with her New World experience: her intimacy with Amerindian women; her "rude" convent life, with its smells, its smoke, and its common pot so disgusting to French manners; and her speaking and writing in Algonquin, Huron, and Iroquois, languages which delighted her but which Claude maintained would not interest the French because they were both "useless and despised."[253] While the literary authorities in France were defining *politesse* for the *Dictionnaire de l'Académie française* as "a certain manner of living, acting, and speaking, *civile, honneste,* et *polie,*" Marie was presumably writing down *aiendaouasti* for her Huron dictionary, the adjective the Hurons applied to people who lived up to the standards for greeting, offering food, and stationing themselves in the proper order for polite deference. But then the academicians were defining *sauvage* so as to exclude the people Marie and the Jesuits saw and thought about every day: "without religion," said the Academy's Dictionary, "without laws, without fixed habitation, and living more like beasts than men, as in *The savage peoples of America*."[254]

Marie de l'Incarnation degreased the bodies of her "savage" girls, but some of the grease got into her own pores. In her general confession of 1633, given to her Director before she became an Ursuline, she wrote of the mortification of her flesh, the self-denial of food, the smelling of infected wounds, and the rest. Now she was in a world where "dirt" and "smells" had a different significance and where the lack of food, the labor of long, heavy trekking, carrying, and canoeing, and the sleeping on hard surfaces were sustained without complaint by everyone. In France the Ursulines composed biographies in which the tranquil comportment of a religious in her final illness was the mark of special heroism: "the razor screamed through her flesh, but not a sigh escaped her."[255] In the North American woodlands, men and women of all kinds endured torture as prisoners without a sigh and, indeed, with a special song.

Marie de l'Incarnation's writing about matters of body and of courage is a mixture of her Ursuline sensibility and a sensibility born of her exchange with Amerindians. The mixture emerges in the strong and concrete prose in which she described the patience and trials of the Québec Ursulines in her obituary-biographies: the servant Sister Anne, doing the wash in the cold Canadian winters, taking care of the pigs for decades with complete tranquillity even though it was beyond her strength; Mother Marie de Saint Joseph, getting up at four A.M. in the cold despite her asthma and weak lungs, serenely supporting her final illness amid the clapping of sandals, the cries of children, and the smell of cooking eel.[256] It emerges in her terrifying description of the late

December fire in 1650: seminarians being led through falling beams to the freezing night, flames barring exits, Ursulines and Amerindian Christians jumping from windows in their shifts, bare feet being frozen in the snow.[257]

Drawing from oral reports in Algonquin, Marie gave an account of the escape of the Christian Marie Kamakateouinouetch from Mohawks who had seized her on a hunting trip after killing her husband and child; and from Onondagas who were claiming her as a past prisoner. For almost three months Kamakateouinouetch walked alone through the spring woods, following the sun by day, gathering roots, ends of corn, and birds' eggs, finding an Iroquois axe and fashioning tools to fish and hunt, always fearing the Iroquois nearby. Once in despair, "by a Savage error," she tried to commit suicide by hanging herself, but God protected her and the cord broke. Finally, she came upon an Iroquois canoe, paddled it to the Saint Lawrence, and then went from island to island till she arrived at Montréal.[258] This is New World writing. The subject of such a tale was not in Marie's repertory before she came to Canada, but, equally important, neither was its narrative vigor, reproducing in part the way autobiographical stories were told to her by the Amerindians.

Reproducing in part—but only in part. Marie de l'Incarnation did not become an Amerindian storyteller. Rather, we see in her a European mental landscape changed by the adoption of new motifs and sensibilities, but with important signposts and paths still in the same place. Let us survey that landscape a last time through a set of stories on a theme dear to both of Marie's worlds: abduction.

The first story has a plot which might have come from the pen of Madeleine de Scudéry, Madame de Lafayette, or other contemporary writers on French manners and marriage. It was told by Claude Martin in his Additions to his mother's *Vie:* the tale of the abduction of his cousin Marie Buisson.

"Never had a person been more attached to things of the world," Claude began. At fifteen, Marie Buisson was beautiful, well educated by the attention of her mother Claude Guyart, and well endowed with an inheritance from her late father. Her qualities won the attention of a noble officer in the king's army, who, rather than courting her, seized her one day as she was going to Mass, took her to a château, and tried against her resistance to persuade her to marry him. Retrieved by her frantic mother, Marie Buisson testified against her abductor before the criminal court in Paris. The gentleman was condemned, then pardoned. Bolstered by his connections with the king's brother, Gaston d'Orléans, he decided to try again the following year after the death of Marie Buisson's mother. Claiming Marie was his wife, he haled her before the Archbishop of Tours. She spoke so forcefully that, young though she was, she convinced the prelate she would never have given her heart to such a man. To stop him definitively, she wrote to the queen that she wanted to become a religious in the Ursuline house from which her aunt had departed for Canada several years before and where she had now taken temporary refuge. It was a ruse, said Claude Martin; her inclinations were still with the world. But having taken the step, her honor kept her from leaving. God then took a hand and changed her soul so that the religious life her aunt had always desired for her became "a Paradise of pleasure."[259]

Such abductions were by no means unheard-of in noble and wealthy circles in seventeenth-century France, and led to much commentary and fashionable fiction. Sometimes the abduction was presented as a stratagem, a device agreed upon by the young to get away from patriarchal domination in choice of a marriage partner. More often the event was seen, as in Claude Martin's account, as a case of a woman defending the knowledge of her heart and her right to choose against a man's violence.[260]

The boundary concerns expressed in the abduction/seduction tales of the North American woodlands were quite different. In a tale type found throughout North and South America, there were stories centering around a married woman and an animal lover. Among the Iroquoian-speaking peoples, the animal is a bear. Sometimes the wife is abducted by the bear and then seduced; other times she goes off willingly. When her husband discovers what is going on, he coaxes the bear to him by using his wife's call, then kills him, cooks his sexual organs, and forces his wife to eat them. In some versions, his wife then turns into a bear and haunts her husband afterward.[261] (This tale helps us understand the Montagnais custom, described by Father Le Jeune, of sending all women of marriageable age and young married women without children away from a dwelling into which a freshly killed bear had been brought and not letting them return till after the feast.)[262]

Such a tale plays with the border between animals and humans and reflects on the sources of sexuality and desire. It gives free rein to the sentiments of jealousy supposedly muted in the easy sexual arrangements of Amerindian divorce and remarriage. It ends in a violent draw, with the husband having slain the bear but with the bear-wife still in pursuit. The bear had connections with the world of spirits, but also reminded listeners of the corporeal world of outsiders: Amerindian captors or Frenchmen who might seize or seek a wife. The tale speaks to the lure and to the danger of the foreign.

In the Europe of Marie Guyart's youth, there were also stories circulating about bears and women. Back in the sixteenth century, in a widely read French work, François de Belleforest recalled a tale he had read about a bear in Sweden who seized a beautiful young woman, took care of her, and had a son by her.[263] Better known was the French/Occitanian tale of the prodigious Jean de l'Ours, son of a woodcutter's wife who had been abducted by a bear and had given birth to Jean in the woods. Then there was the Candlemas bear chase in parts of the Pyrenees, where a lustful bear ran after young men cross-dressed as women until he was captured by costumed hunters.[264] Perhaps Marie Guyart had heard such accounts among the "vanities" of her youth. We know that French *coureurs du bois* recounted the exploits of Jean de l'Ours to Indians in the Québec woodlands.[265] Perhaps a decorous version of the Amerindian tale of the Bear and the Woman was recited by some visitor to the Ursuline convent yard.

Whatever the case, the abduction stories that Marie de l'Incarnation wanted to send her correspondents in France concerned the border between Christian and non-Christian. In 1642, early in her years in Canada, she tells of how a young Huron woman, still unbaptized but the daughter of Christian parents, agreed to marry a man whom she loved but who also had another wife. Her horrified parents assented only on condition that he leave his other wife and convert to Christianity. He did the first but not the second, and so her parents took her from him and put her with the Ursulines. There, after a few days of sadness, she said she wanted to receive Christian instruction and that she would not see her husband again until he did the same. Her parents then took the young wife back to their long-house in a Huron mission village, forbidding her to speak to her husband.

> Sometime afterward [Marie continues], going about her necessities, she met her husband. She started to flee. He ran after. She entered the cabin of a Frenchman; [her husband] came in after her. She hid for fear of speaking to him; he protested that he would not leave unless she did. Finally he spoke to her, using every kind of flattery to get her to return to him, but in vain. He became angry and shouted, threatening to kill everyone if they didn't give him back his wife. While he was carrying on, she ducked out without his noticing it, got back to her parents' cabin, and so delivered herself from the hands of this importunate man. While he was pleading with her, she said in her heart, "It's all good, what I want to believe; I want to be baptized; I love obedience."

Marie ends the story with an account of how the Huron converts were convinced the wife had "disobeyed"—that is, they thought she had wanted to see her husband despite being forbidden to do so—and of how they punished her severely (and to Marie inappropriately) with a public whipping. The next day the young woman came to the Ursulines; there she was instructed by Marie and baptized "Angèle."[266]

A late story, sent by Marie to France in 1667, has a similar theme, though with a somewhat different tone and a different ending. An Algonquin woman, once educated by the Ursulines, had been made a captive by the Iroquois. After the Iroquois were defeated by the French, she was taken back to the convent. Her Iroquois captor had kept her as his wife, "and he had such a passion for her that he was continually at our parlor, fearing that the Algonquins would abduct her. Finally we were compelled to give her back to him on condition [that he would become a Christian] . . . I had never believed that a Barbarian could have such great affection [*amitié*] for a foreigner. We'd see him lamenting, losing his speech, raising his eyes, stamping his feet, coming and going like a crazy person. The young woman did nothing but laugh at him, and that didn't offend him at all." They went off married as husband and wife.[267]

In these two stories, Marie de l'Incarnation is poised between France and the American woodlands. In the first recital, her Huron Angèle resembles the Touraine Marie Buisson in the way she stands out against her "pagan" husband. Not that Marie had yet heard about her niece's abduction; it had occurred that same spring of 1642, and the news seems to have missed the summer boats.[268] But even though Angèle had told Marie much of the story herself, the Ursuline's universalizing simplifies the feelings in the Huron's heart. The angry husband, threatening to kill everyone if they didn't "give him back his wife," could fill the niche of the jealous or desiring husband on either side of the Atlantic. (Marie would use the same phrase eight years later to describe how her son cried for her at the Ursuline convent grill at Tours: "Give me back my mother.")[269]

The second recital has more of the ring of the woodlands, even though Marie separated herself from her subjects by her phrase, "I had never believed that a Barbarian could have such great affection for a foreigner." It is a story of Algonquin and Iroquois more than of Christian and non-Christian. The Algonquin ex-captive laughs at her anxious Iroquois lover without any European explanations. The energy of the lover who shouts and stamps and the sureness of the woman who laughs back are partway to the tale of the Bear and the Woman.

In the Huron creation account, Aataentsic fell through a hole under a tree to the new world, and that birth-canal-like image was used for many an Amerindian hero and trickster who came to new adventures. Following her dream vision, Marie de l'Incarnation jumped through a hole into an alternate world. Some of its landscapes she saw sharply and incorporated into her New World writing. Many others remained obscured by fog. Her converts knew those places. From the present we try to find them. But Marie left them unresolved—she for whom the Incarnate Word had been spoken for all peoples, she who believed herself learned enough to teach it in any language to all the nations of the earth.

Metamorphoses

IN JUNE 1699, about the same time that Glikl bas Judah Leib was deciding to hazard a new life in Metz, Maria Sibylla Merian and her daughter Dorothea were boarding a boat in Amsterdam, bound for America. Their destination was Suriname, where they intended to study and paint the insects, butterflies, and plants of that tropical land.

At age fifty-two, Maria Sibylla Merian was a person of some reputation. As early as 1675, when she was a young mother living with her husband in Nuremberg, the learned painter Joachim Sandrart had included her in his *German Academy,* as he called his history of German art. Not only was she skilled in watercolor and oils, in painting textiles and engraving copperplates; not only could she render flowers, plants, and insects with perfect naturalness; but she also was a knowing observer of the habits of caterpillars, flies, spiders, and other such creatures. A virtuous woman and a fine housekeeper (despite all the insects), Merian, said Sandrart, could be likened to the goddess Minerva.[1] A few years later, when she published the two volumes of her *Wonderful Transformation and Singular Plant-Food of Caterpillars,* a Nuremberg luminary, Christopher Arnold, sang in verse of all the men who were being equaled by this ingenious woman. Her work was *"verwunderns"*—"amazing."[2]

Then, in 1692, another kind of singularity was noted about

Maria Sibylla Merian, for a different set of readers. Petrus Dittelbach, a disaffected member of the Labadists (a radical Protestant community in the Dutch province of Friesland) published an exposé of the conduct of his former coreligionists. Among them was "a woman of Frankfurt am Main" who had left her husband, the painter Johann Andreas Graff, in Germany to find peace among the Labadists of Wieuwerd. When Graff came to get her back, he was informed by the leading Brothers that a believer like Maria Sibylla was freed from marital obligations toward an unbeliever like him. Refused entry into the community, the husband stayed around for a time doing construction work outside its walls, and then left. Dittelbach had heard that he was going to break his matrimonial tie, and indeed, about the time *The Decline and Fall of the Labadists* appeared in print, Graff was asking the Nuremberg town council for a divorce from Maria Sibylla so that he could marry someone else.[3]

These accounts suggest the turnings in the life of the artist-naturalist Maria Sibylla Merian. And there were more changes to come. She sailed back from America laden with specimens, published her great work *Metamorphosis of the Insects of Suriname*, amplified her *European Insects*, and was an important figure in the circle of Amsterdam botanists, scientists, and collectors till her death in 1717.

An adventurous life; and, as with Glikl bas Judah Leib and Marie Guyart de l'Incarnation, a life shaped and expanded by religion, even though the Protestant pilgrimage took a distinctive route of its own. As with the writing of Glikl and Marie, Merian's art—her work of observing and depicting—helped her forge her sense of herself and of foreign and exotic others. But she is a harder person to pin down than they are, since she left behind no autobiography, confessional letters, or artist's self-portrait. Instead, we must make use of the observing "I" in her entomological texts and fill in the picture by attending to the people and places around her. A woman emerges—curious, willful, self-concealing, versatile, carried along through religious and family change by her ardent pursuit of nature's connections and beauty.[4]

Maria Sibylla Merian was born in the free imperial city of Frankfurt am Main in 1647, daughter to the artist and publisher Mathias Merian the Elder and his second wife, Johanna Sibylla Heim. Mathias was then in his fifties, known throughout Europe for his engravings of cityscapes and landscapes, his scientific books, and his editions of the illustrated *Grands Voyages* (accounts of journeys to the New World), begun by his first father-in-law, Théodore de Bry, years before.[5] He died when Maria Sibylla was only three, and her mother soon remarried. Her second husband was the widower Jacob Marrel, a still-life painter, engraver, and art dealer.[6] Meanwhile Maria Sibylla's half-brothers, Mathias the Younger and Caspar Merian, were establishing themselves as engravers, publishers, and painters, producing topographic works in the tradition of their father, recording ceremonial events like the coronation of Emperor Leopold I at Frankfurt, and much else.[7]

Mathias Merian the Elder and Jacob Marrel had both acquired citizenship in Frankfurt, and Maria Sibylla could later claim her own *Bürgerrecht* as Mathias' daughter. Though not members of the city's ruling elite of old patricians, doctors of law, and great bankers, both men enjoyed affluence and prestige and ranked as artists well above all other craftsmen in Frankfurt's ordering of estates.[8] Yet Merian and Marrel had one link to some of the Jews crowded into Frankfurt's ghetto (Haim Hamel's brother Isaac would be among them) and to the resident foreigners in Frankfurt—a link of memory and experience, if not of law and status. They were immigrants, as was Maria Sibylla's mother: Mathias was a native of Basel; Johanna Sibylla came from a Walloon family that had migrated from the Netherlands to nearby Hanau; Marrel had a French grandfather who had moved to Frankfurt, but he himself had been born in Frankenthal and had spent years in Utrecht before settling in the city on the Main river.[9] With these cosmopolitan connections, the Merian and Marrel households resembled Glikl's family more than they did the Touraine-rooted Guyarts and Martins of Marie de l'Incarnation.

Almost all of the women artists of the early modern period were, like Maria Sibylla Merian, born into a family of artists. In that setting their talent could be welcomed, and contemporary beliefs about the dampening effects of the female temperament on genius ignored.[10] Differences did exist, however, between female artists and their brothers. One of them was not important for Maria Sibylla: the usual exclusion of women from large-scale history painting and from the representation of the nude body. These were not projects of either the Merian or the Marrel atelier. While her mother taught her and her stepsister to embroider, Maria Sibylla was able to learn drawing, watercolor, still-life painting, and copperplate engraving from her stepfather along with his male pupils.

Another difference counted: male artists received their training by traveling to different sites and workshops. Mathias Merian the Younger had been to Amsterdam, London, Paris, Nuremberg, and Italy, and Caspar had gone almost as far.[11] Johann Andreas Graff came from Nuremberg to study with Marrel, and, before his betrothal to Maria Sibylla, had traveled from Augsburg to work for a few years in Venice and Rome. When the talented young Frankfurter Abraham Mignon came to study flower painting with Marrel, Jacob sent him off to Utrecht to the workshop of one of his own teachers, Jan Davidsz de Heem.[12]

Maria Sibylla Merian stayed put, as daughters did. At least her visual store in Frankfurt was rich, with large collections of prints, books, and paintings belonging to Jacob Marrel and the Merians.[13] Also available to her in Frankfurt was something more modest: caterpillars. Back in 1653, her half-brothers had done the plates for Jan Jonston's *Natural History of Insects*, but for the most part they were copying illustrations from earlier naturalists rather than working from life.[14] Real caterpillars may have been around Jacob Marrel's workshop, however, because he characteristically included caterpillars, butterflies, and other insects in his pictures of flowers and may sometimes have sketched or painted them from life or from specimens.[15] Certainly caterpillars would not have been hard to get: Marrel's brother in Frankfurt was in the silk trade—not unwinding cocoons himself (that was women's work) but having ready access to those who handled silkworms.[16] Whatever the case, Maria Sibylla was to say later that she had begun her observations when she was only thirteen: "From my youth onward I have been concerned with the study of insects. I began with silkworms in my native city, Frankfurt am Main; then I observed the far more beautiful butterflies and moths that developed from other kinds of caterpillars. This led me to collect all the caterpillars I could find in order to study their metamorphoses ... and to work at my painter's art so that I could sketch them from life and represent them in lifelike colors."[17]

No one seems to have discouraged her passion, though her family may have thought it odd. Another celebrated naturalist of her day, Jan Swammerdam of Amsterdam, also began to study insects at an early age, inspired by his father's cabinet of curiosities.[18] Girls may have been expected to feel the sentiment that an anonymous poem attributed to the daughter of Thomas Mouffet, whose widely read *Theater of Insects or Lesser Living Creatures* was eventually to be part of Maria Sibylla's library:

> Little Miss Muffet
> Sat on a tuffet
> Eating her curds and whey.
> Along came a spider
> And sat down beside her
> And frightened Miss Muffet away.[19]

The man who was to marry Maria Sibylla Merian in 1665 was not frightened away. Johann Andreas Graff was a favorite of Jacob Marrel—pupil and teacher collaborated on an engraving that showed cabinetmakers mumming in a Frankfurt square— and presumably the eighteen-year-old bride welcomed him as her husband. Some ten years her senior, he was at least no stranger to her. Nor was he unaware of how absorbed a woman could be in her work: in an ink drawing of 1658, he portrayed Marrel's daughter Sara intently bowed over her embroidery in her father's atelier. The picture promised well for his relationship with Maria Sibylla.[20]

The couple stayed in Frankfurt for five years, where their daughter Johanna Helena was born, and then moved to Graff's hometown, Nuremberg.[21] There his father had been a poet laureate and rector of the Egidienplatz gymnasium—not a patrician, to be sure, but a notable. There, out of a comfortable house on Milchmarkt Street, Graff produced a series of engraved street scenes, views of Nuremberg architecture, and other cityscapes—subjects that he had pursued in Italy and that were quite unlike those of his teacher Marrel or his wife.[22] And there Maria Sibylla painted on parchment and linen cloth, embroidered and engraved, and took on a group of female pupils, one of them the daughter of a publisher-engraver, and another, Clara Regina Imhoff, from a patrician family. Her letters to Clara show her affectionate, attentive to her pupil's advance in technique, businesslike about the cost of paint and varnish, and appropriately deferential to the Imhoff family as persons of high station.[23]

The couple were far from lonely. They frequented Joachim Sandrart (himself once a pupil of Maria Sibylla's father) and the other Nuremberg artists who were trying to found an Academy. They visited the learned Christopher Arnold, writer on antique monuments and exotic religions and correspondent of Menasseh ben Israel,[24] and it was probably Arnold who was responsible for Maria Sibylla's first exposure to Latin nature books. Frau Gräffin (as she now called herself) numbered among her friends a local woman painter, Dorothea Maria Auerin, who served as godmother to her second daughter, Dorothea Maria.[25] Throughout she continued her observations of insects, finding and sketching caterpillars in her garden, in her friends' gardens, in the town moat of nearby Altdorf, and elsewhere, and bringing them to her workshop to feed them with appropriate plant-leaves, record their behavior, and draw and paint them as they changed.

In short, a seemingly perfect life for a female artist of the time. Nothing to suggest rebellion or startling transformations. Her first book, issued under the name of "Maria Sibylla Graffin, daughter of Mathias Merian the Elder" and published by her husband, was also what one might expect. Appearing in three parts from 1675 to 1680, it was a *Blumenbuch*—that is, a collection of copperplate representations, without text, of single flowers, wreaths, nosegays, and bouquets.[26] The flowers and the occasional caterpillars, butterflies, spiders, and other creatures on the plants were rendered with beauty and accuracy (a resolution to the war between "art" and "nature," *Kunst und Natur,* of which she spoke in an opening poem), but they were done in the established mode of flower painting practiced in oil by her stepfather Marrel and his teachers. Just as her father, Mathias Merian, had published a *Florilegium Renovatum,* so here was her flower collection, "painted from life." Just as Jacob Marrel had produced an anatomical sketchbook of use to students, painters, goldsmiths, and sculptors, so her *Blumenbuch* would provide patterns and models for artists and embroiderers.[27] Her 1680 preface gave anecdotes, some culled from wide reading, about those who loved and prized the beauty of flowers: the current pope had offered a thousand crowns to the church of San Carlo in Milan in return for the present of a single bloom; and not long before, in the Netherlands, two thousand guilders had changed hands for a single bulb of the tulip *Semper Augustus.*[28]

As Maria Sibylla Merian wrote those words, a very different kind of book was appearing: her *Raupen* of 1679, or (to give the title in English) the *Wonderful Transformation and Singular Flower-Food of Caterpillars . . . Painted from Life and Engraved in Copper,* followed by a second volume in 1683.[29] In each of the hundred copperplates (fifty per volume, available in black and white or handcolored, depending on the buyer's wish and purse),[30] one or more species of insect were depicted from life, in their various stages: caterpillar or larva; pupa with or without cocoon; and moth, butterfly, or fly, in flight or at rest (sometimes in both states). Many of the plates included the egg stage as well. Each picture was organized around a single plant, represented most often in the flowering stage and sometimes in the fruit stage; the plant was selected to show the leaves upon which the caterpillar fed and the places on the leaves or stem (or on the ground nearby) where the female laid its eggs. Each plant was identified by its German and Latin names, and a page or two of German text facing the picture gave Maria Sibylla's observations on how her insect specimen had looked and behaved at each stage, often with exact dates, and her reactions to its appearance. She did not give names to individual species of moths and butterflies—in fact, her contemporaries had names for only a small number of them[31]— but her descriptions yielded individual life histories.

Here is what she said of an insect shown in its stages from egg to moth on a cherry plant (pictured in the illustrations in this volume):

Many years ago when I first saw this large moth, so prettily marked by nature, I could not marvel enough over its beautiful gradation of color and varying hue, and I made use of it often in my painting. Later, as through God's grace I discovered the metamorphosis of caterpillars, a long time went by until this beautiful moth appeared. When I caught sight of it, I was enveloped in such great joy and so gratified in my wishes that I can hardly describe it. Then for several years in a row I got hold of its caterpillars and maintained them until July on the leaves of sweet cherries, apples, pears, and plums. They have a beautiful green color, like the young grass of spring, and a lovely straight black stripe the length of the back, and across each segment also a black stripe out of which four little white round beads glisten like pearls. Among them is a yellow-gold oval spot and under them a white pearl. Underneath the first three segments they have three red claws on each side, then two empty segments, after which there are four little green feet of the same color as the caterpillars, and at the end again a foot on both sides. Sprouting out of each pearl are long black hairs, together with other, smaller ones, so stiff that one could almost be pricked by them. Strange to note, when they have no food, this variety of caterpillars devour each other, so great is their hunger; but so soon as they obtain [food], they leave off [eating each other].

When such a caterpillar attains its full size, as you can see [in my picture] on the green leaf and stem, then it makes a tough and lustrous cocoon, bright as silver and oval round, wherein it first sheds and expels its entire skin and changes itself into a liver-colored date stone [*Dattelkern,* her usual word for pupa], which stays together with the cast-off skin over the caterpillar. It remains thus motionless until the middle of August, when finally the moth of such laudable beauty comes out and takes flight. It is white and has gray spotted patches, two yellow eyes, and two brown feelers (Hörner). On each of the four wings are a few round circles in and about each other, which are black and white as well as yellow. The ends of the wings are brown, but near the tips (by which I mean only the ends of the moth's two outer wings) are two beautiful rose-colored spots. By day the moth is quiet, but at night very restless.[32]

Other descriptive entries were more precise about the discovery of the insect ("A very ingenious noble maiden of Nuremberg once took me through her beautiful pleasure garden . . . Our goal was to find unusual worms and, encountering none, we went over to the common weeds and found on the White Dead-Nettle this caterpillar"),[33] or about the timing of the metamorphosis (the black caterpillar spun its cocoon at the end of May and remained a *Dattelkern* hanging from a buttercup leaf "for fourteen days"),[34] or about the way in which a male moth and a female moth differed in appearance.[35] The last she did in a few instances only: in many species of lepidoptera there is no contrast between male and female in conspicuous features like wings, while the differences in genitalia—which she might have seen through a magnifying glass—were too small to portray in the paintings she was doing. But whatever the coverage, all her texts worked in concert with her pictures to place insects together with the plants on which they lived as larvae, to give a full account of their external appearance through the life cycle, and to express her appreciation for beautiful colors and markings.

Her concern with beauty linked her to the still-life tradition in which she had been formed, and she herself acknowledged in her 1679 preface that her juxtaposition of plants and insects owed something to the artist's concern for adornment.[36] She was also building on earlier efforts to achieve "naturalistic" or "mimetic" representations of flora and fauna. Detailed and lifelike pictures of insects and plants can be found in the margins of Netherlandish prayerbooks as early as the late fifteenth century, well before they surfaced in Dutch still-lifes in watercolor and oil.[37] To give an example of the quest for precision close to home, Georg Flegel, Jacob Marrel's first teacher in Frankfurt, did small, careful studies of insects (one of them followed a silkworm from egg to moth); and flies, dragonflies, beetles, and butterflies appear among the foods, fruits, sugars, birds, and wines of Flegel's larger oil paintings.[38]

But Maria Sibylla Merian had something else in mind when she did her insect studies from life. The moths and caterpillars of her *Raupen* did not just add to the "lively" (*"lebendig"*)[39] quality of flower pictures, as in the bouquets and wreaths painted by her stepfather Marrel and his student Abraham Mignon. The insects were there for themselves. When necessary, Merian sacrificed verisimilitude (the way things might look to an observer) for a decorative portrayal of the stripes and spikes and legs the caterpillar actually had (what a nature lover must know about an insect).

Above all, her insects and plants were telling a life story. Time moved in her pictures not to suggest the general transience of things or the year's round of the most precious blossoms,[40] but to evoke a particular and interconnected process of change. Her insects were not placed to convey metaphorical messages, as was the practice of many still-life painters and specifically of her stepfather's Utrecht teacher, Jan Davidsz de Heem (the butterfly as the symbol of the resurrected soul, the fly as the symbol of sinfulness, and so on). The *Ignis* of Joris Hoefnagel, a remarkable collection of insect watercolors by an artist-naturalist of the late sixteenth century, was designed like an emblem book, each picture preceded by a biblical quote or adage and followed by a poem.[41] Merian's work was infused with religious spirit, as we shall see, but, except for a nod at the goodness of the bee, there were no allegorical comments in her texts.[42]

If Maria Sibylla recentered flower painting around the life cycle of moths and butterflies and the plant hosts of their caterpillars, how different were her volumes of 1679 and 1683 from the more narrowly scientific insect books of her day? The 1660s were important years for the history of entomology: sustained observation and improved magnification allowed much new understanding of the anatomy and molting of insects and laid to rest among naturalists the belief in abiogenesis (that is, spontaneous generation of certain insects from decaying matter). New systems of classification were tried out, quite different from those used in Renaissance encyclopedias such as the one the Merian brothers had illustrated and published in 1653. There Jan Jonston had followed Thomas Mouffet (and Aristotle) in making the possession of wings a major criterion for classification: wingless caterpillars were treated along with worms in chapters separate from butterflies and moths, and metamorphosis was accordingly slighted.[43]

The *General History of Insects* of 1669, published in Dutch by the physician Jan Swammerdam, was one of the best products of the new entomology.[44] It is especially appropriate here, since Swammerdam was cited in Christopher Arnold's eulogizing poem about Maria Sibylla in her 1679 *Raupen:* "what Swammerdam promises . . . now comes to the knowledge of all."[45] Swammerdam was a fine observer of insect habits and also bred larvae through the stages of their transformations, but he excelled especially in the dissection of insects under a microscope, developing elaborate means to preserve and display the smallest of parts. The *General History* reported his discoveries (on the internal development of the butterfly pupa, on the reproductive organs of different insects, and much more) and spelled out his debates and agreements with other naturalists. The insects he organized into four "orders of natural mutation" or kinds of metamorphosis (for instance, whether they had incomplete metamorphosis like a grasshopper or complete metamorphosis like a butterfly). Transformation figured in his book less to chronicle the life history of separate species than to make possible a principle of classification. At the back of his text of 170 pages were thirteen anatomical illustrations, showing clearly and elegantly, say, the internal and external development of the louse or the stages of the pupa, but not the plants on which the larvae fed.[46] The plates were in black and white, and there was no color option.

Merian seems to have used only a magnifying glass, not a microscope, and at this stage of her investigations she was doing (or at least reports) no dissection. Her focus was, as we have seen, on the external features of the insects as they changed and on the plants on which the larvae fed at different times of the year. The vision here is what we would call an *ecological* one: she even depicted the holes that caterpillars had left on the leaves of their plants. (She did not, to be sure, refer to the role of insects in pollination; her contemporaries were just beginning to look at the "dust" on flowers under the microscope and to argue about whether plants had sex organs.)[47]

An "ecological" approach might have been encouraged in Merian's day by practical worries about draining fens and deforestation.[48] It could also emerge when naturalists put aside their tasks of classification for a time and reflected on God's hand in what they called "the economy of nature." Thus, in 1691–1692 the Englishman John Ray, keen observer of plants, birds, fish, and insects, published his *Wisdom of God*, in which he stressed both the "instinctual" behavior of animals and insects and the usefulness of different parts of nature to one another. But, as Ray's biographer has insisted, taxonomy was always "his first concern." In contrast, Merian centered on interactions in nature and on transformative organic processes. Specialists disagree about whether an "organic" view of nature is the only path to an ecological vision. Carolyn Merchant says it is; Donald Worster says that organic and mechanical concepts generate alternative ecological traditions, one seeking human peace with nature, the other human dominion over nature. Though Merian cannot be used to settle or reformulate this debate, her attitudes toward nature seem consistent, at that stage of her life, with an organic tradition of a relatively peaceable kind.[49]

As for her relation to other naturalists, she seems to have relied on Caspar Bauhin's botanical studies for her Latin plant names (they were the standard seventeenth-century source for nomenclature),[50] but she did not mention him or any other scientist in her text or make explicit where her findings challenged or supported existing views. Rather, it was Christopher Arnold who mentioned their names in his introductory poems to both volumes: Swammerdam; Mouffet in England, now emulated by Merian in Germany; Francesco Redi, whose discovery of 1668 (on insect generation by eggs) was easily known to her; Marcello Malpighi on the silkworm (1669).[51] Merian must have been familiar with these works, but her strategy was simply to show the eggs being extruded and even insist on her own figurative word, *Dattelkern* ("date stone"), for "pupa" rather than settling for the German *Puppe*.[52]

Artist-naturalist that she was, she was not going to let her text dominate her pictures, nor would she "disfigure" her copperplates with letters A through G or Figures I through IV, as did Swammerdam and Malpighi, to help readers determine their meaning.[53] Her pictures were to be clear without mechanical aids; an occasional jog from the text was all that the viewer needed ("the caterpillar depicted on the leaf")—vital representations, preferably in color, of nature's beauty, processes, and relationships. Perhaps it was this quality about her work that led Christopher Arnold to say, "What Swammerdam promises . . . now comes to the knowledge of all."

Closest in type to Merian is Johannes Goedaert of Middelburg, a watercolor painter and naturalist in the "craft tradition" (to extend to him Londa Schiebinger's phrase for women who came to science without academic training).[54] His *Natural Metamorphosis* of 1662–1669, published in Dutch and in Latin translation, was also based on insects that he had bred and observed and, like Merian's book, was organized around individual pictures and accompanying texts. Yet his pictures, though often carefully drawn, were different from hers, portraying the larvae and adult insects, often but not always the pupa, never the eggs (in fact, he still clung to a belief in the spontaneous generation of insects), and virtually never the plants on which the insects fed.[55] Goedaert's illustrations were oriented toward identifying species rather than representing process and connectedness in nature. About the time that Merian was preparing the second volume of her *Raupen* for the press, a new edition of Goedaert came out in English at the hands of a Cambridge naturalist, who, dissatisfied with the "tumultuous order" of the original book, "methodized [Goedaert's] Historys according to the severall natures of the Insects they treat about."[56] Isolated and decontextualized in their Dutch original, Goedaert's insects were available for such rearrangement.

What of the order in Maria Sibylla's *Raupen?* Was it "tumultuous," a drawback in her volumes, which, if only they had been "methodized" by some scheme of classification, would have furthered her message all the more strongly? Or did her volumes have a rhyme and reason of their own?

Merian herself accounted for her order only twice. Her first volume opened with silkworms and their mulberry leaves because these were what she had started with as an observer. They were also useful. Her second volume opened with bees because of their constancy in remaining in the limited world of the hive where God had placed them. The subsequent arrangement of pictures seemed to fit no contemporary classificatory criteria, botanical or entomological. Common plants did not precede clover plants followed by bushes and trees, as they did in a traditional herbalist ordering; woody plants were not separate from herbaceous ones, as they were in a newer proposal; similar fruits and flowers were not bunched in a row.[57] The 1679 *Raupen* opened with mulberry, had the cherry in its middle, and ended with the oak. Though she distinguished between butterfly and moth (*Sommer-vogel* and *Motte*, and sometimes affectionately *Sommer-vögelein* and *Motte-vögelein*) and noted whether they were night-flying or day-flying, their life histories were interspersed. The most important "ordering" in her index at the back of each volume was for the *Dattelkerne*—the pupae—which she sorted out by their color (brown, dark brown, gold, black, and so on); but, if anything, she separated like-colored chrysalises in her sequence. Nor were the several insects she treated outside the "order of Lepidoptera" (as Linnaeus would later call it) in a group by themselves: bees and wasps, caddisflies, flies, and thrips were often undergoing metamorphosis in the same picture with moths and butterflies, because Merian observed their caterpillars or maggots feeding on the same plants.

Merian's goal was simply ill-served by boundary classifications. Her subject was a set of events—"you'll find in this volume more than a hundred transformations *[Verwandlungen]*," she said in 1683—and to represent them properly meant crossing the line between orders and putting the plant and animal kingdoms in the same picture. Yet even while lacking the logic of classification, her sequence was not "tumultuous." Emerging from the sensibility of two artists, Merian and her publisher-husband Graff, the books moved the reader's eye through the transformations by a visually striking and pleasurable path. The "method" of the *Raupen*—highly particular pictures and accounts strung together by an aesthetic link—had scientific importance quite apart from the new species contained on its pages. It made the little-studied process of metamorphosis easy to visualize and remember, and insisted on nature's connections, a long-term contribution. It also fractured older classification systems by its particularism and surprising mixtures, and so cleared the ground for those like Swammerdam who were proposing a replacement.

Publishing the *Raupen* was "remarkable" for a woman, as Christopher Arnold told readers in his opening poem of 1679—"remarkable that women also venture to write for you / with care / what has given flocks of scholars so much to do."[58] Merian herself drew on her female status only once, perhaps disingenuously: in the midst of her description of the insects on the goose-foot plant, she imagined her readers asking whether the thousands of exceptionally large caterpillars during that year of 1679 would not lead to much damage. "Whereupon, following my womanly simplicity [*meiner Weiblichen Einfalt*] I give this answer: the damage is already evident in empty fruit trees and defective plants."[59]

But can we go deeper than Arnold's "beyond-her-sex" topos and Maria Sibylla's modesty topos? Can we ask whether her experience or cultural habits as a seventeenth-century woman helped generate her ecological vision of nature and the crossing of boundaries in her particular narratives?

For the seventeenth century, Maria Sibylla Merian is a sample of one. Other women still-life painters of her day, such as Margaretha de Heer from Friesland, included insects in their pictures, but did not go so far as to breed and study them (Merian's daughters would do so under her influence, but only much later).[60] Other women of her day collected butterflies, moths, and caterpillars, but did not write about or represent them. John Ray's four daughters all brought him specimens, but it was only he who wrote down the observations, naming each caterpillar after the daughter who had collected it.[61] Moreover, Ray had been attentive to the habitat of insects in his early observations, even while making classification his most important goal, and continued to include metamorphoses in his descriptions of individual insects when he was aware of them.[62]

Still Merian was a pioneer, crossing boundaries of education and gender to acquire learning on insects and nurturing daughters as she observed, painted, and wrote. Her focus on breeding, habitat, and metamorphosis fits nicely with the domestic practice of a seventeenth-century mother and housewife. We have here not a female mind uneasy with analysis or timelessly connected to the organic (images that have been thoroughly challenged in recent scholarship),[63] but a woman perched for scientific enterprise on a creative margin—for her a buzzing ecosystem—between domestic workshop and learned academy.

More explicitly important to Maria Sibylla Merian than her

gender was the legitimation, nay, the sanctification of her ento-mological task by religion: "These wondrous transformations," she wrote in her 1679 preface to the reader, "have happened so many times that one is full of praise for God's mysterious power and his wonderful attention to such insignificant little creatures and unworthy flying things ... Thus I am moved to present God's miracles such as these to the world in a little book. But do not praise and honor me for it; praise God alone, glorifying Him as the creator of even the smallest and most insignificant of these worms." The volume concluded with a seven-verse "Caterpillar Song" *(Raupen-lied)*, composed by Arnold to the tune of "Jesus whom my soul desires." How many flowers and insects attest to God's handiwork, sang Arnold; "Let me, lowly little worm, be at thy command."[64]

Merian was not alone in expressing such sentiments. Johannes Goedaert had opened his *Natural Metamorphosis* with religious discussion and the citation of biblical passages favorable to in-sects.[65] Swammerdam drew only a little on the Lord in his 1669 dedication of the *General History of Insects* to the burgomasters of Amsterdam; but in 1675, when he was under the spiritual guid-ance of the visionary prophet Antoinette Bourignon, he published his study of the mayfly under the title *A Figure of Man's Miserable Life.* Along with his plates on the life cycle of this water insect were poems comparing its long larval stage in the mud and its momentary adulthood with the sorrows of human life.[66]

Maria Sibylla had not yet undergone her conversion experience when she began to publish the *Raupen,* but her stress on God's creativity in nature and her "enthusiasm" in talking about insects and their beauty surely prepared her ears for the prophetic and lyrical cadences that soon were to fill her world. As Jean de Labadie had said some years before: "Everything we hear or see announces God or figures him. The song of a bird, the bleating of a lamb, the voice of a man. The sight of heaven and its stars, the air and its birds, the sea and its fish, the land and its plants and animals ... Everything tells of God, everything represents him, but few ears and eyes try to hear or see him."[67] Maria Sibylla was one of those trying to see.

Flowers, insects, and a view of Frankfurt in a painting by Jacob Marrel, step-father and teacher of Maria Sibylla Merian

The older entomology: caterpillars in Jan Jonston's *Natural
History*, published by Merian's
half-brothers in 1653

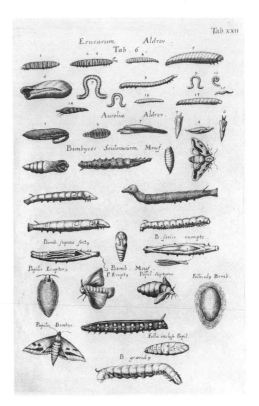

Caterpillar, pupa, and butterfly
in the new entomology of Jan
Swammerdam (1669)

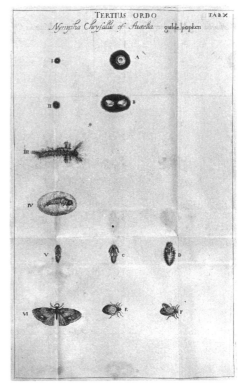

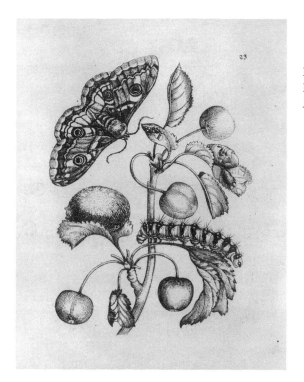

From egg to moth on a
European cherry tree; Merian,
Der Raupen (1679), Plate 23

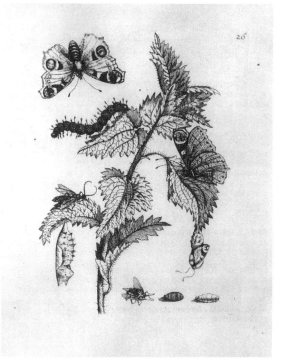

Metamorphoses on the stinging-
nettle plant: Merian, *Der Raupen*
(1679), Plate 26

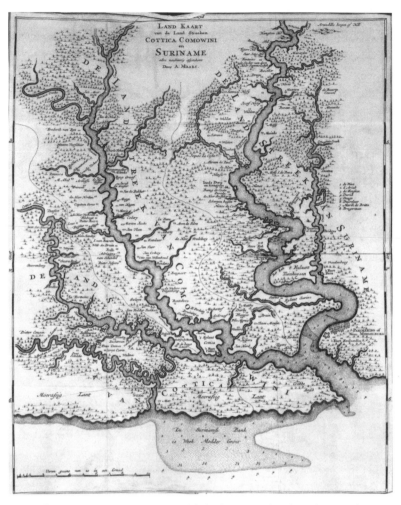

Map of Suriname by A. Maars, published in 1718 but based on earlier information

Caterpillar metamorphoses and moth on a palisade tree in Suriname;
Merian, *Metamorphosis*, Plate 11

Moth, snake, and manioc
bread on a cassava plant;
Merian, *Metamorphosis*,
Plate 5

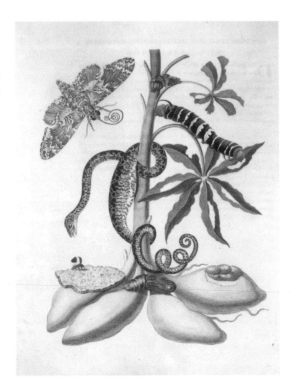

Metamorphoses of the
Great Atlas butterfly and
a wasp, on the branch of
a tree unnamed even by
the Amerindians; Merian,
Metamorphosis, Plate 60

Spiders and ants on a guava tree; Merian, *Metamorphosis*, Plate 18

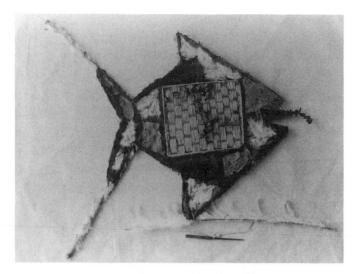

Waiyana wasp mats from Suriname, used for rites of adolescent initiation

Dirk Valkenburg, Africans at a *winti* dance in Suriname (ca. 1707)

AMBOINSCHE
RARITEITKAMER
door
G. E. RUMPHIUS

t AMSTERDAM,
Gedrukt by FRANÇOIS HALMA Boekverkoper. 1705.

Frontispiece of the 1705 Rumphius book on the crustaceans of
Amboina, with kneeling native and naked child

Frontispiece of the posthumous *Metamorphosis* of 1719, with cherubs

MARIA SIBILLA MERIAN
Nat: XII Apr: M D C X L VII. Obiit XIII. Jan: M D C C XVII.

Late portrait of Maria Sibylla Merian, based on a drawing by her son-in-law

The 1683 *Caterpillar* volume was published by Johann Andreas not in Nuremberg but in Frankfurt. The Graffs had returned to that city to attend to matters of family and property. Old Jacob Marrel had died two years before, leaving as heirs to his house, moneys, extensive library, and art collection his widow, Johanna Sibylla, and the husbands of his stepdaughter Maria Sibylla and his own daughter Sara. But the inheritance was also encumbered with debts. With some harshness, Mathias Merian the Younger blamed the situation on his stepmother and her husband: Johanna Sibylla and Jacob had "wasted the good money [left by Mathias Merian the Elder] so that after Marrel's death she had to live off the charity of her daughter."[68] There was soon a lawsuit, with Maria Sibylla joining her mother against Sara's husband—a characteristic seventeenth-century family quarrel.[69] While it was being fought, Maria Sibylla brought out volume two of the *Raupen*, observed new insects, taught painting to a group of Frankfurt maidens, and wrote letters to her painter friend Dorothea Maria Auerin back in Nuremberg. By the summer of 1685 the suit had been won by the women, and Graff, who had been intermittently in Nuremberg designing street scenes, started back definitively to the house on Milchmarkt Street. Instead of following him, Maria Sibylla abruptly took her mother and two daughters up to Wieuwerd in Friesland to seek admission to the Labadist community there. Her widowed half-brother Caspar had been a member of it for several years, and now she went to join him.[70]

The conversion took place in Frankfurt, against this background of family quarreling. There Maria Sibylla had long before been baptized as a Lutheran, and had married, like everyone else in her family, in the Evangelical Lutheran Church. There the Pietist movement had originated around Philipp Jakob Spener, who had been senior minister in Frankfurt since 1666 and whose *Pia desideria* of 1675 had called for a renewal of Lutheran religious feeling and action throughout Germany. Nuremberg had been little affected, but Frankfurt had responded with excitement. Some converts were inspired by Spener to join small groups for biblical study, charitable activity, and mystical fellowship; others harkened to the more radical message of worldly renunciation coming from the new Labadist community up north, at first located in Herford and Altona, and after 1675 in Wieuwerd.[71]

What had Maria Sibylla read and heard? Had she attended Spener's sermons or gone to the holy meetings at someone's house? Could she have met Johanna Eleonore von Merlau? Eleonore had been born a few years before her in Frankfurt and had been married there by Spener in 1680 to an important Pietist; she had been experiencing God's work within her from girlhood and receiving revelations from Jesus Christ about the rooms of heaven—revelations that she then wrote down from the heart.[72] Could Caspar Merian have sent his half-sister one of Jean de Labadie's works in French, or translated into Dutch or German? His denunciations of corruption throughout society and his idyllic portrait of "the kind of Paradise on earth one could have" if one lived with the "simplicity and sincerity" of the ancient faithful? His treatise on "the self" and its remaking? His dedicatory letter to Anna Maria van Schurman, in which he praised her learning in languages and other sciences human and divine and her skill in painting and engraving, and summoned her to write of spiritual things ("Hasten, hasten, my sister, to give birth to spiritual fruit")?[73] Or could Maria Sibylla have seen Anna Maria van Schurman's own spiritual autobiography, *Eukleria, or the Choice of the Better Part*, written from within the Labadist retreat and telling the world that the rewards of philosophy were empty compared to the possession of true Christian friendship?[74]

Caspar Merian's life gives evidence of a change in sensibility when, the year before he left for Wieuwerd, he turned from his usual coronation processions and topographic scenes to sharp satirical illustrations for Erasmus' *Praise of Folly* and Sebastian Brant's *Ship of Fools*.[75] With Maria Sibylla Merian, there is only her response to God's shimmering presence through metamorphosis in nature and a last letter to Clara Imhoff in Nuremberg recommending her husband to that patrician family ("he will probably need good advice").[76] Then there is the fact of her departure.

What followed was a major transformation. Though she did not have to separate herself from her daughters, many of the changes in Maria Sibylla's life were as momentous as those Marie Guyart experienced when she entered the Ursuline convent of Tours. It was not just a matter of accepting Jean de Labadie's teaching that the reign of the great king Jesus Christ was at hand and that Labadie himself was one of its heralds; it was a matter of withdrawing immediately from the violence, pride, and concupiscence of the world and living the life of the regenerate, in full repentance. It was not enough to be part of a Frankfurt Pietist sodality sharing religious enthusiasm twice a week while going about one's everyday business; one had to separate from that sinful everyday existence and move oneself to "the Reformed Church, retired from the world and collected now at Wieuwerd in Friesland."[77]

Labadie had died in 1674, and under the guidance of his successor, Pierre Yvon, the community was to grow into a New Jerusalem. Every tongue was welcome: Maria Sibylla would have heard French, Dutch, German, and even a little English spoken when she arrived, while sermons were in French and Dutch. Every rank was welcome: among the 350 or so men and women there in the mid-1680s were coopers, carpenters, cooks, spinners, merchants, medical practitioners, and pastors; the Wieuwerd estate of Waltha on which the Labadists lived had been donated by three converts from a patrician family, the sisters Aerssen van Sommelsdijk. In a gesture toward worldly hierarchy, the Sommelsdijk sisters always lodged with pastor Yvon and his wife in the manor house rather than in the simpler dwellings with everyone else, but the language of polite social deference, such as that used by Maria Sibylla in her letters to Clara Imhoff, was absent. The significant hierarchy at Waltha was a spiritual one, the "first class" of the elect, all Brothers and Sisters, above the smaller "second class" of aspirants, still imprisoned by self-love.[78]

True repentance brought what Yvon called poverty of spirit, meaning absolute detachment from worldly things. Detachment from pride, for a start—detachment from being praised by learned men for one's ingenuity and skill. Detachment from finery, from elegant clothes and jewelry such as Maria Sibylla had worn as she visited in the patrician houses in Nuremberg. These things would have to be shed like an abandoned skin, and replaced by the rough habit of Waltha. Detachment from property, from houses on Milchmarkt Street and in Frankfurt, from lawsuits about inheritance, from private collections of fine paintings. Whatever possessions one had were given immediately to the community for common use; and to be accepted in the "first class," one had to divest oneself of any property owned in the sinful world. Maria Sibylla Merian was evidently received as one of the elect, for she wrote the Frankfurt authorities in 1690 that she had no property in that city, that everything attributed to her belonged to Johann Andreas Graff.[79]

The marriage by then had ended. She has left us no clues about possible trouble between them before her conversion: he had published her *Raupen*, and she acknowledged in the 1679 volume "the accomplished help of my dear spouse."[80] What is clear is that Johann Andreas had not followed his wife's religious enthusiasm in either his art or his life, and, as we have seen, his visit to Wieuwerd to get her back ended in disappointment. On his knees before her, he had begged to be allowed to live with her and their children. That he was then denied permission "to sleep with her in a holy place" or to stay in the community even among the "second class" must have been based on Maria Sibylla's assessment of him. She was "as hard as iron," said Brother Dittelbach, who then reminded her of 1 Corinthians 7: "Let not the wife depart from her husband . . . For the unbelieving husband is sanctified by the wife." She answered that Pastor Yvon had a different interpretation of that text. As Yvon said in a recently published book, Christian marriage could be sustained only by true believers and by "holy temperance" in regard to matters of sexual union. If these conditions were not met, the believer was freed of the marriage tie (a position different from that of the Lutheran Church, which allowed divorce for adultery, deliberate desertion, or impotence, but not for sexual excess within marriage or for spiritual disagreement). Faced with the choice between divorce and living with a nonbelieving spouse, an English vicar had decided to leave Wieuwerd for his unrepentant wife back home. Merian stayed, and was referred to later by Dittelbach as an example of the Labadist subversion of marriage.[81]

Had there also been malaise in the Graff household about "holy temperance"? Stories circulating years later, when both of them were in their graves, blamed the separation alternately on Graff's "shameful vices" and on Merian's "caprice" to depart.[82] Their paths after the breakup were certainly different. Johann Andreas told the Nuremberg city council that "his wife had left him to join the Labadists," got his divorce, remarried at age fifty-seven, and sired another child. Meanwhile Maria Sibylla had told the Frankfurt city council that her husband "has separated from her and lives with her in falsity [in Unrichtigkeit mit ihr lebt]."[83] Though her daughters kept their father's name, Maria Sibylla retook the name Merian and from the age of thirty-nine lived without a husband. But why should she have feared loneliness? Even after her brother died at Waltha in 1686, she, her daughters, and her mother had Papa Yvon, as everyone called him, and were part of the Labadist holy family, who, in the words of a Sommelsdijk sister, "lived together in love, of one soul, and one spirit."[84]

That holy family also supported one another in the reconstruction of the self—a goal that, as Labadie and Yvon had taught them, the regenerate could achieve even in this life. The "criminal self" (soi criminel), the selfish self, could be destroyed by penitence, discipline, community prayer, and prophetic exercise, and be transformed into "the self made pure," "un Soi non soi," "a supernatural self in the natural man."[85]

How Merian fared in this process, she did not record for us. She may well have appreciated the forms of spirituality cultivated by the Sisters. The pastor and "speaking Brothers" or leaders were all men, but at religious meetings there were "women speaking" in the prophetic tradition, and a woman gave a simultaneous translation of Yvon's sermons into Dutch.[86] Anna Maria van Schurman had died a saintly death several years before Merian's arrival, but she and her *Eukleria* were still looked to as models for lucid theological writing, tranquil living, and a joyful acceptance of death.[87] In 1683, when Papa Yvon published a description of the godly deaths that in their serenity and even laughter could serve as instruction for others, most of the examples were women: Luisa Huygens, from the learned Dutch family to which Constantijn and Christiaan belonged; Magdeleine Henry from Metz; and Elisabeth Sluyter from Westphalia, among others.[88]

In this spiritual economy of love and punishment, some members felt remade and joyous—"How good to be among the children of God"—while others began to resent the mortification. It wasn't so easy for the family whose ornate chest carved with verses was coated with black paint lest they prize it too much; it wasn't so easy for the artisans who were switched from job to job on the estate lest they take too much pride in their work.[89]

Whatever the circumstances of Merian's spiritual growth, the arena of work is the one we can track best during her Labadist years. It helps us understand how she defined and then redefined her religious self. For some converts, the regenerate life meant abandoning their past scholarship or artistic endeavor. Van Schurman put aside her linguistic studies to concentrate on Christian learning. From his religious community in Schleswig, Jan Swammerdam published his book on the mayfly only after receiving a letter of permission from his prophet Antoinette Bourignon; planning to discontinue his entomological research, he tore up his notes on the silkworm and sent his drawings to Malpighi.[90] Labadie and Yvon might never have counseled such a course, but they did warn against corrupting the eyes with "curious books and Paintings."[91]

But this is only one side of the story. Van Schurman did continue some painting and drawing at Wieuwerd, including small portraits of Labadie and a late self-portrait (Yvon said that portraits were permissible so long as they were unassuming and could raise the spectator's heart to God).[92] By the time Maria Sibylla Merian arrived at Waltha, Brother Hendrik van Deventer, a medical practitioner, was using his laboratory to classify chemical salts, invent fever pills, and seek an antidote for vegetable poisons. His profits went into the common treasury.[93] As for nature studies, Maria Sibylla could easily defend their religious significance. Not only were plants and insects God's handiwork, but, as Labadie himself had said, they were examples of the "innocent self": they were beings that had not changed since the moment God created them, that were still united to him, doing what God wanted of them. If there was any stain in plants and insects, it was in the use that sinful humans made of them.[94]

Thus, in addition to performing whatever tasks were assigned her by the community, Maria Sibylla searched for caterpillars and moths on the heaths and moors of Friesland (a terrain quite different from Frankfurt and Nuremberg) and expanded her interest to frogs, which she dissected to see how they were born and bred.[95] Soon after her arrival at Waltha, she invented a systematic way to preserve and add to her findings. She had a book of good blank paper bound, perhaps at the Labadist printing house, and, using blue-gray paper frames, pasted into it her collection of small watercolor studies of insects and their changes. These were not final compositions with beautifully arranged plants and flowers, but studies halfway between the immediacy of sketches and the permanence of her finished watercolors and copperplates. Opposite each insect study she copied down her earlier observations, adding to them when she had something new to say. Fresh observations in Friesland were then pasted in and recorded as they were made.[96]

This study book seems to have been a spiritual exercise as well as an exercise in natural study. It opens with a preface. "With God!" she exclaims, and goes on to tell about her findings on the silkworm and its transformations. She ends, "I began these investigations in 1660 at Frankfurt, God be praised," lists her illustrated volumes of 1679 and 1683, and signs "Maria Sibyla Merianin."[97] This is a kind of life account, a *Lebenslauf*—the sort that a convert would present to a sect to justify entrance.[98] Possibly Merian's assembling of her papers in this fashion was a way of turning them into collective property, something that would belong to the Labadist family when she died.⁹⁹ But it was also a form of personal presentation, though very different from the spiritual confessions of Anna Maria van Schurman and Marie de l'Incarnation. If they enjoyed the sweet freedom of describing the inner self, Merian preferred the freedom of concealment and discretion. Just as she did not arrest insects in their flight to depict their insides, so she did not stop to reveal her own. Describing God's creatures on the outside allowed them to keep moving and changing.

And indeed, after five or six years, she changed her mind about the Labadists and left for the wicked world of Amsterdam. Her mother had died in 1690, leaving her free to rethink her plans. Perhaps, like Petrus Dittelbach, she had become impatient with the spiritual hierarchy at Waltha and its excesses of discipline and control. And she may well have worried about her daughters. Dorothea Maria had turned twelve in 1690. Yvon had called for a holy education for the Wieuwerd children, which meant, in practice, open rebukes from the Aunts and Uncles and the constant fear of a thrashing. Johanna Helena turned twenty-two in 1690 and may already have developed her attachment to Brother Jacob Hendrik Herolt, whom she would eventually marry and who was also openly critical of excessive mortification. Maria Sibylla had taught Johanna and Dorothea how to paint. But what kind of education could they get at Waltha when so many "bad books," inspired by the "spirit of the world," had been forbidden by Yvon? It was one thing to have read them and have put them aside, as had van Schurman and in a sense Maria Sibylla herself; it was another thing never to have read them at all.¹⁰⁰

For an artist-naturalist who had previously resisted all systems of classification, the sharp line drawn between the elect and the world may have begun to lose its charm. Some Brothers and Sisters cared deeply about that distinction: it seemed to them that the very air they breathed began to thicken and stink as they moved away from Waltha.¹⁰¹ Only special visitors were let in to see the community. When John Locke stopped by in 1685, all his conversations took place in a little house outside the gate. He came away quite critical:

Though I believe they are . . . generally speaking people of very good and exemplary lives, yet the tone of voice, manner, and fashion, of those I conversed with, seemed to make one suspect a little of Tartouf. Besides that, all their discourse carries with it a supposition of more purity in them than ordinary, and as if nobody was in the way to heaven but they; not without a mixture of canting, in referring things immediately to the Lord, even on those occasions where one inquires after the rational means and measures of proceeding, as if they did all things by revelation.[102]

Quite apart from the symbolic or affective importance of such a boundary for Merian, it had practical consequences. How could her work ever grow beyond her study book if she stayed at Wieuwerd? The Labadist printing press was employed only for the literature of religious and moral instruction. To use community funds for her expensive copperplates was out of the question; and besides, Pierre Yvon, who in 1684 had published a tract against worldly ornaments and costly painting, might find the beauty of her flowers and plants excessive.[103] And what of exchanges with other naturalists? After the publication of her *Raupen* while she was still in Frankfurt, collectors had begun to bring her specimens.[104] At Waltha, correspondence with the outside world was supposed to be limited to matters of doctrine and the religious life of the elect.[105]

Sometime in the summer of 1691, Maria Sibylla Merian arranged her departure from the New Jerusalem with her two daughters and her paintings, specimens, and copperplates.[106] In all likelihood Yvon followed the practice established earlier for those elect who fell back to the world: he probably returned to her at least part of the money she had given to the community when she came. (Indeed, the next year, in the wake of her departure and the published exposé of the community by Dittelbach, Hendrik van Deventer demanded control over his sizable income from medical practice and sales outside Waltha, and the whole system of communal goods was dismantled.)[107] Merian made no statement about the Labadists afterward—no assessment, appreciation, or denunciation. As always, she protectively kept her inner life to herself. But it is clear that the five years' "retirement" at Wieuwerd turned out to be just that: a time of chrysalis, of hidden growth and learning for a woman who could not be pinned down. It was not the final maturation of "the supernatural self in the natural man."

Amsterdam in the last decade of the seventeenth century was a flourishing commercial, banking, and industrial capital of about 200,000 people, more populous by far than the cities of Maria Sibylla Merian's youth, and a place where a single woman with her skills, connections, and talented daughters could make her way.[108] Her older daughter, Johanna Helena, soon married Jacob Hendrik Herolt, who, putting the community economy of his Labadist days behind him, plunged into the Dutch trade with the West Indies and Suriname.[109] Maria Sibylla resumed the teaching and painting that had brought her income during her Nuremberg and Frankfurt years; her watercolors of flowers, insects, and birds had important buyers, such as the cultivated and well-married Agnes Block. Johanna Helena also began to sell her flower pictures—Agnes Block acquired a splendid foxglove—and was hired as one of the painters doing watercolors of the plants in the Amsterdam Botanical Garden.[110] By 1697 the scandal around Maria Sibylla in Nuremberg had lifted sufficiently for the Imhoff family to contact her in Amsterdam after years of silence, and she replied warmly. By 1698 she could boast of a well-furnished house on Kerkstraat and count on the friendship and help of the painter Michiel van Musscher a few canals away.[111]

Only her status as a woman divorced under unusual circumstances seems to have been hard for her to present to the fallen world: in her will and other acts of 1699, she called herself "Maria Sibilla Merian, the widow of Johann Andreas Graaf," even though that gentleman was alive and married in Nuremberg.[112]

During these same years, her *Raupen* volumes found their way into scientific libraries in England; and her entomological work advanced, as she bred caterpillars from the Amsterdam area and elsewhere and extended her observations to ants and other species.[113] Especially she was welcomed in the circles of naturalists and collectors in Amsterdam. If the anatomy dissections and lectures of Professor Frederick Ruysch and other doctors of medicine were out of bounds for her, the recently founded Botanical Garden was open to women and men both (an idealizing picture of lectures there shows two women in the crowd, perhaps Merian and Block). With Block she could admire the exotic pineapple plant Agnes had managed to grow, and discuss Agnes' long correspondence with a learned botanist at Bologna.[114] With Caspar Commelin, director of the Garden, she could see plants from the Americas, Africa, and the Pacific, whose seeds or specimens had come from Dutch traders and officers of the Dutch East India Company.[115]

Merian visited the museum of anatomical and other "rarities" acquired by Frederick Ruysch, whose daughter Rachel was her most gifted pupil; she saw the shelves of "foreign" insects and other "marvels of nature" in the cabinet of curiosities of Levinus Vincent.[116] And then there was the most energetic collector of all: burgomeister Nicolas Witsen, president of the East India Company. In the 1690s, he was savoring the colored drawings he had just commissioned of plants and insects in the Company's new settlement at the Cape of Good Hope. Of his insect specimens, Merian commented, "I examined with wonder the different kinds of creatures brought back from the East and West Indies."[117]

But as she said later in the preface to her *Metamorphosis,* something important was missing from all these collections: the origins and subsequent transformations of the insects. The beautiful specimens were stilled, wrenched from context, lacking process. Her own collection of "East and West Indies plants and insects," put together with help from her daughter and merchant son-in-law Herolt, was presumably no better. Moreover, these collections were having little impact on contemporary insect books: Stephen Blankaart's *Rupsen* of 1688 had exactly one New World butterfly, a specimen brought from Suriname, and drawn without its transformations. "So I was moved," Merian said, "to take a long and costly journey to Suriname."[118]

By ordinary standards it was a most unusual journey. Respectable women traveled to the Dutch colonies as wives and dependents in the families of plantation owners and administrators or as single women in groups under contract with the Dutch East India Company. The women that managed to get on board ship on their own in hopes of finding a good farmer to marry on the Cape of Good Hope or of setting up a café for sailors in Batavia were thought disreputable, "a pack of prison whores, and thieves," according to one male observer, "stowed away or sailing in men's clothing."[119] Fifty-two-year-old Maria Sibylla Merian and her twenty-one-year-old daughter Dorothea, even though under the protection of their skipper, were anomalous, traveling without men on strange business.

As the project of an artist-scientist, the trip was also unusual. Flora and fauna of the Americas had been described as early as the sixteenth century by figures like Gonzalo Fernández de Oviedo, whose encyclopedic interests were nourished during his decades of service for the Spanish king as overseer of mines on Hispaniola and then governor of Cartagena and Santo Domingo.[120] This pattern continued in the seventeenth century. In Maria Sibylla's day, for example, the remarkable Georg Everard Rumpf (Rumphius) collected and drew plants, shells, and crustaceans throughout the fifty years he served as merchant-administrator for the Dutch East India Company on the island of Amboina in the Moluccas.[121]

By the 1630s, however, a few naturalists were going to distant shores specifically for the purposes of observation: the physicians Willem Piso and Georg Marcgraf accompanied Prince Johan Maurits of Nassau-Siegen on his expedition to Brazil, and their findings were published in 1648 and 1658 in Amsterdam. But Piso and Marcgraf did not have to organize or pay for their trip; they were in the entourage of a prince, who was governor of what was then part of the Dutch empire. And when the 1648 *Natural History of Brazil* came out, it was "under the auspices and with the favor of the illustrious Johann Maurits."[122] Similarly, the Franciscan Charles Plumier, a passionate observer of plants in the Alps and Provence, jumped at the chance to go to the Caribbean "to do research on all the rare and curious things that Nature had produced there." He was part of a team sent over by a former royal Intendant in the French colonies of Martinique and Saint-Domingue. When his illustrated *Description des Plantes de l'Amerique* appeared in 1693, he thanked the secretaries of state who had seen to it that his trip and the publication of his book had been financed by the king's treasury.[123] Across the Channel, when the young Hans Sloane left in 1687 for two years of observing plants, animals, and people in Jamaica, "one of the Largest and most Considerable of Her Majesty's PLANTATIONS in America," he was physician to the island's new governor, the duke of Albemarle, at a substantial salary and advance for equipment.[124]

Maria Sibylla Merian had no such arrangements. To be sure, the existence of a Dutch colony in Suriname was a requirement for her research, just as the existence of a French colony in Québec had been a requirement for Marie de l'Incarnation's apostolic mission, but Merian had no formal connections with government or religious institutions to pave her way. However much Caspar Commelin and other Amsterdam naturalists must have yearned to make use of on-the-spot observations of the plants and insects of Suriname, they probably wondered whether a woman in her fifties and her unmarried daughter could carry off such a feat in the jungle. Burgomeister Nicolas Witsen financed Cornelis de Bruyn's observations as far afield as Egypt, Persia, and India,[125] but at most gave Maria Sibylla only a loan. In the preface to her *Metamorphosis* she noted the beauty of Witsen's collection, remarked on the costs of both her travel and publication, and expressed obligation and gratitude to no one.[126]

At least she was free to make her own decisions. In February 1699 she asked a broker to sell a large collection of her paintings of fruit, plants, and insects, as well as many specimens acquired in Germany, Friesland, and Holland and sent to her from the Indies. She hoped to cover costs also by the sale of rare specimens from Suriname upon her return. In April 1699, "leaving for the Colony of Zuriname," she made her will, with her daughters

Johanna Helena Graff and Dorothea Maria Graff as her joint heirs, and set up her son-in-law Herolt and her friend Michael Musscher as her agents to continue the sale of her household effects. In June, she and Dorothea set sail.[127]

It was an adventure for which her life changes had prepared her. Hadn't the men in her family traveled about Europe in pursuit of their art? Hadn't her father, Mathias Merian, been the publisher of the last great editions of the *Grands Voyages*, the celebrated series of engravings of the New World? In Nuremberg, she had surely talked about distant lands with her friend Christopher Arnold, who had published descriptions of the "heathen religions" of the Caribbean, Guyana, and Brazil, had edited and illustrated accounts of travel to the Pacific, and had written poems in honor of travel literature as he had in honor of her caterpillars.[128]

Hadn't she made her own spiritual and physical journey from Germany to Friesland? There, among the Labadists, she had heard much of Suriname—though, it must be said, in very mixed report. In the years just before Merian's arrival at Wieuwerd, the Brothers and Sisters had sent out two colonies of their own across the ocean.[129] Their goal was not primarily to convert the peoples of America; Louise Huygens had prayed "to the Lord Jesus for the conversion of the poor Indians" before she died in 1680, but her plea was given scant attention.[130] Rather, as Waltha became more crowded, the holy community decided that some of its members must do "the work of the Lord" in a new setting. One group acquired land in Maryland, despite Labadist aversion to growing "that vile tobacco,"[131] and another refuge appeared in 1683, when Cornelis van Sommelsdijk acquired joint ownership of a third of the colony of Suriname and became its new governor. In the next two years, more than forty Labadists came to the colony, the governor giving them land in the name of his sisters Sommelsdijk. It was located farther up the Suriname River than any Europeans had yet settled. They called it Providence Plantation, a perfect place for the gathering of true Christians.

It turned out that life in the jungle was more of a sacrifice than even the regenerate could bear, and, just as Maria Sibylla Merian was settling in to Wieuwerd, letters came back from Providence Plantation complaining of the snakes, mosquitoes, and stinging ants; of illness, death, and dissension among the elect. The Wild Ones (as they called the Amerindians, comparing them to tapirs) were hostile, their language as "bestial" as their behavior. The Labadists' slaves, whom they had bought in large numbers, refused to work when the saints from Wieuwerd were good to them, so they had to resort to the beating and blows used by other fallen planters. The heat was so extreme that the Labadists themselves could hardly work. Rather than dying a holy death, Sister Swem, the cook at Providence Plantation, denounced the lies of the leaders and refused to retract her words as she approached her Maker.[132]

By late 1686 settlers had begun to return to Wieuwerd with their bitter tales, and were facing the reproaches of the faithful for their weakness. A few years later it became clear that the Labadist settlement had failed. In 1688 Governor van Sommelsdijk and his military commander were slain by their own Dutch soldiers, who revolted against being forced to toil on the fortifications and canals of Paramaribo "as if they were slaves" and against inadequate food (Sommelsdijk was not a Labadist, but expected disciplined conduct from his men).[133] Eventually his sisters Lucia and Maria returned to Waltha. A few of the Brothers and Sisters stayed on in Suriname into the 1690s, but Providence Plantation became essentially a rental property for the Wieuwerd Labadists.[134] (This is important to stress in the context of Merian's life, for previous studies have assumed that the Suriname Labadist community remained a going concern and was part of the attraction for her 1699 journey.) In 1694 the Suriname tax list described the "Collegie der Labadisten" as having no resident "whites" (which meant that any whites there were recent arrivals) and fifty-five "red and black slaves"; in 1697 as having seven whites and sixty-one slaves. In 1699–1702 the Labadist name dropped from the list entirely.[135]

The residue of this experience for Maria Sibylla must have

been complex. On the one hand, a dream of heroic self-testing in a dangerous clime and the attraction of an unknown and exotic insect world. (Governor van Sommelsdijk had sent to the Wieuwerd Labadists a long snake stuffed by the Suriname Indians. He may have sent back some butterfly specimens as well.) On the other hand, a sense of the failure of the religious enterprise in the jungle. Her New World adventure was not the simple fulfillment of an original religious excitement, but a redefining of her aspirations in a more worldly way. There is no sign in her 1697 letter to Nuremberg or in her 1699 will of any persistence of Labadist enthusiasm; her preface to the *Metamorphosis* describes the Friesland years disingenuously as if they had been a mere research trip. Yet her divesting herself of property once again and her taking off with her Wieuwerd-raised daughter across the ocean remind one less of the intellectual curiosity of Amsterdam naturalists than of the experimental mobility of Jean de Labadie and Anna Maria van Schurman.[136] Merian would never have produced the *Metamorphosis* if she had stayed with the elect, but she would never have crossed to Suriname if she had not once dared to be a Labadist.

The land to which Maria Sibylla and Dorothea came in the late summer of 1699 was inhabited by Amerindian peoples, of whom the Europeans saw especially the Arawaks and those speaking Carib languages; some 8,000 Africans, most of them born on the western coast of Africa anywhere from Guinea to Angola; some 600 Dutch Protestants, mostly from Holland and Zeeland; around 300 Portuguese Jews and a few German Jews; increasing numbers of Huguenot refugees seeking new lives after the revocation of the Edict of Nantes; a handful of English families who dared to stay on after their colony passed to the Dutch in 1667; and even a young settler from Merian's Frankfurt am Main.[137] The colony was owned and administered by the Society of Suriname, its shares divided equally among the West India Company, the city of Amsterdam, and the heirs of Cornelis van Sommelsdijk. From Fort Zeelandia and the adjacent little town of Paramaribo a few miles from the mouth of the Suriname River, the governor wrote long letters to the honorable directors in Amsterdam about the difficulties of maintaining order when the Amerindians were threatening to violate their peace treaties and revolt and the French to invade from Cayenne; he sent back copies of the proclamations of his council prohibiting, say, any trade or gambling between white persons and "red and black slaves" and any drumming or dancing by slaves on Sundays without his express permission.[138] Three pastors tried to instruct the European Protestants in their Christian duty out of small churches in Paramaribo and elsewhere, while the Portuguese and German Jews, despite their different rites, shared a brick synagogue amid their plantations at Joden Savanna at a bend on the Suriname River.[139]

Sugar was then the colony's only export and its obsession. "People ridiculed me for seeking anything other than sugar," said Maria Sibylla Merian, and indeed the planters boasted that "no soil in the World is so very rich, and proper for the Cultivation of the Sugar cane as is Suriname."[140] Along the shores of the Suriname, the Cottica, the Commewijne, and their creeks, almost two hundred estates stretched out with their cane fields, bruising mills (for pounding the cane to extract the juice), and boiling houses. From March to October hogsheads of glistening brown sugar left Paramaribo on ships for the refineries of Amsterdam. The return boats brought smoked fish and other foods from the Netherlands, so little did the planters want to be distracted from growing their own sweet product. When it came time to collect taxes, householders were assessed in sugar: fifty pounds for every person over twelve, whether white, black, or red; twenty-five pounds for every child.[141]

The labor was provided by slaves, mostly African men and women brought in by the Dutch West India Company, auctioned off in Paramaribo and branded by their owners, and a small number of Amerindians. The estate of Samuel Nassy, not far downriver from Providence Plantation, had some 300 slaves in 1699—

1700, easily the largest number on a single plantation in the colony in his day; the plantation of Abraham van Vredenburg, which Maria Sibylla would visit, had eighty-nine; Esther Gabay, whose name was often on the export lists, produced her sugar with only forty-one.[142] Europeans and Africans on the Dutch plantations talked to each other in a recently created English-based creole, called "Neger-Engels" by contemporaries; on the Jewish plantations, the creole drew heavily on Portuguese.[143]

Back in 1676 a Dutch pamphlet on the profitability of warm lands like Guyana had given biblical quotations justifying the enslavement of heathens, but had recommended that owners treat their slaves mercifully.[144] This counsel was sometimes ignored in Suriname, where ingenious ways of punishing the "red and black slaves" were developed. The Labadist letters of the 1680s had described the "Spanish whip": any slave who tried to escape was tied in a special hand-to-knee position around a hoop or piece of wood, and then whipped. If the slave was recaptured after a few weeks, the Achilles tendon was removed—as we learn from J. D. Herlein, a visitor to Suriname at the same time as Maria Sibylla. After a second escape, the right leg could be amputated ("I myself was a witness to slaves being punished thus," says Herlein). For a less serious offense, the slave was suspended from a tree by the hands and weighted below from the feet, and whipped first by the owner and then by other slaves.[145]

But some slaves got away successfully, and even in the early days, under the English, Africans had set up independent "maroon" villages on the upper Suriname and its creeks. Maria Sibylla Merian may well have heard about two important group escapes in the decade before her arrival: one in 1690 from the plantation of Imanuël Machado near Joden Savanna, and the other in 1693 from Providence Plantation farther upriver. "Labadissa Negroes . . . from the plantation of La Providence" is how the Suriname government referred to the Bush Negro descendants of the second group eighty years later, whereas their twentieth-century descendants, the Abaisas, tell the story this way: "In slavery, there was hardly anything to eat. It was at the place called Providence Plantation. They whipped you there till your ass was burning. Then they would give you a bit of plain rice in a calabash. (That's what we've heard.) And the gods told them [the Africans] that this is no way for human beings to live. They would help them. Let each person go where he could. So they ran."[146]

As for the "red slaves," a few of them escaped with the Africans and even married with them. Most of their compatriots were living in their own Carib and Arawak settlements along the Saramacca and Maroni Rivers or along sections of the coast and of the Suriname and other rivers not occupied by Europeans. The men hunted, fished, made canoes, and fought enemies; the women planted cassava, yams, and other roots (and must have been the teachers of the Europeans who adopted these crops), and made pots, baskets, and hammocks. Relations with the colonists were sometimes hostile (the Amerindians remembered Sommelsdijk's burning of five of their villages, while the Dutch recalled raids and poisoned arrows), but the two groups often traded in peace, the Amerindians bringing jungle birds, plants and roots, canoes, hammocks, and captives, the Europeans bringing cloth, firearms, knives, scissors, and combs.[147] The world that Merian wanted to discover, the Caribs, Arawaks, and Africans knew very well indeed.

Maria Sibylla settled with Dorothea in a house in Paramaribo, where in October 1699, at the height of the dry season, she painted and recorded her first metamorphosis.[148] She had some connections to help her get started, including some with elite families: the household of the late Governor Sommelsdijk (where along with his heirs lived his Carib concubine, a chief's daughter taken "in marriage" as a gesture of peace with the Caribs);[149] the household of his slain military commander Laurens Verboom, whose young daughter would later travel with Merian to Amsterdam. Maria Sibylla bought or perhaps was given a few slaves ("myne Slaven" is her term), an Indian man and an Indian woman among them.[150] No "bestial" incomprehensible language here, for she quoted them often. They communicated presumably in the common creole of Neger-Engels, which she and Dorothea learned as they had learned Dutch years before in Friesland.

Merian plunged into the work of discovering, breeding, and

recording, and Africans and Amerindians were more useful to her than European planters. She observed in her own garden, and also went into the bird-filled forest right outside Paramaribo, "sending my slaves ahead with ax in hand to hack an opening." When she found an unknown plant so delicate that its cut leaves would wither in the heat, she had "my Indian" dig it up by the roots and replant it in her garden for study.[151] In search of new caterpillars, she, Dorothea, and her Africans and Amerindians visited plantations along the Suriname River, starting with a forty-mile paddle upstream to Providence Plantation during the rainy season of April 1700. Chrysalises and cocoons were some-how packed up when the journey had to resume and were watched for metamorphoses during the trip. On the way back the party probably stopped at one of the Nassy plantations: Samuel Nassy had given an arum plant to Caspar Commelin for the Amsterdam Botanical Garden, and perhaps Merian urged the Nassy family to start a botanical garden in Suriname. The Dutch East India Company had one for medicinal reasons at the Cape of Good Hope, as she would have known from Nicolas Witsen. Why shouldn't the Society of Suriname have one in Paramaribo, along with its dispensary?[152] In June 1700, at the estate of Abra-ham van Vredenburg, military commander of the colony, she especially studied the caterpillars feeding on the cassava leaves. Maybe she also seized the occasion to tell him how much she disapproved of the colony's monoculture of sugar.[153]

Traveling or in Paramaribo, she talked about insects and plant use with her workers and other Amerindians and Africans. Word about her spread, and since women in the native communities of Africa and the Americas often played the role of herbal and mag-ical healers, the Amerindians and Africans may have thought her less crazy than the colonists did. "A black slave woman" (*"een swarte Slavinne"*) brought her a maggot, promising a beautiful metamorphosis ahead; "Indians" brought her a host of lantern flies, whose fiery light and "hurdy-gurdy" (*"Lierman"*) music astonished her and Dorothea. Even more than in Friesland her eye was extended to many insects beyond lepidoptera, and to spiders, birds, lizards, snakes, and toads as well. Shells she had fished up from the bottom of the Atlantic by "a slave" ("*ab servo*") so that she could see what was inside them.[154]

Beyond her endless curiosity remained the task of representation. Everything was first sketched from life, and then as soon as possible she and Dorothea painted on vellum the caterpillars, the chrysalises, and their food. The buzz of insects never stopped:

> When I painted, [wasps] flew before my eyes and hummed around my head. Near my paint-box they built a nest out of mud, which was as round as if it had been made on a potter's wheel; it stood on a small base over which they made a cover of mud to protect the interior from anything unsuitable. The wasps bored a small hole in it for them to crawl in and out. Every day I saw them carry in small caterpillars, doubtless as nourishment for themselves and for their young or worms, just as the ants do. Eventually, when their company became too troublesome, I chased them away by breaking up their house, which allowed me to see all that they had made.[155]

At the same time, the butterflies, moths, and beetles, as well as anything else that could be preserved in brandy or pressed, were labeled so they could be grouped with their larvae (in a few cases, alas, inaccurately labeled) and saved so she could paint them in Amsterdam.[156]

Then after almost two years, she could not bear the heat any longer—"I almost had to pay for it with my life," she wrote a fellow naturalist[157]—and she cut her trip short. She and Dorothea departed on June 18, 1701, loaded with rolled vellum paintings, brandied butterflies, bottles with crocodiles and snakes, lizards' eggs, bulbs, chrysalises that had not yet opened, and many round boxes full of pressed insects for sale. Before leaving she arranged with a local man to send her specimens to market in the future. Young Laurentia Maria Verboom was picked up, to be delivered to a relative in the Netherlands. But Merian also took someone else on board *The Peace* with her to Amsterdam: her *Indianin*— her "Indian woman."[158] This nameless woman from Suriname would be part of the creation of her new book on America.

Four years later the *Metamorphosis of the Insects of Suriname* appeared in Amsterdam. The intervening period had been a busy one. Reinstalled in her old neighborhood, Merian soon saw her daughter Dorothea Maria marry Philip Hendriks, a surgeon from Heidelberg practicing in Amsterdam; and in December 1701 she must have heard that her former husband, Johann Andreas Graff, had died in Nuremberg.[159] There had surely been no resolution between them, and her letters to the Nuremberg naturalist Johann Georg Volkamer in October 1702 made no mention of him. Rather, she talked of painting "in perfection on vellum" what she had brought back from America; of her plans for the new book and whether subscribers could be found to help pay for its copper engravings, even larger in format than the recent *Hortus Medicus* of the Amsterdam Botanical Garden; of the snakes, iguanas, hummingbirds, and tortoises that he might buy from her and the best liquid to preserve them in; of whether he was interested in creatures from the East Indies, for her new son-in-law had just gone there to procure them. Letters to James Petiver in England had the same themes: sales of her specimens, subscribers for her book. Would it not be appropriate, when the book was finished, to send a specially illuminated copy and dedication to Queen Anne of England, "coming from a woman to a personage of the same sex"?[160]

And still there was not enough money to cover costs and pay back her travel loans. She took out time from supplying paintings to her engravers (for with the Suriname book she was able to do the strenuous work of copper engraving herself for only a few of her plates) and did paintings at a price for a book by someone else. Georg Everard Rumpf, now blind, had sent his last great work on the crustaceans, shells, and minerals of Amboina to be published in the Netherlands, but without many of the drawings; he died in 1702 before his assistants could provide them. Together with Simon Schynvoet, an important Amsterdam collector, Merian found examples of Rumpf's specimens in local curiosity cabinets and prepared sixty paintings for copperplates. They were done in Rumpf's expository style, not hers: rows of shells, crabs, or crystals with letters and numbers referring back to the text. *D'Amboinische Rariteitkamer* was published in 1705, the same year as her own book, and shows the extent to which her way of representing nature was a choice, not a matter of skill or habit.[161]

The *Metamorphosis of the Insects of Suriname* came out in Dutch and Latin (Merian did the Dutch, and probably had some assistance with the Latin), a folio edition of sixty copperplates, with copies available for purchase in black and white or hand-colored by her. Once again, as in the days of her father and half-brothers, the name Merian took over the title page: she was publisher as well as author, the engravers and printer having worked out of her house on Kerkstraat. And she marketed the books, which were also sold at the shop of the art dealer Gerard Valck.[162]

"The most beautiful work ever painted in America," naturalists had said about her vellums,[163] and this beauty carried over into the printed edition. (Some of her plates are reproduced in the illustrations here.) Here her characteristic way of showing nature's processes and relationships—the origin and transformation of insects, and the food on which their larvae lived—was applied to creatures and plants that were strange or unknown to people in Europe: cassava, guava, batatas, sweet sop, oil tree, pawpaw, and some for which even the Amerindians of Suriname had no names. Here New World insects, which had been granted only a few pages in the great Marcgraf nature studies of Brazil, were at center stage, observed by a knowing eye, and described by someone in close contact with scientific communities in Europe. Charles Plumier had recently played this role for the plants of the French Antilles; Hans Sloane would shortly play this role for the fauna and especially the flora of Jamaica; Maria Sibylla Merian (with her publishing expertise and Amsterdam friendships) was playing this role for the insects of Suriname, even without the benefit of being a Royal Botanist or a Fellow of the Royal Society.[164]

Her system for ordering her life histories was the same one

she used in the *Raupen:* each picture, with its accompanying text, stood on its own. As before, different species of moths and butterflies might be in the same picture if their larvae fed on the same plant, and bees, wasps, and flies as well. Deepening the break with classification was the presence in six pictures of a lizard, snake, frog, or toad. They were either located in the habitat where they had been observed or added to the insects and plant food explicitly "to decorate the plate," while the text gave information about their reproduction or food.[165] The sequence of plants was not organized according to petal type, leaves, or fruit (as Plumier and Sloane would have done). Nor were plants and insects grouped according to their resemblance to or difference from European species: American grapes, cherries, and plums were interspersed among cassava roots, okra, and "tabrouba" (a tropical tree with green fruit, now called "taproepa" in Suriname).

The overall narrative strategy was, as in the *Raupen,* an aesthetic one, here artfully moving the European reader back and forth between the familiar and the strange. The opening plate of the already known pineapple and the surprisingly huge cockroach evoked the distinctive sweetness and destructiveness of America. The text for the last plate reminded the reader how much there was still to learn: "In January 1701 I set out into the forest of Suriname to see what I could discover. Searching about, I found this graceful red blossom in a tree; neither the name nor the qualities of this tree are known to the inhabitants of this country. Here I came upon a beautiful and very large red caterpillar with three blue beads on each segment and a black feather protruding from each of the beads." It had an extremely strange chrysalis, but the butterfly that emerged was like the Great Atlas seen in Holland.[166]

Mary Louise Pratt has described the work of European naturalists who went abroad in the era of Linnaeus and afterward as "a new form . . . of planetary consciousness among Europeans": "One by one the plant's life forms were to be drawn out of the tangled threads of their life surroundings and rewoven into European-based patterns of global unity and order. The (lettered, male, European) eye that held the system could familiarize ('naturalize') new sites/sights immediately upon contact, by incorporating them into the language of the system." Pratt suggests that this vision of the world is simultaneously "innocent and imperial," helping European economic expansion but doing nothing more violent than naming and classifying.[167] Merian's *Metamorphosis* is surely part of the early stages of this project of European looking and describing. But her ecological eye and hand leave much space for Surinamese insects and plants to flourish in local terms and relations.

Merian's strategy had its critics. James Petiver, planning to translate the Suriname book, intended to "methodize" it. Everything was to be switched around and sorted out into three chapters, one "Of Lizards, Frogs and Serpents"; one "Of Butterflies"; one "Of Moths."[168] As much as Maria Sibylla wanted her *Metamorphosis* to appear in English, she would never have approved this grotesque distortion of her project: as in the *Raupen*, her lack of "method" put all the attention on the process of transformation. In 1705 she returned some specimens Petiver had sent her, saying she was interested "only in the formation, propagation, and metamorphosis of creatures, how one emerges from the other, and the nature of their diet, as the esteemed gentleman can see in my book." Would he please not send her any more dead insects?[169]

The *Metamorphosis* also differed from her European caterpillar book in important ways. To begin with, Merian made an explicit effort to link her findings with those of other naturalists. No idiosyncratic terms like the German *Dattelkern* of the *Raupen*, but rather the *poppetjens* and *aureliae* (or *nymphae*) used by her contemporaries. To each plant she gave the title in the Amerindian and/or Dutch vocabularies of Suriname. Then Caspar Commelin supplied a Latin name for any plant he could, and indicated whether it was also in the Amsterdam Botanical Garden and whether or not it had been included in earlier works on non-European plants. His brief commentaries, in small type at the bottom of about two-thirds of the texts, brought a learned male voice into the book but not in a way that undermined Merian's authority in regard to insects. Merian herself mentioned four entomologists in her preface (Mouffet, Goedaert, Swammerdam, and Blankaart), saying somewhat disingenuously that, like them, she was giving only observations and leaving it to readers to draw their own conclusions. But her "womanly simplicity" was a thing of the past: she simply asserted straight out that Leeuwenhoek's opinion that the fifty red warts on the sides of a certain caterpillar were eyes did not at all correspond with her observations—the warts could not be eyes. (She was right.)[170]

Could one still listen for the Lord amid the new scholarly voices and new authorial tone of the *Metamorphosis?* He was invoked in a formulaic phrase in Merian's preface to the reader: "So long as God grant me health and life, I plan to add the observations I made in Friesland and Holland to those I made in Germany and to publish them in Latin and Dutch." But that was the only time the Lord was mentioned in the text: the natural world of Suriname stood on its own. To be sure, Merian still believed in God the creator. As she had written Volkamer in 1702, her book would show "the wonderful animals and works created by the Lord God in America." Similarly, in the revision and expansion of her European *Caterpillars* for a Dutch edition some years after the *Metamorphosis,* she spoke in her foreword of "the government of the Creator, which has put such wonderful life and beauty into such small animals that no painter with a brush and paint could achieve as much." Those she had found in America had enflamed her desire to observe all the more. But apart from this, the divine presence had become much less evident in her work since the first edition of the *Raupen;* there were certainly no more caterpillar hymns.[171] Maria Sibylla Merian had gone beyond mere coolness regarding Labadist separatism to a detached sense of God's presence and power in the world. She had done so quietly, gradually, and perhaps without direct participation in the intense debates about deism, atheism, and vitalism swirling around her in Amsterdam. God was no longer a force constantly sustaining nature's changes; he was a transcendent Creator. Instead of enthusiasm for God's presence, she had admiration for his handiwork.[172]

The two years in South America seem to have confirmed her change of mind. Organic nature there seemed both more beautiful and more dangerous than in Europe. In the *Raupen* she had spoken of how destructive a caterpillar horde had been in 1679, and in her plates had shown holes on some of the leaves eaten by the larvae; but generally the visual impression was of an "innocent" nature (to use Labadie's word)—a nature suitable to God's constant presence. In contrast, nature in Suriname was represented not only as being more threatening to people, who had to suffer the incursion of cockroaches on their clothes and food and be careful not to touch certain hairy caterpillars (as Merian did) lest their hands swell up painfully, but also as wreaking more havoc within the animal kingdom at large.[173] The terrifying Plate 18 depicting spiders and ants (it can be seen among the illustrations here) had no equivalent in the *Raupen* or in the additions she made to the book on European caterpillars. From a sorry-looking guava tree, brown web-spiders are catching prey and enormous black spiders are depicted on a branch: "They do not spin long webs, as some travelers would have us believe. They are covered with hair all over and supplied with sharp teeth, with which they give deep dangerous bites, at the same time injecting a fluid into the wound. Their habitual food and prey are ants, who find it difficult to escape them as they move over the tree. These spiders (like all others) have eight eyes; with two they see upward, with two downward, with two to the right, and two to the left. When they fail to find ants they take small birds from their nests and suck all the blood from their bodies."[174] In the plate, the black spiders are eating ants and devouring a hummingbird (of which more later).

The ants are busy in Plate 18, too, eating a beetle and counterattacking spiders. Merian's text does not omit the traditional "industriousness" and cooperation of the ants—they construct insect bridges and build cellars "so well formed that you'd say they were the work of human beings"—but they are violent: "They burst forth once a year in countless numbers from their cellars. They fill up the houses, moving from one chamber to the next, sucking the blood out of any creature they meet, large or small. They gobble up a large spider in the blink of an eye, for so many ants attack at once that it cannot get away. They run through one room after another, and even people have to flee. When they have eaten the whole house clean, they make for the next one, and then finally return to their cellar." Merian describes reproduction and metamorphosis in ants, but her main tale here is of destruction.[175]

The emotional and intellectual space that had been emptied by the retreat of God from nature was filled in two ways. First, by Merian's projects for plant and insect use: many fruits, such as plums, grapes, and vanilla, which could be cultivated if the Dutch were not so preoccupied with sugar; green and yellow caterpillars, whose cocoon thread was so strong that "if someone were to take the trouble to gather these caterpillars it would provide good silk and yield much profit."[176]

Second, and more substantial, that space was filled by Merian's observations on the Amerindians and Africans of Suriname. We have already seen that the *Metamorphosis* contains mention of "my slaves" and "my Indians." Merian presented herself to readers as a slave owner, even while she criticized the monoculture of sugar that depended on slavery, and she also accepted the legitimacy of the Dutch in Suriname. Nonetheless, the construction of her relation with Africans and Amerindians had some very unusual features to it, which (like her representations of insects and plants) opened fissures in the ground of argument for European domination.

European scientists and naturalists in the seventeenth and early eighteenth centuries rarely mentioned in their publications the various "servants" who assisted them with their research, as Steven Shapin has told us in his pioneering article, "The Invisible Technician."[177] This was true also of publications on American, African, and Pacific flora and fauna. Charles Plumier described his botanical investigations in Martinique as if they were solitary rambles. (Father Labat, the local Dominican missionary, made fun of him for saying he had discovered the secret of an ancient purple dye, when every black fisherman along the Martinique shore knew what mollusk it came from.) Hans Sloane, whose *Voyage to Jamaica* would appear two years after the *Metamorphosis,* recorded in his Introduction many conversations with "Negroes" and "Indians" about illness and plant foods and remedies, but acknowledged scientific aid only from an English clergyman whom he took along to "draw Figures" of fish, birds, and insects.[178]

In contrast, Merian recognized the help of Africans and Amerindians in finding and handling specimens. They even provided "testimony" about insects: "all [these creatures] I myself observed and sketched from life, except for a few that I added on the testimony of the Indians." The green grasshopper in Plate 27 was drawn wholly from such African and Indian report, so she said, for the chrysalis she had collected died before the adult insect could emerge.[179] At least one English naturalist was made uneasy by Merian's slave helpers, for translating the Latin text into English in a personal copy, he or she preferred to call the "serva Nigrita" *("swarte Slavinne")* who brought the orange maggot of Plate 27 "my Negro serving maid" and dropped entirely the "mancipia" *("myne slaven")* who opened a path through the forest for Maria Sibylla.[180]

But Merian herself prompted the reader's disquietude about the conditions of slavery, in her entry on the *Flos pavonis,* the "peacock flower":

Its seeds are used by women who are in childbirth in order to promote labor quickly. Indians, who are not well treated in their servitude by the Dutch, use it to abort their children so that they will not become slaves like them. The black slaves from Guinea and Angola must be treated benignly *[heel heuslyk, benigne],* otherwise they will produce no children at all in their state of slavery. Nor do they have any. Indeed, they even kill themselves on account of the harsh treatment to which they are ordinarily subject. For they feel that they will be born again with their friends in a free state in their own country, so they instructed me out of their own mouths.[181]

Merian's report of the African belief in rebirth after death, their conviction that one was reborn free and in one's own land, was not new in European accounts of American slavery. George Warren had talked of it in 1667 in his *Impartial Description of Surinam*, commenting that "[this] Conceit makes many of them over-fondly wooe their Deaths, not otherwise hoping to be freed from that indeed un-equall'd Slavery." Charles de Rochefort said the same about the people of the French islands, and Richard Ligon about those of Barbados, both of them also mentioning flight or slave revolt as another effort at achieving freedom from cruel masters. Hans Sloane would add the detail that the Negroes cut their throats, "imagining they shall change their condition by that means from servile to free."[182]

What is distinctive about Merian's account is that it is framed as a conversation—"so they instructed me out of their own mouths"—and as a conversation with women, who spoke also about aborting their children rather than bringing them into the world as slaves. Spanish friars had long ago mentioned in their letters Indian women who, overworked and in despair, used "plant poisons" to destroy the fruit in their wombs.[183] And in 1707 the physician Hans Sloane would say of Wild Sena, which he had seen in damp fields and near streams in Jamaica, "It provokes the Menstrua extremely, causes Abortion, etc. and does whatever Savin and powerful Emmenzgogues will do."[184]

In the *Metamorphosis*, the Amerindian women themselves identify the abortifacient to Maria Sibylla Merian: the peacock flower, whose seeds can also speed delivery. Here is a public sharing of the "secrets of women," reported with some sympathy by a European in whose world abortions were illegal and sinful. *I listen to African women; I report abortion without condemnation.* (Merian may well have spaced her own children, born in 1668 and 1678, by some form of birth control such as coitus interruptus, but probably not by abortion.) As for her statement that the African slave women did not have children, it is hyperbole, but it lends support to those historians who explain the low fertility among the slaves as being, in at least small part, a matter of the women's choice.[185]

If this was the only moment in the *Metamorphosis* in which Merian expressed feeling for the slaves or referred to their plight, it was by no means the only "instruction" given her by Africans and Amerindians. Her texts were filled with ethnographic nuggets of information, much of it women's information: about which plants, fruits, insects, and animals were eaten and by whom ("These toads are eaten by the blacks *[de Swarten]*, who consider them to be a good dish"; "These worms are placed on charcoal to roast and are eaten by them [the Indians, *de Indianen*] as a very fine delicacy");[186] about which plants were used for dressing wounds or for treating diarrhea, worms, and scalp maggots; about which plants yielded seed capsules to make brooms, seeds to string for pretty armbands for the unmarried women, fiber to be spun into thread for hammocks, and dyes to decorate the bodies of the Indian men. Merian entered the world of the Africans and Amerindians now and again by reporting how things tasted to a European—that is, how plants and fruits tasted, never insects, toads, or snakes' eggs.[187]

Such information about medicinal plant use and foodstuffs had been part of European descriptions of the New World from the beginning. If several of the items in the *Metamorphosis* were described for the first time, Merian's account of the making of bread from the cassava root had been anticipated in Piso's writing on Brazil.[188] What is noteworthy about her text is its ethnographic tone. Just as she did not classify the species of flora and fauna, so she did not classify the customs of Amerindians and Africans. Her observations were particular, linked to individual plants and insects, an extension of her sense of the relationships in nature. She once made an analogy between Amerindians and insects ("these caterpillars hang like Indians in their hammocks, from which they never completely emerge"), but then she sometimes talked the same way about herself, as when she thought of how much she had to tell her old friend Dorothea Auerin ("I would give a ducat to be turned into a fly so that I could fly to her").[189] There was at most one slighting remark in her book, about the lack of industry of the Amerindian men, and her imprecise language here—"people"—may have been referring instead to lazy Dutch settlers.[190] The strong generalizing judgments in the *Metamorphosis* were about the sugar-possessed Europeans. She did not concern herself about whether Christianity would or would not improve Amerindians and Africans (and in view of her current state of mind about religion, we can see why). The word "savage" she used not at all.

Now, "savage" was not readily abandoned in Maria Sibylla Merian's day. When Father Labat wrote up his years on Martinique and other Antilles islands, J. D. Herlein his observations of Suriname,[191] and the astronomer Peter Kolben his stay on the Cape of Good Hope, they all drew upon contemporary assumptions about higher and lower cultures and peoples. Labat reserved the term *sauvages* for the Caribs, very few of whom were Christian converts, and simply called his African slaves, parishioners, and penitents *"nègres."* His description of their ways was attentive and sometimes approving: he especially admired the blacks' respect for their elders and the Carib wives' willing obedience in a work rhythm much more strenuous than that of their husbands. But the Africans were marked by their natural "libertinage" ("there is no nation in the world more inclined to the vice of the flesh than theirs") and by their religious "inconstancy": "Their hot temperament, their inconstant and libertine humor, the facility and sense of impunity with which they commit all kinds of crimes hardly make them suitable for embracing a Religion whose foundations are justice, mortification, humility, continence, flight from pleasures, the love of enemies, contempt for riches, etc." The Africans converted easily but not deeply, and mixed idolatry and sorcery with their Christianity. As for the Amerindians, it was hopeless: they had a "natural indifference to religion."[192]

Kolben thought the "Hottentots" (as he and his contemporaries called the Khoikhoi) were "by no means as stupid and senseless" as Europeans had claimed, and noted—in contrast to those who found them "incapable of Religion"— that they had "some sense of God." As Pratt has reminded us, Kolben used European categories such as "government" to describe the "Hottentots" rather than seeing mere disorder among them. Yet he still placed them on a scale of civilization, and the best he could imagine for them was as "excellent servants and perhaps the faithfullest in the world."[193]

Cultural classification was in part produced by the very genre of travel literature, where chapters such as "The Disposition, Nature, and Attributes of the Black Slaves" and "Diverse Customs of the Savages" were expected (as they had been in the Jesuit relations on the Amerindians of Québec at the time of Marie de l'Incarnation).[194] The naturalist's pen might be less impelled to insert explicit judgments, depending on what kind of scientific frame was given to the material. Hans Sloane had more than one genre in his *Voyage to Jamaica,* and his use of cultural classification varied accordingly. In his long Introduction, full of chatty observations about the inhabitants and about his various medical patients, he found, for example, that the Indians and Negroes of Jamaica "have no manner of Religion by what I could observe of them. 'Tis true they have several Ceremonies . . . but these for the most part are so far from being Acts of Adoration of a God, that they are for the most part mixt with a great deal of Bawdry and Lewdness." The scientific body of his text was made up of individual entries on plants and their local uses, organized by numbers of petals. If a long chapter on tobacco included the comment, "In all places where it has come, [tobacco] has very much bewitched the Inhabitants from the more polite Europeans to the barbarous Hottentots," the word "savage" appeared rather sparingly in the two folio volumes. In most of the entries, plant or animal uses were conveyed without evaluation (as on the cotton-tree worms: "sought after by Negroes and Indians and boy'led in their Soups").[195]

Much more than Sloane's approach, Merian's scientific style and conversational exchange encouraged ethnographic writing indifferent to the civilized/savage boundary. Would they have encouraged an ethnographic style of painting as well? No picture of persons, European or non-European, has come down to us from the hand of Maria Sibylla Merian.[196] But if we want to get some idea of the spirit with which she would have represented the African women and men among whom she lived, perhaps we can do so from a picture by Dirk Valkenburg, a student of her close friend Michiel van Musscher. The year after the *Metamorphosis* appeared, Jonas Witsen—one of the Amsterdam notables whose collection Merian had visited and who surely had acquired (or been given) her book—hired Valkenburg to serve as bookkeeper and artist on the three plantations his wife had recently inherited in Suriname. Valkenburg obliged with a set of drawings of the buildings and trees on these properties, as well as an oil painting of the Africans on one of them, perhaps Palmeniribo, from which there was to be a slave escape a few years later.[197] Valkenburg's canvas followed some of the conventions of Dutch genre painting, but also gave expression to the artist's ethnographic eye.

As we can see in the illustration of Valkenburg's painting reproduced in this book, about three dozen Africans—men, women, and some children—are pictured in a clearing next to the thatched huts reserved for slaves. It is late afternoon, and the sunlight gleams on deep black and brown skin. The people are not working or serving Europeans (as in earlier paintings by Frans Post depicting the sugar mills in Brazil),[198] but are collected for what appears to be a *winti* dance—that is, a dance in which some of the participants are possessed by their gods.[199] Drummers are at work, and people have begun the pipe smoking and the drinking needed for ecstatic trance. Two women and a few men are dancing, while others watch or talk among themselves. A man kisses a woman, as happens in the usual Dutch dance scene. Was the kiss observed by Valkenburg or not? Father Labat said that men and women kissed in certain African dances ("such is this dance opposed to modesty"), whereas John Gabriel Stedman was later to claim that he had never seen a public kiss among the Africans ("such is their delicacy"). In any case, the man's kiss here is gentle, and the woman has a baby on her back—the kind of household described in the Suriname slave rolls in these years, which Valkenburg was himself keeping.[200] A man is vomiting, as happens in the usual Dutch dance scene. Observed by Valkenburg or not? The potion special to the *winti* could induce vomiting. The only real concession to the "Bawdry-and-Lewdness" commonplace about blacks is a man making a pass in the background at an older woman with breasts hanging below her waist. Even then, the distance is considerable between Valkenburg's serious and relatively decorous Africans and the rowdy kermis peasants and village merrymakers of Dutch low-life art.[201]

Two persons stand aloof from the rest at the front of the clearing. One is a tall young man wearing a European hat and standing with dignity (a captive prince?), his pipe stowed in his loincloth belt, the kind of man who might lead his fellows in escape. The other is a young woman with an infant on her back; seated on a drum, she is looking away from the dancing and out at the spectator. An older child leans on her drum, pointing at her and her baby. The accoutrements of the *winti* dance are around her feet—a pipe, a bowl, a calabash—and perhaps she is waiting for the god to come. But she is pensive and sober as she looks beyond our viewer's eye, the kind of woman who might have told Maria Sibylla Merian about the hardships of slavery.

Like Marie de l'Incarnation's *Relation* and letters, the *Metamorphosis* was a text that came from a woman's pen and that unsettled the colonial encounter. But it also showed how diverse women's perspectives could be: Merian offered a particularistic recognition of customs and informants different from the ones she was used to; Sister Marie imaged a universalizing dream of likeness to Amerindian women, who had been remade in their souls as Christians.

A third vision by a woman mediates between the two: Aphra

Behn's *Oroonoko or the History of the Royal Slave*, published in 1688 some twenty-four years after its author had spent a year or two on the plantations of Parham Hill and nearby Saint John's Hill in what was then the English colony of Suriname.[202] (The Labadists' Providence Plantation would be built not far away.) This tale of the Gold Coast prince Oroonoko and his beauteous wife Imoinda, cruelly enslaved and sent to Suriname, is recounted as a series of events to which Behn was for the most part "an Eye-witness" and in which she played a role. Oroonoko speaks eloquently to the male slaves on Parham Plantation about the indignities and burdens of their life: its drudgery and the whip; the fact that they have been sold, not even conquered in honorable war; the fact that they are owned and humiliated by an "unknown" and "degenerate" people. Men, women, and children follow Oroonoko to escape to the jungle (that is, to live as maroons),[203] but are finally recaptured by a large militia under the deputy governor. Oroonoko is whipped mercilessly and duplicitously, at the hands both of the governor and of his former African comrades, and his wounds are afterward rubbed with pepper. Planning suicidal revenge against the governor, Oroonoko kills his pregnant wife (who expects by death "to be sent into her own Country"), but he is then too weak and sorrowful to leave her corpse. The governor has him executed and sends his body parts to different plantations as a warning to the slaves.

Behn's attitudes—and those she gives to Oroonoko—are mixed throughout. Oroonoko speaks against slavery, but back in Africa he has sold his captives to European slavers. When his fellow rebels desert him, he says bitterly that they are cowardly, "by Nature Slaves . . . fit to be used as Christians' Tools." Behn represents herself as Oroonoko's confidante and supporter and opposes his dreadful punishment, yet she also tries to divert him from mutiny, keeps him under surveillance, and, once he has led the escape, fears with the other womenfolk that he will come back from the woods and cut their throats. Though she uses "Indian slaves" as her rowers, the nonenslaved Amerindians she portrays almost as noble savages, better off in their natural innocence than if they had been instructed by Religion or Law. Oroonoko's greatness comes, however, not only from his African royal nature and fine wit, but also from the education in "Morals, Language and Science" he has received from his French tutor. Though "perfect Ebony or polished jet" in color, his features are more those of a European than of an African. The tragedy of his death is of such magnitude that, as Laura Brown has shown in an astute essay, Behn implies a comparison between the "mangled King" Oroonoko and the martyred English king Charles I.[204]

If Maria Sibylla Merian ever read *Oroonoko* (either in the English original or in the German translation published in Hamburg in 1709),[205] she might have been amused or irritated by the "mixed" reality in Aphra Behn's natural history: Behn and her party sit down to a meal in an Indian village where unlikely buffalo is served with a plausible abundance of pepper;[206] and the Suriname weather is described as "eternal Spring," without mention of trying heat and threatening insects. But the German/Dutch entomologist might have sensed a kinship with the English author nonetheless. Both were, and characterized themselves in their publications as, slave owners or slave users for a time. Both benefited from some of the exotic products of imperial trade (Merian, from specimens; Behn, from feathers and butterflies, which she presented as gifts to the king's theater and royal collections in England).[207] Both were deeply troubled by what they saw and heard on Suriname plantations, without directly questioning the right of the English and Dutch to settle there.

Yet there was a difference in the treatment of their subjects. Behn shaped Oroonoko's life story in Africa and Suriname into a heroic romance which could appeal to Europeans,[208] while depicting some of the cruelty of slavery and giving Oroonoko an independent voice to denounce it. Merian recorded certain practices of women (Amerindians and red and black slaves) in concrete fragments and allowed a sympathetic account of abortion as resistance—an intractable fact that would not have appealed to Europeans at all.

There are two other women we have not heard from: the Carib

or Arawak woman whom Maria Sibylla Merian took back with her to Amsterdam (and whom Merian most likely kept as a servant rather than as a slave)[209] and the African who brought her the maggot climbing up the stalk of an apple of Sodom. As for their response to *Oroonoko*, the Amerindian woman would probably have found much of its description of the English visit to the Indians bizarre, from Behn's silence about female-produced cassava at the meal to her dismissal of the shaman as a mere deceiver. The African woman might well have found it fitting that the slaves escaped at the instigation of a great leader. That is how it was told in the maroons' own stories of First Time, though always with the presence of some *obia*, or supportive spirit, not mentioned by Oroonoko (maybe that's why he was recaptured).[210] The African might also have assigned more initiative to Imoinda and more backbone to the other slave women than did Behn. Indeed, she would have recalled that the recent escape from Providence Plantation in 1693 was attributed to Mother Kaàla, whose *obia* talked with the water spirits.[211]

But what would the Amerindian and African women have said of Merian's *Metamorphosis*, to which, after all, they had contributed? To begin with, they might have wanted their names and/ or peoples mentioned, as Marie de l'Incarnation always did for the Québecois Amerindians whose lives, conversations, and speeches she described in her letters. Merian included the names of naturalists and those of two plantation owners on whose land she saw certain insects, but of her non-European helpers she simply said "black slave" rather than Jacoba, Wamba, Sibilla, Tara, Wora, or Grietje (to give some names from a 1699 Paramaribo list of recent arrivals from Africa)[212] and "Indians" rather than Caribs, Arawaks, Waraos, Tairas, Accawaus, or Waiyana.

More broadly, the Amerindian woman might have found it strange, if one were passing on knowledge about plants and insects to one's own kind, not to include what Europeans called magical and ritual uses. For the Peii, or shaman ("priest," to use Merian's word), tobacco was associated with powerful spirits which he drew upon in tobacco juice and smoke for his own ritual of purification and for curing, and he had other special plants as well. His secrets may not have been known to a Carib woman, and in any case the Peii did much of his work by sucking harmful things out of the sick person's body, falling into trances, and shaking the calabash.[213] Available to all the Caribs, however, were certain plants that were used along with incantations to protect against dangerous spirits everywhere in nature and to obtain good results in hunting, planting cassava, and family life.[214]

The Amerindian woman would also have been through ceremonies using insects quite different from anything in Maria Sibylla's past. Among many of the Carib-speaking peoples and the Arawaks, ants and wasps were part of one of the rites of passage into adolescence for both boys and girls. The young person's hand might be plunged into stinging ants, or ants and/or wasps might be bound to the chest. (By the nineteenth century, only the males were undergoing the wasp test, and this may have been true earlier.) The Waiyana developed a fiber mat, braided into the rough shape of a tiger, crab, or mythic animal or spirit and decorated with feathers, on which were placed wasps that had been drugged with a plant juice. (Pictures of such mats are given in the illustrations.) The mat was then bound onto the young person's body for the ceremony, during which the wasps would revive.[215] Thus, endurance for hunting and the strength of fertility were passed on to the next generation. Insects were also part of a Carib postpartum ceremony for males following the birth of a first child. After eight days in his hammock, eating only cassava bread and water, the father underwent a test of stinging ants and then moved to a joyous drinking feast.[216]

For the African woman, too, there were special uses of the natural world that it would seem odd to isolate from a repository of information. She would have thought of the deities and spirits associated with the great silk-cotton tree in Suriname and the offerings placed under its boughs. Her mother might have been one of the custodians and charmers of the *papa* snake (boa constrictor), a sacred vehicle for the gods, and the African woman would know not to harm one lest the gods seek vengeance. Her brother would have learned what his father's taboo food was (this knowledge was the sign of paternity); the toad, which in Merian's account was simply "considered as a good dish by the Blacks," might have been *trefu* (forbidden) for the men in her family.[217]

For the African woman, the power of arthropods was especially great in the realm of story. "[The Negroes] are naturally eloquent," Father Labat was to write about his years in Martinique.[218] The central hero of the stories that the Africans brought across the ocean and developed was Anansi the spider, trickster par excellence, after whom all stories are named. Europeans sometimes heard about him. The Dutch commercial agent Willem Bosman, who was on the Guinea Coast from 1690 to 1702, said of a "hideous great Spider" in his room: "the Negroes call this spider Ananse, and believe that the first Men were made by that creature."[219] In Suriname, "Anansi-tori" were told during the rites for the dead, interspersed over the course of a year with offerings for the dead and with feasting and mourning practices; they could be told at other times as well, but not during the day. Anansi does ingenious, cunning, and sometimes mean things to protect himself and get what he wants; his targets and victims may sometimes be smaller than he is (cockroaches) and sometimes bigger (tigers and kings).[220]

A story that the African woman of the Sodom-apple maggot might have heard in some version tells how the spider Anansi tricked Tiger into allowing Anansi to ride him like a horse. Anansi had boasted to the King that he could do this; the doubting King passed on the claim to Tiger, who was angry at such an affront. Tiger stormed to Anansi, who said the King had lied about the boast. He would be glad to set the record straight before the King, he said; but he was so sick he could not get there on his own feet. So Tiger took Anansi to the King on his back. On the way, Anansi used other tricks to get Tiger to wear a bridle, and by the time they got to the King's house, the spider was even whipping Tiger.[221]

But Anansi did not win out every time, as the African woman might have heard or told in another tale. To keep himself the most cunning man/spider on earth, Anansi acquired all the cunning he could find from others, put it in a gourd, and then tried vainly to take it to the top of a silk-cotton tree. When his son helpfully told him the right way to carry the gourd, Anansi realized he had not amassed all the cunning in the world and never could. He angrily broke the gourd to pieces.[222]

Glikl of the Bird Story would have enjoyed this tale of How Cunning Was Spread and would perhaps have made her own version; Marie de l'Incarnation, impatient with Indian creation stories that told of muskrats and tortoises, might have found Anansi no help to moral discussion. Maria Sibylla Merian, insofar as she was interested in cultural comparisons ("Batatas . . . can be cooked like carrots; their taste is very much like chestnuts . . . but sweeter"),[223] would have noticed that the magical use of plants by Amerindians and Africans was analogous to herbal magic in rural medicine in Germany; that arthropods played a role in Aesop's fables, though nowhere near as important as Anansi's role; that Anansi Rides Tiger had some analogies to the upside-down in the old European legend of Phyllis' riding Aristotle.[224] And she would have been aware of sharp differences, as between adolescent rites of passage in Carib lands and those in Europe.

How much Maria Sibylla Merian actually learned of the ritual practices of the Caribs and Africans we do not know. Very possibly, her "Indian woman" did tell her about some magical uses of plants and her "African woman" about the sacrality of certain snakes, just as they told her about abortifacients; but Merian decided not to record these things in the *Metamorphosis*. We are unable to test her on the cases most readily known to Europeans, for she found or at least described no caterpillars on a silk-cotton tree, and the beautiful snake hiding under the jasmine hedge in her Plate 46 was not a boa constrictor. But she might well have feared that her credentials as a woman naturalist would be undermined by magical reports. Here perhaps was a boundary that was practical for her to draw.

Yet in an indirect way, Anansi's spirit is present for a moment in the *Metamorphosis* (just as Amerindian sensibilities and plot lines found their way into Marie de l'Incarnation's letters). Let us return to the great spiders and the hummingbird of Plate 18, a surprising picture that soon inspired European copies and prompted Linnaeus later to name the species *Aranea avicularia,* "little-bird spider."[225] (The reader can see it in the illustrations here.) "When they fail to find ants," said Maria Sibylla, "they take small birds from their nests and suck all the blood from their bodies." She then specified that the birds were hummingbirds, "otherwise the nourishment of the priests in Suriname, who (so I was told) are forbidden to eat other food."

That the Peii had food taboos, and especially meat taboos, is certain,[226] but whether Merian ever *saw* a great hairy tarantula suck a hummingbird's blood is not. If she did see it, what are those four eggs doing in the hummingbird's nest, rather than the characteristic two?[227] The great nineteenth-century naturalist Henry Walter Bates did observe a *Mygale avicularia* (as they came to be called in the nineteenth century) killing a finch along a tributary of the Amazon, but added that the event was "quite a novelty" to the local Brazilian residents. Present-day experts in tropical biology point out that such an attack, though it can occur, is exceptional—that a bird would not be the main prey or an ordinary alternate prey for a "bird-spider."[228] In Merian's case, then, the event seems to have been something she was told about—and told about by an Anansi-teller. Whatever trace of actual natural history is present in the text and picture, here Anansi gets his food, and the best food—food fit for a shaman.

"She is sixty-two years old, but still very lively . . . and hard-working, a very courteous woman." Thus Zacharias Conrad von Uffenbach, a learned young scholar from Merian's birthplace, recorded in his notes in 1711 after visiting the artist-naturalist and buying her books and watercolors. She was now one of the international figures of Amsterdam, a person one had to meet, the way one had to attend Frederick Ruysch's anatomy lectures, see

Nicolas Witsen's collection, and view the great maps in the Town Hall. When Peter the Great visited the city, his physician stopped by Kerkstraat and acquired some of her paintings for the czar.[229] Though the German and English subscriptions for the Suriname book were never sufficient for published translations in those languages in her lifetime, the *Metamorphosis* was widely read by naturalists. Around 1714, using her old copperplates, she published a Dutch translation of the two volumes of her European *Caterpillars (Der Rupsen)* with a few additional observations but with a more succinct and impersonal text. "The ingenious noble maiden" in the Nuremberg garden and many other lyrical expressions had disappeared.[230]

She now had her own marking, an informal title that regularized her anomalous status: she was Juffrouw Merian—Mistress Merian—ordinarily the term of address for a young unmarried woman, but in special cases a title of honor for a mature woman on her own. The report of her young visitor from Frankfurt reveals that her memory of her marriage was still bitter, and that she still concealed the truth about the divorce and her Labadist years. "Evil and miserable" *("übel und kümmerlich"):* such was Uffenbach's impression of her life with Graff. "After her husband died, she moved to Holland"—clearly not what had happened.[231] One suspects that she passed on to her daughters, at the expense of their father, the feeling that they were Merians first and foremost. Widowed from her surgeon-husband, Philip Hendriks, around 1715, Dorothea Maria took the name Merian for a time, rather than her father's name, Graff.[232]

Maria Sibylla's relations with Dorothea Maria and Johanna Helena have their mysteries, if only because we have no autobiographies or letters written by the mother to her children, as we do in the case of Glikl and Marie Guyart. But there exist letters in which Merian talks about her daughters, and texts in which they talk about her. Some of the time, Merian seems to perceive herself as head of a far-flung family economy: in 1702 Philip Hendriks was expected to supply creatures from the East Indies for her to sell, and in 1712 Johanna Helena was to do the same from Suriname; in 1703 one of the daughters, probably Dorothea Maria, was expected to help with an English translation of the *Metamorphosis,* and of course we know Dorothea had already helped with the painting in Suriname.[233] But Merian, who acknowledged her African and Amerindian informants in the *Metamorphosis* and credited her slave assistants, said not a word in it about her daughters. Can it be that she thought of them as simply subsumed under her? Or that a husband-wife team (one was acknowledged in the *Raupen*) was acceptable in a nature study, whereas a mother-daughter team might be seen as lacking seriousness?

Whatever the case, her daughters had it their own way in the third volume of the *Rupsen,* which was prepared by Maria Sibylla from her unpublished European observations, but printed just after her death in 1717. It was indeed a family affair: "Dorothea Maria Henricie [*sic* for Hendriks], the youngest daughter," was given on the title page as publisher of the book by her late mother Merian, and the text promised an appendix on insects of Suriname, "observed there by her daughter Johanna Helena Herolt, at present living in Suriname." God had now taken her mother, said Dorothea's preface, and had given rest to the woman who had been so active. Had it not been for Maria Sibylla's two years of ill-health, the book would have been out sooner; Dorothea was completing her mother's work for the benefit of all insect lovers.[234] Some editions of the *Rupsen* have, bound into their pages, a late portrait of Maria Sibylla in which the family element is stressed once again. She points to a plant with a chrysalis and caterpillar on its leaves, and the emblem of the Merians is prominently displayed above her head.[235]

Just as the mother was adventurous, so too were the daughters. Johanna Helena had left for Suriname by 1711. While her husband, Jacob Herolt, served as one of the rectors of the Paramaribo orphanage and administrator of the goods of the orphans' deceased parents, Johanna collected specimens of reptiles, fish, and insects, which she hoped to sell for a good price in Europe, and studied and painted insects and plants.[236] Some of her pictures, promised but never appearing in the *Rupsen,* seem to have been published without identification in her mother's posthumous publications (more family economy). Johanna Helena and Jacob Hendrik Herolt may have stayed in Suriname the rest of their lives.[237] Meanwhile, in the fall of 1717, Dorothea Maria departed for Saint Petersburg, becoming the second wife of the Swiss painter Georg Gsell (who had been boarding with his two daughters at the Merian house on Kerkstraat). She taught with him in the new art classes at the Petrine Academy of Sciences, and painted flowers and birds for the czar's cabinet of curiosities. Before leaving the Netherlands, she sold all of the pictures, plates, and texts for her mother's Suriname and European books to the Amsterdam publisher Johannes Oosterwijk.[238]

In the next two years, Oosterwijk was to give a new twist to the image of the woman naturalist, through his Latin editions of the European *Caterpillars* and the Suriname *Metamorphosis.* Both books had laudatory poems and prefaces from learned men. The couplets of the Jewish physician Salomon Perez went well beyond Christopher Arnold's paeon to the wonderwoman of the 1679 *Raupen.* Both books celebrated women observing insects. In the frontispiece to the European book, designed by Simon Schynvoet, a learned goddess lectures to an idealized Maria Sibylla Merian and her daughters amid insect specimens. In the frontispiece to the Suriname book, an idealized young Merian looks at specimens in the foreground, while through a window in an imagined Suriname Merian runs after creatures with her butterfly net.[239]

But Oosterwijk made some choices. The nature books published in the Netherlands in the late seventeenth and early eighteenth centuries usually included a sign of the Dutch colonial empire in their opening pages: non-European peoples are depicted in a posture of tribute as they present gifts from their homelands—objects that will be studied by the Europeans. In the frontispiece to Jan Commelin's *History of the Rare Plants at the Amsterdam Medical Garden* (1697), an African man and an Asian man kneel to present their plants to a personified queenly Amsterdam, while an American Indian awaits her turn. The sources for an imperial catalogue are the willing gifts from indigenous populations.[240] In the Rumphius *Amboina* (for which Merian did the illustrations but did not design the frontispiece), a dark-skinned man bows low to present a large basket of shells to a group of male naturalists, while a naked boy kneels amid shellfish and turtles.[241]

In Merian's *Metamorphosis* of 1719, no African or Carib kneels before her with a tribute of insects and plants. Rather, in a traditional Renaissance conceit, little cherubs show her specimens and insect paintings. Perhaps Oosterwijk thought the imperial image inappropriate for a woman's book. Perhaps the choice reflected Merian's own disquiet (passed on, say, by her friend Schynvoet, who served as consultant for the 1719 *Metamorphosis*)[242] at placing her book at the center of an imperial enterprise. Once again Merian takes her own flight. Once again we cannot pin the woman down.

CONCLUSION

VARIED LIVES, but produced within a common field. The hazards of plague, the pains of illness, and the early death of relatives—all affected the fortunes of Glikl bas Judah Leib, Marie Guyart de l'Incarnation, and Maria Sibylla Merian. All three knew the ferment of urban voices and printed words. All three experienced the hierarchical structures that placed an added weight on women. All were summoned, if only for a time, by sudden spiritual openings that promised a better future. The trajectories of their lives had some common features, including the good luck of much energy and a long life. The divergent features came from chance and temperament, but even more from patterns established by the religious cultures and vocational expectations of the seventeenth century.

The most important similarity among the three is in their manner of work, a women's version of an artisanal-commercial style. All of them had a sure expertise: they could tell a good jewel, a good embroidery design, a good insect specimen, among other judgments. All three were adept accountants, recording loans and children's dowries, or sales of books, paintings, and specimens, as the occasion required; switching from records of horses, wagons, and carters to records of church ornaments, food supplies, nuns' dowries, and land swaps as they changed vocation and location. They were quick to jump into action, to draw on whatever skills they had to meet the needs of the moment, whether coping with the crisis of credit loss and fire damage or heeding the desire to embark on a new venture.

For townsmen, flexibility in work skills was often seen as accompanying poverty: the man had to abandon his trade to survive; he was a *gagne-denier*, available for any kind of job. For city women, well-off or indigent, flexibility was essential and was encouraged by the way they were brought up.[1] More often than their brothers, girls were taught general trade and domestic skills rather than having several years of formal apprenticeship; they picked up whatever craft techniques they observed in the household of their parents, master, or mistress. Weren't they expected to adapt their work energies one day to whatever household they entered as wife, servant, or second wife? Glikl bas Judah Leib and Marie Guyart certainly lived that way, and their flexibility received additional impetus from religion. Jews needed to be good at improvising rapidly, amid the uncertainties of Christian Europe. And a heroic Catholic had to be available to serve wherever and whenever God called.

Maria Sibylla Merian was a little different, for even though she learned to breed and observe insects on her own, she had had years of training as an artist from her family. Her flexibility might stretch to farming during her days among the Labadist elect, but mostly she moved among the crafts that belonged to the versatile artist's shop of the seventeenth century. She became a painter, an engraver, a publisher, an art dealer, a teacher like her admired father Merian and her stepfather Marrel, and an embroiderer like her mother.

Sure expertise is an artisanal trait, often reinforced for men by the institutional approval of their guilds. Women's guilds existed for certain female trades, and women were sometimes subsidiary members of guilds in mixed trades. Glikl, Marie, and Maria Sibylla were among the many women who, for one reason or another, did not belong to such organizations. In Hamburg, trade guilds existed for Christians but not for Jews (let alone Jewish women); a woman helping her brother-in-law run a trucking business in Tours was not in a guild, though the brother-in-law was. Merian had the best chance for guild membership as a painter, but was in fact part of a Nuremberg circle trying to found an art academy. Thus, for Glikl, Marie, and Maria Sibylla their sense of expertise as young adults came from their own practice in a setting where they were also household managers—a setting in which caterpillar-breeding boxes were scattered among cooking utensils, and advice on seed pearls was given while nursing a child. Confirmation (say, from convent sisters or fellow naturalists) came later.

Perhaps, too, this sense of craft figured in the attentiveness that all three women devoted to their writing and describing. Merian evidently regarded her books as the continuation of her handwork and observation, whereas Marie de l'Incarnation's pedagogic books put her teaching on paper. But Marie and Glikl bas Judah Leib both came to writing without formal training in rhetoric, grammar, or the construction of texts. They had models—storytellers, sermons, popular books, and (in Marie's case) the language of the Ursuline convent—but composing their manuscripts required judgments about narrative and dialogue. Maybe, as Marie claimed, the "spirit of Grace" made her write as it wished; but if so, it worked through the nerves and muscle of her skill.

Religion influenced all three women enormously. The situation of being a Jew gave Glikl bas Judah Leib a constrained and vulnerable status in Christian Europe. Her self-image as one of the children of Israel gave her a profound identity, through which was filtered other identities—that of woman, merchant, resident of a German-speaking land. She took advantage of what a decentralized rabbinic religion left open for women: prayer, the sanctification of the household and her body as a married woman, charity, reading, and, in her case, writing. Of the religious novelties that excited the Jewish communities of Europe in the seventeenth century—the coming of Sabbatai Zevi, Kabbalah, and radical thought—only the first played much of a role in her life. This, too, may be a gender-related variable. News of the hoped-for messiah sped to everyone, but kabbalistic ideas and debates about Spinozan and conversos heresies did not extensively permeate the texts available to women (or so it seems; perhaps wives heard more about these matters than we know).

It was the printing press and Yiddish translators that expanded Glikl's access to central elements in Jewish thought. And we have seen how this nourished not only her moral arguments but also her subjectivity. Thinking about the Book of Job helped her recognize her own unyielding restlessness over the years.

Marie Guyart de l'Incarnation took advantage of two of the paths left open for women by the hierarchical church of the Catholic Reformation: the elaboration of holiness while living in the world as wife and widowed mother; and the development of a teaching vocation in a new Order for celibate women. She took each as far as it would go, flowering in ascetic discipline and mystical vision, then expanding teaching into a heroic apostolate in a distant place.

From the beginning, these practices had consequences for Marie's eloquence and sense of self. Punishment of her body, conversations with Christ, and theological visions were translated early into conversations with her confessor and writings about an "I" who shifted from intense activity to passivity. Along the way, religion provided her with words to interpret her abandonment of her son and her periods of despair. By the end, she had composed the story of an "I" who was active and passive at the same time, and she had learned to speak and write of God's mysteries in four languages. The proximity of an earthly Paradise, which Glikl had had to relinquish early, had not totally flickered out for Marie de l'Incarnation when she died in the Canadian woodlands.

Forms of Protestant radical spirituality—open to both men and women—erupted in Maria Sibylla Merian's life with special force when she was in her thirties and forties. First there was a rapturous sense of God's presence in nature—a sense that infused her work on lowly crawling things. Then there was her conversion to the Labadist sect, and her rupture with husband, family property, and worldly pride. Years after she had left the community and settled into the cooler detachment of deism, a Labadist-like energy and conviction informed her outlandish plan to travel to the jungles of Suriname for the sake of research.

Surely these religious moves led Maria Sibylla to self-reflection and inner dialogue. Among the Labadists, wasn't commentary required from each member on his or her own status as a penitent and remade person? But on paper she seems to have left only her workbook with its preface about her past research, not an autobiography like Anna Maria van Schurman's *Eukleria*. After the Labadist years, she gave out fragments for public consumption: her Merian lineage, her nature studies and travel. Regarding her marriage and religious experiment, she offered vague references, misrepresentations, even lies.

With Glikl bas Judah Leib and Marie de l'Incarnation, the writing of an autobiography did not threaten commercial enterprise or a teaching vocation. Sensitive events were alluded to without details that would compromise the mother or embarrass the children, and some matters were skipped over entirely.[2] With Maria Sibylla Merian, the "scandals" that marked the life were not side affairs. Spelling them out might have been a threat to her identity as naturalist, painter, and woman. Nor, she may well have thought, did her children need to have a record of what she had been through. Unlike Claude Martin, who sought from Marie de l'Incarnation the secrets of a father he had never known, Merian's daughters had seen it all at her side. Her self-concealment, I have suggested, was a condition of her liberty.

Family relations and experiences gave central shape to seventeenth-century lives, but displayed great range in practice. The reproductive rates of the three women show how culture and personal choice could affect the conditions of early modern fertility: Glikl with her fourteen pregnancies and twelve children; the young widow Marie, never remarried, with her one son; Maria Sibylla with her two daughters (and, as far as we know, only two pregnancies) stretched over twenty years of marriage. The amazing fecundity of Glikl and Haim is partly due to the seventeenth-century Jewish practice of very early marriage. The Graffs' decision to use some form of birth control took place in the decades during which Protestant couples in Geneva and England were trying the same thing.

Within all three marriages, hierarchical prescriptions for the wife's obedience were somewhat eroded by the experience of shared enterprise: the Hamburg jewelry and loan business, the Tours silk-making shop, the engraving and publishing of Nuremberg and Frankfurt. The way Marie Guyart told it, her husband also left her free for hours of religious devotion; and Johann Andreas Graff

clearly respected his wife's insect discoveries. But such accommo-
dations do not necessarily a contented marriage make. Only Glikl,
who first saw her husband the day of her betrothal, described years
of affectionate intimacy with a current of passion running through.
Marie "loved" her husband during their brief year or two together,
but there was also the dark cloud of his "disgrace" involving another
woman. As for Maria Sibylla, the marriage to a man she had known
for some years was ultimately a disaster, foundering perhaps on a
deep sexual incompatibility and surely on the religious split of her
conversion.

The unfeeling and distant parent who once frequented the histories of the early modern family does not appear in these households. The tone and pitch of mothering did vary, however. Counting
on early marriage rather than on delayed inheritance to set her
children off on a Jewish life, Glikl gave much open expression to
love, anxiety, anger, and grief to let her children know how she felt
and what she wanted of them. Not a quiet household. Unsuccessfully
feigning detachment from her son, Marie Guyart discussed him and
her responsibilities toward him endlessly with her confessors, and
finally with him through the safe medium of correspondence. The
childhood scenes they both recalled were of him crying and pro-
testing while she calmly stated God's will. Maria Sibylla's maternal
tone is harder to hear, though the affection with which Dorothea
spoke of her after her death may echo Maria Sibylla's own voice.
What is sure is that Merian won her daughters' loyalty as against
their father, even while giving them the wherewithal ultimately to
live lives of their own.

Merian also bequeathed to her daughters continuing ease in their
roles as artists and naturalists. Beyond that and her own impressive
example, she made no generalizations about women's capacities.
Marie de l'Incarnation went farther, not only inspiring her niece
Marie Buisson to be an Ursuline, but also drawing portrait after
portrait of French Ursulines and Amerindian women converts as
apostolic preachers and teachers. Glikl bas Judah Leib was charitable
and *"melumedet"* ("learned"), as her memorial notice called her,
and stepped beyond the limit of most Jewish women in her literary

experiment of "arguing with God." But the praise she bestowed on her daughter was only for Esther's generosity and piety. Glikl would serve as a stimulus to feminist innovation only to a relative two hundred years later.

There were some seventeenth-century contemporaries for whom the improvement of the status of women was the heart of all reform. In the wake of many *salonnière* claims about women's merits, the Cartesian François Poullain de La Barre published *De l'égalité des deux sexes* in Paris in 1673, the year after Marie de l'Incarnation's death in Québec. Mary Astell's *Serious Proposal to the Ladies for the Advancement of Their True and Greatest Interest* appeared in London in 1694, arguing for the establishment of a seminary to give "Learned Education" to women.[3]

Glikl, Marie, and Maria Sibylla, devoted though they were to female friends and relatives, did not have the promotion of women per se as their uppermost goal. But their stories reveal other possibilities in the seventeenth century, as they carved out their novel ways of living on the margins.

"Margins" in what sense? To begin with, these women were removed from the centers of political power, royal, civic, and senatorial, Glikl as a Jewish woman and Marie and Maria Sibylla as nonaristocratic women. They were certainly touched by the state and its rulers in important ways. Glikl bas Judah Leib and other Jews needed some kind of protecting monarch or government to survive. Credit agreements with court Jews like the Oppenheimers in Vienna could bring havoc or profit into Glikl's life; and with her second marriage to the royal trader Hirsch Levy in Metz, her economic stability was tied for a time to the French king. Marie de l'Incarnation and Marie Sibylla Merian could not have carried out their callings in Québec and Suriname without some European political presence in those lands. Merian wondered about patronage from Queen Anne of England for her *Metamorphosis*, looked for readers among the burgomeisters of Amsterdam, and surely must have appreciated Czar Peter's interest in her just before she died. As for actual political influence, only Marie de l'Incarnation had the chance to give advice to governors—and that in an informal way during her years in Canada. Glikl was limited to asking a court Jew for a favor.

The women were also at considerable remove from formal centers of learning and institutions for cultural definition. Glikl talked with scholars of Talmud mostly around a dinner table and heard them give sermons from the women's balcony. Marie de l'Incarnation talked with doctors of theology in the course of confession or in the convent yard or in correspondence (as with her son), and heard them preach as she sat in the convent chapel. Merian's learning came from books in the family library and then from a scholarly patron in Nuremberg. Closer to centers of scholarly exchange in her later years in Amsterdam—the botanical garden, cabinets of curiosities—she still could not frequent the university. In all three cases, cultural visions and artifacts—the storied autobiography, the mystical expression and New World writing, the life histories of insects on their plants—were created from a marginal place. But that place did not have the sterility or low quality assigned to the word "margin" in the modern economic usage that thinks in terms of profits. Rather, it was a borderland between cultural deposits that allowed new growth and surprising hybrids.

In their own way, each woman appreciated or embraced a marginal place, reconstituting it as a locally defined center. For Glikl, it was Jewish networks and *Gemeinde* that counted most. For Marie, it was her Ursuline house and convent yard of Amerindians and French in the Canadian woodlands far from the *politesse* of France. For Maria Sibylla, it was a Labadist settlement on the fringes of the Netherlands and then the rivers and rain forests of Suriname—not permanent stopping places, but life-changing nonetheless. In each case, the individual freed herself somewhat from the constrictions of European hierarchies by sidestepping them.

Margins were not, of course, just for women. Many European men were distanced from power centers for reasons of birth, wealth, occupation, and religion, and men sometimes chose or embraced marginal locations for themselves. Such were the male Jews (other than the court Jews) and missionary Jesuits, Labadists, and enthusiast-naturalists whom we have met in the pages of this book. But "women on the margins"—the case with the stronger suppression—can reveal with particular clarity what was at stake for the men and women both.

Centers and hierarchies cannot be escaped entirely. Michel Foucault had a good insight about the locus of power in the seventeenth century when he said that it should be conceptualized not only "in the primary existence of a central point, in a unique source of sovereignty," but as omnipresent in "force relations" throughout society.[4] Glikl bas Judah Leib, Marie Guyart de l'Incarnation, and Maria Sibylla Merian also carried power relations with them. In the case of Glikl, we looked at her relation with non-Jews; in the cases of all three women, we looked at their connections, imagined or real, with non-European peoples. Glikl put her energy into elaborating a bounded field, a literary *eruv*, that would sustain her, her family, and her fellow Jews within a world of Christian domination and danger. That was what was paramount for her in the tale of the pious Talmudist, in which she even devised an inverted world where Jews were on top. She did not stretch herself further in her storytelling to rethink the assumed superiority of Europeans to "savages." Her empathy with suffering did not flow to unseen places that lay so far beyond the *eruv*. (Would she perhaps have recast such a tale if she had been one of the Jewish women on a Suriname plantation, described as "chattering" all day with their African house-slaves? Or one of the members of an eighteenth-century congregation in Suriname, where a noticeable number of Jews were now *courlingen*—that is, free persons of color?)[5]

Marie de l'Incarnation and Maria Sibylla Merian found that the margins entailed real power relations with non-European peoples, Marie as matriarchal teacher to Amerindian women and men, Maria Sibylla as owner of African, Carib, and Arawak slaves. Drawing both from their experience as women, including conversations with women, and from their vocational stance—the missionary enthusiasm of the one, the scientific style of the other—they elaborated ways of thinking about non-Europeans that moderated European claims of superiority made by their male contemporaries: the extravagance of Marie de l'Incarnation's universalism, the indifference to savage/civilized classification in Maria Sibylla Merian's ethnographic observation.

Some historical perspectives might push us to seek a single set of rules about knowledge or representation that underlie the three approaches. Or failing that, to arrange the three approaches in a scale as "older" and "newer" or as more or less viable over time. Such interpretation should be resisted in favor of the full simultaneity of the three patterns. Variant patterns alert us to mobility, mixture, and contention in European cultures. They also leave space for the insertion of non-European eyes that return the Europeans' gaze, as we've seen in reconstructing the response of Khionrea and Uthirdchich to Marie de l'Incarnation and of Carib, Arawak, and African women to Merian.

The narrative order of this book—from Glikl bas Judah Leib to Marie de l'Incarnation to Maria Sibylla Merian—is different from the chronological one of history: the woman of Tours was born at least a generation before the two female contemporaries of Hamburg and Frankfurt. It seemed useful to portray the strategies of a Jewish life within Europe's uneasy confines before considering the paradoxes of Christian lives that expanded across the Atlantic into uncertain relations with Amerindians and Africans. But this analytical order is not a Woman's Progress, as though one style of life superseded the other the way Christians thought the church superseded the synagogue, the new covenant the old. Each life stands as an example, with its own virtues, initiatives, and faults, and seventeenth-century European motifs run through them all: melancholy, enhanced sense of self, curiosity, eschatological hope, the pondering of God's presence in and intentions for the universe. I have no favorite.

AT ONE TIME THEY were flesh and blood; then, what was left were memories, portraits, their writings, and their art. While Marie de l'Incarnation was being wrapped for the grave, all her prayer books, rosaries, medals, and garments were borne off as precious relics. Across the Atlantic in the Ursuline convent of Tours, her niece Marie Buisson saw her one last time in a vision.[6] The spiritual autobiography that she wanted burned was copied by Ursulines and, as we have seen, edited, added to, and published by her son, Claude Martin, along with her letters and other works. Thus, they spread to Ursuline houses and to other religious, such as the sisters of the Rosary and the Carmelites, whose signatures adorn the title pages of editions in convent libraries and rare-book rooms.[7] A manuscript of the autobiography was in the bags of a young Sulpician priest from France, Pierre Sartelon, when he came to Montréal in 1734, and it passed to the Ursulines of Trois-Rivières after a disastrous fire in 1806.[8] More than a century later Dom Albert Jamet published the Trois-Rivières manuscript, having been attracted to Marie by her mysticism, not by her role as a teacher. As for the Hurons, Algonquins, and Iroquois, whose souls it had been her mission to save, Jamet said elsewhere: "The northern Indian would never be anything but a big child . . . Today the facts are there. The Savages were refractory to civilization . . . They were not Christians by nature."[9]

Marie's manuscripts in Algonquin, Huron, and Iroquois, the most important testimony of her relation to the woodlands people, were given in the nineteenth century to missionaries for the Canadian north, according to Dom Guy Oury (who has written about Marie de l'Incarnation with great learning and without the racism of Jamet).[10] I hope that they found their way into Amerindian hands. Perhaps they exist somewhere, with a family history like that written by Paul Tsaouenkiki on a manuscript of Father Chaumonot's Huron-French dictionary: "This document was bequeathed to me by my father Paul Tahourhench, great captain of the Huron tribe established in 1697 at Notre Dame de la Jeune Lorette, near Québec. My father had it from his mother, La Ouinonkie, wife of Paul Ondaouenhout, who died around 1871 at the age of eighty-four."[11]

Maria Sibylla Merian's watercolors and publications were already widely known in Europe at the time she died, and this awareness spread as editions of the European *Caterpillars* and the Suriname *Metamorphosis* came out in Dutch, French, and Latin, two of them appearing as late as the 1770s.[12] Linnaeus referred to her books, used

"Merianella" as a trivial (or specific) name for one of the moths in his classification, and approved Queen Louisa Ulrika's collection of Merian insect pictures. He also listed Merian's copperplate editions among those that were threatening the natural sciences by their cost; "not a few Sons of Botany who are reared in modest circumstances are compelled to do without such high-priced books."[13]

Cost was no consideration for Peter the Great and his successors, who sent Dorothea Maria Gsell back to Amsterdam in 1736 to acquire more of her mother's watercolors for the collection of the Academy of Sciences in Saint Petersburg.[14] Displayed along with the Rembrandts in the *Kunstkammer*, Merian's paintings were surely a source for the subsequent interest in lepidoptera among the Russian military and officerial elites. Indeed, they were an inspiration to the writer Vladimir Nabokov in his life-long passion for collecting butterflies. He was about eight in 1907 when, rummaging around in the attic of the family country home not far from Saint Petersburg, he came across some books that had belonged to his maternal grandmother, herself something of a naturalist. He came downstairs with "glorious loads of fantastically attractive volumes," Maria Sibylla Merian's book on the insects of Suriname the first among them.[15]

In the Suriname of Johanna Helena Herolt, her mother's work also has some presence. There are two editions of the *Metamorphosis* today in the library of the Surinaams Museum. That institution got its start in the cabinets of curiosities of the eighteenth century, and persisted after Suriname's independence in 1975 in the remarkable seventeenth-century Fort Zeelandia. But survival of the objects and books in the museum was no simple matter in 1982, when the military regime that had seized power two years before took over Fort Zeelandia and ordered it cleared immediately. Curators had to pack up everything in great haste and defend their objects from theft. Since then the museum has had to operate out of reduced and provisional quarters, at least once with violence swirling outside its doors. Nonetheless, the Merian volumes, together with Waiyana wasp mats, Saramaka talking drums, and Javanese shadow puppets, are now part of a collection that Suriname intellectuals consider a "national heritage" for a multiethnic postcolonial society.[16]

The book of Glikl bas Judah Leib has also had its adventures. Passed down in family copies, the manuscript was printed in Yiddish in 1896 by the scholar David Kaufmann. Then, in 1910, Bertha Pappenheim took time out from her busy schedule as Jewish feminist, social worker, and reformer in Frankfurt to publish a German translation.[17] Much had changed in her life since, as a young woman, Pappenheim had been treated for nervous ailments by Marcel Breuer and he and Sigmund Freud had published her case as "Anna O." in their 1895 *Studies on Hysteria*. A few years later, she had translated Mary Wollstonecraft's *Vindication of the Rights of Women* into German.[18] Then it was Glikl's turn. "Glückel von Hameln," as Pappenheim called her (following the 1896 Yiddish edition), was a collateral relative: through her mother, Pappenheim was a descendant of Haim Hamel's sister Yenta.[19] More important, Glikl exemplified both the energetic independence and the family commitment that Pappenheim wanted to encourage in Jewish women in Germany in the first decades of the twentieth century. And, like Glikl, Pappenheim believed in the uses of storytelling, publishing a book of family stories for children in 1890 and a German translation of the Yiddish *Mayse Bukh* in 1929. Perhaps her own psychological suffering and the efforts to cure it left her open to the violence, passion, and insight of the Jewish tales. So closely did Bertha Pappenheim identify with Glikl that she had herself painted in what she imagined as Glikl's garb.[20]

Pappenheim's translation, published by her brother and a cousin in Vienna, was a complete version of Glikl's Yiddish. Occasionally Pappenheim germanified Glikl; for instance, "I turned down marriage offers from the most distinguished men in the whole of Ashkenaz" became "the whole of Germany" *("in ganz Deutschland")*.[21] But she was attentive to Glikl's text and kept many Yiddish features of her language.

Three years later, Alfred Feilchenfeld, a specialist in Jewish history, brought out another translation of Glikl. Since he thought her autobiography important only for what it revealed about Jewish families and how they lived in Germany, he eliminated all the folktales and moral commentary that "repeatedly interrupted" the biographical account.[22] Instead, he put two stories, wrenched from context, in an appendix as examples. (One psychoanalyst in Freud's circle, Theodor Reik, cited the Bird Story from his edition.)[23] Feilchenfeld also omitted Glikl's formulaic modifiers ("may the memory of his merits be a blessing") and changed the breaks between some of the books. This mutilation of Glikl's text may not have troubled assimilating middle-class German-Jewish readers and scholars of the "Science of Judaism." They may have been delighted to explore a German family past, but embarrassed by the Yiddish questioning of a seventeenth-century woman.[24]

Bertha Pappenheim had a different idea of what constituted a modern identity for the German-Jewish woman. She must have regretted the popularity of this other Glikl, which, published by the Jewish Publishing House of Berlin, went through four editions to 1923.[25] Then in Nazi times, all the editions of Glikl's autobiography—truncated, whole, Yiddish, German—got packed away in "poison coffers" with other undesirable books. I was glad to find they were on the shelves of the libraries in East and West Berlin in March 1990. I take it as a sign for the good that, like the third fledgling in the Bird Story, they made it to the other side.

NOTES

ACKNOWLEDGMENTS

ILLUSTRATION CREDITS

INDEX

NOTES

ARAH   Algemeen Rijksarchief, The Hague

ADM   Archives Départementales de la Moselle

ADIL   Archives Départementales d'Indre-et-Loire

AL   *The Life of Glückel of Hameln, 1646–1724, Written by Herself,* trans. and ed. Beth-Zion Abrahams (London: Horovitz Publishing, 1962; New York: Thomas Yoseloff, 1963)

AUQ   Archives des Ursulines de Québec

BN   Bibliothèque Nationale de France, Paris

Cor   Marie de l'Incarnation, *Correspondance,* ed. Dom Guy Oury (Solesmes: Abbaye de Saint-Pierre, 1971)

GAA   Gemeentearchief Amsterdam

JJ   Abbé Laverdière and Abbé Casgrain, eds., *Le Journal des Jésuites publié d'après le manuscrit original conservé aux archives du Séminaire de Québec,* 2nd ed. (Montréal: J. M. Valois, 1892)

JR   Reuben Gold Thwaites, ed., *The Jesuit Relations and Allied Documents,* 73 vols. (Cleveland: Burrows Brothers, 1896–1901)

JTS   Jewish Theological Seminary of America, New York

KM   *Die Memoiren der Glückel von Hameln, 1645–1719* (Yiddish), ed. David Kaufmann (Frankfurt am Main: J. Kaufmann, 1896)

MetD   Maria Sibylla Merian, *Metamorphosis Insectorum Surinamensium: ofte verandering der Surinaamsche Insecten* (Amsterdam: Maria Sibylla Merian and Gerard Valck, n.d. [1705])

MetL   Maria Sibylla Merian, *Metamorphosis Insectorum Surinamensium* (Amsterdam: Maria Sibylla Merian and Gerard Valck, 1705)

PM   *Die Memoiren der Glückel von Hameln,* trans. Bertha Pappenheim (Vienna: Stefan Meyer and Wilhelm Pappenheim, 1910)

Rau79   Maria Sibylla Merian, *Der Raupen wunderbare Verwandelung und sonderbare Blumen-nahrung* (Nuremberg: Johann Andreas Graff, 1679; Frankfurt and Leipzig: David Funk, 1679)

Rau83   Maria Sibylla Merian, *Der Raupen wunderbare Verwandelung und sonderbare Blumen-nahrung: Anderer Theil* (Frankfurt: Johann Andreas Graff, 1683; Nuremberg and Leipzig: David Funk, 1683)

Rel   Marie de l'Incarnation, "La Relation de 1654" in Dom Albert Jamet, ed., *Ecrits spirituels et historiques*, vol. 2 (Paris: Desclée de Brouwer, 1930; facsimile edition, Québec: Les Ursulines de Québec, 1985)

RSMer   Elizabeth Rücker and William T. Stearn, *Maria Sibylla Merian in Surinam* (London: Pion, 1982)

Rup13   Maria Sibylla Merian, *Der Rupsen Begin, Voedzel, En Wonderbaare Verandering* (Amsterdam: Maria Sibylla Merian and Gerard Valck, n.d. [1713?])

Rup14   Maria Sibylla Merian, *Der Rupsen . . . Tweede Deel* (Amsterdam: Maria Sibylla Merian and Gerard Valck, n.d. [1714?])

Rup17   Maria Sibylla Merian, *Derde En Laatste Deel Der Rupsen*, ed. Dorothea Maria Hendriks (Amsterdam: Dorothea Maria Hendriks, n.d. [1717])

SocSur   Archives of the Sociëteit van Suriname, Algemeen Rijksarchief, The Hague

StAF   Stadtarchiv, Frankfurt am Main

StAH   Staatsarchiv, Hamburg

Stud   Maria Sibylla Merian, *Schmetterlinge, Käfer und andere Insekten: Leningrader Studienbuch*, ed. Irina Lebedeva, Wolf-Dietrich Beer, and Gerrit Friese (Leipzig: Edition Leipzig, 1976; Lucerne: Reich Verlag, 1976)

SUBF   Stadt- und Universitätsbibliothek, Frankfurt am Main

SUBH   Staats- und Universitätsbibliothek, Hamburg

Vie   Marie de l'Incarnation and Claude Martin, *La Vie de venerable Mere Marie de l'Incarnation, Premiere Superieure des Ursulines de la Nouvelle France: Tirée de ses Lettres et de ses Ecrits* (Paris: Louis Billaine, 1677; facsimile edition Solesmes: Abbaye Saint-Pierre, 1981)

Arguing with God

1. The Yiddish text of Glikl's autobiography was first published by David Kaufmann, ed., *Die Memoiren der Glückel von Hameln, 1645–1719* (Frankfurt am Main: J. Kaufmann, 1896). A full and on the whole careful translation into German was done by Bertha Pappenheim, *Die Memoiren der Glückel von Hameln* (Vienna: Stefan Meyer and Wilhelm Pappenheim, 1910). A truncated German translation, with her stories omitted from the text (two are present, but only as appendixes) and with changes in Glikl's division of her books, was made not long afterward by Alfred Feilchenfeld, *Denkwürdigkeiten der Glückel von Hameln aus dem Jüdisch-*

Deutschen übersetzt (Berlin: Jüdischer Verlag, 1913), with further printings in 1914, 1920, 1923 (by the Jüdischer Verlag); in 1979 (Berlin: Verlag Darmstädter Blätter); and 1987 (Frankfurt am Main: Athenäum). Two English translations exist. One is by Marvin Lowenthal, with some of Glikl's stories restored to her text, but still incomplete and with some bowdlerizing of Glikl's words: *The Memoirs of Glückel of Hameln* (New York: Harper, 1932), new ed. with introduction by Robert S. Rosen (New York: Schocken Books, 1977; Schocken now plans a new translation). The other, made directly from the Yiddish by Beth-Zion Abrahams, is usually attentive to Glikl's meanings and ordering but omits one moral tale, a long quotation from an ethical text, and a reference to demons, among other brief excisions: *The Life of Glückel of Hameln, 1646–1724, Written by Herself* (London: Horovitz Publishing, 1962; New York: Thomas Yoseloff, 1963). For further discussion of these editions, see Dorothy Bilik, "The Memoirs of Glikl of Hameln: The Archaeology of the Text," *Yiddish*, 8 (Spring 1992): 1–18. Chava Turniansky of Israel is currently preparing a new and definitive Yiddish edition with Hebrew translation.

My citations from Glikl are assisted by the translations of Abrahams and Pappenheim, but in every case checked against and modified by the Kaufmann Yiddish edition. This is especially important in regard to translations that modernize or assimilate Glikl too much: for example, where Glikl says "the circumcised and the non-circumcised," Abrahams and Pappenheim translate "Jews and non-Jews" (KM, p. 160; PM, p. 149; AL, p. 87). Pappenheim keeps the formulaic modifiers that Glikl appends to many names—"may the memory of his merits be a blessing"—whereas Abrahams rarely includes these. For the bird story: KM, pp. 15–17; PM, pp. 13–14; AL, pp. 8–9.

2. Pierre Favre, *Mémorial*, trans. and ed. Michel de Certeau (Paris: Desclée de Brouwer, 1959), pp. 76–82, 208–209, 217–218. Michel de Certeau, *The Mystic Fable*, vol. 1: *The Sixteenth and Seventeenth Centuries*, trans. Michael B. Smith (Chicago: University of Chicago Press, 1992), pp. 188–193. In his approbation of the *Libro de la Vida*, Teresa's confessor wrote that it should be shown only to "men of learning and experience and Christian discretion" (Alison Weber, *Teresa of Avila and the Rhetoric of Femininity* [Princeton, N.J.: Princeton University Press, 1990], p. 77, n. 1). But this recommendation could not eliminate Teresa's female readers from her imagination as she wrote, nor the enthusiastic female readership her autobiography enjoyed in France. Michel de Certeau, "Jeanne des Anges," in Soeur Jeanne des Anges, *Autobiographie d'une hystérique possédée*, ed. Gabriel Legué and Gilles de la Tourette (Grenoble: Jérome Millon, 1990), pp. 300–344.

3. Michel de Certeau, *The Practice of Everyday Life*, trans. Steven F. Rendall (Berkeley: University of California Press, 1984), pp. 68–90.

4. On Glikl, see ML, pp. xiii–xl; N. B. Minkoff, *Glickel Hamel (1645–1724)* (New York: M. Vaxer Publishing, 1952; in Yiddish and praised by specialists);

Encyclopaedia Judaica, 16 vols. (Jerusalem: Keter Publishing, 1972), vol. 7, pp. 629–630; the bibliography at the back of Glikl Hamil, *Zichroines* (Buenos Aires: Arenes Literario en el Instituto Cientifico Judio, 1967); Daniel S. Milo, "L'Histoire juive entre sens et référence," in Daniel S. Milo and Alain Boureau, eds. *Alter histoire: Essais d'histoire expérimentale* (Paris: Les Belles Lettres, 1991), pp. 145–167; and the important essays by Dorothy Bilik, Günter Marwedel, and Chava Turniansky cited elsewhere in these notes. An overview of Jewish women in Germany in the seventeenth through nineteenth centuries is Monika Richarz, "In Familie, Handel und Salon: Jüdische Frauen vor und nach der Emanzipation des deutschen Juden," in Karin Hausen and Heidi Wunder, eds., *Frauen Geschichte-Geschlechtergeschichte* (Frankfurt am Main: Campos Verlag, 1992), pp. 57–66. On the history of Jewish women more generally, see Judith R. Baskin, ed., *Jewish Women in Historical Perspective* (Detroit: Wayne State University Press, 1991).

5. I follow here the spellings of Glikl's name by the recordkeeper of the Jewish Gemeinde (community) of Altona/Hamburg (Günter Marwedel, "Glückel von Hameln und ihre Familie in den Steuerkontenbüchern der Aschkenasischen Gemeinde Altona," in Peter Freimark, Ina Lorenz, and Günter Marwedel, *Judentore, Kuggel, Steuerkonten: Untersuchungen zur Geschichte der deutschen Juden, vornehmlich im Hamburger Raum* [Hamburg: Hans Christians Verlag, 1983], fig. 4a) and by the recordkeeper of the Jewish community at Metz in Glikl's death notice ("Pinkas Kehilat Mets," JTS, ms. 3670, fol. 3A).

6. ADM, 3E3708, no. 68, and 3E3728, no. 333: in Hebrew, "Esther, daughter of our teacher Haim Segal"; in the Latin alphabet, "Esther Goldschmidt." In both marriage contracts the French notary referred to her as "Esther Goldschmidt" with variant spellings. ADM, 3E4150, no. 761: in Hebrew, "Miriam, daughter of our teacher Haim." The French notary referred to her as "Marie Golschmit." Other Jewish women in Metz followed the same practice in signing marriage and other family contracts, whereas for business contracts they signed in Hebrew characters their Yiddish first names and their father's last names (ADM, 3E3692, 31 March 1701, 28 November 1701, 22 January 1702). Ashkenazic women in the Prague-Vienna area in the early seventeenth century signed their letters with reference to their fathers (Alfred Landau and Bernhard Wachstein, *Jüdische Privatbriefe aus dem Jahre 1619* [Vienna and Leipzig: Wilhelm Braumüller, 1911], p. xxv). Haim appeared on the list of Jews attending the Leipzig fairs as Hain Goldschmidt (Max Freudenthal, "Leipziger Messgäste," *Monatsschrift für Geschichte und Wissenschaft des Judentums*, 45 [1901]: 485), and at least some of his male descendants passed on that name. His son Moses, later rabbi of Baiersdorf, called himself Moses Hamel.

7. Marwedel, "Glückel von Hameln," pp. 72, 78, 91. ADM, 5E11115, fol. 46r. "Pinkas Kehilat Mets," JTS, ms. 3670, fol. 3A. Haim's gravestone in Altona reads: "Reb Haim of blessed memory, son of the leader Joseph Hamel Segal, may the memory of the righteous one be a blessing" (photograph, Institut für die Geschichte der deutschen Juden, Hamburg).

8. KM, p. 168; PM, p. 157; AL, p. 91. In the early modern period, Judah (Yehudah) was always associated with Leib in Yiddish speech, as in the Lion (that is, *leib* in Yiddish) of Judah. In the Grabbuch of the Jewish cemetery at Altona, the entry for Glikl's son Leib is "Jehuda Levi Hamel ben Haim," showing a further connection between the names of Glikl's father and Leib (Duplicat der Grabbücher of Altona, Institut für die Geschichte der deutschen Juden, Hamburg, no. 1221; Max Grunwald, *Hamburgs deutsche Juden bis zur Auflösung der Dreigemeinden 1811* [Hamburg: Alfred Janssen, 1904], p. 256, no. 1547).

9. KM, pp. 27–30; PM, pp. 25–29; AL, pp. 15–18. Glikl's memorial notice in Metz called her "daughter of Judah Joseph of Hamburg" (JTS, ms. 3670, fol. 3A). Kaufmann said the last name of Glikl's father was Pinkerle (KM, p. xvi), but did not give any grounds for that choice. Examining the list of Altona gravestones and other bits of not wholly consistent evidence, D. Simonsen concluded that Glikl's father was Joseph Judah Levi, son of Nathan, and that his family name was Pheiwel or Pheiweles, which became Philipps (D. Simonsen, "Eine Confrontation zwischen Glückel Hameln's Memoiren und den alten Hamburger Grabbüchern," *Monatsschrift für Geschichte und Wissenschaft des Judentums*, 49 [1905]: pp. 96–106). Since the evidence here is still quite uncertain, I am not referring to Glikl by her father's last name.

10. Werner Joachmann and Hans-Dieter Loose, eds., *Hamburg: Geschichte der Stadt und ihrer Bewohner*, vol. 1: *Von den Anfängen bis zur Reichsgründig*, ed. Hans-Dieter Loose (Hamburg: Hoffmann und Campe, 1982), pp. 259–350; Martin Reissmann, *Die hamburgische Kaufmannschaft des 17. Jahrhunderts in sozialgeschichtlicher Sicht* (Hamburg: Hans Christians Verlag, 1975); Mary Lindemann, *Patriots and Paupers: Hamburg, 1712–1830* (New York: Oxford University Press, 1990), especially the opening chapters.

11. Hermann Kellenbenz, *Sephardim an der unteren Elbe: Ihre wirtschaftliche und politische Bedeutung vom Ende des 16. bis zum Beginn des 18. Jahrhunderts* (Wiesbaden: Franz Steiner Verlag, 1958); Joachim Whaley, *Religious Toleration and Social Change in Hamburg, 1529–1819* (Cambridge: Cambridge University Press, 1985), pp. 70–80; Günter Böhm, "Die Sephardim in Hamburg," in Arno Herzig and Saskia Rohde, eds., *Die Juden in Hamburg, 1590 bis 1990* (Hamburg: Dölling und Galitz Verlag, 1991), pp. 21–40.

12. Irmgard Stein, *Jüdische Baudenkmäler in Hamburg* (Hamburg: Hans Christians Verlag, 1984), p. 39. On Isaac/Manuel Teixeira dining and gaming with a Danish general in Hamburg in the late 1680s, see Johann Dietz, *Master Johann Dietz*, trans. Bernard Miall (London: George Allen & Unwin, 1923), p. 176.

13. Johan Müller (Senior of the Lutheran clergy of Hamburg and pastor of Saint Peter's), *Einfältiges Bedenken von dem im Grund verderbten und erbärmlichen Zustande der Kirche Christi in Hamburg* (1648), in Christian Ziegra, *Sammlung von Urkunden, Theologischen und juristischen Bedenken . . . zur hamburgischen Kirchenhistorie*, 4 vols. (Hamburg: C. S. Schröder, 1764–1770), vol. 1, pp. 10–11; and *Bedenken wegen Duldung der Juden* (1649), ibid., pp. 98–114. More criticism from

the Lutheran clergy on 9 April 1650 (their open activities are "blasphemy to the sacrament of Our Lord"), StAH, Senat, Cl. VII, Lit. Hf., no. 5, vol. 1b, fasc. 1, fol. 13r; and during April 1669, Whaley, *Religious Toleration*, p. 78.

14. Grunwald, *Hamburgs deutsche Juden;* Whaley, *Religious Toleration*, pp. 80–93; and Günter Marwedel, "Die aschkenasischen Juden im Hamburger Raum (bis 1780)," in Herzig and Rohde, eds., *Juden in Hamburg*, pp. 61–75. The catalogue to which the Herzig and Rohde volume is an accompaniment is *Vierhundert Jahre Juden in Hamburg: Eine Ausstellung des Museums für Hamburgische Geschichte vom 8. 11. 1991 bis 29. 3. 1992* (Hamburg: Dölling und Galitz Verlag, 1991).

15. Stein, *Jüdische Baudenkmäler*, pp. 27, 48.

16. Günter Marwedel, ed., *Die Privilegien der Juden in Altona* (Hamburg: Hans Christians Verlag, 1976). Heinz Mosche Graupe, ed., *Die Statuten der drei Gemeinden Altona, Hamburg und Wandsbek* (Hamburg: Hans Christians Verlag, 1973), especially pp. 65–172. KM, pp. 23–27; PM, pp. 21–25; AL, pp. 13–15.

17. StAH, Cl. VII, Lit. Hf., no. 5, vol. 1b, fasc. 2, 37r–42r (depositions against the Jews, 1 March 1698). Whaley, *Religious Toleration*, pp. 82–83, 86–87. Graupe, *Statuten*, pp. 53–55, 209–251.

18. KM, pp. 26–33; PM, pp. 24–30; AL, pp. 15–19.

19. A. Lewinsky, "Die Kinder des Hildesheimer Rabbiners Samuel Hameln," *Monatsschrift für Geschichte und Wissenschaft des Judentums*, 44 (1900): 250, n. 1. Marwedel, "Glückel von Hameln," p. 72. On Hameln in the seventeenth century, a town of less than 5,000 persons, see Percy Ernst Schramm, *Neun Generationen: Dreihundert Jahre deutscher "Kulturgeschichte" im Lichte der Schicksale einer Hamburger Bürgerfamilie (1640–1948)*, 2 vols. (Göttingen: Vandenhoeck und Ruprecht, 1963–1964), vol. 1, pp. 59–74.

20. Figures on Christian German women and men marrying in their mid-twenties can be found in Heide Wunder, *"Er ist die Sonn,' sie ist der Mond": Frauen in der Frühen Neuzeit* (Munich: Verlag C. H. Beck, 1992), p. 48. The intendant Marc Antoine Turgot said of the Jews of Metz in 1699: "Ils marient leurs garçons à quinze ans et leurs filles à douze" (BN, ms. fr. nouv. acq. 4473, quoted by Robert Anchel, *Les Juifs de France* [Paris: J. B. Janin, 1946], pp. 154, 160). The Jewish Haim Hamel and the Lutheran Jobst Schramm, both traders born in Hameln and subsequently moving to Hamburg, make an amusing comparison: Haim, marrying Glikl when he was in his mid-teens, Jobst marrying Dorothea Lübke of Hamburg at age thirty-nine (Schramm, *Neun Generationen*, pp. 101–104). In Poland in the mid-eighteenth century, Jews were still marrying "in the thirteenth year" (Gershon Hundert, *The Jews in a Polish Private Town: The Case of Opatów in the Eighteenth Century* [Baltimore: Johns Hopkins University Press, 1992], p. 76), whereas a demographic study of the Jews of Lunéville in Lorraine at the end of the eighteenth century shows a shift toward a later age of marriage (Françoise Job, "Les Juifs dans l'état civil de Lunéville, 1792–1891:

Etude démographique—nuptialité, fécondité," in Gilbert Dahan, ed., *Les Juifs au regard de l'histoire: Mélanges en l'honneur de Bernhard Blumenkranz* [Paris: Picard, 1985], pp. 345–347).

21. Whaley, *Religious Toleration*, p. 84. KM, p. 190; PM, pp. 178–179; AL, p. 103.

22. Of the twelve children of Glikl and Haim who lived long enough to marry, Hendele died seventeen weeks after her marriage in Berlin and Zanvil died in Bamberg while his wife was pregnant with their first child. A daughter was born after Zanvil's death, and was flourishing at age thirteen in 1715, when Glikl was writing the opening pages of Book 7 of her *Life*.

23. Glikl mentions a "wet nurse" only once, when she was sick for a time after the birth of Hannah, but her health improved and she dismissed her. She specifically mentions nursing Zipporah at her breast, and there are other indications of direct nursing. KM, pp. 71–72, 129; PM, pp. 64–65, 119; AL, pp. 39–40, 71. On the death rates of children and the use of wet nurses in Germany, especially by Christian women of noble and prosperous families, see Wunder, *Frauen*, pp. 36–38.

24. KM, pp. 75, 80, 108–111 (p. 108: "gut gidanken" from "min Gliklikhen," "good thoughts" from "my little Glikl"); PM, pp. 69, 74, 98–102; AL, pp. 42, 44, 59–62. Marwedel, "Glückel von Hameln," p. 78. The ledger of contracts kept by the Jewish community of Worms in the seventeenth century shows women as storekeepers and as regular participants with their husbands in commercial transactions (Shlomo Eidelberg, *R. Juspa, Shammash of Warmaisa (Worms): Jewish Life in Seventeenth-Century Worms* [Jerusalem: Magnes Press, 1991], p. 98).

25. Zipporah married Kossman Gompertz, son of Elias Cleve, alias Gompertz, of Cleve, and resided in Amsterdam; Nathan married Miriam, the daughter of the late Elias Ballin, merchant and parnas of Hamburg; Hannah married the son of Haim's brother Abraham Hamel, who lived in Hannover and Hameln; Mordecai married the daughter of Moses ben Nathan, parnas of Hamburg, and resided in Hamburg, moving to London sometime after Glikl's departure; Esther married Moses Krumbach, alias Schwabe, son of the banker Abraham and the businesswoman Jachet/Agathe Gompertz, of Metz; Leib married the daughter of Hirschel Ries of Berlin, an in-law of Glikl's sister Mattie, and resided in Berlin until his business failure; Joseph married the daughter of Meyer Stadthagen of Copenhagen and resided in Copenhagen; Hendele married the son of the late Baruch, alias Benedikt Veit, a Viennese Jew who had moved to Berlin; Zanvil married the daughter of Moses Brillin of Bamberg and resided in Bamberg; Moses married the daughter of Samson Baiersdorf and resided in Baiersdorf as rabbi; Freudchen married Mordecai, son of the learned Moses ben Leib of Hamburg, and resided with him in Hamburg and eventually in London; on Miriam's marriage in Metz, see n. 48 below.

26. KM, p. 271; PM, p. 254; AL, p. 148.

27. KM, p. 199; PM, p. 189; AL, p. 108.

28. KM, pp. 124–125, 230; PM, pp. 114–115, 217; AL, pp. 69, 126. Glikl did not date the episode in which a Christian merchant, under advice from a Jewish merchant, brought a court case against Mordecai; but from its placement in her text and her comments, it seems to have happened quite soon after Haim's death. Early modern creditors always pressed on widows and "orphans." On the range in annual profits of the Christian merchants of Hamburg, see Reissmann, *Kaufmannschaft*, p. 241, n. 163.

29. Freudenthal, "Leipziger Messgäste," p. 485.

30. KM, pp. 30–31, 33; PM, pp. 28–29, 31; AL, pp. 17–19. Simonsen, "Confrontation," p. 100.

31. KM, pp. 30, 216; PM, pp. 27–28, 204; AL, pp. 17, 117. Cecilia, widow of Michel Hinrichsen, carried on his substantial business after he died in 1710 (Kellenbenz, *Sephardim*, p. 444). The widow of Jacob Sostmann, originally of Altona, carried on his tobacco-dressing establishment in Naskov, Denmark, after his death (Marwedel, *Privilegien*, p. 159, no. 22b, n. 1). Women were a small minority among Jewish traders attending the Leipzig fairs, but they were present: from 1668 to 1699 five Jewish women from Hamburg were named, along with about 240 Jewish men from Hamburg (Freudenthal, "Leipziger Messgäste," pp. 468, 484–487).

32. On Christian women in the urban economies of Germany, see Merry E. Wiesner, *Working Women in Renaissance Germany* (New Brunswick, N.J.: Rutgers University Press, 1986); Wunder, *Frauen*, ch. 5; and Rita Bake, *Vorindustrielle Frauenerwerbsarbeit: Arbeits- und Lebensweise von Manufactur arbeiterinnen im Deutschland des 18. Jahrhunderts unter besonderer Berücksichtigung Hamburgs* (Cologne: Pahl-Rugenstein Verlag, 1984), pp. 79–83, 145–148.

33. Selma Stern, *The Court Jew: A Contribution to the History of the Period of Absolutism in Central Europe*, trans. Ralph Weiman (Philadelphia: Jewish Publication Society of America, 1950), pp. 47–55, 184–185. Esther Schulhoff is the only woman mentioned in Selma Stern's book on the "court Jew." Heinrich Schnee, a specialist on court finance in the seventeenth and eighteenth centuries, says that "only a few women" can be found among the "thousands" of persons in the office of court factor (Heinrich Schnee, *Die Hoffinanz und der moderne Staat: Geschichte und System der Hoffaktoren an deutschen Fürstenhöfen im zeitalter des Absolutismus*, 4 vols. [Berlin: Duncker und Humblot, 1963] vol. 4, p. 148).

34. KM, p. 269; PM, p. 252; AL, p. 147: "With a heavy heart I myself went round the Börse, and then gave [the bills] to the brokers to sell for me." Eidelberg, *Juspa*, p. 40.

35. J. Dircksen's copperplate of the Hamburg Börse in 1661 has one woman sitting by herself within the yard (reproduced in Jochmann and Loose, eds., *Hamburg Geschichte*, vol. 1, pp. 240–241). Elias Galli's painting of the Börse, weigh house, and town hall (ca. 1680, Museum für Hamburgische Geschichte),

reproduced in this book, appears to have only one woman near the Börse yard. In contrast, in Galli's painting of street trade (*Der Messberg*, ca. 1670, Museum für Hamburgische Geschichte), most of the retail buyers and sellers are women. For an account of a Christian serving-woman at the Börse seeking a Jew with funds to lend her master, see KM, p. 240; PM, p. 226; AL, p. 132.

36. KM, pp. 275–277; PM, pp. 260–262; AL, pp. 150–152. StAH, Cl. VII, Lit. Hf, no. 5, vol. 1b, fasc. 2, fol. 5v; Marwedel, "Glückel von Hameln," pp. 79, 91. About the same time, many Sephardic Jews were moving away from Hamburg without paying their exit fees to the Sephardic Gemeinde, as we learn from a question put to the rabbi of Hamburg/Altona by the Gemeinde (Zevi Hirsch Ashkenazi, *Sefer She'elot u-Teshovot Chakham Zevi* [Amsterdam, 1712; reprinted New York: Gross Brothers, 1960], responsa 14).

37. François Yves Le Moigne, ed., *Histoire de Metz* (Toulouse: Privat, 1986), chs. 8–10; Patricia E. Behre, "Religion and the Central State in Metz, 1633–1700," Diss., Yale University, 1991.

38. Le Moigne, ed., *Metz*, pp. 227, 250, 260, 278. *Recueil des Loix, coutumes et usages observés par les Juifs de Metz* (Metz: Veuve Antoine et Fils, 1786). A. Cahen, "Le rabbinat de Metz de 1567 à 1871," *Revue des études juives*, 7 (1883): 103–116, 204–254; 8 (1884): 255–274. D. Kaufmann, "Extraits de l'ancien livre de la communauté de Metz," *Revue des études juives*, 18 (1889): 115–130. M. Ginsburger, "Samuel Levy, ein Stiefsohn der Glückel von Hameln," *Monatsschrift für Geschichte und Wissenschaft des Judentums*, 51 (1907) : 481–484. Gilbert Cahen, "La Région lorraine," in Bernhard Blumenkranz, ed., *Histoire des Juifs en France* (Toulouse: Privat, 1972), pp. 77–136; and Frances Malino, "Competition and Confrontation: The Jews and the Parlement of Metz," in Dahan, ed., *Juifs*, pp. 321–341. *Les Juifs lorrains: Du ghetto à la nation, 1721–1871. Exposition . . . organisée . . . par les Archives départementales de la Moselle . . . du 30 juin au 24 septembre 1990* (Metz: Association Mosellane pour la Conservation du Patrimoine Juif, 1990), pp. 9–52.

39. BN, N. acq. fr. 22705, fols. 95v–96r: Letter of 18 October 1707 on Jewish building; *Factum pour le corps et communauté des Marchands de la ville de Metz . . . Contre Joseph Levy et Lion de Bonne et Consorts, Juifs Habitans de Metz* (1695), fols. 62r–67r: *Factum, Pour Esther Norden, veuve de Joseph Cahen Iuif, Habitant de la ville de Metz, Plaignante et Appellante: Contre Jacques Durand Marchand Boucher* (1701); *Factum . . . Pour Iacques Durand marchand boucher Bourgeois de cette ville de Metz, Christine Perin sa Femme, et Iean François Durand . . . Prisonniers* (1701). Anchel, *Juifs*, pp. 170–174; Patricia E. Behre, "Jews and Christians in the Marketplace: The Politics of Kosher Meat in Metz," Paper presented to the annual meeting of the American Historical Association, Washington D.C., December 1992.

40. Joseph Reinach, *Une erreur judiciaire sous Louis XIV: Raphaël Lévy* (Paris: Librairie Charles Delagrave, 1898), contemporary Christian and Jewish texts on

the ritual-murder case of 1669 published at an important moment in the *affaire Dreyfus*. Patricia E. Behre, "Raphael Levy—'A Criminal in the Mouths of the People,'" *Religion*, 23 (1993): 19–44. Meyer Schwabe, the accused, was the father of Abraham Schwabe (*Un obituaire israélite: Le "Memorbuch" de Metz (vers 1575–1724)*, trans. Simon Schwarfuchs [Metz: Société d'Histoire d'Archéologie de la Lorraine, n.d.], p. 54, no. 611) and grandfather of Moses Schwabe, husband of Esther bas Chaim. *Memoire pour Me Jean Aubry, Procureur du Roy au . . . Siège Presidial . . . de Metz, Opposant; Contre M. Lamy, Conseiller Honoraire au Parlement . . .* (BN, N. acq. fr. 22705, fols. 97v–98v): "he spread a rumor in town that the Jews had slit the throat of a Christian child and had killed him, which led to insults from the *menu peuple* against the Jews in this town and even against those living in the countryside." This charge did not lead to a prosecution.

41. Marc Antoine Turgot, *Mémoire rédigé pour l'instruction du Dauphin* (1700) cited in *Juifs lorrains*, p. 43, no. 123; and Anchel, *Juifs*, pp. 154, 169–170.

42. Anchel, *Juifs*, ch. 7; Cahen, "La Région lorraine."

43. From ADM, 3E3692: Loans made by Catherine Morhange (1701, fol. 75r), Ainée or Enée Zaye (signs in Hebrew "Hindele Zaye," 1701, fol. 199r; 1702, fols. 22v, 167r); the wife of David Lorey, Jew (1702, fol. 41v); the wife of Lyon de Nofve, Jew (1702, fol. 78v), wife of Aron Alphen (1702, fol. 169v). From 3E3693, no. 8, 10 May 1702: Magdelaine, widow of Josué Trenel, Jew, summons Dame Suzanne Lespinal, wife separated from Pierre de Sorneville, regarding debts of 50£ and 56£. The 1715 memorial notice of Nentche Asnat, daughter of Abraham Halphen, describes her as supporting her whole household and trading in honesty so that her husband could study (*Memorbuch*, p. 71, no. 777). Glikl does not mention any business activity on the part of her daughter Esther or the daughters or daughters-in-law of Hirsch Levy. On the other hand, in the 1717 proceedings against Samuel Levy for fraudulent bankruptcy in Lunéville, his Jewish and Christian creditors had both Samuel and his wife, Anne Schwabe, imprisoned, which suggests that at least her money was involved, though she is not described as an active partner. *Responses de Samuel Levy, Juif, détenu és Prisons Civiles de la Conciergerie du Palais, Défendeur; Aux Contredits Des Syndics de ses Créanciers Chrétiens, Demandeurs* (1717), p. 2 (BN, N. acq. fr. 22705).

44. KM, p. 296: "rikhtig taytsh ars mir ays geleyrnt hot." Kaufmann explicates this as "die aufrichtige deutsche Art, im Gegensatz zu dem französischen Metz" (n. 1) and Pappenheim accepts this translation, PM, p. 278: "the frank German way I had been taught," AL, p. 160. Glikl uses "taytsh" to mean both "Yiddish" and "German," but here (as Kaufmann suggests) she must mean German ways that she had learned back in Hamburg. The women she was responding to when she used the phrase could all speak Yiddish. The contrast here is with styles of politeness in the two areas.

45. KM, pp. 183–184, 210, 295–302; PM, pp. 172–173, 199–200, 278–284; AL, pp. 98–99, 114, 116, 160–164. The first wife of Hirsch ben Isaac Abraham

was Blumchen bas Joshua, who died 13 May 1699 (*Memorbuch*, pp. 48–49, no. 556). See Ginsburger, "Samuel Levy," pp. 484–485, on the two sons and five daughters of Hirsch Levy. By 1700 Samuel was already married to Hendele/Anne Schwabe, by a contract drawn up between the Levys and the Schwabes in 1681, when Samuel was three (ADM, 3E3694, no. 153, 1 May 1703). By 1700 Hendele Sarah/Anne was already married to Isaiah Willstadt, also known as Isaye Lambert the Younger, and by 1709 the couple were arranging a marriage for their daughter Rachel (ADM, 3E4108, no. 92, Hebrew contract of 22 July 1709, French contract of 26 June 1710). Gittele Bilhah, also known as Frumet, seems also to have been married and in her own household well before her death in 1709 (KM, p. 298; *Memorbuch*, p. 60, no. 668). The other three daughters, Hannah, Sarah Rebecca, and Ellechen, were probably still at home with Glikl's Miriam.

46. KM, pp. 300–301, 310; PM, pp. 282, 292; AL, pp. 163, 169. Kaufmann, "Einführendes," in KM, p. xxv, n. 1 (a number of "good Christians" who had lent to Levy lost money at his bankruptcy); Anchel, *Juifs*, p. 196. For the acts in which Cerf Levy was summoned by his creditors, failed to appear, and then through his agent Abraham Schwabe settled his debts, see ADM B2729, Audience of the Bailliage of Metz, January–April 1702, fols. 16r–19v, 22r; 3E3692, fol. 63r, 26 February 1702; 3E3694, nos. 16–17, 74, 115 (12 December 1702), 132 (14 February 1703).

47. "Pinkas Kehilat Metz," JTS, ms. 3670, fol. 3A.

48. Sometime in these years Miriam bas Chaim married Moses, son of the horse dealer Isaiah Willstadt, known also as Isaye Lambert the Elder, and of Sarah Cahen (parents identified in ADM, 3E3695, 1704–1705, fols. 22v–23r, 20 September 1720, and 3E4108, 104bis, 1712). Her father-in-law is not to be confused with a younger relative named Isaye Lambert, alias Isaiah Willstadt, the wealthy banker who married Hirsch Levy's daughter Hendele/Anne. Miriam's husband, Moses, is described in the marriage contract of their son as having horses, carriages, and other equipment for his business (ADM, 3E4150, no. 761, 14 December 1730). Miriam's marriage was not as brilliant as that of her older sister Esther, who wed the banker Moses Schwabe.

49. KM, pp. 313–318; PM, pp. 294–300; AL, pp. 171–174. Samuel was initially joined in Lorraine by his brother-in-law Isaye Lambert the Younger. Lambert returned to Metz, however, in the wake of Louis XIV's order. See Anchel, *Juifs*, pp. 194–203, on the whole affair.

50. *Memorbuch*, p. 65, no. 712, death notice of Hirsch Levy, 24 July 1712. ADM, 3E4150, no. 761: marriage contract for Haim Lambert, son of Moses Lambert and Miriam Goldschmidt, in 1730. Betrothal (1712) and marriage (1716–1717) of Elias Schwabe, son of Moses Schwabe and Esther Goldschmidt, to Karen Lemlen, daughter of Mayer Lemlen of Mannheim (KM, p. 313; PM, p. 294; AL, p. 171; ADM, 3E3709, no. 305). *Responses de Samuel Levy, Juif*, p. 3. ADM, 5E11115, fol. 46r: "Guelic veuve de Cerf Levy decedée Ledit jour, 19 septembre

1724" and "Pinkas Kehilat Mets," JTS, ms. 3670, fol. 3A: "She died and was buried with a good name on the second day of Rosh Hashanah, 5485."

51. KM, pp. 1, 3–4; PM, pp. 1, 3; AL, pp. 1–2. Also on her writing and melancholy, "Although perhaps the whole affair [between Haim and Judah Berlin] was not worth writing, like my whole book, I write to while away the time when vain melancholy thoughts [*misige malekuleshe gedanken*] come to plague me." (KM, p. 121; PM, p. 112; AL, p. 67).

52. Leon Modena, *The Autobiography of a Seventeenth-Century Venetian Rabbi: Leon Modena's "Life of Judah,"* trans. and ed. Mark R. Cohen (Princeton, N.J.: Princeton University Press, 1988). I have considered some of the issues in Jewish autobiography of the early modern period in "Fame and Secrecy: Leon Modena's *Life* as an Early Modern Autobiography," ibid., pp. 50–70. An autobiographical fragment by Abraham Yagel is found in *A Valley of Vision: The Heavenly Journey of Abraham ben Hananiah Yagel*, trans. and ed. with an important introduction by David Ruderman (Philadelphia: University of Pennsylvania Press, 1990), pp. 1–70. Asher Halevi, *Die Memoiren des Ascher Levy aus Reichshofen im Elsass (1598–1635)*, trans. and ed. M. Ginsburger (Berlin: Louis Lamm, 1913). Samuel ben Jishaq Tausk, *Megillat Samuel* (in a beautiful flowered-paper binding from the early eighteenth century, SUB, ms. hebr. oct. 37), is discussed, along with other autobiographical texts in Yiddish, by Israel Zinberg, *A History of Jewish Literature*, vol. 7: *Old Yiddish Literature from Its Origins to the Haskalah Period*, trans. Bernard Martin (Cincinnati and New York: Hebrew Union College Press and Ktav Publishing, 1975), pp. 240–241. On *Megillat Sefer*, the eighteenth-century autobiography of the rabbi Jacob Emden, son of Zevi Hirsch Ashkenazi, rabbi of Altona/Hamburg, see David Kaufmann, "Zu R. Jakob Emdens Selbstbiographie," in *Gesammelte Schriften*, ed. M. Brann (Frankfurt am Main: Kommissions-Verlag von J. Kauffmann, 1915), pp. 138–149; and Alan Mintz, *"Banished from Their Father's Table": Loss of Faith and Hebrew Autobiography* (Bloomington, Ind.: Indiana University Press, 1989), pp. 9–10. A French translation of the *Megillat Sefer* is now available: Jacob Emden, *Mémoires de Jacob Emden ou l'anti-Sabbataï Zevi*, trans. Maurice-Ruben Hayoun (Paris: Les Editions du Cerf, 1992).

53. Leon Modena, *Autobiography*, p. 75. KM, pp. 67–68; PM, p. 60: AL, p. 37. The copy of Glikl bas Judah Leib's autobiography made by her son Moses Hamel, rabbi of Baiersdorf, is at the SUBF, ms. hebr. oct. 2. It remained in the hands of his son Haim, who added a note on the title page, and then passed to other relatives in the late eighteenth century. By the middle of the nineteenth century, the manuscript belonged to the great collector Rabbi Abraham Merzbacher of Munich and was used by Kaufmann for his 1896 edition. Only later did it go to Frankfurt with the rest of the Merzbacher collection. In Kaufmann's day, a second manuscript copy was extant, then in the possession of Theodor Hecht of Frankfurt am Main and now lost (Kaufmann, "Vorwort," vii–viii). There must have been other copies in the eighteenth century, starting with the now lost original, which

was presumably in the possession of Esther bas Haim. Jacob Emden's autobiography began with a life of his grandfather and especially of his father, the noted rabbi Zevi Hirsch Ashkenazi; among his reasons for writing "the account of [his] own life" was "the imperious need to relate to my descendants what has happened to me insofar as it is possible" (Emden, *Mémoires*, pp. 66–146, 150–151).

54. StAH, 622–1, Familie Rotermundt, vols. 1–2: twelve calendars, all printed in Nuremberg, from 1660 to 1682, in which Rotermundt has recorded various pieces of family, personal, and business news. StAH, 622–1, Familie Peter Lütkens, BVIII, two printed calendars for 1687 and 1688, with family and other news recorded in the blank column.

55. A Jewish account book in Yiddish, with some French entries, from Metz, 1694–1705, is at the JTS, ms. 3945. A seventeenth-century travel ledger in Yiddish, with listings of the value of currency in different places and the prices of books, is at SUBF, cod. hebr. 221.

56. Israel Abrahams, ed., *Hebrew Ethical Wills* (Philadelphia: Jewish Publication Society of America, 1976), foreword by Judah Goldin; Davis, "Fame and Secrecy," pp. 56–57. KM, pp. 170, 264–267; PM, pp. 159, 249–251; AL, p. 92, excerpt from the *Yesh Nochalin* omitted from p. 146. The *Yesh Nochalin* was a widely read work by the learned Abraham Halevi Horowitz: "a kind of testament which the aged Horowitz left for his children and in which he gives them ethical instruction and teaches them how to follow the right path" (Zinberg, *Jewish Literature*, vol. 6: *The German-Polish Cultural Center*, p. 56). Glikl misidentified the author as Abraham's son Isaiah, who had edited at least one of his father's moral works and perhaps was responsible for the edition of the *Yesh Nochalin* published at Prague in 1615. See below, on her relation to this text.

57. Anna Maria van Schurman, *Eukleria, seu melioris partis electio: Tractatus Brevem Vitae ejus Delineationem exhibens* (Altona: Cornelius van der Meulen, 1673). Schurman wrote a second part to her *Eukleria*, which was published posthumously in Amsterdam in 1684. On the text, see most recently Mirjam de Baar, " 'Wat nu het kleine eergeruchtje van mijn naam betreft . . .': De Eukleria als autobiografie," in Mirjam de Baar, Machteld Löwensteyn, Marit Monteiro, and A. Agnes Sneller, eds., *Anna Maria van Schurman, 1607–1678: Een uitzonderlijk geleerde vrouw* (Zutphen: Walburg Pers, 1992), pp. 98–107. The Labadist community lived in Altona from 1672 to 1674. They did some moneychanging through a Jewish family of Altona/Hamburg and ended up prosecuting a Hamburg Jew for withholding their money (T. J. Saxby, *The Quest for the New Jerusalem: Jean de Labadie and the Labadists, 1610–1744* [Dordrecht: Martinus Nijhoff, 1987], p. 227).

58. *Leben Frauen Johanna Eleonora Petersen, Gebohrner von und zu Merlau, Hrn D. Jo. Wilh. Petersens Ehe liebsten; Von Ihr selbst mit eigener Hand aufgesetzet, und vieler erbaulichen Merckwürdigkeiten wegen zum Druck übergeben* (no place or publisher, 1718). The revelation of 1664 about the conversion of the Jews is on p. 49,

paragraph 33. The *Leben* is printed with separate title page, frontispiece, and pagination after the *Lebens-Beschreibung* of her husband, the celebrated Pietist Johann Wilhelm Petersen (n.p.: "At the expense of a good Friend," 1717). There was a second anonymous printing of both works in 1719. On religious autobiography in seventeenth- and eighteenth-century Germany, see Georg Misch, *Geschichte der Autobiographie*, 4 vols. (Frankfurt am Main: G. Schulte-Bulmke, 1949–1970), vol. 4, pp. 807–817. On autobiographies and family histories by women, see Wunder, *Frauen*, pp. 27–31; and on the *Lebensläufe* developed by the German Pietists and carried across the ocean to America, see Katherine M. Faull, "The American *Lebenslauf*: Women's Autobiography in Eighteenth-Century Moravian Bethlehem," *Yearbook of German-American Studies*, 27 (1992): 23–48.

59. Yosef H. Yerushalmi, *Zakhor: Jewish History and Jewish Memory* (Seattle: University of Washington Press, 1982), chs. 1–2. Davis, "Fame and Secrecy."

60. Yosef Kaplan, *From Christianity to Judaism: The Story of Isaac Orobio de Castro*, trans. Raphael Loewe (Oxford: Oxford University Press, 1989), pp. 212–215, 328–343, 362–377. Uriel da Costa's *Exemplar humanae vitae* of 1640 is built around his conversion to the religion of his ancestors and his subsequent disenchantment with rabbinically controlled Judaism (first published in Philippus van Limborch, *De Veritate Religionis Christianae Amica Collatio cum Erudito Judaeo* [Gouda: Justus ab Hoeve, 1687], pp. 346–354; reprinted with translation in Uriel da Costa, *Três Escritos*, ed. A. Moreira de Sa [Lisbon: Instituto de Alta Cultura, 1963], pp. 36–69).

61. J. Kracauer, "Rabbi Joselmann de Rosheim," *Revue des études juives*, 16 (1888): 84–105. The journal opens in 1471 with the terrible actions against his relatives or other Jews that he has heard about from his parents or read about; from 1510 on, the entries recount what he has seen or experienced, including imprisonment, and his many efforts as a Jewish leader to protect the Jews. Yagel, *Valley of Vision*, pp. 1–2, 16–20.

62. Zinberg, *Jewish Literature*, vol. 6, pp. 50, 56. Davis, "Fame and Secrecy," pp. 58–60.

63. Leon Modena, *Autobiography*, pp. 122–124, 222–239.

64. Emden, *Mémoires*, p. 92; David Kaufmann, "Rabbi Zevi Ashkenazi and His Family in London," *Transactions of the Jewish Historical Society of England*, 3 (1896–98): 112 and n. 54. The reading of the Talmud was prohibited in ordinances of 1650 and 1710: *Neue-Reglement der Judenschafft in Hamburg* (Hamburg: Conrad Neumann, 1710), p. 14, article 5; and Ziegra, *Sammlung*, pp. 63, 131. The Jews were supposed to confine themselves to the Old Testament.

65. David Hanau, "our teacher, the scholar, and our master," had been rabbi of the Ashkenazic community of Hamburg/Altona during Glikl's youth and married to her maternal aunt Ulka (KM, pp. 31–32; PM, pp. 29–30; AL, p. 18). But the first rabbi of European prominence to come to Altona was Zevi Hirsch ben Jacob Ashkenazi (1660–1718). After studying under his father and maternal

grandfather in Hungary, Zevi Hirsch was sent to Salonika to be trained by Sephardic scholars. In 1685 the Jews of Constantinople bestowed the title of "hakham" upon Zevi Hirsch and subsequently he used that Sephardic title instead of
rabbi, while simultaneously adding "Ashkenazi" to his name. After a time as
hakham to the Sephardic community at Sarajevo, he went briefly to Berlin, where
he took as his second wife the daughter of Zalman Mirels, rabbi of the Ashkenazic
Jews of the three communities of Altona, Hamburg, and nearby Wandsbeck.
Hakham Zevi then lived in Altona from 1690 to 1710, teaching in a yeshivah
created for him by the Gemeinde and sending responsa to congregations all over
Europe. Ashkenazi, *Sefer She'olot*, responsa 93, on the golem. (Zevi Hirsch's
ancestor Elijah of Chelm had created a golem through kabbalistic incantations
and then had killed it. Elijah would not have killed it if it had been human; since
it was not human, a golem could not be part of a minyan.) On Zevi Hirsch
Ashkenazi, see the introductory essay by Maurice-Ruben Hayoun in Emden, *Mémoires*, pp. 10–40; and the biography by his son Jacob Emden, ibid., pp. 65–146.
See also *Encylopaedia Judaica*, vol. 3, pp. 734–735; and Kaufmann, "Rabbi Zevi
Ashkenazi."

66. Haim's studious brother Abraham had already been sent to school in
Poland and had himself become a celebrated teacher in Poznan. After Haim's
death Glikl sent her son Joseph to Poland to study the Talmud, but when the
teacher turned out to be a crook she hired "an honest teacher" to teach him in
Hamburg. Zanvil refused to study, but Moses "studied well," so Glikl sent him
to Frankfurt to study in the talmudic school there (KM, pp. 62, 231–234, 248–
249; PM, pp. 55, 218–221, 234; AL, pp. 34, 126–128, 137). Glikl says nothing
specifically about the education of her daughters. She does mention, in talking of
her husband's final illness, that she had "a worthy teacher" in the house and
summoned him to Haim's deathbed (KM, p. 199; PM, p. 189; AL, p. 108). Presumably he was instructing the younger children in the family, girls as well as
boys.

67. KM, pp. 24, 26, line 3: "Heder"; KM, pp. 22, 23; AL, p. 13 ("had his
daughters taught," rather than the correct "sons as well as his daughters"), p. 14.
Reference to the Heder in the 1685 statutes of the Ashkenazic Gemeinde in
Graupe, *Die Statuten*, no. 142, p. 148; no. 145, p. 149; to private teachers in the
household, no. 189, p. 130.

68. KM, p. 13: "oym taytshen," p. 264: "taytsh." On the state of the Yiddish
language in Glikl's day, and on its history in general, see the classic study by
Max Weinreich, *History of the Yiddish Language*, trans. Shlomo Noble and Joshua
A. Fishman (Chicago: University of Chicago Press, 1980), pp. 315–321, especially
on the difference between Yiddish and German in the "Middle Yiddish" period
(1500–1750) and on names for Yiddish. See also Leo Fuks, "On the Oldest Dated
Work in Yiddish Literature," in Uriel Weinreich, ed., *The Field of Yiddish:
Studies in Yiddish Language, Folklore, and Literature* (New York: Linguistic Circle

of New York, 1954), p. 269; and Jerold C. Frakes, *The Politics of Interpretation: Alterity and Ideology in Old Yiddish Studies* (Albany: SUNY Press, 1989). An important historical and linguistic view of Yiddish is Benjamin Harshav, *The Meaning of Yiddish* (Berkeley: University of California Press, 1990). Harshav would name the language of Glikl and her contemporaries in Hamburg and Metz "Western Yiddish," since it was still relatively free of the Slavic borrowings characterizing central and eastern European Yiddish after her day (pp. 29–30).

69. In general on this literature, see M. Steinschneider, *Jewish Literature from the Eighth to the Eighteenth Century* (London: Longman, 1857; reprint New York: Hermon Press, 1970), pp. 224–225, 235–238, 243–250; Max Grünbaum, *Jüdisch-deutsche Chrestomathie: Zugleich ein Beitrag zur Kunde der hebräischen Literatur* (Leipzig: F. A. Brockhaus, 1882); Zinberg, *Jewish Literature*, vol. 7: *Old Yiddish Literature from Its Origins to the Haskalah Period;* and Menahem Schmelzer, "Hebrew Printing and Publishing in Germany, 1650–1750: On Jewish Book Culture and the Emergence of Modern Jewry," *Leo Baeck Institute Year Book*, 3 (1988): 369–383.

70. Glickl on the *Brantshpigl* and the *Lev Tov*, KM, p. 13; PM, p. 11; AL, p. 7. Grünbaum, *Chrestomathie*, pp. 230–238; Zinberg, *Jewish Literature*, vol. 7, pp. 157–164, 241–242.

71. On *Ayn Schoyn Fraun Buchlayn*, see Grünbaum, *Chrestomathie*, pp. 265–277; and Zinberg, *Jewish Literature*, vol. 7, pp. 142–144. An edition of the *Korbonets* (that is, "oblation," a name given to this kind of prayer book for women) was prepared by Avigdor ben Moses, also known as Rabbi Izmuns; see Ulf Haxen, "Manuscripts and Printed Books from the Collection of The Royal Library, Copenhagen," in *Kings and Citizens: The History of the Jews in Denmark* (New York: Jewish Museum, 1983), vol. 2, pp. 27–28, no. 26. On Yiddish translations from and paraphrases of the Bible and the *Tse'enah u-re'enah*, see Johann Christoph Wolf, *Bibliotheca Hebraea*, 4 vols. (Hamburg and Leipzig, 1715–1732), vol. 2 (Hamburg: Theodor. Christoph. Felginer, 1721), pp. 453–460; Grünbaum, *Chrestomathie*, pp. 192–223; Zinberg, *Jewish Literature*, vol. 7, chs. 4–5; *Tzeenah U-Reenah: A Jewish Commentary on the Book of Exodus*, trans. Norman C. Gore (New York: Vantage Press, 1965), Introduction; and Dorothy Bilik, "*Tsene-rene:* A Yiddish Literary Success," *Jewish Book Annual*, 51 (1993–1994): 96–111. A well-worn copy of the *Tse'enah u-re'enah* at the Royal Library of Copenhagen (Jid-1422) has woodcut illustrations of biblical events, including one of the Tower of Babel colored in by an owner, and much marginalia.

72. Zinberg, *Jewish Literature*, vol. 7, pp. 229–241, 267–272, and ch. 7; Grunwald, *Hamburgs deutsche Juden*, p. 155, no. 54a; Grünbaum, *Chrestomathie*, pp. 385–458; Reinach, *Raphaël Lévy*, pp. 139–194. *Ma'aseh Book: Book of Jewish Tales and Legends*, trans. and introd. Moses Gaster (Philadelphia: Jewish Publication Society, 1981). The first known edition of the *Mayse Bukh* was printed in Basel in 1602, but it is likely that there were earlier editions. Already in 1611,

there was a German translation by the Christian Hebraist Christoph Helwig (Helvicius): *Jüdische Historien oder Thalmudische Rabbinische wunderbarliche Legenden* (Giessen: Caspar Chemlein, 1611).

73. Chava Weissler, " 'For Women and for Men Who Are Like Women': The Construction of Gender in Yiddish Devotional Literature," *Journal of Feminist Studies in Religion*, 5 (Fall 1989): 8–13. Zinberg, *Jewish Literature*, vol. 7, pp. 69, 87, 96, 124–126.

74. On the cursive Hebrew characters, called Weiber-Taitsh, or wayberish-Daytsh, or Vayber-Taytsh, taught to women and used for printing in Yiddish, see *Ma'aseh Book*, pp. xxviii–xxix; Zinberg, *Jewish Literature*, vol. 7, p. 27, n. 27, and p. 133; and Harshav, *Meaning of Yiddish*, p. 81. *Ayn Schoyn Fraun Buchlayn* (Basel, 1602; copy Bayerische Staatsbibliothek, Munich) is printed in this cursive, with paragraph headings and numbers in the semicursive typeface. In letters by Prague Jews in 1619, the handwriting of women and men can be distinguished (Landau and Wachstein, *Privatbriefe*, xx).

75. Marc Saperstein, *Jewish Preaching, 1200–1800: An Anthology* (New Haven, Conn.: Yale University Press, 1989), pp. 39–44, and p. 40, n. 37. "Vernacular sermons" were frequent and had this mixture of Yiddish (or other vernacular) and Hebrew.

76. KM, p. 264; PM, p. 249; passage not translated in AL, p. 146, n. 1. Glikl used the Hebrew word *seyfer* to refer to the *Yesh Nochalin* as she would use it for any religious book in the Holy Tongue, reserving the word *bukh* for books in Yiddish or German (see Harshav, *Yiddish*, 14). On the "worthy teacher" in the employ of Haim and Glikl and the tutor hired later for Joseph, see n. 66 above.

77. KM, p. 279; PM, p. 264; AL, p. 153. *Memorbuch*, p. 80, no. 851; p. 54, no. 611; p. 61, no. 676; and A. Cahen, "Le rabbinat de Metz pendant la période française," *Revue des études juives*, 8 (1884): 259–260 (school founded by Jachet's husband, Abraham Schwabe, in their residence). Baron David Guenzburg Collection, Moscow, Russian State Library, ms. 765, section of the Talmud copied by Hendele Schwabe, wife of Samuel Levy, Colmar [1705–1706], Institute of Microfilmed Hebrew Manuscripts, National University Library, Jerusalem. According to Abraham David, curator of the Institute, almost all the treatises of the Talmud in Guenzburg 754–755 were also copied by Hendele.

78. Chava Turniansky, "Literary Sources in the Memoirs of Glikl Hamel [in Yiddish]," in Israel Bartal, Ezra Mendelsohn, and Chava Turniansky, *Studies in Honour of Chone Shmeruk* (Jerusalem: Zalman Shazar Center for Jewish History, 1993), pp. 153–177. Similar doubts were expressed by Alfred Landau, "Die Sprache der Memoiren Glückels von Hameln," *Mittelungen der Gesellschaft für Jüdische Volkskunde*, 7 (1907): 20–68, especially 23–29.

79. The notes throughout Kaufmann, *Memoiren*, give some idea of the breadth of Glikl's reference. Leon, *Life of Judah*, p. 79. Yizkor notice for Glikl: JTS, ms. 3670, fol. 3A. There are roughly 425 memorial notices for women from

the end of the sixteenth century to 1724 in the published *Memorbuch*. In the first years, a number of women are referred to as *rabbine*, but this is a conventional reference for the daughter or sometimes the wife of a rabbi or parnas of the Gemeinde. In a memorial notice of 1657, the daughter of rabbi Baruch Coblenz, parnas and shtadlan, was described as "the wise-hearted [*hakhamat lev*], eminent, humble and honorable woman Golda Naomi." (Schwarzfuchs translates *hakhamat lev* as "intelligent" [*Memorbuch*, p. 17, no. 225], but the phrase is actually a quotation of Exodus 35:25 and 35:35 and is better translated as "wise-hearted.") This appears to be the only use of the honorific "wise-hearted" for a woman in the *Memorbuch*, and it does not necessarily carry with it an idea of learning. Cherele bas Mechoulam Abraham (d. 1697), said to have helped women on the point of giving birth (she was presumably a midwife), was described as "attending the synagogue morning and night an hour before service, and reading the Psalms in their entirety along with the commentary" (p. 48, no. 550). Brainele Rachel (d. 1710), daughter of a parnas, helped her husband in his study of law and teaching and "devoted herself to study, prayer, and charity" (p. 61, no. 678). In 1715 Nentsche Asnat, daughter of Abraham Halphen and probably an acquaintance of Glikl's, was described as supporting her household as a trader so her husband could study; being a member of several women's confraternities, including one for providing candles to the women's gallery (among other uses, this would make it possible for women to read during service); being among the first to arrive at synagogue every day and staying till the very end; and "completing the reading of the Psalms every day" (p. 71, no. 777).

80. Weinreich, *Yiddish Language*, pp. 316–318.

81. Helwig (Helvicius), *Jüdische Historien*, fol. Aiiir. Johann Christoph Wagenseil, *Belehrung der Juedisch-Teutschen Red- und Schreibart* (Koenigsberg: Paul Friedrich Rhode, 1699), p. 4.

82. KM, 94; PM, 86–87; AL, 52.

83. A. Grabois, "Le souvenir et la légende de Charlemagne dans les textes hébraïques médiévaux," *Le Moyen Age*, 72 (1966): 5–41. Dan Ben-Amos, ed., *Mimekor Yisrael: Classical Jewish Folktales*, collected by Micha Joseph bin Gorion, trans. I. M. Lask, abridged and annotated by Dan Ben-Amos (Bloomington: Indiana University Press, 1990), p. 232.

84. Glikl's account of Charlemagne's marriage proposal to Empress Irene of Constantinople and the subsequent overthrow and banishment of Irene derives from the sole contemporary source: the Greek *Chronographia* of Theophanes (d. ca. 807). See *The Chronicle of Theophanes*, trans. Harry Turtledove (Philadelphia: University of Pennsylvania Press, 1982), pp. 157–161, Annus mundi 6293–Annus mundi 6295 (1 September 800–1 August 803). In the second half of the ninth century, the papal librarian Anastasius made a Latin translation of Theophanes, incorporating it into his own *History;* in the eleventh century Georgius Cedrenus drew heavily upon Theophanes for his Greek *Compendium historiarum*. These

manuscript versions were known to the learned in the Middle Ages, but were not the source of popular legends about Charlemagne in the medieval period (Charlemagne's proposal to Irene and her downfall are not found in Robert Folz, *Le Souvenir et la légende de Charlemagne dans l'Empire Germanique médiéval* [Paris: Les Belles Lettres, 1950; Geneva: Slatkine Reprints, 1973], pp. 41, 145, 261, n. 13, 144, 324, 476). With the invention of the printing press, Theophanes was published in Greek (Heidelberg, 1595) and there were also learned editions of Cedrenus and Anastasius in the sixteenth century. Finally, as part of a major publishing venture in Byzantine history and the Greek church in seventeenth-century Paris, the Dominican I. Goar brought out a Latin translation of Theophanes' *Chronographia* in 1648, and the Jesuit Simon brought out a new edition of Anastasius' *Historia* in 1649. These texts were used as sources for the "universal histories" which were so popular in seventeenth-century Germany and which always devoted much attention to Charlemagne and his hope to "translate" the empire from Irene to himself. For instance, Andreas Lazarus von Imhof (1656–1704), *Neu-eröffneter historischer Bilder-Saal, das ist: Kurtze, deutliche und unpassionirte Beschreibung der Historiae Universalis*, 8 vols. (Nuremberg: J. J. Felsecker, 1692–1715). The reign of Constantine VI with his mother, Irene, and the reign of Irene and her downfall are treated in the first volume, and Imhof says he has used Theophanes for a source (*Neu-eröffneter Historien-Saal*, 10 vols. [Basel: Johann Brandmüller, 1736–1769], vol. 1, pp. 692–700, 891).

85. Landau, "Sprache," p. 27. Compare the view of Turniansky, who considers it unlikely that Glikl ever worked from German written sources and thinks we should assume that for tales such as the one about Irene there is a lost Yiddish account ("Literary Sources"). Indeed, there could be such an account, but Turniansky does not consider in her essay the evidence on the origin of the tale reported here. See also below, on the likelihood Glikl had read the travel account by Jean Mocquet, published in German translation in Lüneberg in 1688.

86. KM, p. 155; PM, p. 144; AL, p. 84. The dukes of Hannover in Glikl's day were from the house of Lüneburg: Johann Friedrich, residing in Hannover as duke from 1665 to 1679, and Ernst August, from 1679 to 1698. The cultural connections of Glikl bas Judah Leib and Jews of her status and activities in Hamburg and Metz seem somewhat different from the situation described by Chone Shmeruk in Poland at the same time. Religious differences raised a virtual wall between Jewish and Christian Poland, he says, and Jews had no access to any written expression of Polish culture. Chone Shmeruk, *The Esterke Story in Yiddish and Polish Literature: A Case Study in the Mutual Relations of Two Cultural Traditions* (Jerusalem: Zalman Shazar Center for the Furtherance of the Study of Jewish History, 1985), pp. 46–47.

87. *Relations-Courier* (SUBH, X/3239). Founded by the publisher Thomas von Wiering (d. 1703) and the Hamburg writer, encyclopedist, and publicist Eberhard Werner Happel (d. 1690), the *Relations-Courier* was published with about

eight pages of news on Tuesdays and Fridays. 1676, no. 155, 28 September: political and military news about the emperor; 1683, no. 18, 2 March, fol. 1r: news of the lost ship, which had in fact been at the Cape of Good Hope and the Canary Islands; 1683, no. 87, 30 October: scientific news from London of a benefit to traders and travelers—namely, the discovery of a new way to get longitude; 1685, no. 59, 24 July: news of Monmouth's rebellion in England; 1685, no. 2, 6 January: news of the burning of Jews in Lisbon in December 1684; 1687, no. 88, 7 June: reports of a new Jewish prophet in Cairo. On the major publishing houses and popular genres in Hamburg, see Werner Kayser, ed., *Hamburger Bücher, 1491–1850* (Hamburg: Ernst Hauswedell, 1973). Hamburg was the first city in German-speaking lands where *Zeitungen* were published regularly (pp. 15, 72–73).

88. KM, p. 307; PM, p. 288; AL, p. 167. Pappenheim translated "because of our many sins" as *leider* ("I am sorry to say"). Abrahams simply leaves it out.

89. For examples of the use of French among the Hamburg patriciate, see letters from Vinzent Rumpf to Peter Lütkens, 1661–1662 (StAH, Archiv des Familie Lütkens, 622–1, BVId); letter of Hamburg merchant Nicolaus Vegesack to the syndics of Hamburg, 1683 (Schramm, *Neun Generationen*, p. 92). KM, pp. 34–35; PM, pp. 32–33; AL, pp. 19–20; KM, p. 28, line 20: the wedding of her sister Hendele was "*magnifique*"; KM, p. 69, line 18: "*travail*"; KM, p. 299; PM, p. 281; AL, p. 162.

90. Cornelia Niekus Moore, *The Maiden's Mirror: Reading Material for German Girls in the Sixteenth and Seventeenth Centuries*, Wolfenbüttler Forschungen, 36 (Wiesbaden: Otto Harrassowitz, 1987). Moore stresses the central importance of religious and ethical works in the reading by young women. Rita Bake et al., " 'Finsteres Mittelalter'?—'Gute alte Zeit'? Zur Situation der Frauen bis zum 19. Jahrhundert," in *Hammonias Töchter: Frauen und Frauenbewegung in Hamburgs Geschichte*, special issue of *Hamburg Porträt*, 21 (1985); Jochmann and Loose, eds., *Hamburg*, vol. 1, pp. 335–340; Franklin Kopitzsch, *Grundzüge einer Sozialgeschichte der Aufklärung in Hamburg und Altona* (Hamburg: Verlag Verein für Hamburgische Geschichte, 1990), pp. 247–259. The mental world of women of the Hamburg patriciate in the seventeenth century can be seen in the letters to Peter Lütkens from his sister Anna Maria Lütkens and his stepmother, Anna Elisabeth Lütkens; the letters primarily give family news within a Christian frame, and contrast with those sent him by his father and male friends (StAH, Archiv des Familie Lütkens, BVIa, BVIc, BVId). For a comparison similar to the one I am making here, see Judith R. Baskin, "Some Parallels in the Education of Medieval Jewish and Christian Women," *Jewish History*, 5, no. 1 (Spring 1991): 41–51.

91. Jochmann and Loose, eds., *Hamburg*, vol. 1, pp. 340–342; Gisela Jaacks, *Musikleben in Hamburg zur Barockzeit*, special issue of *Hamburg Porträt*, 8 (1978). A 1674 painting by Johannes Voorhout of a "Musizierende Gesellschaft" at the Museum für Hamburgische Geschichte includes a woman among the musicians.

KM, pp. 34, 145–147; PM, pp. 32, 136–137; AL, pp. 19, 78–79. Graupe, *Statuten*, no. 34, p. 86 (1685 and 1726).

92. KM, p. 69; PM, p. 62; AL, p. 38.

93. These three duties, well known to all Jewish women, were spelled out on the opening pages of books like *Ayn Schoyn Fraun Buchlayn*, fol. 2r. On the practice of the Jewish women of Hamburg/Altona in regard to the timing of their baths of purification after childbirth, see n. 215 below.

94. KM, p. 302; PM, p. 284; AL, p. 164. Glikl reported that until he had begun to take long business trips, Haim had fasted on the days of the Torah lesson (KM, p. 69; PM, p. 62, AL, p. 38), which were Monday and Thursday. Both women and men might adhere to this or other voluntary fast schedules. *Memorbuch*, p. 9, no. 136; p. 48, no. 556; p. 60, no. 668; pp. 61–62, no. 680; p. 77, no. 829; p. 80, no. 851.

95. Barbara Kirshenblatt-Gimblett and Cissy Grossman, *Fabric of Jewish Life: Textiles from the Jewish Museum Collection* (New York: Jewish Museum, 1977), pp. 18–19, 34, 36, 38, 46–48, 96–101; Rolf Hagen, David Davidovitch, and Ralf Busch, *Tora-Wimpel: Zeugnisse jüdischer Volkskunst aus dem Braunschweigischen Landesmuseum* (Braunschweig: Braunschweig Landesmuseum, 1984); *Vierhundert Jahre Juden in Hamburg*, pp. 122–125. *Memorbuch*, p. 15, no. 199; p. 34, no. 416; p. 36, no. 436.

96. On the *tkhines* prayers, see the excellent work by Chava Weissler, "The Traditional Piety of Ashkenazic Women," in Arthur Green, ed., *Jewish Spirituality from the Sixteenth-Century Revival to the Present* (New York: Crossroad, 1987), pp. 245–275; idem, "Traditional Yiddish Literature: A Source of the Study of Women's Religious Lives" (Cambridge, Mass.: Harvard University Library, 1987); idem, " 'For Women and for Men Who Are Like Women' ": "Prayers in Yiddish and the Religious World of Ashkenazic Women," in Baskin, ed., *Jewish Women*, pp. 159–181; idem, "Woman as High Priest: A Kabbalistic Prayer in Yiddish for Lighting Sabbath Candles," *Jewish History*, 5, no. 1 (Spring 1991): 9–26. A recent collection of *tkhines* in Yiddish and in English translation, drawn from nineteenth-century Yiddish editions but with prayers that go back much earlier, is Tracy Guren Klirs, ed., *The Merit of Our Mothers: A Bilingual Anthology of Jewish Women's Prayers* (Cincinnati: Hebrew Union College, 1992).

97. The second book opens, "While I am yet in good health, I shall with God's help leave all in seven small books." Early in the first book, she says, "There is a limit of seventy years in this toilsome world ... Hundreds of thousands of people do not reach even this age." KM, pp. 23, 2; PM, pp. 21, 2; AL, pp. 13, 1. The span of seventy years was a commonplace of early modern European thought. Ephraim Kanarfogel has pointed out to me that two important ethical books of the medieval period were divided into seven parts by their authors so as to fit into a study program for each day of the week: the *Iggeret ha-Teshuvah* of R. Jonah of Gerona and the *Sefer Miẓvot Qatan* of R. Isaac of Corbeil (letter

of 15 March 1993). Zinberg does not report a Yiddish translation for either of these books (*Jewish Literature*, vol. 7, pp. 142–148), but if Glikl had heard that ethical literature was sometimes divided into seven books, this might have reinforced her own organizing plan.

98. There is an affective and narrative continuity between the melancholy statement with which Book 1 begins and the opening sections of Book 5—that is, a continuity running through the account of Haim's last illness, Glikl's first mourning, and the True Friendship story that follows it. Then there seems to be a break in the writing, as Glikl goes on to recount the decade of her widowhood, 1689–1699, with a liveliness and detail that suggest early and immediate drafts, but also with sentences that suggest distance: "at that time, I was still quite energetic in business"; "although many fine matches were proposed for me . . . as will be related later, I refused them all"; "nevertheless, a whole year passed before the marriage could be celebrated." In her description of the marriage of her daughter Esther to Moses Krumbach of Metz, she does not foreshadow her own move to that city; this suggests a draft written before 1699. She has, however, added memorial formulas—"may he rest in peace," "may the memory of the righteous be a blessing"—after some of the mentions of her sons, Reb Leib, who died in 1701, and Reb Zanvil, who died in 1702 (KM, pp. 215, 217, 229, 248; PM, pp. 203, 206, 216, 233–234; AL, pp. 115, 136.

99. In Book 6, Glikl writes from the point of view of the disaster that has befallen her in marrying Hirsch Levy, even though she does not yet recount it in detail ("I had to . . . live the shame against which I had hoped to protect myself"). She also writes with a very strong sense of financial insecurity ("I do not know if in old age I shall have a place to rest overnight, or a slice of bread to eat"), which was moderated a few years after the bankruptcy when her daughter Esther, son-in-law Moses, and stepson Samuel helped her and Hirsch survive. In addition, throughout Book 6 she speaks of Miriam as not yet married; uses none of the memorial formulas for Hirsch Levy (d. 1712) which she employs regularly in Book 7; and refers to Abraham Schwabe/Krumbach (d. 1704; *Memorbuch*, p. 54, no. 611) as alive. In Book 7 she gives indication several times that she is writing in 1715, but the last paragraph is dated 5479/1719. KM, pp. 277–278, 296, 310, 325, 333; PM, pp. 263, 278, 291, 300, 306, 313; AL, pp. 152, 160, 169, 175, 178, 182.

100. KM, p. 198, line 7: "may the memory of the righteous be a blessing" is added to the name of Glikl's son Leib (d. 1701) early in Book 5, while she is recounting Haim's final illness (recorded initially in the months or year after his death in 1689). "May she live" is used for Glikl's mother in KM, pp. 31, 33, 73, line 1. Glikl's mother, Beila bas Nathan, died in 1704 at the age of about seventy-four (Simonsen, "Eine Confrontation," p. 99), well before Glikl wrote her seventh book. Thus, if she had wished to, Glikl could have gone back over earlier books and changed "May she live" to memorial formulas for her mother, as she did in some mentions of her son Leib in Book 5.

101. KM, pp. 119, 120, 163, 179, 184; PM, pp. 110, 111, 152, 167, 173; AL, pp. 66, 67, 88, 96, 100. Glikl gave her birth date as 5407 (1646–1647), yet said that in the summer of 1699, when she was fifty-four, she received the proposal to marry Hirsch Levy. Her widowhood lasted eleven years (1689–1700), yet she opens Book 6 saying, "I will write of the change in my state that I had avoided for fourteen years." Günter Marwedel, "Problems of Chronology in Glikl Hamel's Memoirs," presented at the Fourth International Congress on Research in Yiddish, Jerusalem, 31 May–5 June 1992.

102. KM, p. 119; PM, p. 110; AL, p. 66.

103. Autobiographies by men tend to be organized around the stages of a vocation or career, with the events of marriage and children winding through this other narrative. In the autobiography by Leon Modena the relations with his children and his wife are important, but are interpreted as part of a larger relation between his writings, his sins, and his sufferings (Davis, "Fame and Secrecy"). The autobiography of the barber-surgeon Johann Dietz (1665–1738) moves from his early life in Halle and his apprenticeship, through his travels and adventures (*Master Johann Dietz*).

104. KM, pp. 194, 309; PM, pp. 183, 291; AL, pp. 105, 169.

105. KM, pp. 128, 309–310; PM, pp. 118, 291; AL, pp. 71, 169. On the death of her daughter Hendele just after Hendele's marriage in Berlin: "Oh, my God! it was a heavy blow! Such a dear and fine young person, like a fir-tree. Such innocent love and piety were hers as you might find in our Matriarchs. Everyone in Berlin and especially her mother-in-law loved her so—their grief cannot be described. But what help is this for my bereaved maternal heart?" (KM, p. 228; PM, pp. 215–216; AL, p. 124). For the death of Leib at twenty-seven, see below. On the death of an unnamed child (presumably a daughter, since there is no mention of circumcision) two weeks after birth: "It was a beautiful well-shaped child, but, unfortunately, had the same fever from which I suffered. Though we brought in doctors and all human aid, nothing helped. The child lived fourteen days and then God—may he be praised—took it to himself as his portion . . . and left us our earthly portion of affliction and me grieving in my childbed without a child" (KM, p. 191; PM, p. 180; AL, p. 104). Glikl also showed great sorrow at the death of her sister Hendele at twenty-four (KM, pp. 148–149; PM, p. 138; AL, p. 80). Formally, Jewish law required the same mourning for a child as for an adult (Ephraim Kanarfogel, "Attitudes toward Childhood and Children in Medieval Jewish Society," in David R. Blumenthal, ed., *Approaches to Judaism in Medieval Times*, 2 vols. [Chico, Calif.: Scholars Press, 1985], vol. 1, p. 27, n. 55).

106. KM, pp. 73, 179, 181–182; PM, pp. 66, 168, 170; AL, pp. 40, 97, 98.

107. KM, pp. 84, 193–194, 200–202; PM, pp. 78, 182–183, 190–192; AL, pp. 47–48, 105, 109–110.

108. KM, pp. 28, 25, 144, 313; PM, pp. 25–26, 23, 134, 294; AL, pp. 16, 14, 77, 171. In the marriage contract of Glikl's Metz grandson Elias ben Moses with Kolen Lemlen from Mannheim, the parents of the bride provided her with a dowry of

20,000 reichstaler and clothing; the parents of the groom, in addition to giving him half their house, promised to support the young couple for three years and to provide Elias with a teacher whose expenses would be paid for ten years (ADM, 3E3709, no. 305).

109. KM, pp. 145–146; PM, p. 136; AL, p. 78.

110. KM, pp. 136–137; PM, p. 126; AL, p. 76.

111. KM, p. 13; PM, p. 12; AL, p. 7.

112. KM, p. 32; PM, p. 30; AL, p. 18 (translates "dung" as "dust").

113. KM, pp. 14, 25, 138; PM, pp. 12, 23, 128; AL, pp. 8, 14. For another reference to the fact that people were content with less in her father's day, see KM, p. 58; PM, p. 52; AL, p. 32.

114. KM, pp. 170, 175, 125; PM, pp. 160, 164, 116; AL, pp. 92, 95, 69. The pairing *oysher un koved* is found in several places in the Hebrew Bible, *osher ve-kavod* (e.g., Proverbs 3:16, 8:18, 22:4).

115. KM, pp. 121, 77, 115, 274; PM, pp. 112, 72, 105, 259; AL, pp. 67, 63, 69, 150. On the importance of an honorable commercial reputation and the shame of bankruptcy among Parisian merchants in the eighteenth century, see Thomas Manley Luckett, "Credit and Commercial Society in France, 1740–1789" (Diss., Princeton University, 1992), chs. 2–3.

116. KM, pp. 153, 170–171, 252–253; PM, pp. 142, 160, 237–238; AL, pp. 82, 93, 139–140.

117. KM, pp. 321–322, 324, 38; PM, pp. 302, 304–305, 36; AL, pp. 176–177, 21.

118. William Shakespeare, *The Merchant of Venice*, Act 3, sc. 1, lines 55–59. Also Act 1, sc. 3, lines 107–130. Standard seventeenth-century Christian accounts of Jewish beliefs and customs have little to say about a Jewish sense of honor. The commonplaces of "blindness," "obstinacy," and "ingratitude" are found in the *Synagoga Judaica* of the Basel Hebraist Johann Buxtorf, first published in German in 1603 and reprinted subsequently in German, Latin, Dutch, and English (*The Jewish Synagogue: Or an Historical Narration of the State of the Jews* [London: Thomas Young, 1657], fol. A2a, p. 25). When Jews are praised in Christian writing, it is usually for their charitable benevolence toward their own kind or for their sobriety and temperance (see, for example, Lancelot Addison, *The Present State of the Jews* [London: William Crooke, 1675], p. 13). Claude Fleury spoke of the politeness of the biblical Israelites and the "honor" they showed their notables, but declared that the Jews had declined from the qualities of ancient times (*Les Moeurs des Israelites* [Paris: Widow Gervais Clouzier, 1681], pp. 169–170 and concluding chapters). The English deist John Toland was exceptional in his balanced and comparative observation: "There are among the *Jews*, to be sure, sordid wretches, sharpers, extortioners, villains of all sorts and degrees: and where is that happy nation, where is that religious profession, of which the same may not be as truely affirm'd? They have likewise their men of probity and worth, persons

of courage and conduct, of liberal and generous spirits." John Toland, *Reasons for Naturalizing the Jews in Great Britain and Ireland, On the same foot with all other Nations* (London: J. Roberts, 1714; facsimile reprint Jerusalem: Hebrew University, Department of the History of the Jewish People, 1964), p. 20. For a recent study on attitudes toward the Jews in early modern Europe, see Myriam Yardeni, *Anti-Jewish Mentalities in Early Modern Europe* (Lanham, Md.: University Press of America, 1990).

119. There are about sixty instances where the noun "honor" is used by Abrahams and *Ehre* by Pappenheim; in only six cases did Glikl use the word *er* rather than *koved*. She used *er* at the opening of Book 1 to refer to the glory or honor of God (KM, p. 1); twice in a retelling in Book 6 of the biblical tale of David and Absalom under the names of Jedidiah and Emunis (KM, pp. 280, 288); and in Book 6 where she quotes herself early in her stay in Metz as saying to a woman who greeted her graciously, "I know not from whom this honor comes" (KM, p. 292). The other two uses of *er* are formulaic, a Yiddish rendering of the phrase *Zucht und Ehre* to describe the propriety of charitable action in her daughter's house in Metz (KM, p. 296). *Koved* is found in KM, pp. 15, 36, 38, 67, 120, 125–126, 137, 145, 148, 153, 170–172, 175–176, 193–194, 212, 214, 224, 226, 247–248, 252–253, 264, 270–271, 274, 278, 291–293, 295, 312, 319–322, 324. On some of the criteria that lead Yiddish speakers to choose a Hebrew origin-word over a German origin-word, see Harshav, *Meaning of Yiddish*, pp. 39–40. Weinreich gives *ern-koved* as one of several examples of later Yiddish compounds involving synonyms from different sources that are put together for emphasis (*Yiddish Language*, p. 642). This was not the case in the Middle Yiddish of Glikl's day.

120. KM, pp. 160 ("circumcised and uncircumcised"), 274, 277, 307.

121. KM, pp. 274, 30, 160; PM, pp. 259, 28, 149; AL, pp. 150, 17, 87.

122. KM, p. 314; PM, p. 296; AL, p. 172.

123. KM, pp. 146–148; PM, pp. 136–138; AL, pp. 78–80.

124. KM, p. 26; PM, p. 24; AL, p. 15.

125. KM, pp. 157, 27; PM, pp. 146, 25; AL, pp. 85, 15. Also on the particular hazards of Leipzig if a Jew died and required burial while at the fair, KM, pp. 107, 177; PM, pp. 98, 165–166; AL, pp. 59, 95–96.

126. KM, pp. 75–78; PM, pp. 69–73; AL, pp. 42–44.

127. Perhaps Glikl took the details from the slaying of Haim's oldest brother, Moses, who was attacked and wounded by thieves on his way to his wedding (KM, pp. 61–162; PM, pp. 54–55; AL, p. 34). He and a companion survived a few days to tell the tale, and the servant who was with them subsequently became a servant to Glikl and Haim.

128. KM, pp. 134–142; PM, pp. 122–132; AL, pp. 74–75 (Abrahams omits the material from Hillel and other sages).

129. KM, pp. 234–246; PM, pp. 221–231; AL, pp. 128–135.

130. This tale is found in Solomon Ibn Verga, *Sefer Shebet Yehudah* (published

in Hebrew in the early sixteenth century; Yiddish edition, Krakow, 1591; English translation and analysis given in Yosef Hayim Yerushalmi, *The Lisbon Massacre of 1506 and the Royal Image in the Shebet Yehudah* [Cincinnati: Hebrew Union College, 1976], pp. 46–47). There is also a version of Glikl's tale in the *Mayse Bukh*, the great Yiddish collection of stories (*Ma'aseh Book*, no. 185, pp. 400–401). In the *Sefer Shebet Yehudah* the king is ruler of Spain, as he is in Glikl's telling. In the *Mayse Bukh* he is sultan of Constantinople, but Glikl may have read and used this version as well. Glikl added a touch of her own, identifying the corpse as a child's body which the sleepless king himself saw thrown into a Jewish house, whereas the *Shebet Yehuda* and the *Mayse Bukh* simply speak of a corpse seen by servants whom the king sent out in the streets to find out what was happening.

131. KM, p. 246; PM, p. 231; AL, p. 135 (several sentences omitted). The harassment of the Jews in connection with the execution is mentioned and prohibited in a printed ordinance issued by the Senate of Hamburg about the affair (StAH, Senat, Cl. VII, Lit. Hf., no. 5, vol. 1b, fasc. 1, printed act of 19 September 1687 inserted at end).

132. Grunwald, *Hamburgs deutsche Juden*, p. 17. KM, p. 234; PM, p. 231; AL, p. 128. Marwedel uses this placement as one of several instances where Glikl's "chronological placement of the events in question [is] clearly wrong" (Marwedel, "Problems of Chronology," p. 6). I here offer an explanation, literary and psychological, for that placement.

133. In addition to the sociable exchange of Haim and Glikl with non-Jews on the way back from Wittmund to Hamburg (above), Glikl also describes the drinking bouts of her servant Jacob and his companion, Herr Petersen, on a trip from Hannover to Hamburg. KM, pp. 101–106; PM, pp. 92–97; AL, pp. 55–58.

134. KM, p. 312; PM, p. 293; AL, p. 170.

135. KM, p. 277; PM, pp. 262–263; AL, p. 152: "I thank and praise the Lord that I left Hamburg owing not a single reichstaler to Jew or non-Jew"; "I feared that if I remained single longer, I might lose everything and be disgraced so that—God forbid—I would harm other people, Jews and non-Jews." On Glikl's "Sabbath-woman": KM, pp. 187–188; PM, pp. 176–177; AL, pp. 101–102. In some towns, the magistrates prohibited Jews from hiring Christian servants to do errands on the Sabbath (Buxtorf, *Jewish Synagogue*, p. 171). It seems that there was no such prohibition in Hamburg, though in 1698 several Lutheran students of theology protested to the Senate that Christian maidservants in Jewish employ were going with the children to synagogue (StAH, Senat, Cl. VII, Lit. Hf., no. 5, vol. 1b, fasc. 2, fols. 37r–42r). Glikl mentions only Jewish household servants.

136. KM, pp. 39–57; PM, pp. 37–50; AL, pp. 22–31. "The Man Who Would Not Take an Oath," A. Aarne and Stith Thompson, *The Types of the Folk-Tale: A Classification and Bibliography*, 2nd ed. (Helsinki: Suomalainen Tiedeakatemia, 1964), Tale type 938, Placidas, pp. 331–332. A Christian version of the story is

found in the life of Saint Eustace, known as Placidus before he converted to Christianity during the reign of the emperor Trajan (Jacques de Voragine, *The Golden Legend,* trans. Granger Ryan and Helmut Ripperger [New York: Arno Press, 1969], pp. 555–561; Alain Boureau, "Placido tramite: La Légende d'Eustache, empreinte fossile d'un mythe carolingien?" *Annales: Economies, Sociétés, Civilisations,* 37 [1982]: 682–699). Jewish versions: "The Reward of Virtue, or the Story of the Man Who Never Took an Oath," in *Ma'aseh Book,* no. 222, pp. 542–546; Angelo S. Rappoport, *The Folklore of the Jews* (London: Soncino Press, 1937), pp. 147–151; E. Yassif, "From Jewish Oicotype to Israeli Oicotype: The Tale of 'The Man Who Never Swore an Oath,' " *Fabula,* 27 (1986): 216–236.

137. KM, p. 49 ("gar tsart . . . gar far shtendig"); PM, p. 44; AL, pp. 26–27, with some departure from the Yiddish text.

138. The savage-princess episode, the riddle tests, and the Jewish dukedom do not figure in any of the versions described in note 136. Glikl says of the tale, "I found this story in a book written by an important and respected man of Prague," but his name is missing from the Yiddish manuscript (KM, p. 57). The distinctiveness of Glikl's version is consistent with the notion that she mixed in these motifs herself—or at least that she chose such a version over the one in the *Mayse Bukh,* which does not have them. For a bibliography on riddles in the Jewish tradition, see Haim Schwarzbaum, *Studies in Jewish and World Folklore* (Berlin: Walter de Gruyter, 1967), pp. 423–424.

139. Jean Mocquet, *Voyages en Afrique, Asie, Indes Orientales et Occidentales: Faits par Iean Mocquet, Garde du Cabinet des singularitez du Roy, aux Tuilleries* (Rouen: Jacques Callové, 1645; first edition 1616), pp. 148–150. German translation: *Wunderbare jedoch gründlich- und warhaffte geschichte und reise begebnisse in Africa, Asia, Ost- und West-Indien,* trans. Johann Georg Schoch (Lüneburg: J. G. Lippers, 1688), pp. 82–86 (a picture of the woman tearing her child in half is on p. 85). Mocquet's account is one of the several origins of the much-told eighteenth-century story of Jarico and Inkle. Inkle is a shipwrecked Englishman who is saved by an Indian maiden, Yarico, when he is washed up on her shores; she protects him from being slain by her fellows and loves and cares for him. They live together in a cave. He persuades her to go and live in England with him if they should see a ship. They do finally leave, but when they get to Barbados, he sells her for a slave. For an important discussion of this tale, its origins and variants, see Peter Hulme, *Colonial Encounters: Europe and the Native Caribbean, 1492–1797* (London: Methuen, 1986), ch. 6. The episode involving the pious Talmudist and the savage princess adds a Jewish version to this major story of failed connection between Europe and the Caribbean. On ill-fated "transracial love stories" in the eighteenth century, see also Mary Louise Pratt, *Imperial Eyes: Travel Writing and Transculturation* (London: Routledge, 1992), ch. 5.

140. Eldad the Danite, a learned wanderer of the ninth century, recounted his

story to the Jews of Spain. He had been shipwrecked near Ethiopia and then was cast up with a companion "among a people called Romranos who are black . . . tall, without garment . . . who eat persons." His companion, who was fat and healthy, was immediately killed and eaten, but since Eldad was sick, he was put in chains until he should get fat and well. Instead he hid his food. He remained with them until an army of fire-worshipers attacked the man-eaters and took him captive. After four years with the fire-worshipers, he was redeemed by a Jewish merchant from Persia. This tale was known over the centuries along with Eldad's other narratives, and had a printed edition in Hebrew in Mantua ca. 1480 (Elkan Nathan Adler, ed., *Jewish Travellers: A Treasury of Travelogues from Nine Centuries*, 2nd. ed. [New York, 1966], pp. 4–7; D. H. Müller, "Die Recensionen und Versionen des Eldad Had-Dâni," *Denkschriften der Kaiserlichen Academie der Wissenschaften: Philosophisch-Historische Classe*, 41 [Vienna, 1892]: 70–73. A bibliography of Jewish travel literature by Leopold Zunz can be found in Benjamin of Tudela, *The Itinerary*, trans. A. Asher, 2 vols. (New York: Hakesheth, n.d.), vol. 2, pp. 230–317; perhaps one of these works was at the origin of some of Glikl's motifs. More likely is a geographic storybook such as the Yiddish *Mayse Amsterdam*, the adventures of one Rabbi Levi, who in 1678 departed on a boat from Amsterdam for the East Indies with nine other Jews to find islands where "there are Jews of whom we did not as yet know" (Zinberg, *Jewish Literature*, vol. 7, p. 237). Island episodes were the organizing theme of a widely read German book published in Hamburg in Glikl's day by one of the city's best-known writers: Eberhard Werner Happel, *Der insulanische Mandorell* (Hamburg and Frankfurt: Z. Hertel and the heirs of M. Weyrauch, 1682).

141. The shipwrecked man and his she-demon wife: "The Story of the Jerusalemite," in Ben Gorion, *Mimekor Yisrael*, abridged ed., no. 200, pp. 373–384 (a Yiddish version was printed in Hamburg, 1711); another version can be found in "The Kiss," ibid., no. 201, pp. 384–386. Also in the Jewish tradition is the motif of the "she-demon" wife, who, like Medea, kills her children when she is neglected or deceived by her husband (Juspa Shammash, *Mayse Nissim* [Amsterdam, 1696], no. 21: "The Queen of Sheba in the House 'Zur Sonne,' " translated in Eidelberg, *R. Juspa*, pp. 87–88); the variations on this theme are described in a Hebrew study by Sara Zfatman, *The Marriage of a Mortal Man and a She-Demon* (Jerusalem: Akademon Press, 1987). The archetype of the she-demon in the Jewish tradition is Lilith, Adam's first wife, who in one of her avatars threatens the newborn children of the living (Raphael Patai, *The Hebrew Goddess*, 3rd enlarged ed. [Detroit: Wayne State University Press, 1990], ch. 10). Glikl did not mention Lilith in her autobiography, but her grandson Moses Marcus the Younger did so in a book on the customs of the Jews, published in 1728: "When a Man has a Son born, his Friends wish him Joy, and some use to put little Papers in the four Corners of the Woman's Chamber that is in Childbed, upon which they write *Adam and Eve, away Lilit*, together with the Names of three Angels, to preserve

the Woman and Child from Witch-craft." [Moses Marcus], *The Ceremonies of the Present Jews* (London: J. Roberts, 1728), p. 14. Perhaps Moses Marcus had seen this at the home of his mother Freudchen bas Chaim. On these paper amulets, see Joshua Trachtenberg, *Jewish Magic and Superstition: A Study in Folk Religion* (New York: Atheneum, 1977), pp. 139, 169.

142. Cecil Roth, *The House of Nasi: The Duke of Naxos* (Philadelphia: Jewish Publication Society of America, 1948), especially ch. 4 and, on his fame, pp. 182–186. Nasi maintained his own residence in Istanbul, and the island was governed by his lieutenant, Francisco Coronel or Coronello (a Catholic of conversos origin) and by Christian officials. Both Moslems and Jews were tolerated on the island. Gedalia Yogev, *Diamonds and Coral: Anglo-Dutch Jews and Eighteenth-Century Trade* [Leicester: Leicester University Press and New York: Holmes and Meier, 1978], pp. 156–158; Emden, *Mémoires*, p. 183.

143. On the Jewish communities and plantations in Suriname in the late seventeenth and early eighteenth centuries, see the chapter "Metamorphoses," below.

144. KM, pp. 71–72; PM, pp. 64–65; AL, pp. 39–40. Howard Eilberg-Schwartz, *The Savage in Judaism: An Anthropology of Israelite Religion and Ancient Judaism* (Bloomington: Indiana University Press, 1990), pp. 31–41; Richard H. Popkin, "The Rise and Fall of the Jewish Indian Theory," in Yosef Kaplan, Henry Méchoulan, and Richard H. Popkin, eds., *Menasseh ben Israel and His World* (Leiden: E. J. Brill, 1989), pp. 63–82. Menasseh ben Israel's view, based on the report of a Portuguese Marrano explorer who claimed to have met Jews in the Andes mountains, was circumspect: Menasseh thought that a part of a Lost Tribe had migrated to America while other Amerindians had come from Asia (pp. 68–69). A similar reference to indigenous Jews occurs in a mid-seventeenth-century Yiddish text, *Mayse vestindie*; see Weinreich, *Yiddish Language*, p. 315.

145. Johann Müller, *Judaismus oder Jüdenthumb: Das ist Ausführlicher Bericht von des Jüdischen Volckes Unglauben Blindheit und Verstockung* (Hamburg: Printed by Jacob Rebenlein for Zacharias Hertel, 1644). Whaley, *Religious Toleration*, pp. 86–88.

146. Johann Jacob Schudt, *Jüdische Merckwürdigkeiten*, 4 vols. (Frankfurt and Leipzig: Samuel Tobias Hocker, 1715–1718), vol. 4, pp. 135–137. The pros and cons of the London quarrel had been circulating among Jewish communities in Europe in Hebrew pamphlets since 1707. It had first been picked up for German readers by Adam Andreas Cnollen, deacon of Fürth, in his *New Things and Old*, published in German in 1714; Glikl's son Moses Hamel was rabbi of nearby Baiersdorf and may have read this Christian account of his sister's misfortunes in London. Also on the London episode see Emden, *Mémoires*, pp. 183–184; and Kaufmann, "Rabbi Zevi Ashkenazi," pp. 102–125.

147. Schudt, *Jüdische Merckwürdigkeiten*, vol. 1, p. 296. On the *eruvin* in general, see the talmudic tractate *'Erubin*, in Israel Epstein, ed., *The Babylonian Talmud, Seder Mo'ed*, part 2, vol. 3, trans. Israel Slotki (London: Soncino Press,

1938); *Encyclopaedia Judaica*, vol. 6, pp. 849–882; and, for the *eruvin* in Hamburg/Altona, the important study by Peter Freimark, "Eruw/Judentore: Zur Geschichte einer rituellen Institution im Hamburger Raum (und anderswo)," in Freimark et al., *Judentore*, pp. 10–69. Rabbi Zevi Hirsch Ashkenazi described his irritation in the 1690s at the wrong way in which the Hamburg/Altona Ashkenazic Jews handled the *eruv* to permit carrying: they placed bread in all the synagogues and prayer rooms in the area, whereas he thought one loaf of bread in one synagogue was all that was needed to create the *eruv* for the whole region (*Sefer She'elot*, responsa 112).

148. KM, pp. 100, 107; PM, pp. 91, 97; AL, pp. 55, 59. On the rabbinic strategies in the Talmud for "reconquering" space and time so that Jews could live in Exile, see Arnold M. Eisen, *Galut: Modern Jewish Reflection on Homelessness and Homecoming* (Bloomington: Indiana University Press, 1986), pp. 35–42.

149. KM, pp. 32–33; PM, p. 30; AL, pp. 18–19.

150. KM, pp. 268–270; PM, pp. 251–253; AL, pp. 146–147. On Samuel Oppenheimer and this episode, see Stern, *Court Jew*, pp. 19–28, 85–91.

151. KM, pp. 107–121; PM, pp. 98–112; AL, pp. 59–67. Haim had arranged a marriage between the daughter of his brother Samuel and Judah Berlin, so this conflict was not only among Jews but among in-laws.

152. The "Herod" was Issachar Cohen, who was recommended to Haim by his brother Isaac of Frankfurt after the ending of the partnership with Judah Berlin (KM, p. 119; PM, p. 110; AL, p. 66), and who served Haim and Glikl as business agent and commercial servant for ten years. On Herod in the Jewish tradition, see *Encyclopaedia Judaica*, vol. 8, p. 387. The use of "Herod" as an insult among Jews was not special to Glikl. A 1694 quarrel inside the Hildesheim synagogue at Simchas Torah led to an exchange of insults among several men, one of whom was married to Haim's niece. One said to the other that "he regarded him as Herod and Pilate [*sic!*]" (A. Lewinsky, "Die Kinder des Hildesheimer Rabbiners Samuel Hameln," *Monatsschrift für Geschichte und Wissenschaft des Judentums* 44 [1900]: 378).

153. KM, p. 161; PM, p. 150; AL, p. 87 (reference to Moses Helmstedt of Stettin, who had the monopoly of the mint in Stettin and wanted Haim to supply him with silver). Glikl also told a story of cheating within the family: the quarrel between Haim's father Joseph Goldschmidt and a man named Feibusch, to whose stepson Joseph had married his daughter Yenta. Yenta's husband accused his stepfather of stealing his inheritance and seized some of his commercial property, whereupon a major fight ensued in the courts, with Feibusch and Joseph each having the other imprisoned (KM, pp. 64–65; PM, pp. 57–58; AL, pp. 35–36).

154. KM, p. 165; PM, p. 154; AL, p. 89.

155. KM, pp. 211–230, 308; PM, pp. 200–218, 288–289; AL, pp. 114–126, 167–168.

156. KM, p. 143; PM, p. 133; AL, p. 77. Glikl adds that her father-in-law was

then a wealthy man, with all his children married. Was there some ambivalence in her joy over the small jug?

157. KM, pp. 17, 61; PM,, pp. 14, 54; AL, pp. 9, 33–34. Another example of help from beyond the grave can be found in the story of Sulka, the wife of Haim's brother Abraham and childless for seventeen years. Just before her mother died, she said to Sulka, "If I have one merit before God, blessed be he, I shall beg that you should bear children." Sulka became pregnant after her mother's death and gave birth to a daughter, whom she named Sarah after her mother (KM, 62–63; PM, pp. 55–56; AL, p. 34). On Jewish prayers to one's ancestors for assistance in this world and prayers from the other world, see Chava Weissler, "The Living and the Dead: Ashkenazic Family Relations in the Light of Hebrew and Yiddish Cemetery Prayers," in Weissler, *Voices of the Matriarchs*, forthcoming. I have treated the subject of Catholic reciprocity between the living and the dead and the Protestant critique of that reciprocity in "Ghosts, Kin, and Progeny: Some Features of Family Life in Early Modern France," in Alice Rossi, Jerome Kagan, and Tamara Hareven, eds., *The Family* (New York: W. W. Norton, 1978), pp. 87–114.

158. KM, pp. 31–38; PM, pp. 28–36; AL, pp. 17–22. Glikl bas Judah Leib also told how her son Mordecai took care of Haim when he became sick at the Leipzig fair. Though it was Mordecai's "obligation" to do so, still he was very young (KM, p. 192; PM, p. 181; AL, pp. 104–105).

159. KM, pp. 180–181; PM, p. 169; AL, p. 97. Also after Haim's death, Glikl brought in learned men to pray and study Talmud in the house for a whole year (KM, p. 201; PM, pp. 190–191; AL, p. 109). On Jewish prayers for the dead, see Weissler, "The Living and the Dead"; and Israel Lévi, "La commémoration des âmes dans le judaïsme," *Revue des études juives*, 29 (1894): 43–60.

160. KM, pp. 175–176; PM, p. 164; AL, p. 95.

161. KM, pp. 271–272; PM, pp. 257–259; AL, p. 149. Collections were made by the Altona/Hamburg Gemeinde for the Holy Land in Glikl's day, and a few Portuguese and German Jews went to live there. StAH, Jüdische Gemeinde 31, vol. 1, no. 5 (1687, 1699); Emden, *Mémoires*, p. 85; Bernhard Brilling, "Die frühesten Beziehungen der Juden Hamburgs zu Palästina," *Jahrbuch der Jüdisch-Literarischen Gesellschaft*, 21 (1930): 19–38.

162. KM, pp. 124, 202–203; PM, pp. 114–115, 192–193; AL, pp. 69, 110–111.

163. KM, pp. 204–209; PM, pp. 194–198; AL, pp. 111–113, with an error in the translation of the king's advice to his son: "together with a thousand fools," rather than the correct "under a thousand fools." (The Lowenthal translation inaccurately softens the king's advice from killing the thousand fools and the two servants to "thrashing" them; *Memoirs*, p. 157.) Aarne and Thompson, *Types*, Tale type 893: the Unreliable Friend (the Half-Friend); Stith Thompson, *Motif-Index of Folk Literature*, rev. ed., 6 vols. (Bloomington: Indiana University Press, 1989), H1558.1: Test of Friendship, the Half-Friend, vol. 3, pp. 511–512. "Half a

Friend" in Moses Gaster, *The Exempla of the Rabbis* (London and Leipzig: Asia Publishing, 1924), no. 360, pp. 134, 249. Gaster's version, from a seventeenth-century manuscript, is about a father who disproves his son's claim that he has a hundred friends by devising a test with a slain sheep in a bag. It ends with the son's recognizing the truth of his father's warnings; there is no mention of retribution against those who turned him down. "Sincere Friendship," in Angelo S. Rappoport, *Folklore of the Jews* (London: Soncino Press, 1937), pp. 159–163: the story of a wise man and his son, it does not end with the execution of the two servants or any other punishment. Turniansky gives Yiddish variants of the tale in a sixteenth-century manuscript in the Bodleian Library (Hebrew ms. 2213) and in the *Sefer Lev Tov* of Isaac ben Eliakum, first published in 1620, but points out that neither is exactly like Glikl's version ("Literary Sources," p. 172 and nn. 44–45). In the *Mayse Bukh,* there is the tale of a naive king's son who knew nothing of the world, had always stayed at home, "and was therefore like a home-raised calf, a glutton and a drunkard." The king sent his son off with the Master of the Horse to learn the ways of the world (*Ma'aseh Book,* no. 208, pp. 491–503). Though there are some shared motifs in Glikl's tale and this one, the story lines are very different.

164. The story is known in the study of folk literature as "The Matron of Ephesus (Vidua)" (Thompson, *Motif-Index,* K2213.1, vol. 4. p. 483) and has many versions in European languages. The Jewish versions include, first, that of Berechiah ben Natronai ha-Nakdan in his Hebrew *Mishle Shu'alim,* or *Fox Fables,* of the late twelfth or early thirteenth century (Yiddish translation, Freiburg, 1583), where the widow is won over by a knight who has removed his brother's body from the gallows and fears punishment; second, that of the *Mayse Bukh,* where the gallows guard is the seducer; and, third, that of the Yiddish *Ku-Bukh* of Abraham ben Matityahu (Verona, 1594), in which the widow has made her home near her husband's grave and is seduced by the gallows guard to become his lover. Translations can be found in Berechiah ha-Nakdan, *Fables of a Jewish Aesop,* trans. Moses Hadas (New York: Columbia University Press, 1967), no. 80, pp. 145–146; in *Book of Fables: The Yiddish Fable Collection of Reb Moshe Wallich, Frankfurt am Main, 1697,* ed. and trans. Eli Katz (Detroit: Wayne State University Press, 1994), no. 19, pp. 114–118; and in *Ma'aseh Book,* no. 107, pp. 193–195. A full discussion of the fable and its sources can be found in Haim Schwarzbaum, *The Mishle Shu'Alim (Fox Fables) of Rabbi Berechiah ha-Nakdan: A Study in Comparative Folklore and Fable Lore* (Kiron: Institute for Jewish and Arab Folklore Research, 1979), pp. 394–417. For a study of the Jewish widow, see Cheryl Tallan, "The Medieval Jewish Widow: Powerful, Productive and Passionate" (Master's thesis, York University, 1989).

165. KM, pp. 273–274; PM, pp. 259–260; AL, p. 150.

166. KM, pp. 275–277; PM, pp. 260–263; AL, pp. 150–153.

167. KM, pp. 310–311; PM, pp. 292–293; AL, pp. 163, 169–170. Exodus 19:4:

"Ye have seen what I did unto the Egyptians and how I bare you on eagles' wings, and brought you unto myself."

168. KM, pp. 318–319; PM, pp. 299–300; AL, p. 174. Hirsch Levy's house had evidently passed to his daughter Hendele/Anne and her husband, Isaye Lambert, alias Willstadt (see nn. 45, 48, and 49 above).

169. KM, pp. 312, 319; PM, pp. 294, 300; AL, pp. 171, 175. In September–October 1717, Esther bas Haim and Moses Schwabe, alias Krumbach, made a donation of half their house with its furnishings and utensils to their son Elias as part of the arrangements for his marriage to Kolen Lemlen. Esther and Moses reserved, in Elias' part of the house, an upper-floor apartment which they would keep until their death (perhaps as a place in which to stay and be cared for once they were too old to sustain their part of the house). Glikl is not mentioned in the act but was presumably living in the half of the house retained by her daughter and son-in-law (ADM, 3E3709, no. 305).

170. KM, pp. 312, 318–320; PM, pp. 293–294, 299–301; AL, pp. 170–171, 174–175.

171. KM, p. 89; PM, p. 82; AL, p. 50. Midrashic commentary on Genesis 25:21 ("And Isaac entreated the Lord for his wife, because she was barren") noted that the Hebrew phrase "for his wife" could also mean "facing his wife" and that Isaac and Rebecca were thus praying to God in different parts of the room (Midrash Rabbah, Genesis 63 [5]). Rashi's commentary on the text: "He stood in one corner and prayed, whilst she stood in another corner and prayed" (*Chumash with Taragum Onkelos, Haphtaroth and Rashi's Commentary*, trans. A. M. Silbermann and M. Rosenbaum [Jerusalem: Silbermann Family, 1985], p. 114, n. 21). Another of Glikl's prayers: KM, p. 22; PM, p. 19; AL, p. 12).

172. Joseph Dan, " 'No Evil Descends from Heaven': Sixteenth-Century Jewish Concepts of Evil," in Bernard Dov Cooperman, ed., *Jewish Thought in the Sixteenth Century* (Cambridge, Mass.: Harvard University Press, 1983), pp. 89–105; idem, "Manasseh ben Israel's *Nishmat Hayyim* and the Concept of Evil in Seventeenth-Century Jewish Thought," in Isidore Twersky and Bernard Septimus, eds., *Jewish Thought in the Seventeenth Century* (Cambridge, Mass.: Harvard University Press, 1987), pp. 63–75. On Lurianic Kabbalah and its concepts, see Gershom Scholem, *Sabbatai Sevi: The Mystical Messiah* (Princeton, N.J.: Princeton University Press, 1973), pp. 28–44, especially pp. 39–40 on the Anti-Adam.

173. On demons and spirits in Jewish thought and practice, including such works as the *Brantshpigl*, the *Mayse Bukh*, and the *Yesh Nochalin*, see Trachtenberg, *Jewish Magic*, chs. 3–4. *Ma'aseh Book*, no. 152, pp. 301–303. Glikl's reference to the "troops of angels (or demons) of destruction" draws on the *Yesh Nochalin*, but not on a section of that book saturated with the dualistic ideas of the Lurianic Kabbalah (KM, p. 265; PM, p. 249; omitted from AL). On a protective device against Lilith possibly used in Glikl's household, see n. 141 above.

174. KM, pp. 8, 14, 21, 192, 201–202, 209; PM, pp. 7, 12, 19, 180–181, 191,

198; AL, pp. 5, 7, 11, 104, 110, 113. The quotation "as it is said, because of the wicked, the saint is taken away" is drawn from Isaiah 57:1.

175. On the Book of Job, I have learned much from Moshe Greenberg, "Job," in Robert Alter and Frank Kermode, eds., *The Literary Guide to the Bible* (Cambridge, Mass.: Harvard University Press, 1987), pp. 283–304; and Ilana Pardes, *Countertraditions in the Bible: A Feminist Approach* (Cambridge, Mass.: Harvard University Press, 1992), pp. 145–152. Glikl draws twice from Job when describing her own misfortunes: first in regard to the bankruptcy of Hirsch Levy, "For the thing which I greatly feared has come upon me" (Job 3:25; KM, p. 277; PM, p. 263; AL, p. 152), and again when talking of her sorrow at the death of her son Zanvil, "Who will say unto him, 'what doest thou'?" (Job 9:12; KM, p. 310; PM, p. 292; AL, p. 169). She also uses phrases from Job in her moral teachings, e.g., "Naked came I out of my mother's womb and naked shall I return thither" (Job 1:21; KM, p. 14; PM, p. 12; AL, p. 8).

176. KM, pp. 128, 132, 164, 192; PM, pp. 118, 121, 153–154, 180; AL, pp. 71, 73, 89, 104. The Shekhinah is discussed extensively in Raphael Patai, *The Hebrew Goddess,* 3rd enlarged ed. (Detroit: Wayne State University Press, 1990) and Gerson Scholem, *Sabbatai Sevi: The Mystical Messiah,* trans. R. J. Zwi Werblowsky (Princeton, N.J.: Princeton University Press, 1973).

177. KM, p. 34; PM, p. 32; AL, 19.

178. KM, pp. 69–70; PM, pp. 62–63; AL, pp. 38–39.

179. KM, p. 198; PM, p. 188; AL, p. 108.

180. KM, p. 57; PM, p. 50; AL, p. 31. Sometimes Glikl presents the moral recompense as coming only in the next world: KM, pp. 2–3; PM, pp. 2–3; AL, p. 2.

181. KM, pp. 1–2; PM, p. 2; AL, p. 1. Another example: KM, p. 60; PM, pp. 149–150; AL, p. 87: "If God—blessed be his name—had given the young pair good fortune, they might have been as wealthy as Reb Samuel [Oppenheimer] himself, who from day to day rose higher. But the great merciful God portions out his gifts and his indulgences to those whom his Majesty chooses. We humans, lacking understanding, cannot talk of this, but instead must thank the good Creator for everything."

182. On arguing with God through rabbinical argument, "law-court prayers," and poetry, see Anson Laytner, *Arguing with God: A Jewish Tradition* (Northvale, N.J.: Jason Aronson, 1990). Glikl's *Memoirs* add storytelling to the tradition explored by Laytner.

183. Stories of which there is a version in the *Mayse Bukh* include the pious Talmudist (see n. 136 above), the king of Spain who could not sleep (see n. 130). On the *Brantshpigl,* see KM, p. 13; PM, p. 11; AL, p. 7, and n. 70 above. On the Yiddish sources for Glikl's tales, see the important study by Turniansky, "Literary Sources."

184. On Alexander of Macedon in the Jewish tradition, see the introduction

by I. F. Kazis to Immanuel ben Jacob Bonfils, *The Book of the Gests of Alexander of Macedon: Sefer Toledot Alexandros ha-Makdoni* (Cambridge, Mass.: Mediaeval Academy of America, 1962), pp. 2–25; and the commentary of Dan Ben Amos, in Bin Gorion, *Mimekor Yisrael*, abridged and annotated ed., pp. 89–90.

185. The classical treatments of the story of Solon and Croesus, starting with Herodotus, I: 29–33, 86–88, are given in Antonio Martina, ed., *Solone: Testimonianze sulla vita e l'opera* (Rome: Edizioni dell'Ateneo, 1968), pp. 32–50. Herodotus' *History of the Persian Wars* was published in German already in the sixteenth century (Augsburg, 1535; Eisleben, 1555; Frankfurt, 1593), so the story of Solon and Croesus was available for popular collections in German and Yiddish. Though Glikl's moral is similar to that of Herodotus—that one cannot tell whether a life has been happy until its end, for good fortune can be overturned— her narrative diverges from that of the Greek historian in several ways: Croesus' kingdom is not given a geographic location, and Solon is presented by her as a philosopher in Croesus' court, rather than a visiting philosopher-king; Croesus' fateful war with the Persian Cambyses is presented by her as a war about boundaries with an unnamed king (KM, pp. 171–175; PM, pp. 161–164; AL, pp. 93–95). Either her story is drawn from a version which dropped many precise details from the original text or she dropped them herself.

186. See n. 84 above.

187. Kayser, ed., *Hamburger Bücher*, pp. 50–51, 72, 76–77. Eberhard Werner Happel, *Groste Denkwürdigkeiten der Welt: Oder so genannte Relationes Curiosae*, 5 vols. (Hamburg: Thomas von Wiering, 1683–1690); *Der insulanische Mandorell*. In general on editions of stories and writers of tales in seventeenth-century and early eighteenth-century Germany, see Manfred Grätz, *Das Märchen in der deutschen Aufklärung: Vom Feenmärchen zum Volksmärchen* (Stuttgart: Metzler, 1988), pp. 33, 88–89, 102, 108 and passim in the bibliography, pp. 331–397.

188. Charles Perrault's editions of tales began in 1691; the first edition of eight tales is *Histoires ou contes du temps passé; Avec des Moralitez* (Paris: Claude Barbin, 1697). The four volumes of *Les Contes des fées* by the Comtesse d'Aulnoy first appeared in Paris in 1696–1698. Grätz, *Märchen*, pp. 19–25, 337–338.

189. On the characteristic Jewish version of Placidas and its opening, see Yasif, "From Jewish Oicotype to Israeli Oicotype." The *Mayse Bukh* version opens with the deathbed counsel of a rich father (*Ma'aseh Book*, no. 222, p. 542).

190. KM, pp. 39, 124, 202–203; PM, pp. 37, 114–115, 192–193; AL, pp. 22, 69, 110.

191. On Jewish folktales and folklore about birds, see Gaster, *Exempla of the Rabbis*, p. 275; Marie Campbell, "The Three Teachings of the Bird," in Raphael Patai, Francis Lee Utley, and Dov Noy, eds., *Studies in Biblical and Jewish Folklore* (New York: Haskell House Publishers, 1973), pp. 97–107; and Moshe Carmilly, "The Magic Bird," in Victor D. Sanua, ed., *Fields of Offerings: Studies in Honor of Raphael Patai* (Rutherford, N.J.: Fairleigh Dickinson University Press, 1983),

pp. 129–141. The Tale and Motif Types associated with Glikl's father bird and fledglings are Aa-Th Type 244C ("Raven drowns his young who promise to aid him when he becomes old. He saves one who admits he will not help because he will have to carry his own young") and Motif J267.1. The sources in 244 are Finnish and Lithuanian (Aarne and Thompson, *Types*, Tale type 244, p. 78). A nineteenth-century Romanian version concerning a mother partridge and her young is given by Moses Gaster, *Rumanian Bird and Beast Stories* (London: Sidgwick and Jackson, 1915), no. 95, pp. 294–295. Schwarzbaum reports twentieth-century Russian tellings in the Israel Folklore Archives (*Mishle Shu'alim*, p. xxxix, n. 10). Glikl's seems to be the earliest known account. Other tale types that can be associated with the bird story in terms of moral issues are: Modest choice Motif L211, L210 (Modest choice best); L10 Victorious Youngest Son, with a Jewish source recorded by Dov Noy; M21 King Lear Judgment.

192. KM, p. 94; PM, p. 86; AL, p. 52.

193. KM, pp. 19–21; PM, pp. 17–18; AL, pp. 10–11. The visit of Alexander to the Elders of the South is described in the Talmud, Tractate *Tamid*, 32a (I. Epstein, ed., *The Babylonian Talmud*, part 1, vol. 6, *Tamid*, trans. Maurice Simon [London: Soncino Press, 1948] pp. 26–28). In the medieval Hebrew version of Immanuel ben Jacob Bonfils, Alexander does not visit the Brahmins, but only sends them a letter to which they reply (Bonfils, *Book of the Gests*, pp. 13–14, 133–143). Further versions in Micha Joseph bin Gorion, *Mimekor Yisrael: Classical Jewish Folktales*, ed. Emanuel bin Gorion, tr. I. M. Lask, 3 vols. (Bloomington: Indiana University Press, 1976), vol. 1, nos. 116–117, pp. 246–248: "The Wise Men of India." Turniansky ("Literary Sources," pp. 170–171) has identified the text transmitting the story to Glikl as the *Josippon*, written in Hebrew in the tenth–twelfth centuries in Italy and appearing in printed Yiddish translations in Zurich (1546), Prague (1607), and Amsterdam (1661). Excerpts from the story of Alexander's trip to India from the Amsterdam edition are given in Grünbaum, *Chrestomathie*, pp. 346–349.

194. KM, pp. 171–175, 303–305; PM, pp. 161–164, 285–287; AL, pp. 93–95, 165–166. Glikl tells the story of Alexander and the human eye after recounting how her daughter Esther had given many alms during the serious illness of her young son "for the ransom of his soul," but her son-in-law had been reluctant to spend the money. Years later, after she had moved into her children's house, she says that her son-in-law had "received a new heart," did much for his family on both sides, and was generous to the poor (KM, p. 312; PM, p. 294; AL, p. 171). Hebrew versions of the tale of Alexander: "Tribute from Eden," *Mimekor Yisrael*, abridged and annotated ed., no. 48, pp. 103–104; "Alexander at the Gate of the Garden of Eden," in Kazis, Introduction to Bonfils, *Book of the Gests*, pp. 16–17.

195. KM, pp. 94–98; PM, pp. 86–89; AL, pp. 52–53, with some omissions. For a historical account of this episode, see Warren Treadgold, *The Byzantine Revival, 780–842* (Stanford, Calif.: Stanford University Press, 1988), pp. 118–120, 130, 132.

196. Theophanes, *Chronicle*, pp. 157–161, Annus mundi 6293–Annus mundi 6295 (1 September 800–1 August 803).

197. "As a righteous matron must I say with the patient Job, 'The Lord has given, the Lord has taken away, the Lord's Name be praised' " (KM, pp. 96–97; PM, p. 88; AL, p. 53). For examples of the modification of a Christian tale in order to create a Yiddish version "acceptable to Jewish ears," see Gabriele L. Strauch, "Text and Context in the Reading of Medieval Literature—A Case in Point: Dukus Horant," in Peter L. Allen and Jeff Rider, eds., *Reflections in the Frame: New Perspectives on the Study of Medieval Literature*, special issue of *Exemplaria*, 3 (1991): 67–94; and Arnold Paucker, "Yiddish Versions of Early German Prose Novels," *Journal of Jewish Studies*, 10 (1959): 151–167.

198. KM, p. 93; PM, p. 86; AL, p. 52.

199. The application of Psalms 31:12 ("forgotten as a dead one") to the death of a child had been made by the eleventh-century scholar Solomon ben Isaac Rashi in a curious commentary on how Jacob mourned his son Joseph for many days in the false belief that he was dead (*Chumash with . . . Rashi's Commentary*, p. 185, n. 35). The talmudic references to Johanan ben Nappaha's mourning his tenth son are in Berakoth 5b and Baba Bathra 116a (I. Epstein, ed., *The Babylonian Talmud, Seder Zera'im*, vol. 1, part 5: *Berakoth*, trans. Maurice Simon [London: Soncino Press, 1948], pp. 20–22; *Seder Neẓikin*, vol. 4, part 4: *Baba Bathra*, trans. Israel W. Slotki [London: Soncino Press, 1953], pp. 477–478). Neither reference gives a story like Glikl's. In Berakoth 5b, R. Johanan and other scholars discuss in what sense it is true that "if a man busies himself in the study of the Torah and in acts of charity and [nonetheless] buries his children, all his sins are forgiven him." In the course of this discussion, R. Johanan says, "Leprosy and [the lack] of children are not chastisements of love." After discussing leprosy, the text goes on, "But is [the lack of] children not a chastisement of love? How is this to be understood? Shall I say that he had children and they died? Did not R. Johanan himself say, 'This is the bone of my tenth son?' " The reference in Baba Bathra 116a is also very brief. The Arukh, an eleventh-century dictionary of the Talmud composed by Rabbi Nathan of Rome, interprets the bone "to have been a tooth of the last of [Johanan's] sons which he preserved . . . to show to people who suffered bereavement to induce in them a spirit of resignation" (comment of Simon on Berakoth 5b, p. 20, n. 9). Johanan ben Nappaha was a third-century Palestinian sage (c. 180–c. 279) (*Encyclopaedia Judaica*, 10: 144–147). There are stories about him in the *Mayse Bukh*, though not the one about the loss of his tenth son (*Ma'aseh Book*, no. 23, pp. 39–40; no. 66, pp. 111–114). Lowenthal, in translating this section of Glikl's book, identified the mourning father as Johanan ben Zakkai, a first-century Jewish sage (Lowenthal, *Memoirs*, p. 88). Glikl herself had simply said "Reb Johanan," adding at one point "a great *tana*" (KM, p. 130; PM, p. 120). Perhaps Lowenthal's misidentification comes from the word *tana*, for technically it should be reserved for scholars of the first century, whereas Johanan ben Nappaha would be called an *amora* (see also Turniansky, "Literary

Sources," p. 167 and n. 32). Among the stories about Johanan ben Zakkai, there is none about the loss of a tenth son and the saving of a bone, but only a very different tale about how he was consoled by others over the loss of a son (Jacob Neusner, *Development of a Legend: Studies on the Traditions Concerning Yohanan ben Zakkai* [Leiden: Brill, 1970], pp. 124–125).

200. KM, pp. 129–132; PM, pp. 119–121; AL, pp. 71–72. In Glikl's account, the little boy was seated on a bench near the kettle by the servants, who then paid no attention to him. His death by falling into the boiling water while housework was going on was by no means unusual in late medieval accidents to children (Barbara Hanawalt, *The Ties That Bound: Peasant Families in Medieval England* [New York: Oxford University Press, 1986], pp. 157, 180).

201. KM, p. 279; PM, p. 264; AL, p. 153. This is the story that she said she had "written out from the Holy Tongue into Taytsh."

202. Jedidiah, a name cognate with David, is the name given Solomon in 2 Samuel 12:24–25.

203. KM, pp. 279–289; PM, pp. 264–272; AL, pp. 153–157.

204. KM, pp. 132–133, 308; PM, pp. 122–123, 288–289; AL, pp. 73, 167.

205. For an important interpretation of these chapters of 2 Samuel which stresses their treatment of David's expressiveness and of dynastic succession, see Joel Rosenberg, "1 and 2 Samuel," in Alter and Kermode, eds., *Literary Guide*, especially pp. 130–143. In Glikl's telling, the issues are sinfulness, suffering, and succession.

206. "Unresolved tension" is Moshe Greenberg's characterization of the Book of Job, in "Job," p. 301.

207. Gaster, *Exempla of the Rabbis*, pp. 23–29; Nissim Ben Jacob Ibn Shahin, *An Elegant Composition Concerning Relief after Adversity*, trans. William M. Brinner (New Haven: Yale University Press, 1977), Introduction, pp. xv–xx; Schwarzbaum, *Mishle Shu'alim*, pp. i–xviii, on the uses of "fables"; and especially for sermons, Saperstein, *Jewish Preaching*, pp. 89–103.

208. For Germany, see the critique of the Jewish use of legends at synagogue in the foreword to Christoph Helwig's translation of the *Mayse Bukh* (*Jüdische Historien*, fols. Aiiiir–Aviir) and the sympathetic reflections of Johann Christopher Wolf on the truth status of the *meshalim* in Jewish thought and their relation to Jesus' parables (*Bibliotheca Hebreae*, 2: 973–981). For France, see Marc Fumaroli, *L'Age de l'Eloquence: Rhétorique et 'res literaria' de la Renaissance au seuil de l'époque classique* (Geneva: Droz, 1980), pp. 358–359, 388: the Jesuit Le Moyne insisted in his *Peintures Morales* of 1643 that the "dramaturgie pédagogique" of sermons was to be made up of "exemples authentiques et tirés de l'Histoire," without the fictions of the theater or the novel.

209. On the mixed language of Jewish sermons, see n. 75 above. KM, pp. 21, 279; PM, pp. 18, 264; AL, pp. 11, 153.

210. KM, p. 323; PM, p. 304, AL, p. 177. Likewise in Book 1, in the midst of

moral commentary: "I do not intend to write a book of morals *(musar)*, for I am not capable of it. Our wise men have written many such books, and we have the holy Torah" (KM, p. 4; PM, p. 3; AL, p. 2.). But she then goes on to insist that one must hold to the Torah and be instructed by the Torah.

211. Zinberg, *Jewish Literature*, vol. 7, pp. 23–24. Chava Weissler, *Traditional Yiddish Literature*, pp. 16–17; and idem, "Women in Paradise," *Tikkun* 2, no. 2 (April–May 1987): 43–36, 117–120.

212. Zinberg, *Jewish Literature*, vol. 7, pp. 241–242, 285–286. Tiktiner's *Meineket Rivkah* had editions in Prague in 1609 and Krakow in 1618; she was known to the Christian Hebraist Johann Christoph Wagenseil, who in 1674 called Tiktiner "the first woman writer in Yiddish." A *firzogerin*, she also wrote a Yiddish liturgical poem for Simchas Torah.

213. In *Gei Hizzayon (A Valley of Vision)*, by Abraham ven Hananiah Yagel, this learned Italian Jew intersperses a fragment of his life—a period of business troubles and imprisonment—with a long set of stories, recounted while he is visiting the next world from prison, summoned to the heavenly voyage by the soul of his father. This is the only text I know of which resembles Glikl's. In an article entitled "The Jewish Theodicy Legend," Dov Noy reviews the structure of many folktales on the themes of suffering and God's justice, collected in Israel from people in mourning. Whatever human protest occurs along the way in the tales, they always end (like many of Glikl's stories) affirming God's justice, human inability to understand God's ways, and the importance of repentance and acceptance (Sanua, ed., *Fields of Offerings*, pp. 65–84). Glikl's stories do not bring finality, however, both because of disturbing elements in each story and because of the events and comments with which they are juxtaposed.

214. On the Marrano Juan/Daniel de Prado and his stay in Hamburg with his wife and mother, see Kaplan, *From Christianity to Judaism*, pp. 125–142, 146–178.

215. KM, p. 199; PM, p. 189; AL, p. 108. A wider background to Glikl's ambivalence about Niddah (as the laws regarding menstruation were called) is suggested by an interesting statement in Jacob Emden's biography of his father, Zevi Hirsch Ashkenazi, the leading rabbi at Hamburg/Altona from 1690 to 1710. "My father decided to prohibit a custom of the women [of Hamburg/Altona], who were putting off their ritual bath until several months after their delivery; this hindered their cycle and caused much trouble" (*Mémoires*, p. 84). The Jewish law, deriving from Leviticus 12:1–8, declared the newly delivered mother unclean for forty days following the birth of a male child and eighty days following the birth of a female child. The legal prescriptions varied somewhat over the centuries in France and Germany, but none delayed purification for as long as "several months" (*Encyclopaedia Judaica*, vol. 12, pp. 1146–1147). The Hamburg women were evidently making their own decisions about the timing of the ritual purification of their bodies and their resumption of intercourse with their husbands.

216. KM, pp. 23, 80–83; PM, pp. 20, 74–76; AL, pp. 12, 45–46. Other prayers

for the coming of the Messiah and/or the redemption of the people of Israel: KM, pp. 1, 58, 309; PM, pp. 1, 52, 289–290; AL, pp. 1, 32, 168. On reactions to Sabbatai Zevi in Hamburg, see Scholem, *Sabbatai Sevi*, pp. 566–591; and on reactions to the Sabbatian prophet and healer Sabbatai Raphael, who came to Hamburg from October 1667 to Passover 1668, see pp. 787–790.

217. KM, pp. 82–83; PM, p. 76; AL, p. 46.

218. KM, pp. 325–333; PM, pp. 305–313; AL, pp. 178–182. The deaths of the six young women are recorded in the Metz *Memorbuch*, p. 72, no. 685. They died on the Sabbath, the second day of Shevouth 5475, and were buried the next day, 6 June 1715. Another account of the episode is *Ma'ase be-Metz*, in SUBF, ms. hebr. oct. 144, fol. 69r–v.

219. KM, p. 333; PM, p. 313; AL, p. 182.

220. The names of the two women who started the affair are given in *Sommaire pour Salomon Cahen, Juif, Banquier et Consorts Juifs et Juives, Habitans de la Ville de Metz, Demandeurs et Défendeurs: Contre Isaac Spire Levy, Olry Chem, et Consorts Juifs Habitans de la même Ville* . . . (1714; BN, N. acq. fr., 22705, pp. 3–4): they were the wife of Isaye Lambert and the wife of Salomon Cahen. According to Cahen, the two women were at prayer in the women's section, and the trouble started when the wife of Lambert said "in a proud and impertinent tone that it was not suitable for [Cahen's wife] to stand in the posture in which she was standing and that she should hold herself in a different way." The men then picked up the fight. Isaye Lambert's wife was Hendele Levy, daughter of Hirsch Levy (see n. 45 above). Salomon Cahen was judged more in the wrong than Lambert by the rabbi and the parnasim, and was sentenced to heavy fines and religious exclusions, all the more severe when Cahen took the case before the Christian courts. One of Cahen's complaints was that his judges had all been relatives or associates of Isaye Lambert, including a business agent of Moses Schwabe (p. 20). See also on this case Malino, "Competition and Confrontation," pp. 327–330.

221. *Responses de Samuel Levy* (1717; see n. 43 above) and *Factum pour Mayeur Tresnel et Olry Abraham Cahen, Juifs de Metz . . . Contre . . . Ruben Schaube, Juif, cy-devant Banquier à Metz. Accusé* (1717); *Précis de la Cause de Samuël Levy, Juif détenu es Prisons de la Conciergerie du Palais, Appellant et Deffendeur . . . Contre, Les Sindics de ses Créanciers Chrétiens* . . . (N.p.: D. Gaydon, 1718; BN, N. acq. fr. 22705).

222. Moses Marcus, *The Principal Motives and Circumstances That induced Moses Marcus To leave the Jewish, and embrace the Christian Faith: With a short Account of his Sufferings thereupon; Written by Himself* (London: E. Bell, 1724). Moses Marcus the Younger, born in 1701, discusses his relations with his parents both in his dedication to the Archbishop of Canterbury and in his autobiographical preface. "My Father and Mother are of the City of Hamburgh, in Germany, and now live in this City (London) in the greatest Splendor imaginable, for private

Persons." Moses' first interest in Protestantism had been aroused in discussion with "German Protestant Divines" in Hamburg, to which his mother had sent him for talmudic studies for several years after his father left for the Indies. When his father returned from India to London "with immense riches" in 1720, he sent for Moses. Back in England, Moses continued his conversations with Christian divines and revealed his views to his father. Despite fierce opposition from his father (Mordecai Hamburger, also known as Moses Marcus the Elder) and mother (Freudchen, Glikl's next-to-last child, born in the 1680s) and attempts to bribe him if he would stay Jewish and go back to Hamburg and marry, Moses was baptized on New Year's Day 1722–1723. His book opens with an attestation of his learning and conversion from the chaplain to the Archbishop of Canterbury, dated 10 August 1723, which suggests a publication early in 1724. Glikl died on September 19, 1724. Mordecai Hamburger had been in the diamond business in London from 1701 to 1712 before going to the French settlement at Pondicherry (1712–1714) and the English settlement at Madras (1714–1720). When he returned to London loaded with precious stones and an enormous diamond, the news was published in all the London gazettes (Yogev, *Diamonds*, pp. 130–131, 150–152, 156–158; Emden, *Mémoires*, p. 183). Thus, public discussion of the family was already part of the London scene before the conversion of Moses Marcus the Younger. On Jewish conversion, see Deborah Hertz, "Women at the Edge of Judaism: Female Converts in Germany, 1600–1750," in Menachem Mor, ed., *Jewish Assimilation, Acculturation and Accommodation: Past Traditions, Current Issues and Future Prospects*, Studies in Jewish Civilization, 2 (Lanham, Md.: University Press of America, 1992), pp. 87–109; Todd Endelman, *The Jews of Georgian England, 1714–1830: Tradition and Change in a Liberal Society* (Philadelphia: Jewish Publication Society, 1979), ch. 2; and idem, *Radical Assimilation in English Jewish History, 1656–1945* (Bloomington: Indiana University Press, 1990), ch. 2.

223. KM, p. 333; PM, p. 313; AL, p. 182.

New Worlds

1. The original manuscript of the spiritual relation sent by Marie de l'Incarnation to her son, Claude Martin, in 1654 is lost, but a copy made in the last quarter of the seventeenth century is in the archives of the Ursuline house at Trois-Rivières, Québec; I have used it in photocopy at the Ursuline house in Ville de Québec. The manuscript has been published by Dom Albert Jamet as "La Relation de 1654," in Marie de l'Incarnation, *Ecrits spirituels et historiques*, 4 vols. (Paris: Desclée de Brouwer, 1929–1939; facsimile reprinting of vols. 1–2, Québec: Les Ursulines de Québec, 1985), vol. 2. The source and history of the manuscript are discussed by Jamet in *Ecrits*, vol. 2, pp. 26–33; and by Soeur Sainte-Julie, "Marie de l'Incarnation: Sa relation spirituelle manuscrite de l'année 1654," mimeograph (Trois-Rivières, Québec: Archives des Ursulines, 1976). A

slightly revised version of the *Relation* of 1654 was published by Marie's son, Claude Martin, together with much other material, in *La Vie de la venerable Mere Marie de l'Incarnation, Premiere superieure des Ursulines de la Nouvelle France: Tirée de ses Lettres et de ses Ecrits* (Paris: Louis Billaine, 1677; facsimile edition Solesmes: Abbaye de Saint-Pierre, 1981). In quoting from or citing the *Relation*, I will give page references in the notes both to the manuscript version as published by Jamet and to the printed version published by Claude Martin, but unless I indicate otherwise my translations will always be based on the manuscript version. *Rel*, pp. 159–161; *Vie*, pp. 168–170.

2. *Rel*, pp. 165–167; *Vie*, pp. 181–182.

3. Marie de l'Incarnation to Claude Martin, 9 August 1654, 27 September 1654, in *Vie*, fols. 04r–u2v. Also printed in Marie de l'Incarnation, *Correspondance*, ed. Dom Guy Oury (Solesmes: Abbaye Saint-Pierre, 1971), no. 155, p. 526; no. 162, p. 548. References to Marie de l'Incarnation and Claude Martin within *Cor* will be abbreviated MI and CM.

4. Marie-Augustine de Sainte-Paule de Pommereu, *Les Chroniques de l'Ordre des Ursulines, recueillies pour l'usage des Religieuses du mesme ordre*, 2 vols. (Paris: Jean Henault, 1673), vol. 2, part 3, p. 439. The *femme forte* image is used about Saint Ursula herself, ibid., vol. 1, part 1, p. 4. On different uses of the image, see Ian Maclean, *Woman Triumphant: Feminism in French Literature, 1610–1652* (Oxford: Clarendon Press, 1977), ch. 3; and Linda Lierheimer, "Female Eloquence and Maternal Ministry: The Apostolate of Ursuline Nuns in Seventeeth-Century France" (Diss., Princeton University, 1994). In addition to the *Vie* of Marie, edited and expanded by her son, Claude Martin, a life was published by the Jesuit Pierre-François de Charlevoix, who drew primarily from the Martin work: *La Vie de la Mere Marie de l'Incarnation, Institutrice et premiere Superieure des Ursulines de la Nouvelle France* (Paris: Louis-Antoine Thomelin, 1724). The standard modern biography of Marie Guyart de l'Incarnation is Dom Guy-Marie Oury, *Marie de l'Incarnation (1599–1672)* (Québec: Presses de l'Université Laval, 1973; and Solesmes: Abbaye Saint-Pierre, 1973); a recent biography is Françoise Deroy-Pineau, *Marie de l'Incarnation: Marie Guyart, femme d'affaires, mystique, mère de la Nouvelle France, 1599–1672* (Paris: Editions Robert Laffont, 1989). Studies focusing on her spirituality include Henri Brémond, *Histoire littéraire du sentiment religieux en France depuis la fin des Guerres de Religion jusqu'à nos jours*, 11 vols. (Paris: Bloud et Gay, 1920–1933), vol. 6, *La Conquête mystique*, part 1; and Maria-Paul del Rosario Adriazola, *La Connaissance spirituelle chez Marie de l'Incarnation* (Paris: Les Editions du Cerf, 1989). Useful articles include Germain Marc'hadour, "De Tours à Québec: Marie de l'Incarnation," *Impacts*, n.s., 3 (1975): 3–25; Dominique Deslandres, "L'Education des Amérindiennes d'après la correspondance de Marie Guyart de l'Incarnation," *Studies in Religion / Sciences Religieuses* 16 (1987): 91–110; Chantal Théry, "Marie de l'Incarnation, intimée et intime, à travers sa *Correspondance* et ses *Ecrits spirituels*," in Manon Brunet and Serge

Gagnon, eds., *Discours et pratiques de l'Intime* (Québec: IQRC, 1993), pp. 107–118; and Marie-Florine Bruneau, "Feminité sauvage; feminité civilisé: Marie de l'Incarnation entre la clôture et la forêt," *Papers on French Seventeenth-Century Literature*, 19, no. 37 (1992): 347–354; Bruneau also has a longer study of Marie de l'Incarnation forthcoming. In addition, see Claire Gourdeau, *Les délices de nos coeurs: Marie de l'Incarnation et ses pensionnaires amérindiennes* (Sillery: Septentrion, 1994).

5. Bernard Chevalier, ed., *Histoire de Tours* (Toulouse: Privat, 1985), chs. 5–6; Jean-Pierre Surrault, "La Touraine des temps modernes," in Claude Croubois, ed., *L'Indre et Loire: La Touraine des origines à nos jours* (Saint-Jean-d'Angely: Editions Bordessoules, 1982), pp. 195–285.

6. *Rel*, pp. 46–47; *Vie*, pp. 2, 4, 9–10. E. Chambert, "La Famille de la vénérable Marie de l'Incarnation," *Bulletin de la société archéologique de Touraine*, 23 (1926–1927): 91–104; Oury, *Marie*, pp. 6–12. Marie Guyart's father, Florent, is described as a "marchand boulanger" in an act of 1621 (ADIL, 3E2, notary François Nau, 25 September 1621). Jeanne Michelet, Marie Guyart's mother, was distantly related to the Babou family, whose most distinguished member in the early sixteenth century was Philibert Babou, seigneur de la Bourdaisière in Touraine and *contrôleur de l'argenterie du roi* (*Inventaire sommaire des archives départementales antérieures à 1790: Indre-et-Loire*, ed. C. Loizeau de Grandmaison [Paris: Dupont, 1878–1891], E34, E47, E57, E59). On the Abbey of Beaumont-les-Tours, see *Chronique de l'abbaye de Beaumont-lez-Tours*, ed. Charles de Grandmaison, in *Mémoires de la société archéologique de Touraine*, 26 (1877). Philibert's descendants were Beaumont abbesses: Magdelaine Babou, abbess from 1573 to 1577; her sister Anne Babou, abbess from 1578 until her death in 1613; their grandniece Anne Babou, abbess from 1613 to 1647 (ibid., pp. 39, 76, 81). The nuns described in the *Chronique* come from noble families of Touraine and other regions, from families of high royal officers, and perhaps a few from the families of the urban elite. One young woman of nonnoble status was received in 1627 at a time of plague: Marie Gatien, an apothecary's daughter, who herself could serve as pharmacist to the house (ibid., p. 96).

7. *Rel*, pp. 56–59; *Vie*, pp. 7–12, 14–18, 23–25, 638 ("God permitted a certain woman to unleash against her and her husband all the persecutions and actions she could devise, and she succeeded so well that she was the instrument God used to despoil them of all their goods"). On the claims of the widow's dower on the husband's estate in Touraine, see Hubert Gelly, "Soixante-quinze ans de vie tourangelle d'après les décisions du Parlement de Paris," *Bulletin de la Société Archéologique de Touraine*, 39 (1979): 166.

8. *Rel*, pp. 72–75, 88, 99; *Vie*, pp. 30–43, 52–55. Paul Buisson is described in the 1621 marriage contract of his niece Barbe Angerelle as a *"marchant roulyer,"* "merchant wagoner" (ADIL, 3E2, Notaire François Nau, 25 September 1621). Barbe had been living in the Buisson household, and perhaps it was because

of her departure after her marriage to a blacksmith that space was created in the house for Marie Guyart and her son to move in. In a judicial act of 1642, drawn up about ten years after his death, Paul Buisson was characterized as a "capitaine des charrons de l'Artillerie" (AN, X2b, no. 174, 11 September 1642), whereas Claude Martin said that he was "Commissionnaire pour le transport des marchandises dans tous les côtez du Royaume: il estoit encore Officier de l'Artillerie" (*Vie*, p. 54). The success of Buisson's trucking business is suggested by these added titles and royal offices. On the kind of business that would have been conducted in Buisson's household, see E. Levasseur, *Histoire du commerce de la France*, 2 vols. (Paris: A. Rousseau, 1911), vol. 1, pp. 244–250, 313–319.

9. *Rel*, pp. 48–49, 53, 67–71; *Vie*, pp. 3, 13–14, 26–30.

10. *Rel*, p. 78; *Vie*, p. 38. *Introduction A La Vie Devote Par François de Sales, Evesque et Prelat de Geneve* was first published by Pierre Rigaud in Lyon in 1609; a second and third edition, with revisions and corrections, appeared in 1610. The text is addressed to "Philothea." Before 1620, forty French editions had been published (Henri-Jean Martin, *Livre, pouvoirs et société à Paris au XVIIe siècle (1598–1701)*, 2 vols. [Geneva: Librairie Droz, 1969], vol. 1, p. 146). On the importance of the *Introduction* for laywomen, see Elizabeth Rapley, *The Dévotes: Women and Church in Seventeenth-Century France* (Montréal and Kingston: McGill-Queen's University Press, pp. 17–18). Marie de la Nativité, a novice at the Ursuline convent in the 1630s, also got her start when her confessor had her read the work (*Vie*, p. 244). On the early phases of the Catholic Reformation in Tours, see Robert Sauzet, "Le Milieu dévot tourangeau et les débuts de la réforme catholique," *Revue d'histoire de l'Eglise de France*, 75 (1989): 159–166.

11. *Rel*, pp. 88–89, 97–98, 107; *Vie*, pp. 48–49, 64, 93, 490–491, 501–502.

12. *Rel*, p. 128; *Vie*, pp. 93, 115. Claude Guyart has a clear and elegant signature at the bottom of the marriage contract of her husband's niece (ADIL, 3E2, notary François Nau, 25 September 1621). Inventory postmortem of Claude's goods in ADIL, E254, 7 March 1643: pictures of Mary Magdalene, Melchizedek, Our Lady, and "Roman Charity." Her sister Jeanne Guyart, who married the schoolteacher Sylvestre Normand, would have entered the world of literate culture through her husband; she could also sign her name (Chambert, "Famille," p. 93). Claude Martin claimed that Paul Buisson could neither read nor write, and that Marie Guyart had to read to him all his incoming correspondence and write his answers (*Vie*, p. 636); and indeed, he does not sign his niece's marriage contract. It is hard to believe that Buisson obtained the office of military transport without even a shred of literacy, but it could well be that he depended on Marie for most of his secretarial work.

13. *Rel*, p. 147; *Vie*, pp. 51, 52, 128. See Martin, *Livre*, vol. 1, pp. 102–103, 134, on these editions. A corpus of medieval mystical texts was attributed to the first-century Greek Christian Dionysus the Areopagite, believed to be the same as Saint Denis, the first bishop of Paris. On the great importance of his "mystic

theology" to spiritual practice in the first half of the seventeenth century, see Michel de Certeau, *The Mystic Fable*, trans. Michael B. Smith (Chicago: University of Chicago Press, 1992), vol. 1: *The Sixteenth and Seventeenth Centuries*, pp. 90, 102–103, 147–149. The edition available to Marie Guyart was *Les Oeuvres de divin St Denys Aréopagite, traduites du grec en françois par fr. Jean de St François* [Jean Goulu] (Paris: Jean de Heuqueville, 1608), with a second edition in 1629. Goulu was a Feuillant, like Marie's Director, and a friend and biographer of François de Sales. On active and passive methods of mental prayer, see *Rel*, pp. 77–79; *Vie*, pp. 38–39.

14. *Rel*, pp. 116, 123, 140–141, 147; *Vie*, pp. 73, 84, 107, 128. On divine conversation in mystical practice, see de Certeau, *Mystic Fable*, pp. 157–161.

15. *Rel*, pp. 93, 119–122; *Vie*, pp. 45, 77–79, 417.

16. *Rel*, p. 123; *Vie*, pp. 84, 417.

17. *Rel*, pp. 101–102, 113–115; *Vie*, pp. 53–54, 69–72.

18. *Vie*, pp. 51, 88, 115, 130–131, 142–143, 161.

19. *Rel*, pp. 97, 108–110, 114, 149–150; *Vie*, pp. 47–49, 62, 64–65, 70, 135. Caroline Bynum has discussed the uses of painful asceticism in the spirituality of late medieval women, stressing that their practices were based not on simple hatred of inferior female flesh as opposed to spirit, but rather on a desire to use both human flesh and spirit in imitation of Christ (*Holy Feast and Holy Fast: The Religious Significance of Food to Medieval Women* [Berkeley, Calif.: University of California Press, 1987], especially pp. 208–218, 294–296). Marie Guyart, like the figures examined by Bynum, showed no signs of viewing female flesh as inferior to male flesh, though she did describe her heroic asceticism as the action of a divinely aided soul against the body. The fruits for her were the imitation of Christ and especially union with Christ. I am also suggesting a connection between bodily mortification and the ecstasy of writing, both of which are consummations of the loving union with God.

20. *Rel*, p. 110; *Vie*, p. 66.

21. *Rel*, pp. 111, 123; *Vie*, pp. 67–68, 84.

22. Ignatius Loyola, *The Spiritual Exercises*, trans. Anthony Mottola (Garden City, N.Y.: Doubleday Image, 1964), Fourth Week, Three Methods of Prayer, pp. 105–109. French translations of the *Spiritual Exercises* appeared in Lille in 1614 and in Paris in 1619. François de Sales, *Introduction to the Devout Life*, trans. John K. Ryan (Garden City, N.Y.: Doubleday Image, 1955), Second Part, pp. 80–89: a method for mental prayer, with points, preparation, representation by imagination, and other techniques.

23. On hypocrisy, masking, and the quest for authenticity in the latter half of the sixteenth century, see Natalie Zemon Davis, *The Return of Martin Guerre* (Cambridge, Mass.: Harvard University Press, 1983); and Jean Starobinski, *Montaigne in Motion*, trans. Arthur Goldhammer (Chicago: University of Chicago Press, 1985).

24. Teresa of Avila, *The Life of Teresa of Jesus: The Autobiography of St. Teresa of Avila,* trans. E. Allison Peers (Garden City, N.Y.: Doubleday Image, 1960), ch. 7, p. 96; ch. 26, pp. 242–243; ch. 29, pp. 267–275. On Teresa's counsel and rhetorical strategies for dealing with the devil and "melancholy," see Alison Weber, *Teresa of Avila and the Rhetoric of Femininity* (Princeton, N.J.: Princeton University Press, 1990). *Rel,* p. 112; *Vie,* pp. 67–69, 93.

25. François de Sales, *Introduction,* pp. 223–224: "Instruction for Widows." *Rel,* pp. 78, 104–107; *Vie,* pp. 39, 42–43, 58–60.

26. *Vie,* p. 114.

27. *Rel,* pp. 97, 142–143; *Vie,* pp. 48, 112, 621, 628–629, 631. On plague years in Tours during the first part of the seventeenth century, see Brigitte Maillard, "Les Hommes et la mort à Tours au XVIIe siècle," in Monique Bourin, ed., *Villes, bonnes villes, cités et capitales: Etudes d'histoire urbaine (XIIe–XVIIIe siècle) offertes à Bernard Chevalier* (Caen: Paradigme, 1993), p. 79.

28. *Rel,* pp. 114, 142; *Vie,* pp. 70, 11–112, 618.

29. [Jean de Bernières, sieur de Louvigny], *The Interiour Christian; or the Interiour Conformity which Christians Ought to have with Jesus Christ* (Antwerp: n.p., 1684), fol. a3r. *Le Chrétien intérieur* was first published by the sister of Bernières in 1659, after his death. On the piety of Bernières, see Brémond, *Sentiment religieux,* vol. 6, pp. 229–266; and on the remarkable publishing success of *Le Chrétien intérieur,* see Martin, *Livre,* vol. 2, p. 621.

30. *Rel,* pp. 156–158; *Vie,* pp. 123–124, 162–165.

31. *Rel,* pp. 158–161; *Vie,* pp. 168–176. The story of Marie Guyart's neither embracing him after the age of two nor hitting him is retained in the biography of Claude Martin, written by his fellow Benedictine-Maurist Edmond Martene and based on interviews with Martin over many years as well as on other sources. [Edmond Martene], *La Vie du venerable pere Dom Claude Martin, religieux benedictin de la Congregation de S. Maur; Decedé en odeur de sainteté au Monastere de Mairmontier, le 9 du mois d'Aoust 1696* (Tours: Philibert Masson, 1697), p. 4.

32. *Rel,* p. 159; *Vie,* pp. 169, 175, 374.

33. Marie Guyart may well have heard an account of Frémyot's departure to found the order of the Visitation from her friend Gillette Roland, to whom Dom Raymond de Saint Bernard also ministered as Director. Roland had known François de Sales in Savoie, and she was to be one of the founders of the order of the Visitation in Tours in 1633. See MI to Marie-Gillette Roland, religious of the Visitation of Tours, Québec, 4 September 1640, *Cor,* no. 46, pp. 108–110, and 30 August 1642 (the "precious death" of Jeanne de Chantal), no. 63, p. 154. Marie de l'Incarnation's correspondents will be given their religious or ecclesiastical titles at their first appearance in these notes. Subsequently they will be referred to by name only.

34. On the origins of the Visitation and other activist women's orders in seventeenth-century France, see Rapley, *The Dévotes.* On the departure of Jeanne-

Françoise Frémyot, baronne de Chantal (today usually called Jeanne de Chantal) and her relations with her children, see Msgr. Bougaud, *Histoire de Sainte Chantal et des origines de la Visitation*, 2 vols. (Paris: Poussielgue, 1909), vol. 1, ch. 12; and Elisabeth Stopp, *Madame de Chantal: Portrait of a Saint* (Westminster, Md.: Newman Press, 1962), ch. 6. In 1609 Frémyot had married her oldest daughter, aged twelve, to the baron de Thorens, brother of François de Sales; since the young couple resided in Savoie, the mother was able to keep in touch with them. Her second daughter, Françoise, was raised at the Visitation convent in Annecy, and then made a good marriage to the comte de Toulongeon. The youngest child, Charlotte, whom Frémyot had also planned to take with her to the convent, died shortly before Jeanne-Francoise's departure. The son, Celse-Bénigne, had already come under his maternal grandfather's care in Dijon the year before his mother's departure and was receiving instruction from a family tutor. Stopp has suggested the connection between Celse-Bénigne's action at the doorsill and Plutarch's story of the young Pompey, who lay down at the gate of his father's military camp to prevent his father's soldiers from deserting to Cinna (p. 111). Celse-Bénigne's tutor might well have had him read Plutarch, either in Latin or in the French translation by Jacques Amyot. Plutarch, *The Lives of the Noble Grecians and Romains Compared*, trans. Thomas Norton (London: George Miller, 1631), p. 633.

35. *Rel*, p. 161; *Vie*, pp. 170, 176–179.

36. On the history of the Ursulines, see T. Ledochowska, *Angèle Mérici et la Compagnie de Sainte-Ursule à la lumière des documents*, 2 vols. (Rome and Milan: Ancora, 1968); Pommereu, *Chroniques;* Gabrielle Marie de Chantal de Gueudré, *Histoire de l'Ordre des Ursulines en France*, 3 vols. (Paris: Editions Saint-Paul, 1958–1963); Marie André Jégou, *Les Ursulines du faubourg St-Jacques à Paris, 1607–1662* (Paris: Presses Universitaires de France, 1981); and Lierheimer, "Female Eloquence."

37. *Rel*, p. 159; *Vie*, pp. 169, 371. MI to the Ursulines of Tours, 1652, *Cor*, no. 140, p. 457. Oury, *Marie*, p. 293. Dowries in the 1630s were in the range of 4,000–5,000 livres in the Tours house. One of the women who made profession during Marie's years was Claire Grannon, daughter of Cézare Grannon, sieur de la Boyarderie and bourgeois of Tours, with a dowry of 5,500£ (ADIL, H852, acts of 31 March 1637, 10 January 1639 ("Soeur Marie Guiard, assistante," was among the witnesses). Among the novices later taught by Marie were the daughters of an ennobled burgher, of an old noble family of Touraine, and of a grain merchant (*Vie*, pp. 242, 285, 291). On the mixture of social background and the size of dowries among the Paris Ursulines, see Jégou, *Ursulines*, pp. 103–107.

38. Pommereu, *Chroniques*, vol. 1, part 2, p. 195; Jégou, *Ursulines*, ch. 9; Gueudré, *Ursulines*, vol. 2, ch. 5; Roger Chartier, Dominique Julia, and Marie-Madeleine Compère, *L'Education en France du XVIe au XVIIIe siècle* (Paris: Société d'Edition d'Enseignement Supérieur, 1976), ch. 8.; Rapley, *Dévotes*, pp. 58–60; Lierheimer, "Female Eloquence," chs. 4–5.

39. Pommereu, *Chroniques*, vol. 1, part 1, pp. 40–45 (on possessions among the Ursulines in Aix-en-Provence in 1609–1611); part 2, pp. 244–247 (on possessions at the Ursuline house in Auxonne in 1658–1660). Michel de Certeau, *La Possession de Loudon*, 3rd ed. (Paris: Gallimard, 1990).

40. *Rel*, pp. 179–180; *Vie*, pp. 205–206.

41. *Rel*, pp. 165, 176–177; *Vie*, pp. 180–181, 199–200, 502–505. Brémond, *Sentiment religieux*, vol.3, pp. 43–74, a description of the theology and mystical sensibility of Cardinal Pierre de Bérulle (d. 1629), a leader of the Catholic Reformation in France. On the Augustinian origins of the theology of the Word, see A. Vacant et al., *Dictionnaire de théologie catholique*, 15 vols. (Paris: Librairie Letouzey et Ané, 1903–1950), vol. 15, pp. 2664–2666. The Word Incarnate is not central to Saint Teresa's images of Christ in either her *Life* or her guide to prayer, *The Way of Perfection*, trans. E. Allison Peers (Garden City, N.Y.: Doubleday Image, 1964).

42. *Vie*, pp. 217–218. Marie learned later that her son's bad conduct was also an "adroit" ruse to get himself back to Tours at the time of her profession. He had not been allowed to attend her investiture, and did not want to miss the second ceremony (*Rel*, p. 183). Claude Martin omitted the word *finement*— "adroitly"—about himself when he edited the text for publication (*Vie*, p. 216). [Martene], *Claude Martin*, p. 8.

43. *Rel*, pp. 178–179; *Vie*, pp. 204, 208–215, 224–225. On *malaise* and melancholy among the religious, see Jean Delumeau, *Sin and Fear: The Emergence of a Western Guilt Culture, 13th–18th centuries*, trans. Eric Nicholson (New York: St. Martin's Press, 1990), ch. 10; and Weber, *Teresa*, pp. 139–146.

44. *Vie*, pp. 211–212, 218.

45. *Rel*, pp. 182–183; *Vie*, pp. 215–216.

46. Though local efforts to establish a Jesuit college in Tours went back to 1583, it was only in the spring of 1632 that Louis XIII finally authorized the order to have a permanent residence in the town (Oury, *Marie*, pp. 210–212). On the radicals and *illuminati* among the Jesuits, see Brémond, *Sentiment religieux*, vol. 3, pp. 258–279 ("Jésuites Bérulliens") and especially de Certeau, *Mystic Fable*, ch. 8.

47. Dom Raymond de S. Bernard had been called from Tours not long after Marie Guyart de l'Incarnation entered the Ursulines, and there are only a few letters from her to him extant for the years of melancholy, 1631–1633. In contrast, there are numerous letters from the years before and after (*Rel*, pp. 181–182; *Vie*, p. 215; *Cor*, p. 1039). She obtained permission to write a letter to the Ursuline confessor, which he answered only three weeks later with a single sentence (*Vie*, p. 212). On Father La Haye's becoming her director and urging her to write, see *Rel*, pp. 181–185; *Vie*, pp. 215–217, 222–223.

48. *Rel*, pp. 174–175; *Vie*, pp. 198–199. Pommereu, *Chroniques*, vol. 1, part

1, p. 26, on Angela: "Prayer rendered her so learned that she did not learn otherwise to read or write. She even understood Latin by an infused knowledge."

49. *Rel*, pp. 189, 194–196; *Vie*, pp. 202–203, 228, 234–235. Marie's phrase is that she read in "le petit Catéchisme du Concil et dans celuy du Cardinal Bellarmin." The catechism of the Council of Trent was published in Latin and was intended for educated priests, but had editions in French by 1578–1580. Roberto Bellarmin prepared two catechisms—a Grand and a Petit—the second of which had many editions in French (Jean-Claude Dhotel, *Les Origines du catéchisme moderne d'après les premiers manuels imprimés en France* [Paris: Aubier-Montaigne, 1967], pp. 440–441). She had also been reading the *Exercicio de perfeccion y virtudes christianas* of the Spanish Jesuit Alonso Rodriguez, much reprinted in French from 1621 on. She had not found it helpful for her interior meditation, and Father La Haye told her to put it aside and read only her French New Testament. *Rel*, p. 189; *Vie*, p. 228; Martin, *Livre*, vol. 1, p. 140.

50. *Rel*, pp. 194–195; *Vie*, pp. 234–235, 240–242, 519–520. Her Jesuit Director was now Jacques Dinet, one-time rector of the Jesuit College at Rennes, where her son had been a pupil. Dinet had also been a schoolmate and fellow teacher at Rouen with Louis Lallemant, one of the most important of the "spiritual Jesuits" (*Rel*, p. 195; *Vie*, pp. 217, 235; Oury, *Marie*, p. 243, no. 1; Certeau, *Mystic Fable*, pp. 269–270). Marie gave three manuscripts to the Mother Superior of the Tours house when she left France for Canada: a catechism, an exposition of the Song of Songs, and a set of meditations during two retreats (MI to CM, 26 October 1653, *Cor*, no. 153, pp. 516–517). They were published after her death by her son, Claude Martin, with his own modifications and additions, under the titles *L'Ecole sainte ou explication familiere des mysteres de la foy* (Paris: Jean Baptiste Coignard, 1684) and *Retraites de la venerable Mere Marie de l'Incarnation religieuse Ursuline; Avec une exposition succincte du Cantique des Cantiques* (Paris: Louis Billaine, 1682). A modern edition of the latter work with some additions from the *Vie* can be found in *Ecrits spirituels et historiques,* ed. Jamet, vol. 1, pp. 395–525.

51. MI to Raymond de S. Bernard, 3 May 1635, *Cor*, no. 17, pp. 42–43; *Rel*, pp. 189–193; *Vie*, pp. 229–230, 232–234.

52. *Rel*, pp. 198–199, 201–205; *Vie*, pp. 300–301, 305, 309–310, 316; MI to Raymond de S. Bernard, 1635, *Cor*, no. 12, p. 27. Published *Relations* from Jesuit missionaries in North America begin with Pierre Biard's *Relation de la Nouvelle France* (Lyon: Louis Muguet, 1616), which concerned the Abenakis and Micmacs of the Atlantic seaboard, the region that the French called Acadie. Then in 1532 appeared Paul Le Jeune's account from Québec, *Brieve Relation du Voyage de la Nouvelle France, Fait au mois d'Avril dernier par le P. Paul le Ieune de la Compagnie de Iesus* (Paris: Sébastien Cramoisy, 1632). Subsequently the Cramoisy atelier brought out a *Relation* every year until 1672. The *Relations* have been published in French and English translation by Reuben Gold Thwaites, ed., *The Jesuit*

Relations and Allied Documents, 73 vols. (Cleveland, Ohio: Burrows Brothers, 1896–1901).

53. *Vie,* p. 307. Heart imagery was important in Marie's account of her relation to Christ in the years 1635–1638, when she was seeking support for the Canadian adventure (*Rel,* p. 203; *Vie,* p. 306).

54. *JR,* vol. 5, pp. 144–147; vol. 6, pp. 150–153; vol. 7, p. 256. MI to Raymond de S. Bernard, April 1635, *Cor,* no. 12, p. 27. Writing later in her autobiography about crossing the Atlantic, she described how much there had been to suffer "for persons of our sex and condition" (no fresh water, inability to sleep, etc.), but insisted that nonetheless her spirit and heart had been at peace (*Rel,* p. 246; *Vie,* p. 395).

55. Even before Marie had begun to read the *Jesuit Relations,* she was reading Etienne Binet's life of François de Xavier (1506–1552): *L'Abbregé de la vie admirable de S. François Xavier de la Compagnie de Jesus, surnommé l'apostre des Indes* (Paris: S. Chappelet, 1622). His "zeal for the conversion of peoples" may have been one of the sources of her vision (MI to the Ursulines of Tours, spring 1652, *Cor,* no. 140, p. 443).

56. *Rel,* pp. 198–200; *Vie,* pp. 301–302. See Book of Revelation, 1:5, 11:15, and 17:14 for possible quotations from Marie to God the Father. Another Bible quote to Dom Raymond de S. Bernard appears in a letter of April 1635: "I have strongly present in my mind the passage from Saint Paul that *Jesus Christ died for everyone,* and I see with extreme sadness that everyone does not yet live [in Christ] and that so many souls are plunged in death. I am embarrassed all over to dare to aspire and even to think that I can contribute to their finding life" (*Cor,* no. 12, p. 27).

57. Vincent Ferrer, "Traité contre les Juifs" (1414), in Père Fages, O.P., ed., *Oeuvres de Saint Vincent Ferrier* (Paris: A. Picard and A. Savaète, 1909), vol. 1. Jean Seguy, "Monsieur Vincent, la Congrégation de la Mission et les derniers temps," in *Vincent de Paul: Actes du Colloque International d'Etudes Vincentiennes, Paris, 25–26 septembre 1981* (Rome: Edizioni Vincenziane, 1983), pp. 217–238.

58. Guillaume Postel, *De la Republique des Turcs: et là ou l'occasion s'offrera, des meurs et loys de tous Muhamedistes, par Guillaume Postel Cosmopolite* (Poitiers: Enguilbert de Marnef, n.d. [1565?]), dedication to the Dauphin of France, son of Henri II. William Bouwsma, *Concordia Mundi: The Career and Thought of Guillaume Postel (1510–1581)* (Cambridge, Mass.: Harvard University Press, 1957), chs. 5, 7; Maurice de Gandillac, "Le Thème postelien de la concorde universelle," and Marion Kuntz, "Guillaume Postel and the Universal Monarchy: The State as a Work of Art," in *Guillaume Postel, 1581–1981: Actes du Colloque International d'Avranches, 5–9 septembre 1981* (Paris: Maisnie-Trédaniel, 1985), pp. 191–197, 233–256; Frances A. Yates, *Astrea: The Imperial Theme in the Sixteenth Century* (London: Routledge and Kegan Paul, 1975), esp. pp. 1–28, 121–126, 144–146.

59. Psalms 113:3: "From the rising of the sun unto the going down of the

same the Lord's name is to be praised" (*Vie*, p. 320); 2 Corinthians 5:15 (MI to Raymond de S. Bernard, April 1635, *Cor*, no. 12, p. 27).

60. *Rel*, p. 198; *Vie*, p. 300.

61. *Rel*, pp. 211–221; *Vie*, pp. 316–349; MI to Raymond de S. Bernard, late 1638, *Cor*, no. 30, pp. 67–69 (reports news from the Jesuit letters she has received from Canada, including a letter from Father Garnier written on birchbark); *JR*, vol. 7, pp. 256–259.

62. *Rel*, pp. 213–215, 219–221; *Vie*, pp. 322–339; MI to Raymond de S. Bernard, 19 April 1635, 26 October 1637, *Cor*, nos. 14, 28, pp. 33, 65.

63. There had been hope that Noël Brûlant de Sillery would endow a women's convent in New France but nothing came of it (*Vie*, pp. 334, 339; MI to Raymond de S. Bernard, 29 July 1635, *Cor*, no. 20, pp. 48–50 and 49, n. 4). On the career of Isaac de Razilly, administrator for Louis XIII and the Compagnie de la Nouvelle France in Acadia from 1632 to 1635, see Sauzet, "Le Milieu dévot," pp. 160, 162; *Dictionary of Canadian Biography*, ed. George Brown, 12 vols. (Toronto: University of Toronto Press, 1966–1991), vol. 1, pp. 567–569; and Dom Guy Oury, "Les Tourangeaux en Nouvelle-France au temps de Marie de l'Incarnation," *Bulletin trimestriel de la Société archéologique de Touraine*, 37 (1972): 149–151. The two girls were the daughters of a Micmac woman and Charles Saint-Etienne de la Tour, fur trader and coadministrator of Acadia with Razilly. One daughter, baptized Antoinette de Saint Etienne, entered the Benedictine house of Beaumont-les-Tours in 1636, sang so well that she was taken before the queen to perform, and made her profession in 1646, aged about nineteen or twenty (*Chronique . . . de Beaumont*, pp. 139–143, 252). The other daughter entered the Ursuline convent in Tours in 1634 or 1635 at about eight years of age and died several years later. Curiously enough, Marie de l'Incarnation did not mention the métisse girl in her letters of the late 1630s or in her reminiscences.

64. *Rel*, pp. 206–207; *Vie*, pp. 310–315, 733: "her life was very similar to that of our Mother." Dom Guy-Marie Oury, *Madame de la Peltrie et ses fondations canadiennes* (Québec: Presses Université de Laval, 1974), pp. 9–40. MI to Joseph-Antoine Poncet, Québec, 25 October 1670, *Cor*, no. 259, pp. 904–905.

65. *Rel*, pp. 227–228; *Vie*, pp. 350–354, 356–357; Oury, *La Peltrie*, pp. 43–55; MI to Joseph-Antoine Poncet, 25 October 1670, *Cor*, no. 269, pp. 905–907. Marie de l'Incarnation, who had once feared hypocrisy as the worst possible sin in her own inner life, described the Bernières–La Peltrie false marriage in God's cause as "playful and diverting" when she wrote of it after La Peltrie's death (ibid., p. 909). On women's use of stratagems and false scenarios to get around family constraints, see Sarah Hanley, "Engendering the State: Family Formation and State Building in Early Modern France," *French Historical Studies*, 16 (1989): 15–21.

66. *Rel*, pp. 229–232; *Vie*, pp. 357–359; MI to Joseph-Antoine Poncet, 25 October 1670, *Cor*, no. 269, p. 907; Oury, *La Peltrie*, pp. 57–65. On the Com-

pagnie de la Nouvelle France, established in 1627–1628, see Charles W. Cole, *Colbert and a Century of French Mercantilism*, 2 vols. (New York: Columbia University Press, 1939; reprint Hamden, Conn.: Archon Books, 1964), vol. 1, pp. 173–185; and Marcel Trudel, *Histoire de la Nouvelle-France*, 3 vols. (Montréal: Fides, 1963–1983), vol. 3, part 1, *La Seigneurie des Cents-Associés, 1627–1663: Les Evénements*, pp. 1–25. The Company could distribute lands in New France as it pleased.

67. *Rel*, pp. 228–229, 231–235; *Vie*, pp. 357, 359–366, 368–374; MI to Madame de La Peltrie, Tours, November 1638, *Cor*, no. 31, p. 70; Oury, *La Peltrie*, pp. 65–70.

68. *Rel*, p. 235; *Vie*, pp. 366, 374–376; [Martene], *Claude Martin*, pp. 10–12; Dom Guy-Marie Oury, *Claude Martin: Le Fils de Marie de l'Incarnation* (Solesmes: Abbaye Saint-Pierre, 1983), pp. 35–38.

69. *Rel*, p. 239; *Vie*, p. 378. Among other charitable activities, the Duchesse d'Aiguillon sponsored the Daughters of Charity, founded by Louise de Marillac and Vincent de Paul, and financed the foundation of the Hôtel-Dieu of Québec. Paul Ragueneau, *La Vie de la mere Catherine de Saint Augustin, religieuse hospitaliere de la Misericorde de Quebec en la Nouvelle France* (Paris: Florentin Lambert, 1671), dedication to the Duchesse d'Aiguillon, fols. aiir–aiiir; Jeanne-Françoise Juchereau de St-Ignace and Marie Andrée Duplessis de Ste Hélène, *Les Annales de l'Hôtel-Dieu de Québec, 1636–1716*, ed. Albert Jamet (Québec: Hôtel-Dieu, 1939), pp. 8–10; Colin Jones, *The Charitable Imperative: Hospitals and Nursing in Ancien Regime and Revolutionary France* (London: Routledge, 1989), pp. 94, 98.

70. *Rel*, pp. 240–244; *Vie*, pp. 385–386. The two Jesuits were Barthélemy Vimont and Pierre Chaumonot. The three Hospital sisters were Marie de Saint Ignace, Anne de Saint Bernard, and Marie de Saint Bonaventure, all young women in their twenties (Juchereau and Duplessis, *Hôtel-Dieu*, p. 11). MI to Françoise de S. Bernard, Superior of the Ursulines of Tours, "De l'Amirale de S. Joseph sur mer," 20 May 1639, *Cor*, no. 39, pp. 86–87). For an overview of early women's orders in Canada, see Leslie Choquette, " 'Ces Amazones du Grand Dieu': Women and Mission in Seventeenth-Century Canada," *French Historical Studies*, 17 (1992): 626–655.

71. Trudel, *Nouvelle-France*, vol. 3, part 1, pp. 102, 141, 247, 369: between 400 and 500 French persons were in Québec settlements at the end of the 1630s; about 2,000 French in Québec in 1657; about 3,000 French in Québec in the 1660s, with another 500 French settlers in Acadie and Newfoundland. An analysis of this immigration by place of origin, status, and gender is given in Trudel, *Nouvelle-France*, vol. 3, part 2, *La Seigneurie des Cent-Associés, 1627–1663: La Société*, pp. 11–55. Excellent recent bibliographies of the history of New France are found at the beginning of each of Trudel's volumes.

72. MI to CM, Québec, 29 October 1665, in *Cor*, no. 220, p. 759. On the immigration of women and their marriages, see C. H. Laverdière and H. R.

Casgrain, eds. *Le Journal des Jésuites publié d'après le manuscrit original conservé aux archives du Séminaire de Québec*, 2nd ed. (Montréal: J. M. Valois, 1892), p. 335 (2 October 1665); Micheline d'Allaire, *Talon: Textes choisis* (Montréal: Fides, 1970), pp. 23–25; Trudel, *Nouvelle-France*, vol. 3, part 1, pp. 137–138, 154–158, 407–411; part 2, pp. 36–46; William Eccles, *The Canadian Frontier, 1534–1760*, rev. ed. (Albuquerque: University of New Mexico Press, 1984), p. 68. All unmarried male day-workers were enjoined to marry within fifteen days of the arrival of the ships under penalty of losing the right to fish, hunt, or buy pelts from the Indians.

73. Trudel, *Nouvelle-France*, vol. 3, part 2, pp. 344–356, 444–448. The role of the Jesuits in directing religious life in Québec as well as in directing missionary activity during the early years is clear from their *Journal*, kept from 1645 to 1650 by the superior Jérôme Lalemant, from 1650 to 1653 by Paul Ragueneau, and subsequently by other superiors. (This *Journal* is available in consecutive form in *JJ* and chopped-up form by year in *JR;* I have preferred to use and cite *JJ* because one can follow more conveniently the changing attitudes, policies, and writing practices of the various superiors.) For the route of the Québec Rogations Day procession in 1649 (a time when, in France, parish bounds were "beaten" or marked); see *JJ*, p. 125. MI to CM, 11 October 1646, *Cor*, no. 100, p. 295; 27 September 1648, no. 113, p. 344; 22 October 1649, no. 123, p. 378.

74. *JJ*, pp. 146 (8 December 1646), 185–186 (August 1653), 258 (June 1659), 262 (24 August 1659), 269 (November–December 1659); Trudel, *Nouvelle-France*, vol. 3, part 2, pp. 182, 444–453; Cornelius J. Jaenen, *The Role of the Church in New France* (Toronto: McGraw-Hill Ryerson, 1976), pp. 17–21.

75. MI to CM, 24 August 1658, *Cor*, no. 177, p. 597; September–October 1659, no. 183, p. 613. MI to Ursule de Ste. Catherine, Ursuline of Tours, 13 October 1660, *Cor*, no. 189, pp. 643–645; 13 September 1661, no. 193, pp. 652–654 (Bishop Laval alters the Ursuline constitutions without their agreement; they refuse to accept, and win their cause).

76. Trudel, *Nouvelle-France*, vol. 3, part 1, pp. 168–178, part 2, pp. 253–257; Eccles, *Canadian Frontier*, pp. 42–44.

77. Trudel, *Nouvelle-France*, vol. 3, part 1, pp. 363–386; Charles W. Cole, *Colbert and a Century of French Mercantilism*, 2 vols. (New York: Columbia University Press, 1939; reprinted Hamden, Conn.: Archon Books, 1964), vol. 2, pp. 1–6, 56–64. MI to CM, September–October 1663, *Cor*, no. 207, p. 710. The exclusive monopoly of the West India Company over Canadian trade was lifted in 1669, though it still preserved some "rights" over Canadian trade. In 1674 these rights were turned over to the Compagnie d'Occident (Cole, *Colbert*, vol. 2, pp. 80–81).

78. The writings of James Axtell have been pioneering in the study of the American Indians in their encounter with Europeans: *The European and the Indian: Essays in the Ethnohistory of Colonial North America* (Oxford and New York:

Oxford University Press, 1981); *The Invasion Within: The Contest of Cultures in Colonial North America* (New York and Oxford: Oxford University Press, 1988); *Beyond 1492: Encounters in Colonial North America* (New York and Oxford: Oxford University Press, 1992). A general historical and ethnographic orientation to the Amerindian peoples of Canada is R. Bruce Morrison and C. Roderick Wilson, eds., *Native Peoples: The Canadian Experience* (Toronto: McClelland and Stewart, 1986). Bruce G. Trigger, *Natives and Newcomers: Canada's "Heroic Age" Reconsidered* (Kingston and Montréal: McGill-Queen's University Press, 1985), is an excellent presentation of both archeological and historical evidence. Important studies of Iroquoian-speaking peoples include Elisabeth Tooker, *An Ethnography of the Huron Indians, 1615–1649* (Washington, D.C.: Smithsonian Institution for the Huronia Historical Development Council, 1964); Conrad Heidenreich, *Huronia: A History and Geography of the Huron Indians* (Toronto: McClelland and Stewart, 1971); Bruce G. Trigger, *The Children of Aataentsic: A History of the Huron People to 1660*, new ed. (Kingston and Montréal: McGill-Queen's University Press, 1987); Lucien Campeau, *La Mission des Jésuites chez les Hurons, 1634–1650* (Montréal: Editions Bellarmin, 1987), especially pp. 1–113 on the precontact Hurons; Francis Jennings, *The Ambiguous Iroquois Empire: The Covenant Chain Confederation of Indian Tribes with English Colonies from Its Beginnings to the Lancaster Treaty of 1744* (New York: W. W. Norton, 1984); Francis Jennings, William Fenton, Mary Druke, and David R. Miller, eds., *The History and Culture of Iroquois Diplomacy: An Interdisciplinary Guide to the Treaties of the Six Nations and Their League* (Syracuse: Syracuse University Press, 1985); Daniel K. Richter, *The Ordeal of the Longhouse: The Peoples of the Iroquois League in the Era of European Colonization* (Chapel Hill: University of North Carolina Press, 1992); Matthew Dennis, *Cultivating a Landscape of Peace: Iroquois-European Encounters in Seventeenth-Century America* (Ithaca and London: Cornell University Press, 1993); and John Demos, *The Unredeemed Captive: A Family Story from Early America* (New York: Alfred A. Knopf, 1994). Important studies of Algonquian-speaking peoples include Alfred Goldsworthy Bailey, *The Conflict of European and Eastern Algonkian Cultures, 1504–1700*, 2nd ed. (Toronto: University of Toronto Press, 1969); William S. Simmons, *Spirit of the New England Tribes: Indian History and Folklore* (Hanover, N.H.: University Press of New England, 1986); Colin G. Calloway, ed., *Dawnland Encounter: Indians and Europeans in Northern New England* (Hanover, N.H.: University Press of New England, 1991); Richard White, *The Middle Ground: Indians, Empires and Republics in the Great Lakes Region, 1650–1815* (Cambridge: Cambridge University Press, 1991). A major study of the art and material culture of Amerindian peoples, with much historical evidence, is *The Spirit Sings—Artistic Traditions of Canada's First Peoples: A Catalogue of the Exhibition* (Toronto: McClelland and Stewart for the Glebow-Alberta Institute, 1988). Studies of Iroquois women have a long history: a collection of essays from 1884 to 1989 is W. G. Spittal, ed., *Iroquois Women: An Anthology* (Ohsweken, Ont.: Iroqrafts, 1990). Marxist and feminist approaches opened a new chapter in the study of Indian women of northeastern America with the work of Judith K. Brown, "Economic Organization and the Position of Women among the Iroquois," initially published in *Ethnohistory*, 17 (1970), and reprinted in *Iroquois Women*, pp. 182–198; and Eleanor Leacock, "Montagnais Women and the Jesuit Program for Colonization," in Mona Etienne and Eleanor Leacock, eds., *Women and Colonization: Anthropological Perspectives* (New York: Praeger, 1980), pp. 25–42. Karen Anderson's *Chain Her by One Foot: The Subjugation of Women in Seventeenth-Century France* (London and New York: Routledge, 1991) has pulled much information together, but does not carry the conceptual argument beyond Leacock's pioneering essay. Carol Devens has especially stressed the role of Amerindian women's resistance to Christianity in *Countering Colonization: Native American Women and Great Lakes Missions, 1630–1900* (Berkeley and Los Angeles: University of California Press, 1992). I have tried to give a comparative perspective on Amerindian women and European women in the sixteenth and early seventeenth centuries in "Iroquois Women, European Women," in Margo Hendricks and Patricia Parker, eds., *Women, "Race," and Writing in the Early Modern Period* (London: Routledge, 1994), pp. 243–258, 350–362. A new historical and ethnographic study of Iroquois women is now being conducted by Carol Karlsen. The writer Paula Gunn Allen has published works on Indian women that draw on a mix of historical examples, legends, and the values and lore in her own Lakota family: *The Sacred Hoop: Recovering the Feminine in American Indian Traditions*, 2nd ed. (Boston: Beacon Press, 1992); *Grandmothers of the Light: A Medicine Woman's Sourcebook* (Boston: Beacon Press, 1991). Meanwhile, Calvin Martin has published a critique of most current writing on Amerindian history by "whites" and "European-Americans," claiming that such writing fails to understand the mental world of the Indians: "The Metaphysics of Writing Indian-White History," in Calvin Martin, ed., *The American Indian and the Problem of History* (New York and Oxford: Oxford University Press, 1987), pp. 27–34: "Indian-white history is the process of two thoughtworlds that at the time were most often than not mutually unintelligible," p. 33. In trying to find evidence for and understand the "thoughtworld" of the Amerindians of the eastern woodlands, I see and will give examples both of opacity between the two worlds and of intelligibility and exchange (of "middle ground," as Richard White calls it).

79. In using the title "Onontio" for any governor long after Montmagny's departure in 1648, the Indians were following their own practice of continuing or "resuscitating" a person—especially a dead captain—after his death by giving his name to a successor (*JJ*, pp. 214–215, 28 May 1657; *JR*, vol. 23, pp. 164–167; Jennings, *Iroquois Empire*, p. 96; Campeau, *Mission des Jésuites*, pp. 70, 313).

80. Gabriel Sagard, *Le Grand Voyage du pays des Hurons* (1632), ed. Réal Ouellet (Québec: Bibliothèque Québécoise, 1990), part 1, ch. 7, pp. 172–173; Ruth B. Phillips, "Like a Star I Shine: Northern Woodlands Artistic Traditions," in *The Spirit Sings*, pp. 84–85.

81. Jacques Cartier, "Deuxième voyage de Jacques Cartier (1535–1536)," in

Charles A. Julien, René Herval, and Théodore Beauchesne, eds., *Les Français en Amérique pendant la première moitié du XVIe siècle* (Paris: Presses Universitaires de France, 1946), vol. 1, p. 159; *JR*, vol. 3, pp. 100–101; Sagard, *Grand Voyage*, part 1, ch. 7, p. 172.

82. MI to CM, 10 September 1646, *Cor*, no. 97, p. 286.

83. *Vie*, pp. 505–506, 612, 746. *JJ*, p. 42 (April 1646).

84. MI to CM, 17 October 1668, *Cor*, no. 244, pp. 828–829.

85. *Vie*, pp. 548–549. On the plague of 1631 and religious efforts to divert it from the Benedictine house at Tours, see *Chronique . . . de Beaumont*, pp. 108–113. Many notables died, including the mayor of Tours. Maillard, "Les Hommes et la mort à Tours," p. 79.

86. MI to a Lady of quality in France, 3 September 1640, *Cor*, no. 43, p. 98: "It's a special providence of this great God that we have any [Amerindian] girls after the large number of them who died last year. The illness was smallpox, and being widespread among the Savages, it got into our Seminary, which in a few days resembled a hospital. All the girls had the sickness three times, and four of them died of it. We were all expecting to fall sick, since the malady was contagious and we were taking care of them day and night . . . But Our Lord helped us so mightily that none of us was bothered. The Savages who are not Christians are in the error that baptism, instruction, and living among the French were the cause of this mortality." See below on another of Marie's reports concerning an epidemic and its impact on the Indians.

87. For a review of the literature on the timing and impact of the epidemics, see Trigger, *Natives and Newcomers*, pp. 226–251.

88. Sagard, *Grand Voyage*, part 1, ch. 4, pp. 131–132; Trigger, *Natives and Newcomers*, pp. 172–224; Arthur Ray and Donald B. Freeman, *'Give Us Good Measure': An Economic Analysis of Relations between the Indians and the Hudson's Bay Company before 1763* (Toronto: University of Toronto Press, 1978), chs. 2–3; Heidenreich, *Huronia*, ch. 7; Jennings, *Iroquois Empire*, ch. 6; Trudel, *Nouvelle-France*, vol. 3, part 1, pp. 124–154.

89. MI to CM, 26 August 1644, *Cor*, no. 80, p. 221; 1 September 1652, no. 142, p. 479: farming, fishing, and the extraction of fish oils would better advance French interests than the fur trade; 24 September 1654, no. 161, p. 544; 10 August 1662, no. 201, p. 681; August–September 1662, no. 204, p. 691; 12 November 1666, no. 225, p. 775; 27 August 1668, no. 258, p. 873. On the impact of alcohol on the Amerindians, see Peter C. Mancall, " 'The Bewitching Tyranny of Custom': The Social Costs of Indian Drinking in Colonial America," *American Indian Culture and Research Journal*, 17, no. 2 (1993): 15–42.

90. MI to CM, 26 August 1644, *Cor*, no. 80, p. 224.

91. MI to CM, 14–27 September 1645, *Cor*, no. 92, pp. 252–261. Barthélemy Vimont sent his *Relation* from Québec to France on 1 October 1645 (*JR*, vol. 27, pp. 246–273). This is not the only instance of Marie's reading a copy of the *Relations* in manuscript before its publication in France.

92. MI to CM, 1 September 1652, *Cor*, no. 152, p. 478; 14–27 September 1645, *Cor*, no. 92, p. 256.

93. *JR*, vol. 35, pp. 182–205. The Iroquois attack also occurred at a time of famine due to droughts in the Huronia region. Ragueneau talks about this as one of two blows that destroyed the Huron settlements in the "land apart."

94. *JR*, vol. 38, p. 62.

95. *Rel*, pp. 330–332; *Vie*, pp. 588–589. Marie de l'Incarnation comments that in all her years of praying to the Virgin, this was the first time she had had mystical interior union and inner conversations with her.

96. Trudel, *Nouvelle-France*, vol. 3, part 1, pp. 221–224.

97. MI to CM, 11 August 1654, *Cor*, no. 156, p. 531; 24 September 1654, no. 161, pp. 542–547. *JR*, vol. 40, ch. 5.

98. MI to CM, 25 June 1660, *Cor*, no. 184, p. 620; 17 September 1660, no. 185, p. 634; 2 November 1660, no. 192, p. 649.

99. MI to CM, 12 November 1666, *Cor*, no. 225, pp. 772–776; *JJ*, 5–14 November 1666, pp. 351–352; *JR*, vol. 50, pp. 140–147. *Dictionary of Canadian Biography*, vol. 1, p. 554.

100. MI to the Mother Superior of the Ursulines of Dijon, 9 August 1668, *Cor*, no. 236, p. 805.

101. On the assumptions behind and settings for Jesuit conversion, see J. H. Kennedy, *Jesuit and Savage in New France* (New Haven: Yale University Press, 1950), ch. 3; Jaenen, *Church in New France*, ch. 2; Olive Patricia Dickason, *The Myth of the Savage and the Beginnings of French Colonialism in the Americas* (Edmonton: University of Alberta Press, 1984), ch. 12.

102. MI to CM, 29 August–10 September 1646, *Cor*, no. 97, p. 278. Trudel, *Nouvelle-France*, vol. 3, part 2, pp. 380–384. Another example of Jesuit efforts toward settlement of nomadic peoples was at Miscou, far to the east on the Gulf of Saint Lawrence, where the Jesuits tried to convert the fishing-hunting-and-gathering Micmacs. Father Richard was delighted when some of them became Christian and settled down "in separate houses built à la Françoise." *JR*, vol. 30, pp. 126–127.

103. *JR*, vol. 28, pp. 38–101; Campeau, *Mission des Jésuites*, chs. 12–15.

104. *JR*, vol. 43, pp. 156–185. This mission lasted only two years, the Jesuits fleeing in 1658 when warned by a Christian Huron captive adopted into the Onondagas that the young warriors were plotting to kill them (*JR*, vol. 44, pp. 148–183). Marie's electrifying description of this mission and its dénouement can be found in MI to CM, 14 August 1656, *Cor*, no. 172, pp. 582–585; 15 October 1657, no. 175, pp. 591–592; 4 October 1658, no. 179, pp. 602–606. Her son warned in the preface to his edition of her letters that some people who had seen his mother's description of the Jesuit escape from the Onondagas noted its divergence from the account of the event in the Jesuit *Relations* (*Lettres de la venerable Mere Marie de l'Incarnation, premiere superieure des Ursulines de la Nouvelle France* [Paris: Louis Billaine, 1681], fol. eir.)

105. *JR*, vol. 37, pp. 18–43, 96–98. MI to CM, 1 September 1652, *Cor*, no. 142, p. 478.

106. *JR*, vol. 50, pp. 248–295.

107. MI to CM, 26 August 1644, *Cor*, no. 80, pp. 219–220; *Rel*, p. 260; *Vie*, p. 408. An 1840 painting by Joseph Légaré, based on archival research by Abbé Thomas Maguire, shows the wooden fence, the cabins, and the great trees of the convent before the fire of 1650 (a close Ursuline copy made around 1847 is reproduced in this book). The painting and its history are discussed in John R. Porter, *The Works of Joseph Légaré, 1795–1855* (Ottawa: National Gallery of Canada, 1978), no. 41. Oury, *Marie*, pp. 377–381.

108. MI to CM, 3 September 1651, *Cor*, no. 133, p. 415, no. 12, p. 418; MI to Cécile de S. Joseph, superior of the Ursulines of Mons, 1 October 1669, *Cor*, no. 251, p. 853. The twenty-two religious in 1669 were all of French origin, either born in Québec or in France. Examples: Charlotte Barré, initially servant to Madame de La Peltrie, received as Charlotte de S. Ignace, with a dowry set at 3,000 livres but made up of furniture, clothing, and thirteen books of devotion (AUQ, 1/1/1.3, 20 November 1648); Philippe-Gertrude de Boulogne de Saint Domingue, sister of the wife of the governor of Québec, with a dowry of 3,000 livres (AUQ, 1/1/1.3, December 1651; *JJ*, p. 122 [March 1649], p. 146 [8 December 1650]); Anne de Bourdon de Ste. Agnes, daughter of an important member of the Québec Communauté des Habitants, with a dowry of 3,000 livres, 2,000 of which was paid in beaver furs, the rest in silver and land rents (AUQ, 1/1/1.3, 2 January 1658). Anne Bourdon's sister Geneviève had taken the Ursuline habit several years before (*JJ*, p. 177 [8 December 1652]).

109. *Rel*, pp. 296–298; *Vie*, pp. 465–466, 469; MI to Ursule de Ste. Catherine, summer 1656, *Cor*, no. 171, pp. 574–581. AUQ, 1/1/1.4. Oury, *Marie*, ch. 8.

110. MI to CM, 3 September 1651, *Cor*, no. 133, p. 415; 25 June 1660, no. 184, p. 620. *JJ*, 21 January, p. 148 (21 January and 13 February 1651); p. 282 (19–26 May 1660).

111. MI to Marie-Gillette Roland, 24 August 1643, *Cor*, no. 67, p. 181; to the community of the Ursulines of Tours, spring 1652, no. 140, p. 451 ("on l'appelloit la sainte fille"); MI to CM, 30 September 1643, no. 73, pp. 200–201; 24 September 1654, no. 161, p. 544 ("nous qu'ils appellent les Filles saintes"); 18 August 1664, no. 212, pp. 730–732; 18 October 1667, no. 230, p. 786; 1 September 1668, no. 237, p. 809.

112. MI to one of her brothers, 4 September 1640, *Cor*, no. 47, p. 112; to CM, 4 September 1641, no. 56, p. 132; 17 May 1650, no. 126, p. 390; 9 August 1668, no. 235, p. 801; to the Ursulines of Tours, spring 1652, no. 140, p. 451. *Rel*, pp. 319–320; *Vie*, p. 538.

113. MI to a Lady of quality, 3 September 1640, *Cor*, no. 43, p. 95; to CM, 4 September 1641, no. 56, p. 132; 3 September 1651, no. 133, p. 414; 13 September 1651, no. 135, p. 423; 9 August 1668, no. 235, p. 801; 27 August 1670, no. 258,

p. 873; to Ursule de Ste. Catherine, summer 1656, no. 171, p. 579; to Françoise de S. Bernard, 23 September 1660, no. 186, p. 637; to Cécile de S. Joseph, 1 October 1669, no. 252, p. 852; to Victor Le Bouthillier de Rancé, archbishop of Tours, 25 September 1670, no. 266, p. 894; to Marguerite de Saint-François-Xavier, superior of the Ursulines of Dijon, 27 September 1670, no. 268, p. 903. The first register kept for the Amerindian boarders was burned in the fire of 1650. Marcel Trudel has studied the register for boarders of French origin for the years 1641 through 1662: over the 22 years, he found 130 boarders, an average of 5–6 per year. They were of mixed social origin, from the families of nobles, merchants, artisans, and farmers. Some of the French girls came only for Lent, to prepare for Easter Communion. Marcel Trudel, "Les Elèves pensionnaires des Ursulines de Québec et les bourses d'étude, 1641–1662," in *Mélanges de civilisation canadienne-français offerts au professeur Paul Wyczynski*, Cahiers du Centre de Recherche en Civilisation Canadienne-Française, 10 (Ottawa: Editions de l'Université d'Ottawa, 1977), pp. 275–291.

114. MI to a Lady of quality, 3 September 1640, *Cor*, no. 43, p. 95.

115. MI to a Lady of quality, 3 September 1640, *Cor*, no. 43, pp. 95, 97; to CM, 4 September 1641, no. 46, p. 132; to Cécile de S. Joseph, 1 October 1669, no. 251, p. 852.

116. MI to a Lady of quality, 3 September 1640, *Cor*, no. 43, p. 97. Similar comments in *Rel*, pp. 258 261; *Vie*, pp. 402, 408–409. In a late letter, Marie recognizes a protective function of the grease: "they grease themselves because they don't wear linen [undergarments]" (MI to Cécile de S. Joseph, 1 October 1669, *Cor*, no. 251, p. 852).

117. References to the Huron Thérèse Khionrea learning to read and write can be found in MI to Catherine Agnès de S. Paul, Abbess of Port-Royal, 30 August 1642, *Cor*, no. 62, p. 152; to Ursule de Ste. Catherine, 29 September 1642, no. 65, p. 167. In her letter to the abbess of Port-Royal, Marie also says that some of the *filles sauvagesses* are reading a French book about an act of grace that occurred in the life of a young Port-Royal sister. At least by the end of Marie's life, some girls were taught to write in their own language. I have reproduced in this volume a 1676 letter written on birchbark in Huron and in French from seminarians of several nations—the Ouendats (Hurons), Oneidas, Onondagas, "Ouogouens" (along the Hudson?), Algonquins, and Montagnais—to Monsieur Sain, a financial officer at Bourges (BN, N. acq. fr. 6561). On the educational program of the Ursulines, see Deslandres, "Education des Amérindiennes."

118. MI to CM, 4 September 1641, *Cor*, no. 56, p. 132; to Ursule de Ste. Catherine, 29 September 1642, no. 65, pp. 165–166.

119. MI to CM, 24 September 1654, *Cor*, no. 161, p. 544.

120. The collaboration of young Amerindian women with Marie de l'Incarnation on her altar painting is mentioned in a letter of the Ursuline superior of the Québec house after Marie's death (Marguerite de S. Athanase to Paul Rague-

neau, Québec, summer 1572, *Cor*, Appendix, no. 38, p. 1026; also given in *Vie*, p. 746). Was there some mixture of motifs and styles in this altar painting, as there was in the santero paintings surviving in New Mexico from a later period? See Jane Dillenberger and Joshua C. Taylor, *The Hand and the Spirit: Religious Art in America, 1700–1900* (Berkeley, Calif.: University Art Museum, 1972), pp. 123–134.

121. MI to a Lady of quality, 3 September 1640, *Cor*, no. 43, p. 98; to CM, 4 September 1641, no. 66, p. 132 ("plus de sept cent visites de sauvages et sauvagesses"); 30 September 1643, no. 73, p. 200; to Ursule de Ste. Catherine, 16 September 1641, no. 59, p. 144 ("plus de huit cens visites de Sauvages"). *Vie*, p. 626.

122. MI to Marie-Gillette Roland, 4 September 1640, *Cor*, no. 46, p. 108.

123. MI to CM, 29 August–10 September, 1646, *Cor*, no. 97, p. 285.

124. MI to the Ursuline community of Tours, spring 1652, *Cor*, no. 140, p. 452.

125. *JJ*, pp. 34–35 (Lent 1646); p. 46 (23 May 1646); pp. 81 (Lent 1647); p. 98 (Christmas 1647); p. 115 (28 August 1648). On the life of Marie's godson Joseph Onaharé: MI to CM, 30 August 1650, *Cor*, no. 128, p. 399; *JR*, vol. 35, pp. 222–233.

126. *JJ*, pp. 47 (Corpus Christi, 1646); p. 62 (Assumption of Our Lady, 1646); p. 89 (Corpus Christi, 1647); p. 93 (Assumption of Our Lady, 1647); pp. 109–110 (Corpus Christi, 1648); p. 117 (25 October 1649, beginning of the Jubilee); p. 139 (Corpus Christi, 1650). MI to CM, 30 August 1650, *Cor*, no. 128, p. 39.

127. *JJ*, p. 58 (8 July 1646); MI to CM, 29 August–10 September 1646), *Cor*, no. 97, pp. 286–287.

128. MI to CM, 30 August 1644, *Cor*, no. 81, p. 229; also to Ursule de Ste. Catherine, 15 September 1641, no. 58, p. 140: "I find everything concerning the education of our Neophytes . . . full of charm. If I have crosses in Canada, they are only lightened by this holy exercise."

129. *Rel*, pp. 257–258; *Vie*, p. 401. Similar descriptions of learning and mastering Algonquin can be found in MI to one of her brothers, 4 September 1640, *Cor*, no. 47, p. 112; to CM, 4 September 1641, no. 56, p. 132; to Ursule de Ste. Catherine, 15 September 1641, no. 58, p. 140.

130. MI to Marie-Gillette Roland, 30 August 1641, *Cor*, no. 53, p. 125.

131. The *Retraites* are made up of quotations from the Bible followed by lyrical meditations. *L'Ecole sainte* is organized around the symbol of the apostles, the Ten Commandments, the Lord's Prayer, and the sacraments. Statements of belief are given from the Roman catechism and supported with quotations from the Bible. See n. 50 above for full citations for both books.

132. MI to Marie-Gillette Roland, 30 August 1641, *Cor*, no. 53, p. 125.

133. Her list of compositions in Amerindian tongues can be found in MI to CM, 10 August 1662, *Cor*, no. 200, p. 678; 9 August 1668, no. 235, p. 801. An important study of early Jesuit writing in and about Indian languages is Victor

Egon Hanzeli, *Missionary Linguistics in New France: A Study of Seventeenth- and Eighteenth-Century Descriptions of American Indian Languages* (The Hague and Paris: Mouton, 1969). There is no Jesuit work mentioned there that resembles Marie's *Sacred History*. For examples of different modes of speech for women and for men, see [Jean André Cuoq], *Etudes philologiques sur quelques langues sauvages de l'Amérique* (Montréal: Dawson Brothers, 1866; reprinted New York: Johnson Reprint, 1966), pp. 30–31.

134. Marie was often called to the parlor, "being visited and consulted by most people in the country" (*Vie*, p. 460); "consulted on every side" (p. 552). Examples of visitors from whom she drew information: MI to CM, 14 August 1656, *Cor*, no. 172, p. 583 (Zacharie Dupuis, commander of the soldiers who accompanied Father Dablon on his first mission to the Onondagas); 1 September 1668, no. 237, p. 809; 1 September 1669, no. 248, pp. 840–841; 27 August 1670, no. 258, p. 874 (recalling the frequent visits years before of the explorer Médard Chouart, sieur des Groseillers, who was a native of Touraine).

135. Material in the *JR* drawn from or written by Marie de l'Incarnation: *JR*, vol. 20, pp. 124–141; vol. 22, pp. 178–201; vol. 23, pp. 290–301; vol. 25, pp. 222–231, 238–243; vol. 38, pp. 68–165; vol. 40, pp. 222–231. MI to Marie-Alexis Boschet, superior of the Ursulines of Mons, 20 October 1663, *Cor*, no. 209, p. 719; to Renée de Saint-François, Ursuline of Tours, 15 September 1668, no. 240, p. 818: "The Reverend Father du Creux, who is doing the history of Canada, asks me each year for news to insert there." François Du Creux, *Historiae Canadensis, seu Novae-Franciae Libri Decem* (Paris, 1664), translated as *History of Canada or New France* by Percy J. Robinson, ed. J. B. Conacher, 2 vols. (Toronto: Champlain Society, 1951). Material in book 5, pp. 331–337, is drawn both from Marie and from the *JR*. Marie also had a correspondence within Canada itself with colony administrators and the local Jesuits (AUQ, 1/1/1/.1; reprinted in *Cor*, no. 90, pp. 246–247; no. 119, pp. 359–360).

136. *Vie*, p. 241.

137. Oury, *Cor*, p. 680, n. 11; p. 804, n. 5. Marie says to her son in 1644 that she thinks she has written more than 200 letters for the autumn boat departure (15 September 1644, *Cor*, no. 86, p. 240). Only fourteen letters are known from that year, which suggests a very great loss. Oury has published 278 letters, however, many of them with repeated themes. Together with her autobiography and other writings found by Claude Martin, they give us some sense of Marie's perspectives and modes of writing.

138. When Marie describes coming back to a letter, it is not to revise but to add new material, MI to CM, 30 August 1650, *Cor*, no. 128, p. 399.

139. MI to CM, 9 August 1654, printed in *Vie*, fol. o iir–v and *Cor*, no. 155, p. 526.

140. MI to CM, 26 October 1653, *Cor*, no. 153, pp. 515–521; *Vie*, Préface, fol. i iiv.

141. The Ursulines always wrote of the life, manner of dying, and spiritual qualities of their sisters after their deaths, and circulated these accounts in printed form to all the houses. An example is Marie de l'Incarnation's account of Anne Bataille de Saint Laurent, who had come to Québec from the Dieppe house in 1642; it was written on 1 September 1669, and printed in France with Marie's name on it (printed copy in AUQ, 1/1/1.3). Marie wrote her son that she was glad Father Le Jeune had published her account of the life and death of Marie de Saint Joseph in the *Jesuit Relations*, but sorry he had mentioned her name (26 October 1653, *Cor*, no. 153, p. 521; *JR*, vol. 38, pp. 68–69). Thus, she held to the convention of religious modesty in publishing for a large readership.

142. MI to CM, 27 September 1654, *Cor*, no. 162, p. 548; 18 October 1654, no. 163, p. 549.

143. ADIL, H852, Act of 10 January 1639.

144. *Rel*, pp. 262–311; *Vie*, pp. 413–482.

145. Oury, *La Peltrie*, ch. 7; MI to Mademoiselle de Luynes, 29 September 1642, *Cor*, no. 66, pp. 173, 176; *Vie*, pp. 467–469.

146. *Rel*, pp. 308–311; *Vie*, pp. 480–481.

147. *Rel*, pp. 352–353; *Vie*, pp. 403–404, 661, 694–695, 742. In a letter to Father Poncet of 17 September 1670, Marie gave an account of her union with God in her Canadian years: a wholly interior operation, without visions, which left the soul free to continue all its external activities (*Cor*, no. 263, p. 888).

148. *Vie*, p. 563; MI to CM, October–November 1651, *Cor*, no. 136, pp. 425–426.

149. MI to CM, 10 September 1640, *Cor*, no. 49, pp. 115–116. The rightness of her abandonment is also expressed in letters of 4 September 1641, no. 56, pp. 130–133; 9 August 1654, no. 155, p. 527; 16 August 1664, no. 211, p. 725; and in *Vie*, fol. o iiir.

150. MI to CM, 30 August 1650, *Cor*, no. 128, pp. 394 (Claude had wished his mother martyrdom in his last letter, but she is unworthy), 399. She had already written to her son on 3 October 1645, "Oh, my dear Son, how consoled I would be if someone had just said to me that you had lost your life for Jesus Christ" (no. 94, p. 270).

151. After eight years of spiritual and theological training, Claude Martin was ordained a priest in 1649. He then taught philosophy and theology at a Maurist house just outside Rouen and spent another year as subprior of the Maurist house in Vendôme. In 1652 he became prior of Saint-Nicaise in Meulan. From that date until 1668, he was prior of several different houses; Marie's letters must have had trouble catching up with him. In 1668 he was elected one of two assistants to the general of the order (Marie saw this as proof once again that the Savior had kept his promise to her to watch over her son; MI to CM, 12 October 1668, *Cor*, no. 242, p. 823). He continued as assistant until 1675, when he became prior of Saint-Denis in Paris, one of the most important of the Maurist houses. This was his

post at the time he published his mother's *Vie*. On Claude Martin see the fascinating biography by Edmond Martene, a young Maurist to whom Claude recounted his life: *La Vie du venerable pere Dom Claude Martin* (cited n. 31 above); and Guy-Marie Oury, *Dom Claude Martin, Le fils de Marie de l'Incarnation* (Solesmes: Abbaye Saint-Pierre, 1983). Works by Claude Martin finished before his mother's death: *Méditations chrétiennes pour tous les jours et principales fêtes de l'année* (Paris, 1669); *Conduite pour la retraite du mois à l'usage des Religieux de la Congrégation de Saint-Maur* (Paris, 1670). Marie acknowledges receipt of the former in a letter of 21 October 1669, *Cor*, no. 255, p. 867.

152. MI to CM, 23 October 1649, *Cor*, no. 124, p. 384. It is interesting to compare Claude Martin's attentiveness to his mother with his *Maximes spirituelles*, collected by his biographer Edmond Martene: "I will never believe that a religious who loves to see his parents . . . loves his perfection . . . One must live without father, without mother, without relatives, without genealogy." *Maximes spirituelles du venerable pere Dom Claude Martin* (Rouen: François Vaultier, 1698), pp. 238–240.

153. We know his side of the correspondence only from her comments. If he kept copies of his letters, he did not use them for the *Vie* or his edition of her *Lettres*. He had asked her to "suppress" his letters after she had read them ([Martene], *Claude Martin*, Avertissement), but if she kept them, they were evidently burned in the Ursuline fires of 1650 and 1686.

154. [Martene], *Claude Martin*, pp. 52–76. The first episode of temptation began not long after Claude was made prior of the Benedictine abbey at Meulan in 1652; Martin's biographer specifically says that Marie's letters assisted him in his terrible temptations and imaginings (p. 67). MI to CM, 12 August 1654, *Cor*, no. 157, pp. 533–534; 18 October 1654, no. 163, pp. 549–550: Marie sees her son's sexual desire as a temptation of the devil but also as an exercise sent by God, and recommends prayer and mortification. Much earlier, during Claude Martin's novitiate, he had had two years of homoerotic desire—"a particular friendship that he had for a young Religious, in which there was a human element"—but there is no indication whether he sought advice from his mother about it. Here, too, he used nettles to tame the flesh ([Martene], *Claude Martin*, pp. 36–37).

155. *Vie*, fols. a iv, e ivr–v, o vr–v.

156. *Rel*, pp. 50, 178, 372; *Vie*, pp. 8, 204, 208, 210.

157. *Vie*, p. 397. How could Claude have gotten such intimate information from a Québec Ursuline? Would such material have been sent to him in a letter?

158. *Rel*, p. 317; *Vie*, pp. 515, 517. In 1669, when her son sent her a volume of lives of Benedictine saints by the Benedictine prioress Jacqueline de Blémur, Marie wrote him that if he had not told her it was a book by a woman, she would never have believed it. She asks her son to visit Blémur and tell her of Marie's esteem for her, "for truly one can put her among the illustrious persons of our sex." MI to CM, 21 October 1669, *Cor*, no. 255, p. 868.

159. Marie de l'Incarnation, *L'Ecole sainte*, Préface (with approbation from François Camus, doctor of theology and grand-vicar of Tours). In a 1676 work, Claude Martin listed the spiritual achievements of women prior to the heroic efforts of the Canadian Ursulines: women filled with the spirit of prophecy, women who gloriously suffered as martyrs, and women "who have the key to knowledge and wisdom and whom one could place at the rank of Doctors" (*Meditations pour la feste de S. Ursule et des compagnes Vierges et Martyres* [Paris: Louis Billaine, 1676], pp. 81–82). Claude thought God had given his mother "the key to knowledge," but it is unclear whether he would have put her, with her limited learning, fully "at the rank of Doctors."

160. *Vie*, p. 304. Marie used formulas deprecating women's capacities, when such formulas were necessary for decorum. For example, her 1642 letter to the *supérieure* of the French Ursulines to ask for donations for the Ursuline mission in Canada opened, "Divine providence has disposed things so that in these last years our holy Order has come to these countries of Canada so that *according to the small capacity of our sex* we can work to apply the blood of Jesus Christ to the souls whom barbarism and ignorance have seemed to exclude from their salvation" (*Cor*, no. 64, p. 156, emphasis added).

161. Saint Thecla is known only from a second-century romance, *The Acts of Paul and Thecla*. She was supposed to be a young woman of Iconium in Asia Minor who, hearing the apostle Paul preach near her window, converted to Christianity. Refusing all pressures to marry, including painful public torture, she ultimately dressed in men's clothing and rejoined Paul in Asia Minor. He then commissioned her to teach the word of God. Subsequently she lived in a cave in Seleucia, healing and performing miraculous cures. Her cult was suppressed only in 1969. David Hugh Farmer, *The Oxford Dictionary of Saints* (Oxford: Clarendon Press, 1978), p. 369. Claude Martin's *Meditations pour la feste de S. Ursule* was written at his mother's request (MI to CM, 21 October 1669, *Cor*, no. 155, p. 867), but published after her death. The historical preface, fols. iii–cviii, cleared away the many "fables" about the saint, lest the "moral truths" he wished to draw from her life and martyrdom be based on "error and lies." In Martin's narrative, Ursula and her companions resisted the "barbarians" who wanted to rape them at Cologne, but then were simply killed (fol. xxxv). In contrast, the Ursulines' own narrative of 1673 spoke of a "battlefield" and described how Ursula flew on the wings of love "from squadron to squadron" to encourage her "holy Amazons" in "combat" against the attacking army (*Chronique de l'ordre des Ursulines*, vol. 1, pp. 3–5).

162. *Vie*, p. 304. A similar point about all the Ursulines of Canada is made at the end of his *Meditations pour la feste de S. Ursule*, pp. 82–83: "though it is not permitted to give them the title of Apostle, they at least fulfilled the functions as much as their sex permitted."

163. *JR*, vol. 3, pp. 72–85; vol. 6, pp. 156–227; vol. 33, pp. 198–223; vol. 43, pp. 262–273.

164. *JR*, vol. 5, pp. 104–105; vol. 43, pp. 270–271 (de Quen's comment of 1656–1657, "No Hospitals are needed among them," was written after decades of effort to enclose the urban poor in hospitals and during the very same year that the Hôpital Général was established in Paris with the stated intention of saving the poor from "religious ignorance." Other examples: vol. 3, p. 85 (the Abenakis are never in a hurry, quite different from us who can never do anything without hurry and worry); vol. 38, pp. 266–267 (the Hurons have "a certain external seemliness in their behavior, which prevents a thousand levities that are quite common among European youth, especially when both sexes mingle without any external restraint"). Such topical chapters also led to Jesuit reflection on human universals and on cultural differences in everything from sense of smell to posture (e.g., *JR*, vol. 44, pp. 276–309).

165. MI to one of her brothers, 4 September 1640, *Cor*, no. 47, p. 113; to CM, 30 September 1643, no. 73, p. 200; October 1669, no. 254, p. 865; September–November 1671, no. 277, pp. 942–943, drawing from *JR*, vol. 55, pp. 172–179.

166. MI to CM, 26 August 1644, *Cor*, no. 80, pp. 219–222; 1679, no. 270, 915–919.

167. MI to Paul Le Jeune, March 1640, *Cor*, no. 42, p. 93.

168. MI to one of her brothers, 4 September 1640, *Cor*, no. 44, p. 103; MI to Marguerite de Saint-François Xavier, 27 September 1670, no. 268, p. 903.

169. MI to Ursule de Ste. Catherine, 29 September 1632, *Cor*, no. 65, p. 160.

170. MI to CM, 26 August 1644, *Cor*, no. 80, p. 221; 29 August–10 September 1626, no. 97, p. 285: praise for the sensibility of conscience and high quality of confession among the Hurons.

171. MI to Ursule de Ste. Catherine, 15 September 1641, *Cor*, no. 58, p. 139.

172. MI to CM, 30 August 1650, *Cor*, no. 128, p. 398. Marie was watching the procession from a concealed place where she could not be seen.

173. MI to Jeanne-Françoise Le Vassor, superior of the Visitation of Tours, 4 September 1640, *Cor*, no. 45, p. 104; to Ursule de Ste. Catherine, 13 September 1640, no. 50, p. 119; to a woman among her friends, 9 September 1655, no. 164, p. 553: the "unparalleled fervor" of the Hurons, constant to their new religion even in Iroquois captivity, "casts shame on those born in Christianity."

174. MI to Ursule de Ste. Catherine, 5 September 1641, *Cor*, no. 58, p. 139. Marie presents Pigarouich as using the second person singular—*tu*—in addressing God, whereas Jean de Brébeuf reports teaching prayers in Huron in which the Lord was addressed both in the second person singular and the second person plural (*JR*, vol. 10, pp. 68–73). In her own writing, she virtually always quotes herself as addressing the Lord as *vous*. The single exception is in a lyrical address to the adorable Spirit of the Word about the plenitude of love implanted in her heart: "O Amour, tu t'es plu à me martyriser" (*Rel*, p. 148; her son changed this to *vous* in the published version, *Vie*, p. 134). On Pigarouich, see *JR*, vol. 14, pp. 132–133; vol. 18, pp. 188–195; and *Dictionary of Canadian Biography*, vol. 1, pp. 548–549.

175. MI to CM, 26 August 1644, *Cor*, no. 80, pp. 222–223. Marie goes on to describe a conversation with the woman, whose prayer for warriors in an Indian language touched her deeply. *JR*, vol. 25, pp. 238–243, based on a report from Marie.

176. MI to Ursule de Ste. Catherine, 16 September 1641, *Cor*, no. 59, p. 144; 29 September 1642, no. 65, pp. 165–169. MI to CM, 30 September 1643, no. 73, p. 201; 29 August–10 September 1646, no. 97, p. 281. Thérèse Khionrea to MI, Trois-Rivières, 30–31 July 1642, Appendix 11, p. 977. A Québec Ursuline [Marie de l'Incarnation?] to Paul Le Jeune, 1653, Appendix 18, p. 988. Campeau provides the name Khionrea (*La Mission des Jésuites*, p. 86).

177. MI to Marie-Gillette Roland, 24 August 1643, *Cor*, no. 67, p. 181.

178. MI to CM, 18 August 1664, *Cor*, no. 212, pp. 730–732. "She often gave me an account of her adventures." *JR*, vol. 49, pp. 94–101: portrait of Geneviève, based on Marie's report.

179. MI to Ursule de Ste. Catherine, 13 September 1640, *Cor*, no. 50, pp. 117–118.

180. The Jesuit account of this episode at the Huron mission was sent to Paris by Hierosme Lalemant on 27 May 1640 and does not mention the woman's harangue (*JR*, vol. 19, pp. 176–179). Marie worked up her description from the oral report of Father Pierre Pijart, who came down to Québec from the Huron country and visited her (MI to Ursule de Ste. Catherine, 13 September 1640, *Cor*, no. 50, p. 118; on Pijart, see *JR*, vol. 19, pp. 178–181).

181. MI to CM, 26 August 1644, *Cor*, no. 80, pp. 218–219; 30 August 1650, no. 128, p. 399.

182. MI to CM, 24 September 1654, *Cor*, no. 161, p. 546; 12 October 1655, no. 168, pp. 565–566; 8–21 October 1661, no. 191, p. 671. Du Creux, *History of Canada*, vol. 2, pp. 698–700 (section on Aouentohons sent by Marie de l'Incarnation).

183. MI to CM, 18 October 1667, *Cor*, no. 230, p. 786; to Father Poncet, 7 October 1669, no. 252, p. 857; to Marie de Ste. Catherine, superior of the Ursulines of Saint-Denis, 11 October 1669, no. 253, p. 860.

184. MI to CM, 24 September 1654, *Cor*, no. 161, p. 546; 18 October 1667, no. 230, p. 786; 1 September 1668, no. 237, p. 809; to the superior of the Ursulines of Saint-Denis, 21 September 1668, no. 241, p. 821. Du Creux, *History of Canada*, vol. 2, p. 699. Deslandres, "L'Education des Amérindiennes," pp. 91–96.

185. MI to the superior of the Ursulines of Saint-Denis, 21 September 1668, *Cor*, no. 241, p. 821; to CM, 17 October 1668, no. 244, p. 828.

186. MI to CM, 1 September 1668, *Cor*, no. 237, p. 809.

187. MI to CM, 17 October 1668, *Cor*, no. 244, p. 828.

188. See, for instance, Marie's comment on the Algonquin Marie-Magdelaine Amiskvian: "She is sought in marriage by a Frenchman, but we plan to give her to one of her nation because of the example we hope she will give to the Savages" (MI to a Lady of quality, 3 September 1640, *Cor*, no. 43, p. 95; see also *JR*, vol.

20, pp. 126–129). Another example is "Barbe, sauvage seminariste des Ursulines" for four years. She left the convent in February 1647, "strongly" pursued by a Frenchman, but "it turned out the girl . . . preferred a savage and to follow the will of her parents" (*JJ*, p. 77). Marie de l'Incarnation must have approved Barbe's decision.

189. MI to Ursule de Ste. Catherine, 29 September 1642, *Cor*, no. 65, p. 162.

190. An example of a male proselytizer is the Montagnais Charles Meiachkouat, who visited Marie regularly whenever he came to Québec on missions or for Easter and reported on his preaching activities. She describes and quotes him at length: MI to Jeanne-Françoise Le Vassor, 24 August 1641, *Cor*, no. 52, pp. 122–123; to Ursule de Ste. Catherine, 29 September 1642, no. 65, pp. 160–161; to Marie-Gillette Roland, 24 August 1643, no. 67, pp. 181–182.

191. MI to a Lady of quality, 3 September 1640, *Cor*, no. 43, p. 94.

192. MI to CM, 1670, *Cor*, no. 270, pp. 916–917.

193. MI to CM, 26 August 1644, *Cor*, no. 80, p. 220; summer 1647, no. 110, p. 332; to the community of Ursulines of Tours, spring 1652, no. 140, p. 459; to Cécile de S. Joseph, 1 October 1669, no. 251, p. 852.

194. Marie refers to Pigarouich's sexual adventures with great indirection: "one among them having committed a considerable fault against good manners . . ." (MI to Marie-Gillette Roland, 12 August 1644, *Cor*, no. 78, p. 214). Much of the story is given in *JR*, vol. 25, pp. 248–281, along with the tale of an Onontcha-taronon captain who seduced a Christian woman and took her for his third wife.

195. MI to Jeanne-Françoise Le Vassor, 24 August 1641, *Cor*, no. 52, pp. 122–123.

196. *Vie*, pp. 728, 735.

197. MI to Marie-Alexis Boschet, 20 October 1663, *Cor*, no. 209, p. 718. Also, "The Savage humor is made like that: when they are constrained they become melancholy, and melancholy makes them sick" (MI to CM, 1 September 1668, no. 237, p. 809). In a letter to her son of 30 August 1650, written in a rare moment of pessimism at the height of the Iroquois success against the Hurons, Marie quoted the Jesuit Adrien Daran in regard to a limit to the religious capacity of Amerindian men. Daran is on his way to France and will see Claude Martin: "he will tell you that . . . it will always be necessary to depend on Europe to provide workers for the Gospel, the nature of the American Savages, even the most holy and spiritual among them, being not at all suitable for Ecclesiastical functions, but suitable simply to be taught and gently led" (no. 128, p. 396). Marie did not put this view in her own voice; she did not repeat it in other letters. It concerned men's capacity rather than women's, of which she had more knowledge; it conflicted with her positive images of Apostolic Indians like Charles Meiachkouat. On the whole, the limits to Marie's optimistic universalizing came from her own observations of Amerindian women's relation to a convent vocation, not from Jesuit views.

198. Katharine Tekakwitha was a Mohawk convert who refused marriage at age twenty-two and took a vow of perpetual virginity before her Jesuit confessor at the mission of Sault Saint Louis in 1679—"an unheard-of thing among her people," as Father Cholenec said in his *Life*. But Tekakwitha's life of intense prayer, confessional self-revelation, penitential discipline, and Christian teaching was not carried on in enclosure. Rather, in Cholenec's words, "God gave her a companion," Marie Thérèse Tegaiaguenta, who vowed a life of perpetual widowhood after a traumatic episode of cannibalism during the starvation of a hunting expedition. The two women were always together, carrying on their tasks but also speaking of God and of their spiritual adventures and disciplining their shoulders with rods. By the time of Katharine's death in 1680, a few other women had joined them in a devotional group known as "Katharine's Sisters." (Pierre Cholenec, "The Life of Katharine Tegakouita, First Iroquois Virgin (1696)," in Catholic Church, Sacred Congregation of Rites, *The Positio . . . on the Introduction of the Cause for Beatification and Canonization and on the Virtues of the Servant of God Katharine Tekakwitha, the Lily of the Mohawks* [New York: Fordham University Press, 1940], pp. 239–335. On Tekakwitha, see also Nancy Shoemaker, "Kateri Tekakwitha's Tortuous Path to Sainthood," in Shoemaker, ed., *Negotiators of Change: Historical Perspectives on Native American Women* [New York: Routledge, 1995], pp. 49–71). These Iroquois women invented a way to live as virgins in the woodlands without enclosure, as Angela Merici had tried to do for the Ursulines in European cities a hundred and fifty years before.

199. *JR*, vol. 6, pp. 238–241.

200. *JR*, vol. 28, pp. 48–49.

201. MI to a woman among her friends, 9 September 1655, *Cor*, no. 164, p. 553.

202. *JR*, vol. 10, pp. 12–13, 72–73; vol. 17, pp. 202–203. Also see Sagard, *Grand Voyage*, part 1, ch. 18, pp. 257–264.

203. *JR*, vol. 49, pp. 112–115.

204. *JR*, vol. 20, pp. 202–203.

205. *JR*, vol. 20, pp. 184–213.

206. *JR*, vol. 20, pp. 190–191.

207. *JR*, vol. 29, pp. 122–143.

208. On the scholarly literature on the nature of "savagery" and "barbarism," see Dickason, *The Myth of the Savage*, part 1; Anthony Pagden, *The Fall of Natural Man: The American Indian and the Origins of Comparative Ethnology* (Cambridge: Cambridge University Press, 1982); and idem, *European Encounters with the New World* (New Haven and London: Yale University Press, 1993). For French historical theory on the effect of climate and geography on character, see Jean Bodin, *Method for the Easy Comprehension of History*, trans. Beatrice Reynolds (New York: Columbia University Press, 1945; reprint New York: Octagon Books, 1966), especially ch. 5. The Ursuline convent was destroyed by fire in 1650 and severely burned in 1686, and much if not all of the library must have been lost.

We can get some sense of what it contained from the reestablishment of the collection that began in 1687. Of 162 works published before 1672 in the catalogue of the Ursuline convent, all but three are devotional works, works on liturgy or Scripture, lives of saintly persons, especially of women, and other religious texts. The exceptions have nothing to do with travel literature or non-European peoples: *Histoire de la Guerre sous le regne de Henri IIII* (Paris: Jean Richer, 1608); Jean-Marie de Vernon, *Le Roy tres-chrestien, ou la vie de St Louis Roy de France* (Paris: Georges Iosse, 1662), which is partly a religious study; and a book of popular medicine by Philibert Guybert of the Paris Faculty of Medicine, *Toutes les oeuvres charitables* (Paris: Pierre Le Mercier, 1670). Among books printed in the twenty years after Marie's death are two more popular medical books and a late seventeenth-century reprint of a sixteenth-century commercial arithmetic by Jean Trenchant. I have examined a number of these editions in the Ursuline convent library, and have found several hand-inscribed with the date 1687.

209. *JR*, vol. 8, pp. 92–93; vol. 16, pp. 238–239; vol. 50, pp. 170–171; Tooker, *Ethnography of the Hurons*, pp. 44–45.

210. Kennedy, *Jesuit and Savage*, pp. 74–75, 83.

211. MI to Ursule de Ste. Catherine, 29 September 1642, *Cor*, no. 65, p. 61; to CM, 29 August–10 September 1646, no. 97, p. 286; to CM, 24 September 1654, no. 161, p. 544; to the community of the Ursulines of Tours, spring 1652, no. 140, p. 451. Madame de La Peltrie to Paul Le Jeune, summer 1640, Appendix 5, p. 965. [Cuoq], *Etudes philologiques*, p. 137; *JR*, vol. 10, pp. 116–119.

212. MI to the community of the Ursulines of Tours, spring 1652, *Cor*, no. 140, pp. 436–467; to Father Poncet, 25 October 1670, no. 269, pp. 904–911. AUQ, 1/1/1.3: Marie de l'Incarnation, printed letter on the life and death of Sister Anne de Saint Laurens, 1669.

213. *JR*, vol. 22, pp. 170–171.

214. MI to Paul Le Jeune, summer 1640, *Cor*, Appendix 4, pp. 962–963; Madame de La Peltrie to Paul Le Jeune, summer 1640, Appendix 5, p. 965.

215. Juchereau and Duplessis, *Hôtel-Dieu*, pp. 85–86, 95–96, 129–132, 161–163.

216. Ragueneau, *La Vie de la mere Catherine de Saint Augustin* (cited n. 69 above), pp. 64–66, 249, 238, 255, 289–294 (the *sorcier* described here is presumably French, for his body was examined for devil's marks and he was described as holding a "Sabbath," neither of which was considered a sign of shamanic activity or witchcraft among the Amerindians). Ragueneau says that "this life is composed almost entirely from a journal taken from certain papers that her Directors and Confessors ordered her to write on what was going on within her every day" (p. 1). Often Ragueneau quotes the journal directly. Catherine de Saint Augustin, born into a minor seigneurial and officerial family of Cherbourg, joined the Hospitalières of Bayeux when she was twelve, came to Québec at eighteen, and died there at thirty-six.

217. Marie Morin, *Histoire simple et véritable,* ed. Ghislaine Legendre (Montréal: Presses de l'Université de Montréal, 1979), pp. 54, 63, 132, 137, 153, 183–184. Jeanne Mance, one of the founders of the hospital in Montréal, is described as caring for "the salvation of perhaps a million Savages" when she first left Langres for Canada (p. 41), but Morin does not make this a subject of her history. On Morin, see Esther Lefebvre, *Marie Morin, premier historien canadien de Villemarie* (Montréal and Paris: Fides, 1959).

218. Albert Jamet, Introduction to Juchereau and Duplessis, *Annales de l'Hôtel-Dieu,* p. xli, quoting a letter of Mother de Ste. Hélène, 25 October 1740.

219. Sagard, *Grand Voyage,* part 1, ch. 18, p. 253. *JR,* vol. 6, pp. 156–157; vol. 10, pp. 132–133.

220. *JR,* vol. 8, pp. 118–119. A similar point is made by some Abenakis to Father Ennemond Massé around 1612–1613 (*JR,* vol. 3, pp. 123–124) and by some Montagnais to Father Le Jeune in 1633 (vol. 5, pp. 158–161). Le Jeune was arguing against the significance that the Montagnais attached to dreams. A "Savage" had come to him saying that his son-in-law had dreamed that the Jesuits would give him a piece of tobacco as long as his hand. "I refused him saying that I didn't give anything for dreams, and that this was only folly and that I would explain to them how dreams were made when I knew their language better. He responded that every nation had something special to themselves and that if our dreams were not true, theirs were . . . Just as he believed us when we said something to him or showed him some picture, so in the same way, we should believe him when he told us something special to his nation."

221. *JR,* vol. 10, pp. 304–305.

222. Marie de Saint Joseph to Paul Le Jeune, summer 1640, *Cor,* no. 43, p. 962: "they compose and model themselves after our actions, except for bows, where they imitate Madame de La Peltrie." Juchereau and Duplessis, *Hôtel-Dieu,* p. 131, drawing from *JR,* vol. 49, pp. 80–83.

223. *JR,* vol. 8, pp. 22–23; vol. 10, pp. 140–141, 168–173; vol. 17, pp. 152–155;, vol. 33, pp. 188–191. Tooker, *Ethnography,* pp. 86–91. On dream interpretation, see Barbara Tedlock, "Zuni and Quiché Dream Sharing and Interpreting," in Barbara Tedlock, ed., *Dreaming: Anthropological and Psychological Interpretations* (Cambridge: Cambridge University Press, 1987), pp. 105–131.

224. MI to Cécile de S. Joseph, 1 October 1669, *Cor,* no. 251, p. 855; MI to CM, 1670, no. 270, pp. 916–917.

225. *JR,* vol. 17, pp. 164–187.

226. MI to CM, August–September 1663, *Cor,* no. 204, pp. 687–693; Juchereau and Duplessis, *Hôtel-Dieu,* pp. 122–124; Ragueneau, *Catherine de Saint Augustin,* pp. 238–240.

227. H. David Brumble III, *American Indian Autobiography* (Berkeley: University of California Press, 1988), pp. 32–37. Carlo Ginzburg, *The Night Battles:*

Witchcraft and Agrarian Cults in the Sixteenth and Seventeenth Centuries, trans. John and Anne Tedeschi (London: Routledge and Kegan Paul, 1983); *Ecstasies: Deciphering the Witches' Sabbath,* trans. Raymond Rosenthal (New York: Pantheon Books, 1991).

228. *JR,* vol. 24, pp. 30–33, 170–175 (based on reports from the Hospitalers). *JR,* vol. 8, pp. 120–121: Amerindian gifts to the dead are "superstitions . . . which we hope by the grace of God to change into true Religion"; vol. 10, pp. 300–301: "foolish and useless ceremonies." Another example of Christian converts continuing to bury objects with their deceased and giving a good reason for it is found in *JR,* vol. 39, pp. 30–33.

229. See the discussion of a gradual mixture or "fusion" of Mayan religion with Spanish Catholicism in Yucatan in Nancy M. Farriss, *Maya Society under Colonial Rule: The Collective Enterprise of Survival* (Princeton, N.J.: Princeton University Press, 1984), ch. 10; and the analysis of different mixtures (especially in regard to ancestor worship) in Andean religion in Kenneth Mills, "The Limits of Religious Coercion in Mid-Colonial Peru," *Past and Present,* 145 (November 1994): 84–121. Frank Salomon has given a portrait of the juxtaposition of Andean and Christian elements in the mind and practice of an early seventeenth-century man in such a way that they are both "inseparable," but "irreducibly conflictual" (*Nightmare Victory: The Meanings of Conversion among Peruvian Indians [Huarochirí, 1608?],* Working papers, no. 7 [College Park, Md · University of Maryland Department of Spanish and Portuguese, 1992]). Compare Ramón A. Gutiérrez, *When Jesus Came, the Corn Mothers Went Away: Marriage, Sexuality, and Power in New Mexico, 1500–1846* (Stanford, Calif.: Stanford University Press, 1991), pp. 93–94: he interprets the Christianity of the converted Pueblo not so much in terms of mixture or strained juxtaposition, but as a shallow cover for pre-Christian beliefs: "the meanings attached to these acts [such as offering feathers and corn meal to the Cross] were fundamentally rooted in Pueblo concepts." Conversions were "nominal" and "superficial," assented to out of fear or to acquire the protections, foods, and technology of the Franciscan friars. On the whole, I have found "mixture"—sometimes comfortable, sometimes troublesome—a more helpful interpretive concept than "superficial cover" in the eastern woodlands, including in cases of Amerindian resistance.

230. *JR,* vol. 5, pp. 204–205; vol. 27, pp. 262–263. Further evidence in Davis, "Iroquois Women," pp. 249–250, 252–254, and notes 36–39, 50–55.

231. Ibid, pp. 248–249 and notes 29–35. In contrast to many Jesuit references to male shamans (or *sorciers*), there are only a few to women *sorcières*: *JR,* vol. 8, pp. 182–183; vol. 9, pp. 112–115; vol. 14, pp. 182–183; vol. 21, pp. 242–243. On menstrual separation and the power of the glance of the menstruating woman, see *JR,* vol. 9, pp. 122–123; vol. 29, pp. 108–109; and Raymond D. Fogelson, "On the 'Petticoat Government' of the Eighteenth-Century Cherokee," in David

K. Jordan and Marc J. Swartz, eds., *Personality and the Cultural Construction of Society: Papers in Honor of Melford E. Spiro* (Tuscaloosa: University of Alabama Press, 1990), pp. 172–176.

232. *JR*, vol. 8, pp. 124–127; vol. 38, pp. 36–37: Abenaki "Pythonesses" could see absent things and foretell the future. The role of women as soothsayers explains the suspicion of backsliding in regard to the Huron Christian woman who foretold the 1663 earthquake.

233. *JR*, vol. 10, pp. 132–135; Tooker, *Ethnography*, pp. 143–148.

234. *Vie*, Préface, fol. e 3r; *Retraites*, Préface, fol. e 4r; *Lettres*, Avertissement, fol. a 4r–v. On the importance of *honnêteté* in language according to the criteria of the French court and the Académie, see Ferdinand Brunot, *Histoire de la langue française des origines à nos jours*, ed. Gérald Antoine, 2nd ed., 13 vols. (Paris: Albin Michel, 1966–1968), vol. 4, part 1, pp. 179–197.

235. Préface to the *Vie*, fol. i 3r.

236. *Ecole sainte*, fol. e 2r. On disdain for old or outmoded words among those setting the style of language usage in seventeenth-century France, see Brunot, *Langue française*, vol. 3, part 1, pp. 95–150; vol. 4, part 1, pp. 227–266.

237. Joan DeJean has commented to me that in the last forty years of the seventeenth century, many literary people were editing texts in the same spirit as Claude Martin, including their own youthful works, "to bring them up to standards of civility" (letter of 1 August 1993).

238. The manuscript in the archives of the Ursuline house at Trois-Rivières, Québec, is not in the hand of Marie de l'Incarnation or in the hand of her niece Marie Buisson (I have compared the handwriting with Marie Buisson's signatures on an act concerning the Ursulines of Tours, ADIL, H852, Act of 20 October 1681). Jamet gives evidence that the manuscript is in a female hand and was copied in France in the last quarter of the seventeenth century. He also shows that the *Vie* of Marie de l'Incarnation published by Charlevoix in 1724 (see n. 4 above for full citation) is based on a manuscript of Marie's *Relation* as well as on the *Vie* printed by her son Claude Martin. Charlevoix's quotations are often closer to the manuscript of Trois-Rivières than to Martin's published text. Jamet, *Ecrits*, vol. 2, pp. 28–30, 32–33.

239. In 1641–1643, Marie de l'Incarnation was in correspondence with Catherine-Agnès de S. Paul, daughter of Antoine Arnauld and abbess of Port-Royal. The women exchanged information about the spiritual growth of their young charges and about the Canadian mission, to which the sisters of Port-Royal also sent alms (MI to Catherine-Agnès de S. Paul, 4 September 1641, *Cor*, no. 57, pp. 137–138; 30 August 1642, no. 62, pp. 151–153; 18 September 1643, no. 71, pp. 195–196). After the publication of Antoine Arnauld's Jansenist book against frequent Communion in 1643, there are no letters to Port-Royal known. She herself had had special permission to have daily Communion when Raymond de

Saint Bernard was her Director (*Rel*, p. 108; *Vie*, p. 62). MI to CM, 1648, *Cor*, no. 113, p. 344.

240. Martin was supervising the edition of Augustine at the time he was working on the *Vie*. The first two volumes were published in Paris by François Muguet in 1679. On the edition, and on the vulnerability of the monks of Saint Maur to the accusation that an edition of Augustine made them appear *jansénisants*, see Oury, *Claude Martin*, pp. 160–166.

241. *Rel*, p. 52, line 25; *Vie*, p. 13. *Rel*, p. 141, line 20; *Vie*, p. 111. *Rel*, p. 116, lines 12–13; *Vie*, p. 73. When Marie is grateful to have been born of parents who were Christian, Claude adds "and Catholic" (*Rel*, p. 57, line 2; *Vie*, p. 21). Sometimes longer interpolations are required. The mother, in describing a densely packed vision, is satisfied with: "The Word, by the splendor of its illuminations, communicated itself to the Cherubim." The son goes on, "which gave me to understand that it is all illumination and all truth on its inside through its eternal generation and on its outside when it communicates itself" (*Rel*, p. 121, lines 16–17; *Vie*, p. 78).

242. Certeau, *Mystic Fable*, pp. 108–112. Martin, Préface to the *Retraites*, fols. a 3v–a 4r, a 8v. Oury, Introduction to the facsimile edition of *Vie*, pp. 14–18; Oury, *Claude Martin*, pp. 192–193. Claude was a friend of Pierre Nicole, despite their disagreements.

243. For *expérimenter*: *Rel*, p. 74, line 6, *Vie*, p. 31 ("je voyais clairement"); *Rel*, p. 92, line 1 ("Dieu fait expérimenter à l'âme"); *Vie*, p. 44 ("Dieu lui faisait entendre"); *Rel*, p. 94, line 19 ("elle voit et expérimente"); *Vie*, p. 47 ("elle voyoit clairement et par une experience sensible"); *Vie*, p. 316, line 21; *Vie*, p. 516. For *tendre* and *tendance*: *Rel*, p. 76, line 7, *Vie*, p. 37 ("avoit une inclination"); *Vie*, p. 106, lines 24, 26; *Vie*, p. 59; p. 341, lines 12–13 ("mon âme avoit une tendance"), *Vie*, p. 606 ("mon âme avoit une pente"). Though Claude Martin never eliminated the sections of the *Relation* in which Marie spoke about the difficulty of meditation and systematic mental exercises (they gave her headaches) or concealed her path of passive mental prayer, it is interesting that he once added phrases that made her sound more methodical: *Rel*, p. 292, line 12 ("Il y faut de l'examen, de l'étude, de la fidelité"); *Vie*, p. 457 ("il y faut de la meditation, des motifs, de l'examen, de l'étude, des resolutions, de la fidelité"). Oury comments that Martin's additions supply all the terms used for "methodical meditation" (*Rel*, p. 292, note c).

244. *Rel*, p. 95, lines 9–12, *Vie*, p. 47. A similar modification: she experiences her heart as "ravished" and blended with another heart, while an "interior voice says to [her] 'thus is made this union of hearts' "; Claude adds again that the inner voice speaks "distinctly" (*Rel*, p. 114, lines 22–24, p. 115, lines 1–2; *Vie*, p. 70).

245. *Rel*, p. 101, line 6; *Vie*, p. 53. Similarly, Marie says of a union between

her soul and Christ, "n'étant plus moi, je demeurai lui" ("Being no longer me, I remained him") and Claude rephrases, "n'étant plus à moi, je demeurais toute à lui" ("belonging no more to myself, I belonged wholly to him"), (*Rel*, p. 138, lines 26–27; *Vie*, p. 106. Also, when she broke into a *tutoiement* to the Lord, "O Amour, tu t'es plu à me martyriser," he changed it to "O Amour, vous vous êtes" (*Rel*, p. 148, lines 23–24; *Vie*, p. 134 (see n. 174 above on *tutoiement* in addressing the Lord).

246. *Rel*, p. 343, lines 16–21; *Vie*, pp. 643–644.

247. *Rel*, p. 49, line 13; *Vie*, p. 7. *Rel*, p. 75, line 14; *Vie*, p. 37. *Rel*, p. 102, line 1; *Vie*, p. 54. Brunot, *Langue française*, vol. 4, part 1, pp. 254, 354. Once Claude held on to Marie's "les affaires du tracas" (*Rel*, p. 145, lines 31–32; *Vie*, p. 119). Another example: the homey "strands and prickly stitching" ("brins et piqûres") of Marie's hairshirt become for Claude "knots and thorns" ("noeuds et épines"). *Rel*, p. 109, line 24; *Vie*, p. 62.

248. *Rel*, p. 345, line 21; *Vie*, p. 645. Marie ends her sentence saying that the Spirit of God deprives this "racaille" ("rabble") from its royal table (line 23); Claude uses "puissances basses" ("lower powers") instead of the popular *racaille*.

249. *Rel*, p. 97, lines 10–11; *Vie*, p. 48. *Rel*, p. 114, line 18; *Vie*, p. 70. *Rel*, p. 294, lines 1–7; *Vie*, p. 458. Claude did include, from her relation to her confessor in 1633, her account of how she desired to kiss the wound of one of her brother-in-law's servants but was forbidden by her Director to do any more than smell it (*Vie*, p. 629).

250. *Rel*, p. 260, lines 11–15, 23–25; *Vie*, pp. 408–409.

251. The Québec Ursuline library has Henry de Maupas du Tour, *La Vie de la venerable Mere Ieanne Françoise Fremiot, Fondatrice, Premiere Mere et Religieuse de l'Ordre de la Visitation de Sainte Marie* (Paris: Simeon Piget, 1658), given to the Ursulines by the sisters of the Visitation in 1702, and *Les Epistres spirituelles de la Mere Ieanne Françoise Fremiot* (Lyon: Vincent de Coeursillys, 1644). It seems very likely that these are replacements for editions that had been sent to the Ursuline convent during Marie's lifetime and had been destroyed in the fire of 1686.

252. *JJ*, p. 164 (4 December 1651), p. 166 (16 April 1652). *JR*, vol. 36, p. 148; vol. 37, p. 94.

253. Martin, *L'Ecole sainte*, Préface, fol. e 3v. There were Jesuits who shared Marie's appreciation for Amerindian tongues. Jérome Lalemant said of the "admirable" formation of compound words among the Montagnais that "the economy of the Savage languages" was a sufficient proof of the existence of God (*JR*, vol. 29, pp. 224–226).

254. *Le Dictionnaire de l'Académie françoise*, 2 vols. (Paris: Widow of Jean-Baptiste Coignard, 1694), vol. 2, pp. 272, 445. [Joseph-Marie Chaumonot?], French-Huron dictionary (ca. 1663), John Carter Brown Library, Providence,

R.I., Codex Ind 12, fols. 19r *("civil")*; 76v *("politesse")*. On *"aiendaouasti,"* see also *JR*, vol. 10, pp. 212–215; vol. 44, pp. 296–297.

255. "Vie de la Mère Iaquette Carpentier, dite de Saint Augustin, Religieuse Ursuline à Nevers," in Pommereu, *Chroniques*, p. 232.

256. Marie de l'Incarnation, Printed death notice for Soeur Anne de Saint Laurens, 1 September 1669, AUQ, 1/1/1/.3. MI to the community of Ursulines of Tours, spring 1652, *Cor*, no. 140, pp. 460–461: death notice for Marie de Saint Joseph.

257. MI to CM, 2 September 1651, *Cor*, no. 133, pp. 412–415.

258. MI to CM, summer 1647, *Cor*, no. 110, pp. 327–330. The episode is also recounted by Jérome Lalemant in *JR*, vol. 30, pp. 254–267, but Marie specifically says to Claude that she had learned the details from the escaped woman herself. Oury dates her letter summer 1647; Lalemant's report is dated in its final form 20 October 1647, ready for the last boat back to France. Thus, he might well have used Marie's account as his base. On preliterate styles of Amerindian autobiography, see Brumble, *American Indian Autobiography*, chs. 1–2.

259. *Vie*, pp. 483–488. I am here following Claude Martin's version, where the name and religion of the *ravisseur* and the precise date of the events are not given. The villain was François Musset, Sieur de Pray, captain of a company of carabineers. He was related through his mother to the Arnauld family, but was himself a Protestant (Oury, *Marie de l'Incarnation*, p. 397). Requests and appeals in the case were presented to the Parlement of Paris in 1642 by Claude Guyart, widow of Paul Buisson, and her second husband, the merchant Antoine Laguiolle; and by François Musset and his collaborators in the abduction, Antoinette Péan and the sergeant Michel Moulin (AN, X^{2a} 271, 11 July, 2 August, 6 August, 11 September, 20 September 1642; X^{2b} 468, 7 July, 11 July, 2 August, 7 August 1642; X^{2b} 469, 11 September, 20 September 1642). It would be interesting to know Musset's side of the story, but I have been unable to find his letter of remission. He later made a good marriage to a woman of higher station than Marie Buisson.

260. There was another abduction case before the Criminal Chamber of the Parlement of Paris at the same time as that of Musset-Buisson (AN, X^{2a} 271, 7 October 1642). Danielle Haase-Dubosc, "Ravie et enlevée au XVIIe siècle," in Danielle Haase-Dubosc and Elaine Viennot, eds., *Femmes et pouvoirs sous l'ancien régime* (Paris: Editions Rivage, 1991), pp. 135–152: an examination of the abduction of the young widow Madame de Miramion by Roger de Rabutin, Comte de Bussy, in 1648. Christian Biet and Jean Bart, "Les *Illustres françaises,* roman moderne, exemple d'un romanesque juridique: 'L'Histoire de Monsieur de Terny et de Mademoiselle de Bernay' " (unpublished paper ENS Fontenay-Saint-Cloud, seminar on "Droit et littérature," 1992): examination of a story by Robert Challe in which abduction is a strategy against unjust patriarchal power.

261. Stith Thompson, *Tales of the North American Indians* (Cambridge, Mass.:

Harvard University Press, 1929), no. 64, pp. 164–167 (The Bear-Woman), and p. 345, n. 244 (The Bear-Woman), n. 245 (Bear paramour); Stith Thompson, *The Folktale* (Berkeley: University of California Press, 1977), pp. 356–358. Claude Lévi-Strauss, *Histoire de lynx* (Paris: Plon, 1991), pp. 146–147: "one of the most widespread myths in the two Americas has as its heroine a woman who goes away under different pretexts to find her animal seducer." Lévi-Strauss's analysis of the myth in the case of the tapir-seducer is in *From Honey to Ashes*, trans. John and Doreen Weightman (London: Jonathan Cape, 1973), pp. 296–308. Jeremiah Curtin and J. N. B. Hewitt, *Seneca Fiction, Legends, and Myths*, 32nd Annual Report of the Bureau of American Ethnology, 1910–1911 (Washington: Government Printing Office, 1918), pp. 102–104, no. 9: "A Woman and Her Bear Lover" (collected in the 1880s). Herbert T. Schwarz, *Tales from the Smokehouse* (Edmonton, Alberta: Hurtig Publishers, 1974), pp. 31–35: "The Bear Walker" (Mohawk, collected 1969). See also the related Tiwa tale collected by Elsie Clews Parsons in 1940, where the lover is a buffalo; in Richard Erdoes and Alfonso Ortiz, eds., *American Indian Myths and Legends* (New York: Pantheon Books, 1984), pp. 291–294.

262. *JR*, vol. 6, pp. 216–219.

263. François de Belleforest told this story in his translation and continuation of the *Histoires tragiques* of Matteo Bandello. This tale is not from Bandello but was added by Belleforest himself as part of a story entitled "Actes cruels et detestables de quelques ieunes citoyens, sur une Damoiselle." It first appeared in François de Belleforest, *Le cinquieme livre des Histoires Tragiques* (Lyon: Benoît Rigaud, 1576). I have used *Histoires tragiques: Recueillies des histoires tant anciennes que modernes, et mises en lumiere*, vol. 6 (Rouen: Adrian de Launay, 1604); the Swedish bear story appears on p. 258 as part of Histoire 109. Belleforest gave as his source Saxo Grammaticus, *Histoire des Danois*, book 10, a work which had appeared in Latin (Saxo Grammaticus, *Danica Historia Libris XVI* [Frankfurt am Main: A. Wechel, 1576], book 10, pp. 174–175; copy at Princeton University has marginalia about the bear and the bear child).

264. On the tale of Jean de l'Ours and its dissemination in various forms, see Paul Delaure and M. L. Tenèze, *Le Conte populaire français*, 2 vols. (Paris: Editions Erasme and Editions G. P. Maisonneuve and Larose, 1957–1964), vol. 1, pp. 110–133; and Daniel Fabre and Jacques Lacroix, *La Tradition orale du conte occitan*, 2 vols. (Paris: Presses Universitaires de France, 1974), vol. 1, pp. 331–346. The earliest printed record of a version of this tale type, according to Delaure, is at the opening of the eighteenth century, but specialists assume that in its oral form it is much older. For the Candlemas ceremony of the dancing bear in the Pyrenees, see Violet Alford, *Pyrenean Festivals* (London: Chatto and Windus, 1937), pp. 16–25; Arnold Van Gennep, *Manuel de folklore français contemporain*, 4 vols. (Paris: A. and J. Picard, 1943–1947), vol. 1, pp. 908–918; N. Z. Davis, *Society and Culture in Early Modern France* (Stanford, Calif.: Stanford University Press, 1975), p. 137.

265. Lévi-Strauss considers the impact of the story of Jean de l'Ours, especially of his prodigious animal energy, on the Amerindians who heard it from *coureurs du bois* in the seventeenth century and who incorporated some of his adventures into their own tales (*Histoire de lynx*, pp. 242–245).

266. MI to Ursule de Ste. Catherine, 29 September 1642, *Cor*, no. 65, pp. 163–165. Marie heard the account from Father du Quen's report and also from the woman herself. There is also an account by Barthélemy Vimont in the *Relations;* it is based on du Quen's report and has different details and emphases from that given by Marie (*JR*, vol. 22, pp. 114–125).

267. MI to CM, 18 October 1667, *Cor*, no. 230, pp. 786–787.

268. The Buisson abduction is not mentioned in a letter to a sister-in-law of 28 August 1642; it is referred to indirectly in a letter to her niece of 14 September 1643; and it is mentioned directly in a letter to her son of 2 August 1644 (*Cor*, no. 61, p. 149; no. 70, p. 192; no. 76, p. 206).

269. MI to Ursule de Ste. Catherine, 29 September 1642, *Cor*, no. 65, p. 163. *Rel*, p. 166; *Vie*, p. 181.

Metamorphoses

1. Joachim Sandrart, *L'Academia Todesca della Architectura, Scultura e Pittura: Oder Teutsche Academia der Edlen Bau-, Bild- und Mahleren-Künste*, 2 vols. (Nuremberg: Jacob von Sandrart, 1675–1679; and Frankfurt: Mathias Merian the Younger, 1675–1679), vol. 1, no. 283, p. 339.

2. Christoph Arnold, introductory poem to *Rau* 79, verso of title page.

3. Petrus Dittelbach, *Verval en Val der Labadisten, of Derselver Leydinge, en wyse van doen in haare Huys-houdinge, en Kerk-formering, als ook huren op-en nedergang, in hare Colonien of volk plantingen, nader intdekt* (Amsterdam: Daniel van den Dalen, 1692), pp. 18–19. RS*Mer*, p. 13. The Senate's decree of divorce is dated 12 August 1692.

4. An early bibliography of the works of Maria Sibylla Merian is Max Adolf Pfeiffer, *Die werke der Maria Sibylle [sic] Merian bibliographisch zusammengestellt* (Meissen: M. A. Pfeiffer, 1931). In the growing bibliography on Maria Sibylla Merian, one can cite the still useful biography by J. Stuldreher-Nienhuis, *Verborgen Paradijszen: Het Leven en de Werken van Maria Sibylla Merian, 1647–1717* (Arnhem: Van Loghum Slater, 1945). RS*Mer* includes Rücker's biographical study, "The Life and Personality of Maria Sibylla Merian," and her study of Merian's book on the insects of Suriname, a study by Stearn entitled "The Plants, the Insects and Other Animals of Merian's *Metamorphosis Insectorum Surinamensium*," the extant letters of Merian, a bibliography of her publications and of works about her, and much other useful information. Helmut Deckert has an appreciation of Merian as an introduction to his facsimile edition of the 1705 Suriname book: *Metamorphosis Insectorum Surinamensium (Amsterdam 1705)* (fac-

simile edition; Leipzig: Insel Verlag, 1975), pp. 5–35. See the valuable essays by Irina Lebedeva, Wolf-Dietrich Beer, and Gerrit Friese in *Stud*. There is also useful commentary by Helga Ullmann, Wolf-Dietrich Beer, and Boris Vladimo-rivic Lukin in Maria Sibylla Merian, *Leningrader Aquarelle* (Leipzig: Editions Le-ipzig, 1974; Lucerne: C. J. Bucher, 1974). T. A. Lukina has written a very inter-esting biography in Russian, *Maria Sibylla Merian, 1647–1717* (Leningrad: Nauka, 1980). Other studies since 1980 include Charlotte Kerner, *Seidenraupe, Dschun-gelblüte: Die Lebensgeschichte der Maria Sibylla Merian* (Weinheim and Basel: Beltz and Gelberg, 1989); Uwe George, "Der Raupen wunderbare Verwandelung: Auf den Spuren der naturforschenden Malerin Maria Sibylla Merian im südamerikan-ischen Surinam," *Geo*, 7 (July 1990): 11–36; Wilhelm Treue, *Eine Frau, drei Männer und eine Kunstfigur: Barocke Lebensläufe* (Munich: C. H. Beck, 1992); and Sharon Valiant, "Maria Sibylla Merian: Recovering an Eighteenth-Century Leg-end," *Eighteenth-Century Studies*, 3 (Spring 1993): 467–479. Londa Schiebinger has some important pages on Merian in *The Mind Has No Sex? Women in the Origins of Modern Science* (Cambridge, Mass.: Harvard University Press, 1989), pp. 68–78; and idem, *Nature's Body: Gender in the Making of Modern Science* (Boston: Beacon Press, 1993), pp. 203–205. David Freedberg gives valuable con-text to her scientific painting in "Science, Commerce, and Art: Neglected Topics at the Junction of History and Art History," in David Freedberg and Jan de Vries, eds., *Art in History, History in Art: Studies in Seventeenth-Century Dutch Culture* (Santa Monica, Calif.: Getty Center for the History of Art and the Hu-manities, 1991), pp. 377–386. In a dissertation on nature painting in Nuremberg, Heidrun Ludwig gives a detailed discussion of the work of Maria Sibylla Merian during her Nuremberg years: "Nürnberger naturgeschichtliche Malerei im 17. und 18. Jahrhundert" (Diss., Technische Universität Berlin, 1992). See also Heidrun Ludwig, "Von der Betrachtung zur Beobachtung: Die künstlerische Entwicklung der Blumen- und Insektenmalerin Maria Sibylla Merian in Nürnberg (1670–1682)," in John Roger Paas, ed., *"Der Franken Rom": Nürnbergs Blütezeit in der zweiten Hälfte des 17. Jahrhunderts* (Wiesbaden: Harrassowitz, 1995).

5. StAF, Bücher des Standesamts. Heiratsregister Evang. Kirche Frankfurt am Main, 1635–1657, fol. 228r, marriage of 27 January 1646. Merian's first wife was Maria Magdalena de Bry, whom he married in 1617 when he was working for a few years in Oppenheim. Of the large bibliography on Mathias Merian the Elder, see Ulrich Thieme and Felix Becker, *Allgemeines Lexikon der bildenden Künstler Lexikon*, 37 vols. (Leipzig: W. Engelmann, 1907–1950), vol. 24, p. 413; Walther Karl Zülch, *Frankfurter Künstler, 1223–1700* (Frankfurt am Main: Sauer und Auvermann, 1967), pp. 500–502; Lucas Heinrich Wüthrich, *Die Handzeich-nungen von Matthaeus Merian d. Ae.* (Basel: Bärenreiter-Verlag, 1963), pp. 12–25; and idem, *Das Druckgraphische Werk von Matthaeus Merian d. Ae.*, 2 vols. (Basel: Bärenreiter-Verlag, 1966–1972). Merian's publications, often with copperplate title pages and illustrations by him, are very wide-ranging: works on medicine, cosmology, botany; Bible pictures; emblem books; and others.

6. StAF, Bücher des Standeamts. Heiratsregister Evang. Kirche Frankfurt am Main, 1635–1657, fol. 325r, marriage of 5 August 1651. On Jacob Marrel, see Thieme and Becker, *Lexikon*, vol. 24, p. 137; Zulch, *Frankfurter Künstler*, pp. 537–540; Sam Segal, *Jan Davidsz de Heem en zijn Kring* (The Hague: Sdu Uitgeverij and Utrecht: Centraal Museum, 1991), pp. 20, 29–30, 44, and colorplate 45; and Kurt Wettengl, ed., *Georg Flegel, 1566–1638: Stilleben* (Frankfurt am Main: Historisches Museum and Schirn Kunsthalle, 1993; Stuttgart: Gerd Hatje, 1993), pp. 27, 254–261.

7. Thieme and Becker, *Lexikon*, vol. 24, pp. 412–413; Zülch, *Frankfurter Künstler*, pp. 548, 550. *Beschreibung und Abbildung Aller Königl. und Churfürst: Ein-Züge wahlund Crönungs Acta, so geschehen zu Franckfurt am Mayn im Jahr 1658* (Frankfurt am Main: Caspar Merian, 1658). A short autobiography by Mathias the Younger is given in Rudolf Wackernagel, ed., "Selbstbiographie des jüngern Matthäus Merian," *Basler Jahrbuch* (1895): 227–244.

8. On Frankfurt am Main in the seventeenth century, see Gerald L. Soliday, *A Community in Conflict: Frankfurt Society in the Seventeenth and Early Eighteenth Centuries* (Hanover, N.H.: University Press of New England, 1974); and Alexander Dietz, *Frankfurter Handelsgeschichte*, 4 vols. (Frankfurt am Main, 1925; reprint Glashütten im Taunus: Verlag Detler Auvermann, 1970), vols. 3, 4, part 1 (the Merian business is described in vol. 3, pp. 120–129).

9. Soliday, *Frankfurt*, chs. 2, 7–8; RSMer, p. 10; Zülch, *Frankfurter Künstler*, pp. 537–538; Segal, *De Heem*, pp. 29–30, 44. On Isaac Goldschmidt, also known as Hamel, moneylender and jewel merchant of Frankfurt, and his descendants, see Alexander Dietz, *Stammbuch der Frankfurter Juden: Geschichtliche Mitteilungen über die Frankfurter jüdischen Familien von 1349–1849* (Frankfurt am Main: J. St. Goar, 1907), pp. 121–126.

10. Two general studies of women artists in the early modern period are Ann Sutherland Harris and Linda Nochlin, *Women Artists: 1550–1950* (Los Angeles: Los Angeles County Museum of Art, 1976; New York: Alfred A. Knopf, 1976); and Rozsika Parker and Griselda Pollock, *Old Mistresses: Women, Art and Ideology* (New York: Pantheon Books, 1981). Other women painters in Joachim Sandrart's *Academia Todesca*, besides Maria Sibylla Merian, include Anna Maria Printin (no. 284) and Susanna Mayrin, a flower painter of Augsburg (no. 262, p. 328). Several seventeenth-century woman painters are listed in Nuremberg alone in Johann Gabriel Doppelmayr, *Historische Nachricht von den Nürnbergischen Mathematicis und Kunstlern* (Nuremberg: Peter Conrad Monaths, 1730), pp. 223, 233, 253, 259–260, 266, 270. Also on women painters in Germany, see Heide Wunder, *"Er ist die Sonn,' sie ist der Mond": Frauen in der Frühen Neuzeit* (Munich: C. H. Beck, 1992), pp. 145–146. The classical discussion of genius and gender is the frequently reprinted and translated Juan Huarte de San Juan, *Examen de ingenios para las sciencias* (Valencia: Pedro de Huete, 1580; 1st ed. 1575), ch. 15, with a Latin translation in Leipzig in 1622, *Scrutinium ingeniorum pro iis, qui excellere cupiunt*, and further Latin editions in German areas in the seventeenth century.

11. The importance of travel years is suggested by the space Mathias Merian the Younger gave to them in his brief autobiography, "Selbstbiographie," pp. 230–238.

12. Thieme and Becker, *Lexikon*, vol. 24, p. 548; Zülch, *Frankfurter Künstler*, p. 563; Segal, *De Heem*, pp. 30, 44.

13. On Jacob Marrel's collection at the time of his death in 1681, see Zülch, *Frankfurter Künstler*, p. 539. In addition to many engravings and books, he owned 320 oil paintings.

14. Jan Jonston, *Historia Naturalis de Insectis Libri III [sic for IV]: De Serpentibus et Draconibus Libri II cum aenis Figuris—Iohannes Ionstonus Med. Doctor Concinnavit* (Frankfurt am Main: Heirs of Mathias Merian, 1653). At the bottom of the title-page engraving of dragons and insects: "M. Merian Jun. Invinter [*sic* for inventor]." Jonston was drawing his material on butterflies, moths, and caterpillars mostly from Thomas Mouffet and Ulisse Aldrovandi, sometimes quoting them directly, and the plates often specify "from Mouffet," "Papiliones Aldrovandi," "Raup. Mouf.," "Erucarum Aldrov.," "Bombyces Aldrov. Seidenwürm" (Book I, pp. 46–47, 56, and plates 5–8; Book II, pp. 142, 147, and plates 20, 22–23). The Polish-born Jan Jonston (1603–1675) lived in England, the Netherlands, and Germany, and published numerous books of natural philosophy.

15. An example of Marrel's use of insects with flowers is the garland cartouche around a view of Frankfurt, painted in 1651 at the time of Marrel's marriage to the widow of Mathias Merian the Elder (the view of Frankfurt is itself taken from a representation by Mathias Merian the Elder, to which Marrel has added a swimming scene in the midst of the Main). It is reproduced in the illustrations here. There are three butterflies, a dragonfly, and a bee next to or on the flowers, and caterpillars and other insects among them (Frankfurt am Main, Historisches Museum).

16. Zülch, *Frankfurter Künstler*, p. 538. Dietz, *Handelsgeschichte*, vol. 4, part 1, pp. 76–77, 347–348; Soliday, *Community*, p. 146, n. 25.

17. *Stud*, p. 141: "These investigations I began in Frankfurt in 1660 . . ." Maria Sibylla Merian, *Metamorphosis Insectorum Surinamensium* (Amsterdam: Gerard Valck, 1705; facsimile edition with the original paintings from the collection in the Royal Library at Windsor Castle, London: Pion, 1980), "Ad lectorem."

18. G. A. Lindeboom, "A Short Biography of Jan Swammerdam (1637–1680)," in *The Letters of Jan Swammerdam to Melchisedec Thévenot* (Amsterdam: Swets and Zeitlinger, 1975), p. 3.

19. Thomas Mouffet (also Moufet, Moffet, Muffet) was a physician who lived from 1553 to 1604 and published works on health as well as a poem on silkworms dedicated to the Countess of Pembroke: *The Silkewormes, and Their Flies* (London: Nicholas Ling, 1599). His compendium on insects first appeared posthumously in Latin, edited by Theodore de Mayerne, *Insectorum sive Minimorum Animalium Theatrum* (London: Thomas Cotes, 1634); and then in English as *The*

Theater of Insects or Lesser Living Creatures: As Bees, Flies, Caterpillars, Spiders, Worms, etc.—a most Elaborate Work (London: E. Cotes, 1658). The rhyme is supposed to be about his daughter Patience. The earliest dated record of the verse is 1805 (Iona Opie and Peter Opie, eds., *The Oxford Dictionary of Nursery Rhymes* [Oxford: Clarendon Press, 1966], pp. 323–324), but the Opies trace analogous poems back to the seventeenth century,

20. StAF, Bücher des Standesamts, series 1658–1677, fol. 104r: marriage of 16 May 1665. Jacob Marrel, designer, and Johann Andreas Graff, engraver, "Umzug der Frankfurter Schreiner vor dem Romer," 1659 (Germanisches Nationalmuseum Nürnberg, Kupferstich-Kabinett, HB1659/1302). "Daughter Sara of the painter Jacob Marrel, Ao 1658," by J. Graff (Frankfurt am Main, Städl, Print room, Inventory Number 5744). Sara, Jacob Marrel's daughter by his first wife, was sixteen at the time of the drawing; Maria Sibylla was then eleven.

21. The Merians already had some Nuremberg connections, for in 1652 Caspar Merian had married Rachel, daughter of Jacob Morian of Nuremberg (StAF, Bücher des Standesamts, series 1653–1657, 2 November 1652). For an overview of Nuremberg and its cultural life in the seventeenth century, see Gerhard Pfeiffer, ed., *Nürnberg: Geschichte einer europäischen Stadt* (Munich: C. H. Beck, 1971), pp. 303–357.

22. Graff's street scenes of Nuremberg can be found in Nuremberg in the Germanisches Nationalmuseum, Kupferstich-Kabinett, SP6590 (K7373); HB6584 (1065a); HB2320 (K1338). Sandrart, *Academia Todesca*, vol. 1, no. 283, p. 339; Doppelmayr, *Historische Nachricht*, pp. 255–256.

23. Sandrart, *Academia Todesca*, vol. 1, no. 283, p. 339. Doppelmayr, *Historische Nachricht*, pp. 268–270. Maria Sibylla Merian to Clara Regina Imhoff, 25 July 1682, 24 March 1683, 8 December 1684, 8 May 1685, in RS*Mer*, nos. 1–4, pp. 61–63. Henceforth all references to Merian in this collection of letters will be abbreviated MSM.

24. On 3 April 1679, Maria Sibylla Merian painted a spray of roses for the *album amicorum* of Andreas Arnold, son of Christopher Arnold (RS*Mer*, p. 9); the same year, the elder Arnold contributed dedicatory poems to Merian's book on European caterpillars. Works by Christopher Arnold include *Joh. Henrici Ursini De Zorastre Bactriam, Hermete Trismegisto . . . Quibus Christophori Arnoldi spicilegium accessit* (Nuremberg: Michael Endter, 1661); *XXX Epistolae Philologicae et Historicae de Flavii Josephi Testimonio* (Nuremberg: Michael and Johann Frederic Endter, 1661); among the letters of Arnold is a 1651 exchange with Menasseh ben Israel about Flavius Josephus and Josippon. *Inclutae Bibliothecae Norimbergensis Memorabilia . . . Accedit Christophori Arnoldi, V.C. De Hydriotaphia* (Nuremberg: Wolfgang Mauritius Endter and heirs of Johann Andreas Endter, 1674): engravings of urns, references to Thomas Brown and other English writers. *Mensia Fureriana* (Nuremberg: Christopher Gerhard, 1677): a funeral oration for a Nuremberg notable; Arnoldus is described as Historian, Orator, Poet, and learned

in Greek and Latin (fol. A2r). In the exchange with Menasseh ben Israel he quotes Hebrew as well.

25. RS*Mer*, p. 9: baptism 2 February 1678.

26. The volumes of 1675, 1677, and 1680 had titles in Latin or partly in Latin (reproduced in RS*Mer*, pp. 186–187). In 1680 all three volumes were also printed in a single edition with a German title page and a German preface: *M. S. Gräffin, M. Merians des Aeltern seel. Tochter: Neues Blumen Buch allen Kunstverständigen Liebhabern su Lust, Nutz und Dienst, mit Fleiss verfertiget zu finden bey Joh. Andrea Graffen, Mahlern in Nürnberg, im Jahr 1680.* I have used the copy of the composite edition in the Botanical Library at Copenhagen (black and white, with the German plant names from the printed Register added by hand at the bottom of each picture). A facsimile of the 1680 composite edition in the Sächsischen Landes-bibliothek, Dresden, has been published by Helmut Deckert (*Maria Sibylla Merians "Neues Blumenbuch" [Nürnberg 1680]* [Leipzig: Insel Verlag, 1966]). See Ludwig, "Von der Betrachtung zur Beobachtung."

27. Mathias Merian the Elder, *Florilegium Renovatum et Auctum: Das ist, Vernewertes und vermehrtes Blumenbuch* (Frankfurt am Main: Mathias Merian the Elder, 1641), described by Wüthrich, *Druckgraphische Werk*, vol. 2, p. 19, no. 18. Jacob Marrel, *Artliches und Kunstreichs Reissbüchlein für die ankommende Jugendt zu lehren, insonderheit für Mahler, Goldschmidt, und Bildhauer* (Frankfurt am Main: Jacob Marrel, 1661).

28. *Neues Blumen Buch*, Foreword. She dates the papal flower purchase 12 November 1679, when the reigning pope was Innocent XI. (On the tulip mania in the seventeenth century, see Antoine Schnapper, *Le Géant, la licorne, et la tulipe* [Paris: Flammarion, 1988], pp. 47–51.) Merian's references in this foreword indicate something of her learning in 1679. For the tulip sales in the Netherlands, she refers to "Meteran, Bk. 55"—that is, one of the continuations of the history of Emanuel van Meteren (d. 1612), such as *Historien der Nederlanderen* (Leyden, 1647). For a plant from Asia, she refers to "Joh. Neuhoff in Beschreibung Sina, Cap. X6, Bl. 327.328"—that is, a German translation of Johan Nieuhof's much-printed work on the 1655–1657 embassy of the Dutch East India Company to the emperor of China. Talking of an Angelica plant taller than a man and thicker than a man's arm, she refers to "P. Bohusl. Balbinus, lib. I Miscell Hist R. Bohem. cap. 6 paragr. 5"—that is, the just-published first volume of Bohuslaus Aloysius Balbinus, *Miscellanea historica regni Bohemiae* (Prague: G. Czernoch, 1679–1688). These learned books may well have come to her from Christopher Arnold, who among other things edited travel accounts similar to the one written by Johan Nieuhof. See below, n. 128.

29. *Der Raupen wunderbare Verwandelung und sonderbare Blumen-nahrung worinnen durch eine gantz-neue Erfindung: Der Raupen, Würmer, Sommer-vögelein, Motten, Fliegen und anderer dergleichen Thierlein: Ursprung speisen und Veränderungen samt ihrer Zeit, Ort, und Eigenschaften: Den Naturkündigern, Kunstmahlern, und Gartenliebhabern zu Dienst fleissig untersucht kürtzlich beschrieben nach dem*

Leben abgemahlt ins Kupfer gestochen und selbst verlegt von Maria Sibylla Gräffin, Matthaei Merians des Eltern Seel. Tochter ("In Nuremberg the book is available from Johann Andreas Graff, painter, and in Frankfurt and Leipzig from David Funk. Printed by Andreas Knortz, 1679"). Also: *Der Raupen wunderbare Verwandlung und sonderbare Blumen-nahrung Anderer Theil . . . von Maria Sibylla Gräffin, Matthaei Merians des Eltern Seel. Tochter* ("The book is available in Frankfurt am Main from Johann Andreas Graff, painter, and in Leipzig and Nuremberg from David Funk. Printed by Johann Michael Spörlin, 1683").

30. A colored edition: SUBF, Frankfurt Abteilung W 58. A black-and-white edition: SUBF, Senckenberg collection Q353.5535/1.

31. The entomological notes of the great English naturalist John Ray (1627–1705) sometimes give a common name for a species, but as often simply describe the way the butterfly or moth looked. For instance, the butterfly today known as *Vanessa urticae* is described by Maria Sibylla Merian as a butterfly whose caterpillar feeds on nettle leaves (she depicts the caterpillar, cocoon, and butterfly on the nettle plant and also describes appearance and color in her text; *Rau*83, plate 41). John Ray describes it as "Butterfly of the nettle," "the lesser Tortoise-shell Butterfly" (Charles Raven, *John Ray, Naturalist: His Life and Works* [Cambridge: Cambridge University Press, 1950], p. 409, quoting from Ray's posthumous *Historia Insectorum* of 1710).

32. *Rau*79, pp. 47–48, plate 23.

33. *Rau*83, p. 15, plate 8: Taub- oder Todten-Nessel mit der weissen Blüe, *Galeopsis florens* (today White Dead-Nettle, *Lamium album*).

34. *Rau*79, p. 13, plate 6.

35. *Rau*79, p. 21, plate 10 (she knew which was the female because it laid eggs). Years later Hans Sloane said that, in her Surinamc book, Merian had mistakenly depicted the male and female of one butterfly as two butterflies (*A Voyage . . . to Jamaica* [for full title see n. 124 below], 2 vols. [London: Printed by B.M. for the Author, 1707–1725], vol. 2, p. 213). John Ray noted fairly often (though not always accurately) differences in appearance between male and female butterflies (Raven, *Ray*, pp. 407–415. On the importance of sexual dimorphism in the debate about classificatory systems in the eighteenth century, see Schiebinger, *Nature's Body*.

36. *Rau*79, fol. 3r. Her 1679 title includes *Kunstmahlern* among those to whom she hoped her book would be of service.

37. Marjorie Lee Hendrix, "Joris Hoefnagel and the *Four Elements:* A Study in Sixteenth-Century Nature Painting" (Diss., Princeton University, 1984). Thomas DaCosta Kaufmann, *The Mastery of Nature: Aspects of Art, Science, and Humanism in the Renaissance* (Princeton, N.J.: Princeton University Press, 1993), esp. ch. 1, coauthored with Virginia Roehrig Kaufmann. In one of Hoefnagel's manuscripts, actual insect wings are glued onto the page next to the thorax of the insect (pp. 45–47 and fig. 27).

38. Wettengl, ed., *Flegel*, Katalogteil II, "Georg Flegel, Stilleben"; Katal-

ogteil III, "Aquarelle Georg Flegels und Zeitgenösse Naturstudien." Catalogue numbers 67, 99, and 100 are studies of the silkworm.

39. Hendrix, "Hoefnagel," pp. 75, 90. *Rau*79, fol. 3r: *"lebendig."*

40. In the still-lifes of Ambrosius Bosschaert (1573–1621), beautiful specimens of flowers that bloom at different times of the year are placed in the same vase (*Floral Still-Life*, The Hague, Mauritshuis, Inventory number 679; *Bouquet of Flowers in a Stone Niche*, Copenhagen, Statens Museum for Kunst). Georg Flegel, too, put flowers that bloomed at different times of year and in different places together in the same vase (Hana Seifertová, "Stilleben Georg Flegels: Themen, Kompositionen, Bedeutungen," in Wettengl, ed. *Flegel*, p. 64).

41. Segal, *De Heem*, p. 40; Hendrix, "Hoefnagel," pp. 71–74, 216, 266–278. *Ignis* is the first book of Joris Hoefnagel's *Four Elements*, a vellum manuscript done by the artist in Antwerp in the 1570s. On moral and metaphorical messages in the still-life paintings of Georg Flegel, see Kurt Wettengl, "Die 'Gedeckten Tische' des Georg Flegel," in Wettengl, ed., *Flegel*, pp. 84—90.

42. *Rau*83, fol. 3r. Years later, in the posthumously published volume 3 of the *Raupen* in Dutch, Merian made a brief moral reference to the placement of ants on the decorative wreath prepared as a title page for the book. After describing how she was given an ants' nest and discovered that their metamorphosis was like that of caterpillars, she said, "I placed them here [on the wreath] in order to investigate with Solomon their virtues" (*Derde en Laatse Deel der Rupsen Begin, Voedʒel, en Wonderbaare Verandering* [Amsterdam: Dorothea Maria Hendriks, born Gräffin, 1717], introductory matter). This is the only such remark in the text.

43. Mouffet, *Insectorum . . . Theatrum* (1634); *Theater of Insects* (1658). Book I is on winged insects, beetles, bees; Book II on wingless insects—that is, caterpillars, worms, spiders, and others. On Mouffet's book, a compendium of the observations made by Edward Wotton, Conrad Gesner, Thomas Penny, and by Mouffet himself, see the assessment in Raven, *John Ray*, pp. 390–391; and Max Beier, "The Early Naturalists and Anatomists during the Renaissance and Seventeenth Century," in Ray F. Smith, Thomas E. Mittler, and Carroll N. Smith, eds., *History of Entomology* (Palo Alto, Calif.: Annual Reviews, 1973), p. 86. Günter Morge, "Entomology in the Western World in Antiquity and in Medieval Times," ibid., p. 41 (Aristotle classifies first according to whether the insect is winged or wingless, and second according to mouth parts). Jonston, *De Insectis*, Book I, "De Insectis Terrestribus Pedatis et Alatis"; Book II, "De Insectis Terrestribus Pedatis et Non Alatis." On the general social and moral issues in early modern systems of classification, see Keith Thomas, *Man and the Natural World: A History of the Modern Sensibility* (New York: Pantheon Books, 1983), pp. 51–70.

44. Jan Swammerdam, *Historia Insectorum Generalis, ofte Algemeene Verhandeling van de Bloedeloose Dierkens* (Utrecht: Meinardus van Dreunen, 1669). The

work was issued in Latin and French not long after Swammerdam's death in 1680: *Historia Insectorum Generalis* (Leyden: Jordanus Luchtmans, 1685); *Histoire generale des Insectes* (Utrecht: G. de Walcheren, 1682; Utrecht: Jean Ribbius, 1685). On his contribution to entomology, see Beier, "Naturalists and Anatomists," in Smith et al., eds., *Entomology*, p. 90; and S. L. Tuxen, "Entomology Systematizes and Describes," ibid., pp. 106–107; Raven, *John Ray*, p. 392; and S. Schierbeek, *Jan Swammerdam (12 February 1637–17 February 1680): His Life and Works* (Amsterdam: Swets and Zeitlinger, 1967), chs. 4, 9.

45. *Rau*79, verso of title page. Arnold referred to Swammerdam's work again in his introductory poem to the second volume of *Raupen* (*Rau*83, verso of title page).

46. Swammerdam, *Algemeene Verhandeling*, fold-out illustrations at the end of the text. In plate 44 of his posthumous *Bybel der Natur* (1737–1738), Swammerdam pictured the worms on the leaves of the willow tree, which had emerged from the eggs deposited by a fly, but the rest of the remarkable illustrations are anatomical (*Bibel der natur, Worinnen die insekten in gewisse classen vertheilt*, ed. Herman Boerhaave, trans. from the Dutch [Leipzig: J. F. Gleditsch, 1752]).

47. Raven, *John Ray*, p. 223; Schiebinger, *Nature's Body*, pp. 13–23; Alice Stroup, *A Company of Scientists: Botany, Patronage, and Community at the Seventeenth-Century Parisian Royal Academy of Sciences* (Berkeley: University of California Press, 1990), pp. 145–154. On examining pollen under a microscope at the Royal Academy of Sciences in Paris in 1678–1679, see ibid., p. 158. Christian Huygens noted that the "dust" of crocus flowers resembled the dust on the feet of bees, and suggested that the bees were using it to make wax.

48. Carolyn Merchant, *The Death of Nature: Women, Ecology, and the Scientific Revolution* (San Francisco: Harper and Row, 1980), ch. 2, esp. pp. 59–60 on responses to the draining of the Pontine marshes in Italy and of the fens in England; Thomas, *Natural World*, pp. 192–201.

49. John Ray, *The Wisdom of God Manifested in the Works of the Creation, in Two Parts*, 2nd ed. (London: Samuel Smith, 1692), vol. 1, pp. 37–41, 90ff., 103–109, 116, 122; vol. 2, p. 76; Raven, *John Ray*, ch. 17; Donald Worster, *Nature's Economy: A History of Ecological Ideas* (Cambridge: Cambridge University Press, 1977), pp. 42–44. Merchant discusses "organic" views of nature, hierarchical and egalitarian, in *Death of Nature*, chs. 3–4; Worster treats alternative ecological traditions in *Nature's Economy*, chs. 1–2. Recent studies on the economy of nature in Linnaeus suggest that the issues need reformulation: Wolf Lepenies, *Autoren und Wissenschaftler im 18. Jahrhundert: Buffon, Linné, Winckelmann, Georg Forster, Erasmus Darwin* (Munich and Vienna: Carl Hanser Verlag, 1988), pp. 30–31; and Lisbet Koerner, "Nature and Nation in Linnaean Travel" (Diss., Harvard University, 1993), ch. 4), to be published as *Nature and Nation in Linnaeus's Travel* (Cambridge, Mass.: Harvard University Press, forthcoming).

50. Caspar Bauhin (1560–1624), *Pinax Theatri Botanici* (Basel: L. Regis, 1623;

Basel: Joannis Regis, 1671). Merian may well have used the cumulative edition first put together by Jacob Theodorus: *Neu Vollkommen Kräuter-Buch . . . erstlichen durch Casparum Bauhinum . . . gebesset . . . durch Hieronymum Bauhinum . . . vermehrt* (Basel: Jacob Werenfels, 1664), with appendixes with plant names in German, Latin, English, French, Italian, and Arabic. On Bauhin's importance in the seventeenth century, see John Lewis Heller, *Studies in Linnaean Method and Nomenclature* (Frankfurt am Main: Verlag Peter Lang, 1983), pp. 41, 49, 67–69; and Scott Atran, *Fondements de l'histoire naturelle: Pour une anthropologie de la science* (Paris: Editions Complexe, 1986), pp. 67–71.

51. *Rau*79, verso of title page; *Rau*83, verso of title page. Francesco Redi, *Esperienze Intorno alla Generazione degli Insetti* (Florence: All'Insegna della Stella, 1668). Marcello Malpighi, *Dissertatio Epistolica de Bombyce* (London: John Martin and James Allestry, 1669). Among other naturalists mentioned in the 1683 poem was Martin Lister on spiders (*Historiae Animalium Angliae Tres Tractatus* [London: J. Martin, 1678], Tract I).

52. *Rau*79, plate 47. The dictionary of Caspar von Stieler, published in Nuremberg in 1691, gives no metaphorical meaning for "Dattel-kern," but only "caryotae, ossa dactylorum," meaning "date stones" (*Der Teutschen Sprache* [Nuremberg: Johann Hofmann, 1691], p. 121). According to the Grimm brothers, the earliest use of *Dattelkern* to refer to pupae is 1721, in a religious poem published in Hamburg by Barthold Heinrich Brockes (Jacob and Wilhelm Grimm, *Deutsches Wörterbuch* [Leipzig: S. Hirzel, 1860], vol. 2, p. 827). Perhaps Brockes was influenced by Merian's *Raupen*. Johann Leonhard Frisch (1666–1743), a philologist and naturalist, used *Puppe* for the quiescent pupa (*Beschreibung von allerley Insecten in Teutschland*, 13 vols. [Berlin: Christoph Gottlieb Nicolai, 1732], vol. 3, pp. 18–19, 24–26; *Nouveau Dictionnaire des passagers François-Allemand et Allemand-François* [Leipzig: Johann Friedrich Gledischen, 1780], p. 437).

53. On graphic illustration in entomology, see Claus Nissen, *Die Zoologische Buchillustration: Ihre Bibliographie und Geschichte*, 2 vols. (Stuttgart: Anton Hiersemann, 1969–1978), especially Theodor A. Wohlfahrt, "Schmetterlinge in der Illustration," vol. 2, pp. 306–326.

54. Schiebinger, *The Mind Has No Sex?* pp. 66–67. Christopher Arnold also compares Merian to Goedaert in his poetic eulogy: "What Gudart . . . in Seeland once wrote one reads certainly with pleasure; yet it is praiseworthy that a woman desires to do this for you also" (*Rau*79, verso of title page).

55. Johannes Goedaert, *Metamorphosis Naturalis, ofte Historische Beschryvinge van den Orrspronk, aerd, eygenschappen ende vreemde veranderinghen der wormen, rupsen, maeden, vliegen, witjem, byen, motten ende dierghelijcke dierkens meer*, 3 vols. (Middelburg: Jacobus Fierens, n.d. [1662–1669]); *Metamorphosis et Historia Naturalis Insectorum Autore Joanne Goedartio, Cum Commentariis D. Joannis de Mey*, 3 vols. (Middleburg: Jacobus Fierens, n.d. [1662–1669?]). On Goedaert, see Beier, "Renaissance Naturalists," p. 92; Schierbeck, *Swammerdam*, pp. 140–144, 166, 172.

56. Johannes Godartius, *Of Insects: Done into English, and Methodized, with the Addition of Notes; The Figures Etched upon Copper, by Mr Fr Pl [Francis Place]* (York: printed by John White for M.L. [Martin Lister], 1682), preface by Martin Lister. A Latin edition followed three years later: *De Insectis in methodum redactus* (London: S. Smith, 1685). On Lister, a collaborator of John Ray's, see Raven, *John Ray,* pp. 137–142; and n. 51 above.

57. For pre-Linnaean systems for classifying and ordering plants, see James L. Larson, *Reason and Experience: The Representation of Natural Order in the Work of Carl von Linné* (Berkeley: University of California Press, 1971), ch. 1; Atran, *Fondements,* ch. 2; Raven, *John Ray,* pp. 189–200; and Allen J. Grieco, "The Social Politics of Pre-Linnaean Botanical Classification," *I Tatti Studies: Essays in the Renaissance,* 4 (1991): 131–149.

58. *Rau79,* verso of title page.

59. *Rau79,* plate 41, pp. 83–84.

60. Working in the mid-seventeenth century, Margaretha de Heer did fine studies of insects, moths, and butterflies with a bloom or two, but they do not show metamorphoses or food habits or comparative anatomy (*Roses and Butterflies,* 1651, Amsterdam, Amsterdams Historisch Museum; *Butterflies, Insects, and a Hyacinth,* Groningen, Groninger Museum; *Still Life with Insects, Shells, and a Beetle,* 1654, Hartford, Wadsworth Atheneum). Rachel Ruysch of Amsterdam (1664–1750) included many insects in her still-life paintings, and would merit a study as an artist-naturalist. She was the daughter of an important Amsterdam anatomist and botanist, and in the 1690s was a pupil of Maria Sibylla Merian (see further on in this chapter). Sutherland and Nochlin, *Women Artists,* pp. 144, 158–160.

61. Raven, *John Ray,* pp. 394–395. At least once Ray's wife, Margaret Oakley Ray, caught moths for him, but the daughters were the more regular collectors. James Petiver was sent several specimens by Elizabeth Glanville, "a person extremely curious in the knowledge of English Insects" (James Petiver, *Musei Petiveriani Centuria Prima, Rariora Naturae* [London: Samuel Smith and Christopher Bateman, 1703], Addendum no. 10: *Gazophylacii Naturae et Artis Decas Prima* [London: Christopher Bateman, 1702], p. 12). But Glanville left no writings. Petiver also received butterfly specimens from Madame Williams in the Carolinas. Martin Lister's wife, Anna, and his daughter Susannah did more than a thousand drawings for his book on shells, *Historia Conchyliorum* (1685), but he provided the texts and observations (Raven, *John Ray,* p. 139). René-Antoine de Réaumur (1683–1757) employed a woman to draw for his six volumes of *Mémoires pour servir à l'histoire des insectes* (1734–1742), saying that her "modesty" prevented him from publishing her name (Tuxen, "Entomology," p. 98). A figure whose entomological writing would be interesting to examine in relation to gender perspectives is Priscilla Bell Wakefield (1751–1832). Author of travel accounts and popular works on botany, she also published *An Introduction to the Natural History and Classification of Insects, in a Series of Familiar Letters* (London: Darton, Harvey

and Darton, 1816). On her botany and style of writing, see Ann B. Shteir, *Flora's English Daughters: Women and the Culture of Botany, 1760–1860* (Baltimore: Johns Hopkins University Press, 1996).

62. Raven, *John Ray*, pp. 396–397, 407–416. A later male figure, Antonio Vallisnieri (1661–1730), tried to devise a system for classification of all insects by their general habitat and food: those living on plants, in water, on land, on animals or meat ("Idea nuova d'una Divisione generale degli Insetti," *Opera Fisico-Mediche*, 3 vols. [Venice: Sebastian Coleti, 1733], vol. 1, pp. 196–212). See also Beier, "Renaissance Naturalists," p. 91; and Tuxen, "Entomology," pp. 106–107.

63. For reviews of the literature, see Londa Schiebinger, "The History and Philosophy of Women in Science: A Review Essay," *Signs* 12 (1987): 305–322; L. J. Jordanova, "Gender, Science and Creativity," in Maureen McNeil, ed., *Gender and Expertise* (London: Free Association Books, 1987), pp. 152–157; Paula Findlen, "Essay Review: Gender and the Scientific 'Civilizing Process,'" *Journal of the History of Biology*, 24 (1991): 331–338. In addition to the work of Schiebinger (full reference in note 4 above) and Carolyn Merchant (full reference in note 48), gender issues and science in the context of the early modern period are also discussed in L. J. Jordanova, *Sexual Visions: Images of Gender in Science and Medicine between the Eighteenth and Twentieth Centuries* (New York: Harvester Wheatsheaf, 1990); David F. Noble, *A World without Women: The Christian Clerical Culture of Western Science* (New York: Alfred A. Knopf, 1992); Paula Findlen, "Science as a Career in Enlightenment Italy: The Strategies of Laura Bassi," *Isis* (1993): 441–469; and Lisbet Koerner, "Goethe's Botany: Lessons of a Feminine Science," ibid., pp. 470–495. Though these authors are not always in accord about women's roles in scientific inquiry or about gender, creativity, and scientific style, they do agree that all these matters are the product of historical arrangements and changing cultural categories. Even Carolyn Merchant, who claims there is an "age old association" between women and organic nature, sees this as a "historical interconnection" (*Death of Nature*, pp. xv–xvii).

64. *Rau*79, fols. 3r, N4r–v. In the 1683 edition, Merian's goal is "to increase God's praise through his creatures" (fol. C3r). Often looked down on by humans as inconsiderable and useless, these insects "represent to Men's eyes the Glory and Wisdom of God" (fragment of a translation of the opening of the 1683 *Raupen* by James Petiver, British Library, Manuscripts, Sloane 2352, fol. 17v).

65. Goedaert, *Metamorphosis naturalis*, "Aen den goedtwilligen Leser." Middelburg, where Goedaert lived, was an important Calvinist center and also had circles of Reformed pietism and conventicles. See also Raven, *John Ray*, p. 407.

66. Swammerdam, *Algemeene Verhandeling van de Bloedeloose Dierkens*, dedication. Schierbeek, *Swammerdam*, pp. 32–36 and plate 10.

67. Jean de Labadie, *Les Entretiens d'Esprit du Jour Chretien, ou les Reflexions Importantes du Fidele* (Amsterdam: Laurans Autein, 1671), p. 4.

68. Mathias Merian the Younger, "Selbstbiographie," p. 239. See also Dietz,

Frankfurter Handelsgeschichte, vol. 3, pp. 128–129, for further evidence on the family quarrels.

69. Jacob Marrel had had some financial difficulties during the years that Maria Sibylla Merian had spent in Nuremberg. Despite his debts, his will and inventory postmortem (studied before it was lost during the World War II bombing of Frankfurt) indicated that he had a substantial inheritance to pass on. Zülch, *Frankfurter Künstler*, pp. 538–539. Suit of Johanna Sibylla and Maria Sibylla against Heinrich Ruppert, the husband of Sara Marrel: StAF, Ratssupplication 144 (1685), fol. 148r–v. During the same years, Antonetta Margretha, wife of Mathias Merian the Younger, was conducting a suit over the will of her late father, Remy Barthels: StAF, Schöffer-Gerichtsbücher 806, vol. 795 (1683).

70. On Maria Sibylla Merian's observations of insects during these Frankfurt years: Frankfurt, June 1685 (*Stud*, no. 169, fol. 62); May 1683, 18 June 1684 (Frankfurt), 24 June 1684 (*Rup*17, nos. 12, 22, 23, 44). MSM to Clara Regina Imhoff, 25 July 1682; 8 December 1684; 3 June 1685: "my husband would like to go to Nuremberg, but I do not know how soon this will happen" (RS*Mer*, nos. 1, 3, 5, pp. 61–63. Graff's picture of the Egidienplatz in Nuremberg, dated 1682, Nuremberg, Germanisches Nationalmuseum, Kupferstich-Kabinett, SP6590, K7373. By April 1686, Maria Sibylla Merian was recording observations of insects in Friesland (*Stud*, no. 203, fol. 76).

71. Philipp Jakob Spener, *Pia desideria*, trans. Theodore G. Tappert (Philadelphia: Fortress Press, 1964). Johannes Wallmann, *Philipp Jakob Spener und die Anfänge des Pietismus* (Tübingen: J. C. B. Mohr, 1986), part 3 on the Frankfurt years; idem, *Der Pietismus* (Göttingen: Vandenhoeck and Ruprecht, 1990), especially chs. 3, 5. Labadist thought had much influence on Spener, but Spener always argued for remaining within the Church and leavening religious life from within. K. Leder, "Die religiöse und kirchliche Entwicklung im 18. Jahrhundert," in Pfeiffer, ed., *Nürnberg-Geschichte*, pp. 324–325.

72. Johanna Eleanore von Merlau Petersen (b. 1644), *Leben Frauen Joh. Eleonora Petersen Gebohrner von und zu Merlau* (no place or publisher, 1718), bound with the autobiography of her husband, Johann Wilhelm Petersen, *Das Leben Jo. Wilhelmi Petersen* (no place or publisher, 1717), Herzog August Bibliothek, Wolfenbüttel. The two autobiographies were republished together in 1719 (copy at Princeton Theological Seminary). Eleanore had spent much of her youth in Frankfurt, where Petersen had first seen her, and had been in Frankfurt as well as nearby Hanau in the years before her marriage. Sometime after her marriage in 1680 she and Johann Wilhelm left for Amsterdam and elsewhere, so it is uncertain whether she and Maria Sibylla could have talked in 1681–1685.

73. Jean de Labadie, *Entretiens d'Esprit*, pp. 38ff. on the faithful in the early Christian Church (Dutch edition noted in T. J. Saxby, *The Quest for the New Jerusalem: Jean de Labadie and the Labadists, 1610–1744* [Dordrecht: Martinus Nijhoff, 1987], p. 442, no. 27). Jean de Labadie, *Les divins herauts De la penitence*

au Monde . . . pour servir à la grande oeuvre d'une Reformation universelle et d'un general Renouvellement (Amsterdam: Daniel Elzevier, 1667), pp. 41–49. Idem, *La Reformation de l'Eglise Par le Pastorat* (Middleburg, Netherlands: Henry Smidt, 1667), p. 46 on women's lack of modesty (Anna Maria van Schurman sent a copy of this to Philipp Spener in Frankfurt; see Saxby, *New Jerusalem*, p. 234). Idem, *Traité du Soi et Des diverses sortes de Soi, ou Le Renoncement à Soi meme* (Herford, Germany: Laurans Autein, 1672); German translation by Hermann Strauch: *Tractelein von der Selbst-Verläugnung* (Herford: Cornelis van der Meulen, 1672). Idem, *Le Triomphe de l'Eucharistie* (Amsterdam: Abraham Wolfgang, 1667), fols. *2r–*8v: "A Mademoiselle Anne Marie de Schurman, Humble et Fidelle Servante de Dieu." Maria Sibylla Merian became adept at Dutch and French during her years in Friesland, but with her family connections, she may well have been able to read them in the 1680s.

74. Anna Maria van Schurman, *Eukleria seu Melioris Partis Electio* (Altona: Cornelius van der Meulen, 1673); *Eukleria, seu Melioris Partis Electio: pars secunda* (Amsterdam: Jacques van de Velde, 1684, with a second edition in 1685). Saxby, *New Jerusalem*, pp. 117–118, 148, 176–177, 189–190, 224–235; Joyce Irwin, "Anna Maria van Schurman: From Feminism to Pietism," *Church History*, 46 (1977): 48–62; idem, "Anna Maria van Schurman and Antoinette Bourignon: Contrasting Examples of Seventeenth-Century Pietism," *Church History*, 60 (1991): 301–315; Mirjam de Baar et al., eds., *Anna Maria van Schurman (1607–1678): Een uitzonderlijk geleerde vrouw* (Zutphen: Walburg Pers, 1992). Van Schurman corresponded with other female spiritual figures, such as the visionary Antoinette Bourignon (*Euklaria . . . pars secunda*, p. 113) and Eleanore von Merlau Petersen, who had been influenced by her autobiography (Saxby, *New Jerusalem*, pp. 225, 233).

75. Erasmus, *Laus stulitiae* (Basel, 1676), listed in Zülch, *Frankfurter Künstler*, p. 550. Sebastian Brant, *Wol-geschliffener Narren-Spiegel* ("Freystadt," n.d. [Nuremberg, 1730?]), published with Caspar Merian's illustrations posthumously (copy SUBF, N. libr. Ff. 5520).

76. MSM to Clara Regina Imhoff, 3 June 1685, Frankfurt, in RS*Mer*, no. 5, p. 63.

77. Jean de Labadie, *Le Heraut du Grand Roy Jesus* (Amsterdam: Daniel Elzevir, 1667); idem, *Les divins herauts De la penitence au Monde*. Pierre Yvon [and Pierre Dulignon], *L'Homme penitent en trois traitez: Mis au jour Par Pierre Yvon, Pasteur de l'Eglise Reformée retirée du monde, et recueüeillie maintenant à Wiwert en Frise* (Amsterdam: Jaques van de Velde, 1683). Pierre Yvon, *L'Homme pecheur proposé selon tous ses caracteres et sur tout selon son amour propre criminel* (Amsterdam: Jacques van de Velde, 1683; Dutch edition, Amsterdam, 1684). Jean de Labadie (1610–1674) was first a Jesuit in France, then a Protestant minister in France, Geneva, and the Netherlands, and finally the founder of a separate community of penitent Christians "retired from the world." On his remarkable life, see Saxby, *New Jerusalem;* and Michel de Certeau, *The Mystic Fable*, vol. 1: *The*

Sixteenth and Seventeenth Centuries, trans. Michael B. Smith (Chicago: University of Chicago Press, 1992), ch. 9. Pierre Yvon had been influenced in his boyhood by Labadie's sermons to the Protestant community of Montauban, joined Labadie for study in Geneva in 1662, and from then on was his companion in all his religious ventures. He took over the leadership of the community at Wieuwerd after Labadie's death in 1674 and died in Friesland in 1707. Pierre Dulignon was also from a Protestant family in France and fell under Labadie's spell during his studies in Geneva. Saxby, *New Jerusalem*.

78. Saxby, *New Jerusalem*, ch. 11.

79. Pierre Yvon, *Des Ornemens mondains, ou le Luxe du siècle: Condamné par l'Ecriture Sainte at les Premiers Docteurs de l'Eglise* (Amsterdam: Jaques van de Velde, 1684), especially chs. 8–9; Dutch edition, *Van de Wereltsche vercierselen* (Amsterdam: Jaques van de Velde, 1685). Yvon [and Dulignon], *Homme penitent*, especially Dulignon's "De la pauvreté de l'esprit, comme singulierement propre du veritable Penitent," pp. 179–289. Saxby, *New Jerusalem*, pp. 244–247. StAF, Ratssupplication 149 (1690), fol. 78r–v.

80. *Rau79*, fol. 3v.

81. Dittelbach, *Verval en Val*, pp. 18–19. The daughters were also averse to seeing their father. Graff then went mad for a time. Pierre Yvon, *Le Mariage chretien: Sa sainteté et ses devoirs* (Amsterdam: Jaques van de Velde, 1685), chs. 28, 32–33, 36. Labadie's views on lubriciousness and crimes committed within marriage are in *Divins herauts*, pp. 41–43. When the Labadist community was first founded at Herford in 1670, Labadie urged celibacy on all single members and continence on married couples. In 1671, when it was discovered that Catherine Martini was pregnant by Pierre Yvon, the policy was reconsidered and Labadie, Yvon, and other single men and women took partners (Saxby, *New Jerusalem*, pp. 211–213). The English vicar: ibid., pp. 257–258. Thomas Safley, *Let No Man Put Asunder: The Control of Marriage in the German Southwest—A Comparative Study, 1550–1600* (Kirksville, Mo.: Sixteenth Century Journal Publishers, 1984), pp. 33–37.

82. *Neue Zeitungen von Gelehrten Sachen auf des Jahr MDCCXVII*, 23 (20 March 1717): 178 (article occasioned by the posthumous publication of the third volume of the *Rupsen:* Graff a fugitive because of "shameful vices"); and ibid., 95 (November 1717): 767–768 (correction from Nuremberg: Merian left Graff to join the Labadists). Doppelmayr, *Historische Nachricht*, p. 269.

83. Staatsarchiv Nürnberg, Ratsverlässe Nr. 2936, 12 August 1692; RS*Mer*, p. 13. StAF, Ratssupplication 149, 16 September 1690: Merian wants to renounce her citizenship in Frankfurt. Presumably in the wake of her mother's death, she is accounted as having 1,000 guilders' worth of property and is expected to pay a tax on it of 100 guilders. She says that any property she has had in Frankfurt belongs to Graff and that she is separated from him.

84. Mirjam de Baar, " 'En onder 't hennerot het haantje zoekt te blijven': De

betrokkenheid van vrouwen bij het huisgezin van Jean de Labadie (1669–1732)," *Jaarboek voor Vrouwengeschiedenis*, 8 (1987): 11–43, 202. Dittelbach, *Verval en Val*, p. 34. Saxby, *New Jerusalem*, p. 253. Also see the reaction of Jasper Danckaerts on his return to Wieuwerd from a year's trip in North America: "about ten o'clock [we] reached our house, where all arms and hearts were open to receive us, which they did with affection and tenderness, in the love of the Lord" (Jasper Danckaerts, *Journal of a Voyage to New York in 1679–80, by Jasper Dankers and Peter Sluyter of Wiewerd in Friesland*, trans. Henry C. Murphy [Memoirs of the Long Island Historical Society, 1] [Brooklyn: Long Island Historical Society, 1867], p. 428).

85. Labadie, *Traité du Soi*, pp. 1, 75–78, 90–91; Yvon [and Dulignon], *Homme penitent;* Yvon, *L'Homme pecheur;* Saxby, *New Jerusalem*, pp. 246–249.

86. Visiting Wieuwerd in 1677, the Quaker William Penn said, "They are a serious, plain People, and are come nearer to Friends; as in Silence in Meetings, Women-speaking, Preaching by the Spirit, Plainness in Garb, and Furniture in their Houses" (William Penn, *An Account of W. Penn's Travails in Holland and Germany, Anno MDCLXXVII: For the Service of the Gospel of Christ* [London: T. Sowle, 1694], p. 175). Saxby, *New Jerusalem*, p. 251. Mirjam de Baar suggests that Penn mistook women translating for women speaking ("De betrokkenheid van vrouwen," p. 32), but it is unclear why he should do so. The justification for prophetic speaking of women as well as men had been developed by Jean de Labadie in *Traité eclesiastique [sic] Propre de ce tams . . . L'Exercise Profetique selon St. Pol . . . sa Liberté, son Ordre, et sa Pratique* (Amsterdam: Pierre Boeteman, 1668), a text that aroused much controversy and also influenced experiments in Lutheran Pietist meetings in Frankfurt.

87. The *Eukleria* is not only a spiritual autobiography; it is also a history of the Labadists as a movement, including praise of women members and a defense of Labadist doctrines (e.g., *Pars Secunda*, ch. 5 and pp. 34–35, 38). Mirjam de Baar, " 'Wat nu het kleine eergeruchtje van mijn naam betreft . . .': De *Eukleria* als autobiografie," in de Baar et al., eds., *Van Schurman*, pp. 93–107.

88. Pierre Yvon, *Getrouw verhael van den Staet en de Laetste Woorden en Dispositien Sommiger personen die God tot sich genomen heeft* (Amsterdam: Jacob van de Velde, 1681 and 1683). Also in French; and in English: *A Faithful Relation of the State and the Last Words and Dispositions Of certain Persons whom God hath taken to himself* (Amsterdam: Jacob van de Velde, 1685): the godly deaths of eleven women and three men.

89. Saxby, *New Jerusalem*, pp. 245–247.

90. Irwin, "Van Schurman," pp. 58–61; de Baar, "De *Eukleria.*" Lindeboom, *Letters of Swammerdam*, pp. 16–17; Schierbeek, *Swammerdam*, pp. 32–37.

91. Jean de Labadie, *Abregé Du veritable Christianisme et Teorique et Pratique ou Receuil de maximes Chretiennes*, 2nd ed. (Amsterdam: Laurens Autein, 1670), p. 143.

92. A partial list of Van Schurman's artwork, most of it portraits, is given by

G. D. J. Schotel, *Anna Maria van Schurman* (s'Hertogenbosch: Muller, 1853), Appendix B; several self-portraits can be found in de Baar et al., eds., *Van Schurman*. Katlijne Van der Stighelen, " 'Et ses artistes mains . . .': De kunstzinningheid van Anna Maria van Schurman," ibid., pp. 61–74. Yvon, *Ornemens mondains*, pp. 97–98; idem, *Van de wereltsche vercierselen*, p. 91.

93. Saxby, *New Jerusalem*, p. 245.

94. Labadie, *Traité du Soi*, pp. 8–9. Idem, *Abregé Du veritable Christianisme*, pp. 144–145: the eyes can be kept "pure and innocent" by looking at God's creation. Besides appropriate portraits, Yvon allowed painters to "represent the works which came directly from the hand of the Lord" (*Ornemens mondains*, pp. 97–98).

95. *Rup*17, nos. 37 (1690), 38 (1690); *Stud*, no. 173, fol. 63 (August 1689); no. 181, fol. 66 (August 1690); no. 203, fol. 76.

96. I have used the original study book at the Academy of Sciences Library in Saint Petersburg (call number F n. 246).

97. *Stud*, p. 141.

98. On *Lebensläufe* and German spiritual autobiography in Merian's day, see Georg Misch, *Geschichte der Autobiographie*, 4 vols. (Frankfurt am Main: G. Schuylte-Bulmke, 1949–1970), vol. 4, pp. 809–817; and Katherine M. Faull, "The American Lebenslauf: Women's Autobiography in Eighteenth-Century Moravian Bethlehem," *Yearbook of German-American Studies*, 27 (1992): 23–48.

99. This is the suggestion of Irina Lebedeva in her introduction to *Stud*.

100. Yvon, *Mariage chretien*, ch. 39, especially pp. 374–384, 400–402; Dittelbach, *Verval en Val*, pp. 19–22; Saxby, *New Jerusalem*, pp. 248–249. After five years in the community, Dittelbach left around 1688 with his wife and son (ibid., p. 313).

101. Saxby, *New Jerusalem*, p. 247.

102. Peter King, *The Life of John Locke, with Extracts from His Correspondence, Journals and Common-place Books* (London: Henry Colburn, 1829), pp. 162–163, journal entry of 21 August 1685.

103. Yvon, *Ornemens mondains* (1684); idem, *Van de Wereltsche vercierselen* (1685).

104. *Rup*17, no. 14, specimen sent to her from Schwabach (near Nuremberg) in June 1683, when she was in Frankfurt.

105. Saxby, *New Jerusalem*, pp. 268–271, summing up family correspondence in Rijksarchief Utrecht 26.1137 from the years 1689–1692.

106. The last Friesland observation in her study book concerns a gold and black striped caterpillar, which she had found in August 1690 at Wieuwert and which became a butterfly the following June (1691). In a later hand she adds, "On 28 September 1691, I found a like caterpillar in Amsterdam." And in a later hand yet: "This transformation is in my third Caterpillar book" (*Stud*, no. 181, fol. 66; see *Rup*17, no. 18).

107. Saxby, *New Jerusalem*, pp. 245, 247, 314–316.

108. For overall views of the world in which Merian arrived, see Violet Barbour, *Capitalism in Amsterdam in the Seventeenth Century* (Ann Arbor: University of Michigan Press, 1960); J. L. Price, *Culture and Society in the Dutch Republic during the Seventeenth Century* (New York: Scribner, 1974); Svetlana Alpers, *The Art of Describing: Dutch Art in the Seventeenth Century* (Chicago: University of Chicago Press, 1983); Simon Schama, *The Embarrassment of Riches: An Interpretation of Dutch Culture in the Golden Age* (Berkeley: University of California Press, 1988); Dirk J. Struik, *The Land of Stevin and Huygens: A Sketch of Science and Technology in the Dutch Republic during the Golden Century* (Dordrecht: D. Reidel, 1981); Wim de Bell et al., *De "wereld" binnen handbereik: Nederlandse kunst- en rariteitenverzamelingen, 1585–1735*, Catalogue of an exhibit at the Amsterdam Historical Museum, 26 June 1992–11 October 1992 (Amsterdam: Amsterdams Historisch Museum, 1992). For an overview of and bibiliography on women's lives and work in the Netherlands in the late medieval and early modern periods, see Rudolf Dekker, "Vrouwen in middeleeuws en vroeg-modern Nederland," in Georges Duby and Michelle Perrot, eds., *Geschiedenis van de Vrouw*, vol. 3: *Van Renaissance tot de moderne tijd*, ed. Arlette Farge and Natalie Zemon Davis (Amsterdam: Agon, 1992), pp. 415–443.

109. Marriage contract of Joanna Helena Graffin with Jacob Hendrik Herolt, 28 June 1692 (Stuldreher-Nienhuis, *Merian*, p. 100, n. 1). Doppelmayr, *Historische Nachricht*, p. 270: Maria Sibylla Merian's daughter married "Johann [*sic*] Herold," who was "very fortunate in his commerce with Suriname."

110. One of Maria Sibylla Merian's students was Rachel Ruysch (1664–1750), daughter of the anatomist and physician Frederick Ruysch; Rachel Ruysch was to become a still-life painter of note. On Agnes Block, see Cornelia Catharina van de Graft, *Agnes Block, Vondels nicht en vriendin* (Utrecht: A. W. Bruna, 1943), pp. 116, 118; and de Bell et al., eds., *De "wereld,"* pp. 134–136. Valerius Röver had several paintings by Maria Sibylla Merian in his cabinet, including a painting of a bird done in 1697 (de Graft, *Block*, p. 150, no. 7). Fifty Merian watercolors of flowers of the type found in her *Blumenbuch* are recorded in the 1696 inventory of the Rosenberg Slot in Copenhagen, the private collection of the royal house of Denmark; they may well have been acquired from Merian's collection after she got to Amsterdam. Claus Nissen, *Die Botanische Buchillustration: Ihre Geschichte und Bibliographie* (Stuttgart: Anton Hiersemann, 1966), vol. 2, p. 38, no. 389.

111. MSM to Clara Regine Scheurling, born Imhoff, 29 August 1697, Amsterdam, in RS*Mer*, no. 6, p. 64: "[so] many many years have passed since I last heard from all the dear friends I had in Nuremberg." S. A. C. Dudok van Heel, "Honderdvijtig advertenties van Kunstverkopingen uit veertig jaargangen van de Amsterdamsche Courant, 1672–1711," *Amstelodamum*, 67 (1975): 160, no. 52. Connections with Michiel van Musscher, made executor of her will of 1699: ibid., p. 166, no. 91; GAA, Notary Samuel Wijmer, 4830, no. 49, pp. 186–187, act of 23 April 1699; 4864, no. 23, pp. 112–114, act of 23 April 1699. On Michiel van

Musscher (1645–1705) as a genre painter, portraitist, and painter of astronomical instruments, see Arnold Houbraken, *De Groote Schouburgh der Nederlantsche Konstschilders en Schilderessen* (The Hague, 1753; reprint Amsterdam: B. M. Israel, 1976), vol. 3, pp. 210–212; Walther Bernt, *Die niederländischen Maler des 17 Jahrhunderts,* ed. Hans Sauermann, 4 vols. (Munich: Munich Verlag, 1948–1962), vol. 2, nos. 571–572; Peter Sutton, *Masters of Seventeenth-Century Dutch Genre Painting* (Philadelphia: Philadelphia Museum of Art, 1984), pp. 266–267 and plate 124; and de Bell et al., *De "wereld,"* pp. 182–183.

112. GAA, Notary S. Wijmer, 4830, no. 49, 23 April 1699; 4864, no. 23, pp. 112–114, 23 April 1699. Graff did not die until 1701.

113. James Petiver, collector, apothecary, and Fellow of the Royal Society, lists the 1679 and 1683 *Raupen* in his *Musei Petiveriani Centuria Prima, Rariora Naturae Continens: Viz. Animalia, Fossilia, Plantas* (London: S. Smith and B. Walford, 1695), p. 16. John Ray knew of Merian's books in 1703, when he was working on his own *History of Insects,* but decided not to discuss it or other European works because he was confining himself to English species (Raven, *John Ray,* pp. 400–401). Michael Bernhard Valentini, a professor of medicine at Giessen, who had visited Maria Sibylla Merian in Frankfurt, referred to the *Raupen* in his 1704 *Museum Museorum* and said that a Latin translation by Hennike had been sent him in manuscript but never published (*Museum Museorum,* 2nd ed., 3 vols. [Frankfurt am Main: Heirs of Johann David Zunner and Johann Adam Jung, 1714], vol. 1, p. 512). The naturalist Anton van Leeuwenhoek knew of Merian's work by 1697, and spoke of her to Peter the Great during the czar's visit to Delft in 1697 (Lukina, *Merian,* p. 146). On her insect research from 1691 to 1699: *MetD* and *MetL,* "To the Reader"; *Rup*17, Preface (observation of an ant nest, 25 July 1694), no. 4 (observation 8 September 1695, Amsterdam); no. 18 (observation 28 September 1691, Amsterdam).

114. A scientific society in Amsterdam, which had included Swammerdam, ceased meeting after 1672 (Lindebloom, *Letters of Swammerdam,* p. 11). The character of male scientific exchange is suggested by *Johannis Gaubii Epistola problematica, Prima, Ad Virum Clarissimum Fredericum Ruyschium M.D.* (Amsterdam: Johannis Wolters, 1696). Caspar Commelin, *Horti Medici Amstelaedamensis Rariorum tam Africanarum, quam Utriusque Indiae, aliarumque Peregrinarum Plantarum . . . Descriptio et Icones* (Amsterdam: P. and I. Blaeu and the widow of Abraham van Someren, 1701), vol. 2, frontispiece. Jan Weenix, portrait of Agnes Block and her second husband, the silk merchant Sybrand de Flines, with her pineapple and various paintings and objects of interest to a naturalist, including representations of butterflies (Amsterdam Historical Museum). J. J. Poelhekke, "Elf brieven van Agnes Block in de universiteitsbibliotheek te Bologna," *Mededlingen van het Nederlands Historisch Instituut te Rome,* 32 (1963): 3–24.

115. Monique M. C. Nederveen, "De Geschiedenis van de Amsterdamse Hortus," *Tuinjournal* (July 1989): 3–49. Caspar Commelin (1667–1731) succeeded his

uncle Jan Commelin (1629–1692) as director of the Garden and carried on the project of illustrated botanical catalogues that his uncle had founded.

116. *Met*D and *Met*L, "To the Reader." *Catalogus Musaei Ruyschiani . . . Preparatorum Anatomicorum, variorum Animalium, Plantarum, aliarumque Rerum Naturalium . . . collegit . . . Fredericus Ruyschius* (Amsterdam: Janssonio-Waesbergios, 1731); the Ruysch cabinet included a remarkable sequence of human embryos. *Description abregée des Planches, qui representent les cabinets et quelques-unes des Curiosités, Contenuës dans le Theatre des Merveilles de la Nature de Levin Vincent* (Haarlem: Levinus Vincent, 1719): insect section of the cabinet, p. 6 and plate 3; by 1719, it included Suriname specimens from and pictures by Maria Sibylla Merian.

117. Gilbert Waterhouse, Introduction to G. C. de Wet, ed., *Simon van der Stel's Journey to Namaqualand in 1685*, trans. R. H. Pheiffer (Capetown and Pretoria: Human and Rousseau, 1979), pp. 18–20; Graft, *Block,* p. 104. Nicolas Witsen was a frequent recipient of dedications, as in Jan Commelin's botanical editions: *Catalogus Plantarum Horti Medici Amstelodamensis* (Amsterdam: Arnold Oosaen, 1689); and *Horti Medici Amstelodamensis Rariorum Plantarum Historia* (Amsterdam: P. and J. Blaeu and Abraham van Someren, 1697). His role as a collector is treated throughout de Bell et al., *De "wereld,"* pp. 153–155 and passim. Merian, *Met*D and *Met*L, "To the Reader." Though much assisted by the translation of the *Metamorphosis* given by Sarah O'Brien Twohig and William T. Stearn in Rücker and Stearn, *Merian,* pp. 84–137, I have checked all my translations against the Latin and Dutch of the first editions.

118. Dudok van Heel, "Advertenties," p. 160, no. 52. Stephen Blankaart, *Schouburg der Rupsen, Wormen, Maden, en Vliegende Dierkens* (Amsterdam: Jan ten Hoorn, 1688), p. 70 and plate 18. *Met*D and *Met*L, "To the Reader."

119. Jean Gelman Taylor, *The Social World of Batavia: Europe and Eurasian in Dutch Asia* (Madison: University of Wisconsin Press, 1983), pp. 12–15; Rudolf M. Dekker and Lotte C. van de Pol, *The Tradition of Female Transvestism in Early Modern Europe* (London: Macmillan, 1989), pp. 33–34, quoting a 1649 letter of Nicolaus de Graaff to J. K. J. de Jonge. See the difficulties encountered by twenty-one-year-old Elizabeth van der Woude in 1676–1677, after her widowed father died on the boat carrying a small Dutch expedition to establish a settlement on the Oiapoque River, on the border of present-day Brazil and Guyane (Lucy Hotz, "A Young Lady's Diary of Adventure in 1677: Journal of Elizabeth van der Woude," *The Blue Peter,* 9 [1929]: 611–618).

120. Gonzalo Fernández de Oviedo (d. 1557), *De la natural historia de las Indias* (Toledo: Remon de Petras, 1526); idem, *La Historia General de las Indias, primera parte* (Seville: Juan Cromberger, 1535), commissioned by Emperor Charles V. On Oviedo and his work, which appeared in many later editions and translations, see Antonello Gerbi, *La natura delle Indie Nove: Da Cristoforo Colombo a Gonzalo Fernandez de Oviedo* (Milan and Naples: Riccardo Ricciardi, 1975), especially pp. 385–425 on natural history.

121. On Georg Everard Rumpf (Georgius Everhard Rumphius, 1627/28–1702), see J. E. Heeres, "Rumphius' Levensloop" and other essays, in *Rumphius Gedenkboek, 1702–1902* (Haarlem: Koloniaal Museum, 1902); H. C. D. de Wit, "Georgius Everhardus Rumphius" and other essays, in H. C. D. de Wit, ed., *Rumphius Memorial Volume* (Baarn: Uitgeverij en Drukkerij Hollandia, 1959); and Struik, *Land of Stevin,* pp. 128–130. Like Merian, Rumpf was born in Germany—indeed, near Hanau not far from Frankfurt—and moved to the Netherlands as a young man, becoming a merchant in the service of the Dutch East India Company in 1653.

122. Georg Marcgraf died in Africa in 1644. Prince Johan Maurits passed on Marcgraf's manuscript notes and pictures to Johan de Laet, who edited and published them together with Piso's tract *De Medicina Brasiliensis.* See Georg Marcgraf and Willem Piso, *Historia Naturalis Brasiliae, Auspicio et Beneficio Illustriss, I: Mauritii Com. Nassau,* ed. Johan de Laet (Leyden: Franciscus Hackus, 1648; Amsterdam: Ludovicus Elsevier, 1648). Willem Piso published an expanded edition in 1658: see Willem Piso and Georg Marcgraf, *De Indiae utriusque re naturali et medica libri quatuordecim* (Amsterdam: Ludovicus and Daniel Elzevier, 1658). E. van den Boogaart, ed., *Johan Maurits van Nassau-Siegen, 1604–1679: A Humanist Prince in Europe and Brazil* (The Hague: Johan Maurits van Nassau Stichting, 1979), pp. 237–538; Dennis Channing Landis, ed., *The Literature of the Encounter: A Selection of Books from "European Americana"* (Providence, R.I.: John Carter Brown Library, 1991), no. 36.

123. Charles Plumier, *Description des Plantes de l'Amerique avec leurs Figures: Par le R. P. Charles Plumier, Religieux Minime* (Paris: Imprimerie Royale, 1693), Preface. On Plumier and other missionary naturalists in the French Antilles at the end of the seventeenth and in the early eighteenth centuries, see James E. McClellan III, *Colonialism and Science: Saint Domingue in the Old Regime* (Baltimore: Johns Hopkins University Press, 1992), pp. 112–116.

124. Hans Sloane, *Catalogus Plantarum quae in Insula Jamaica Sponte proveniunt, vel vulgò coluntur, cum earundem Synonymis et locis natalibus . . .* (London: D. Brown, 1696), Preface; idem, *A Voyage to the Islands of Madera, Barbados, Nieves, S. Christopher and Jamaica with the Natural History of the Herbs, Trees, Four-Footed Beasts, Fishes, Insects, Reptiles, etc.,* 2 vols. (London: printed by B.M. for the Author, 1707–1725), vol. 1, Preface. E. St. John Brooks, *Sir Hans Sloane: The Great Collector and His Circle* (London: Batchworth Press, 1954), pp. 53–55; G. R. de Beer, *Sir Hans Sloane and the British Museum* (London: Oxford University Press, 1953), pp. 30–31.

125. Zacharias Conrad von Uffenbach, *Merkwürdige Reisen durch Niedersachsen, Holland und Engelland,* 3 vols. (Ulm: Johann Friederich Gaum, 1753–1754), vol. 3, pp. 674–676; Graft, *Agnes Block,* p. 104. Cornelis de Bruyn, *Travels into Muscovy, Persia, a Part of the East Indies . . .* (London: A. Bettesworth et al., 1737), Author's Preface; the stone figure in plate 142 is identified as being in the possession of Mr. Witsen, Burgomaster of Amsterdam.

126. *Met*D and *Met*L, "To the Reader": "a long and costly journey." She had been encouraged by others to publish her paintings, "but at first the expenses of doing such a book deterred me." "I have sought no profit in carrying out this project; rather, I was content only to cover my costs. I spared no expense to complete it."

127. Dudok van Heel, "Advertenties," p. 160, no. 52. GAA, Notary Samuel Wijmer, 4864, no. 23, pp. 112–114; 4830, no. 49, pp. 186–187. MSM to Johann Georg Volkamer of Nuremberg, 8 October 1702, RS*Mer*, no. 7, p. 65. *Met*D and *Met*L, "To the Reader." How do we know that Dorothea Maria was the daughter who went with Maria Sibylla to Suriname, when the passenger list for the return boat from Suriname mentions only Maria Sibylla Merian and "haer dogter [*sic*]"? SocSur, 228, fol. 395. In April 1699, Merian gave her power of attorney to her son-in-law Herolt so he could be her agent in Amsterdam. It seems likely that Johanna Helena would stay with her husband in Amsterdam, rather than accompany her mother to Suriname on a trip which might well have lasted several years, and that the unmarried daughter Dorothea Maria would go with her mother. Indeed, Stuldreher-Nienhuis suggests that the metamorphosis described in volume three of the *Rupsen* as beginning on 10 September 1699 (when Merian had long since left for Suriname) was watched by Johanna Helena (*Rup*17, no. 49; *Verborgen Paradijzen*, p. 90). But there is evidence from Dorothea Maria herself: in 1724, when she was working for the czar in Saint Petersburg, Dorothea Maria told an agent from the Polish court that she "had been with her mother in Suriname" (Jean Le Fort to Duke Ernst Christoph von Manteuffel, 14 October 1724, Saint Petersburg, Sächsisches Hauptstaatsarchiv Dresden, Loc. 3315, vol. 3, fols. 278r–280v: "Il se trouve icy sa fille qui a été avec elle à Surinam, mariée avec un Suisse Peintre d'Histoire de Sa Majesté nommé Gsel" (fol. 278v).

128. Christopher Arnold, ed., *Wahrhaftige Beschreibungen dreyer machtiger Königreiche Japan, Siam und Corea* (Nuremberg: Michael and Johann Friedrich Endter, 1672); Arnold's poem, "Lobgedicht diese Ost-Indianische Reisebeschreibung," pp. 902–903. *Abraham Rogers Offne thür zu dem verborgenen Heydenthum . . . Christoph Arnolds Auserlesenen Zugaben von den Asiatischen, Africanischen und Americanischen Religions-sachen* (Nuremberg: Johann Andreas Endter, 1663), ch. 38: the religion of the peoples of New Spain; ch. 39: the religions of the Caribbean, Guyana, and Brazil. Arnold was interested in comparing exotic religions, perhaps looking for certain shared principles. Merian also might have read two accounts published in Nuremberg in 1669 by the widow and heirs of the publisher-engraver Paul Fürst, whose daughter Magdalena was her pupil: Erasmus Francis, *Guineischer und Americanischer Blumen-Pusch*, on the animals and insects of Peru and Brazil as found in Spanish and Dutch travel literature; and Michael Hemmersam, *Guineische und West-Indianische Reissbeschreibung de An. 1639 bis 1645.*

129. Saxby, *New Jerusalem*, chs. 12–13; L. Knappert, "De Labadisten in Suriname," *De West-Indische Gids*, 8 (1926): 193–218.

130. Yvon, *Faithful Narration*, p. 32. In their scouting trip to North America in 1679–1680, Labadists Jasper Danckaerts and Peter Sluyter showed some interest in the conversion of the Amerindians and sought out John Eliot of Roxbury, Massachusetts, who translated the Bible into an Indian tongue (Danckaerts and Sluyter, *Journal of a Voyage*, pp. 301–315, 379). After this period, Labadist interest in conversion in America waned. Mention of "an approach to the heathens in Suriname" by the first Labadist group there was soon forgotten, according to Dittelbach, when the Brothers and Sisters found out how "barbaric and savage" the Indians were (*Verval en Val*, p. 55).

131. Yvon, *Ornemens mondains*, p. 262: "the abuse of *Tobacco* today, which most people take only to satisfy their sensuality." Danckaerts and Sluyter pitied the indentured servants from England, "compelled to spend their lives here [in Maryland] and in Virginia and elsewhere in planting that vile tobacco, which all vanishes into smoke" (*Journal of a Voyage*, p. 192). Nonetheless, tobacco was one of the crops raised on Bohemia Manor, as the Labadist property in Maryland came to be called. In 1690, slave labor was instituted (Saxby, *New Jerusalem*, pp. 302–303).

132. Dittelbach, *Verval en Val*, pp. 55–59. At best, the Labadists called the Africans "wretched people" and would have preferred treating them mildly. In a journal filled with disapproval of "godless" people and behavior in America, Jaspar Danckaerts made no critique of slavery seen along the way (*Journal of a Voyage*, p. 216).

133. [David Nassy et al.], *Essai historique sur la Colonie de Surinam . . . Avec l'Histoire de la Nation Juive Portugaise et Allemande y Etablie . . . Le tout redigé sur des pieces authentiques . . . par les Régens et Représentans de ladite Nation Juive Portugaise*, 2 vols. (Paramaribo, 1788; facsimile edition, Amsterdam: S. Emmering, 1968), vol. 1, pp. 38–45. John Stedman, *Narrative of a Five Years Expedition against the Revolted Negroes of Surinam*, ed. from the 1790 manuscript by Richard Price and Sally Price (Baltimore: Johns Hopkins University Press, 1988), pp. 61–62.

134. Dittelbach, *Verval en Val*, pp. 55–60; J. D. Herlein, *Beschryvinge van de Volk-Plantinge Zuriname* (Leuuwarden: Meindert Injema, 1718), p. 89; Saxby, *New Jerusalem*, pp. 285–288. Lucia van Sommelsdijk, the governor's sister and widow of Jean de Labadie, is still listed as an exporter of sugar from Suriname in boat lists of 1692, 1693, 1694, and April 1695 (SocSur, 221, fols. 139r, 173r; 222, fols. 144r, 418r; 223, fol. 380r); after that, her name ceases to appear. These shipments were probably arranged by her agents, however, for she was involved in different notarial acts and petitions in the Netherlands in 1692–1693 in connection with the reorganization of the Labadist community there in 1692. In October 1695 she married the widowed Pierre Yvon at Wieuwerd (Saxby, *New Jerusalem*, pp.317–318).

135. SocSur 227, 228, and 229 include several lists of "whites and black and red slaves" by plantation for purposes of taxation: "Liste van de Huisden, de

Blancken, Swarte, en Roodes Slaven." Entries for the "Collegie de Labadisten": SocSur 227, no. 205 (1694), p. 10; no. 206 (1695), p. 9; no. 207 (1696–1697), p. 8. In 1696–1698 they are among those with tax arrears (227, fols. 202r–204r); then in 1698–1702 the Labadist name drops off the list of householders entirely (228, no. 133, no. 134, fols. 383r–391v; 229, fols. 167r–177r). Similarly, "de Labadisten" appear on shipping lists for 1692–1697, exporting to the Netherlands rather small amounts of sugar—sixteen to thirty-two pounds—and receiving smoked fish (221, fol. 144r–v; 222, fols. 140r, 309r; 223, fol. 492r; 225, fol. 455r; 226, fol. 340r). Then they disappear from these lists. The plantation presumably continued under the name of a director or a renter, and in 1715 it appears on the lists as "Plant. La Providence" (SocSur 243, fol. 61v).

136. *MetD* and *MetL*, "To the Reader": "Having moved to Friesland and then to Holland, I continued my study of insects." On Labadie as a wanderer, see the splendid essay by Michel de Certeau in *Mystic Fable*, ch. 9.

137. On Suriname in the late seventeenth and early eighteenth centuries, see R. A. J. van Lier, *Frontier Society: A Social Analysis of the History of Surinam* (The Hague: Martinus Nijhoff, 1971), still an important source even though its social and economic picture of the early period of settlement must be modified by Price and Oostindie; I. C. Koeman, ed., *Links with the Past: The History of the Cartography of Suriname, 1500–1971* (Amsterdam: Theatrum Orbis Terrarum, 1973); Richard Price, *The Guiana Maroons: A Historical and Bibliographical Introduction* (Baltimore: Johns Hopkins University Press, 1976); Richard Price, *First Time: The Historical Vision of an Afro-American People* (Baltimore: Johns Hopkins University Press, 1983); G. W. van der Meiden, *Betwist Bestuur: Een eeuw strijd om de macht in Suriname, 1651–1753* (Amsterdam: De Bataafsche Leeuw, 1987); Neil L. Whitehead, *Lords of the Tiger Spirit: A History of the Caribs in Colonial Venezuela and Guyana, 1498–1820* (Dordrecht and Providence, R.I.: Foris Publications, 1988); Gert Oostindie, *Roosenburg en Mon Bijou: Twee Surinaamse Plantages, 1720–1870* (Dordrecht and Providence: Foris Publications, 1989); Robert Cohen, ed., *The Jewish Nation in Surinam: Historical Essays* (Amsterdam: S. Emmering, 1982); Robert Cohen, *Jews in Another Environment: Surinam in the Second Half of the Eighteenth Century* (Leiden: E. J. Brill, 1991). The range in European and African population can be *roughly* estimated from the tax lists. The totals given for "whites, red and black slaves" for 1701 were 618 whites over twelve years of age; 105 whites under twelve years of age (15 percent of all whites); 7,353 red and black slaves over twelve years of age; 1,193 red and black slaves under twelve years of age (14 percent of all slaves). SocSur 228, fol. 391v. In Paramaribo on 4 October 1699, Benjamin Hemerick, native of Frankfurt am Main, married Elisabeth Dranckiens, native of Suriname. A widower by 11 May 1701, Hemerick married Gertruyt van Aytert, widow of Gerrit Postel (ARAH, Suriname Oudarchief Burgerlijke 9, fols. 72v, 74r). Perhaps Merian was present at the weddings.

138. SocSur 228, fols. 289r–292r (September 1700); 281r (26 March 1701); J. T. de Smidt and T. van der Lee, eds., *Plakaten, Ordonnantiën en ander Wetten,*

uitgevaardigd in Suriname, 1667–1816 (Amsterdam: S. Emmering, 1973), vol. 1, pp. 219–221, no. 85 (8 May 1698); van Lier, *Frontier Society*, pp. 143–145; van der Meiden, *Betwist Bestuur*, ch. 3.

139. Dutch and French pastors signed the baptisms, marriages, and church membership lists in the Generael Kerckeboek van Suriname (1687–1730), ARAH, Suriname Oudarchief Burgerlijke 9. Van Lier, *Frontier Society*, 85–89; Cohen, *Jews*, pp. 147–153.

140. Merian, *MetL* and *MetD*, no. 36. Stedman, *Narrative*, p. 258; [Nassy et al.], *Essai historique*, vol. 1, p. 69. Cotton, coffee, and cocoa were introduced only in the decades after 1720. Oostindie, *Roosenburg en Mon Bijou*.

141. SocSur 227, no. 207: 193 plantations are listed for 1696–1697, with no distinction between adults and children. SocSur 228, fols. 383r–391v: the 1701 list distinguishes between adults and children, with adjusted sugar taxes.

142. SocSur 227, no. 207: on 193 plantations in 1696–1697, the number of red and black slaves ranged from 3 to 183; SocSur 228, document of nine leaves at fol. 133r, showing slave holdings 1698–1700. Van der Meiden (*Betwist Bestuur*, p. 54) gives a finer breakdown of the plantations' adult population for 31 December 1684, when the total slave population above the age of twelve was only 3,332:

Christian plantations	Jewish plantations
Christian men: 362	Jewish men: 105
Christian women: 127	Jewish women: 58
African men: 1,299	African men: 543
African women: 955	African women: 429
Indian men: 29	Indian men: 10
Indian women: 54	Indian women: 13

143. Herlein, *Beschryvinge*, pp. 121–123; Price, *Guiana Maroons*, pp. 20, 35–39. "Neger-Engels" is the source of Sranam, the national language of contemporary Suriname. The Portuguese-based creole is the source of Saramaccan, the language of the present-day Saramakas or Bush Negroes living on the upper Suriname River, many of whom are descendants of slaves escaped from the Portuguese Jewish plantations.

144. [Anon.], *Beschrijvinge van Guiana: Des selfs Cituatie, Gesonthheyt, Vruchtbaerheyt ende ongemeene Profyten en Voordeelen boven andere Landen* (Hoorn: Stoffel Jansz. Kortingh, 1676), pp. 27–30. By means of a dialogue between a farmer, a burgher, a skipper, and a messenger, the pamphlet argues that heathens can be enslaved. See also Otto Keye, *Het Waere Onderscheyt tusschen Koude en Warme Landen* (The Hague: Printed for the author by H. Hondius, 1659), in which New Netherlands in North America was compared unfavorably to Guyana in terms of the profitability of crops, and slavery was defended so long as it was not of Christians.

145. Dittelbach, *Verval en Val*, p. 55. Herlein, *Beschryvinge*, p. 112. Herlein

was in Suriname during the governorship of Paul van der Veen (ibid., fol. *2v), which lasted from 1695 to 1706. He is probably the same as Jan Herlin, who returned from Paramaribo to Amsterdam on 27 July 1704 (SocSur 231, fol. 189r). Van Lier, *Frontier Society*, p. 130. William Blake's engravings of punishments meted out to the slaves of Suriname were created to accompany Stedman's *Narrative of a Five Years Expedition against the Revolted Negroes of Surinam:* "A Female Negro Slave, with a Weight chained to her Ancle" (p. 40), "A Negro hung alive by the Ribs to a Gallows" (p. 105), "The Flagellation of a Samboe Female Slave" (p. 265; she is hanging from a tree and the white planter is directing two African men to beat her).

146. Price, *Guiana Maroons*, pp. 23–24; Price, *First Time*, pp. 51–52, 70–72. [Nassy et al.], *Essai historique*, vol. 1, p. 76.

147. Herlein, *Beschryvinge*, ch. 7; Stedman, *Narrative*, pp. 302–318, 465–469. Peter Kloos, *The Maroni River Caribs of Surinam*, Studies of Developing Countries, 12 (Assen: Van Gorcum, 1971), pp. 1–6 and ch. 3; Whitehead, *Lords of the Tiger Spirit*, chs. 3, 7.

148. *Stud*, no. 232.

149. [Nassy et al.], *Essai historique*, vol. 1, p. 42; van der Meiden, *Betwist Bestuur*, p. 54.

150. *Met*D, no. 36: "door mynen Indiaan," "myne Slaven"; *Met*L, no. 36: "ab Indo servo," "mancipia." On the use of Amerindians as domestic slaves, see Whitehead, *Lords of the Tiger Spirit*, p. 184.

151. *Met*D and *Met*L, no. 36.

152. *Met*D and *Met*L, no. 4, botanical note by Caspar Commelin. Samuel Nassy was in Amsterdam in December 1700 representing the interests of the Jewish community of Suriname to the directors of the Societeit van Suriname ([Nassy et al.], *Essai historique*, vol. 1, pp. 54–55; vol. 2, pp. 126–128) and may not have been at his plantation during the time Merian was making her trip. Peter Kolben, *The Present State of the Cape of Good Hope . . . Written Originally in High German . . . Done into English . . . by Mr. Medley* (London: W. Innys, 1731), vol. 2, p. 216.

153. *Met*D and *Met*L, no. 4. [Nassy et al.], *Essai historique*, vol. 2, pp. 103–104; van der Meiden, *Betwist Bestuur*, pp. 52, 58, 60, 71–72. On the Vredenburg plantation (called Wátambii by the Africans) just off the Suriname River, see Price, *First Time*, pp. 56–57.

154. *Met*D and *Met*L, No. 27 ("serva Nigrita"); no. 49 ("De Indianen," "Indi"); *Met*L, no. 59.

155. *Met*D and *Met*L, no. 54.

156. MSM to Johann Georg Volkamer, 8 October 1702, RS*Mer*, no. 7, pp. 64–65. *Met*D and *Met*L, "To the Reader": "sketched and observed from life" (the section "To the Reader" is in Latin in both editions). Maria Sibylla probably kept special control over the vellums of insects. On some inaccurate labeling, see

William T. Stearn, "The Plants, the Insects and Other Animals of Merian's *Metamorphosis Insectorum Surinamensium*," in RS*Mer*, p. 81.

157. MSM to Johann Georg Volkamer, 8 October 1702, RS*Mer*, no. 7, p. 65.

158. SocSur 228, fol. 395r, 18 June 1701. Laurentia Maria Verboom's father was killed in the soldiers' mutiny of 1688, when she was still very young. She was a teenager at the time of this trip to the Netherlands. She returned to Suriname soon afterward, for she was again on a boat from Suriname to the Netherlands on 12 May 1702 (SocSur 229, fol. 215r). A few other families took Amerindians and Africans back to Suriname each year, often families with children (e.g., SocSur 228, fol. 301r: Moses Henriques, his wife, three children, and "Een neger, een neegerin, en een Indianin," 24 March 1701; 240, fol. 57r–v: Henrik Legerman, his wife, two children and "Een Indianin," 15 June 1713). In the two decades from 1729 to 1749, Gert Oostindie found 8 Amerindians traveling from Suriname to the Netherlands, 87 black slaves, and 7 free blacks (Gert Oostindie and Emy Maduro, *In het Land van de Overheerser, II: Antillianen en Surinamers in Nederland, 1634/1667–1954* [Dordrecht: Foris Publications, 1986], p. 7).

159. GAA, Ondertrouwakte 533, p. 309: betrothal of 14 October 1701. Doppelmayr, *Historische Nachricht*, p. 256. Merian's house is still called the *Roose-tak* (Spray of Roses), as it had been in the 2 February 1699 advertisement for the sale of her specimens; but whereas in 1699 it had been described as on Kerkstraat, in her letters of 1702 to 1704 she gives her address as "In the Spiegelstraat . . . between the Kerkstraat and the Prinsengracht." Then in her letters and title pages from 1705 to 1717, the address is once again at the *Roose-tak* on Kerkstraat. Either this is the same house described with different addresses, or there were two houses, very near each other. See also the investigations of Stuldreher-Nienhuis, *Merian*, p. 130, n. 2.

160. MSM to Johann Georg Volkamer, 8 October 1702 and October 1702; to James Petiver, 4 June 1703, 20 June 1703, 5 October 1703, April 1704, RS*Mer*, nos. 7–12, pp. 64–70. Volkamer was a physician in Nuremberg and author of a botanical work, *Flora Noribergensis sive Catalogus Plantarum in Agro Noribergensi* (Nuremberg: Michaellianis, 1700), dedicated to Peter Hotton, director of the Botanical Garden at Leiden, and to Caspar Commelin, director of the Botanical Garden at Amsterdam. The apothecary James Petiver was an enthusiastic collector of botanical and entomological specimens with an immense correspondence with other naturalists and collectors in England and elsewhere. His publications at this date were catalogues of his collections. In June 1711, during his only trip away from England, he visited Merian as well as other naturalists in the Netherlands. Raven, *John Ray*, pp. 233 and 417, no. 2; Raymond P. Stearns, "James Petiver: Promoter of Natural Science, c. 1663–1718," *Proceedings of the American Antiquarian Society*, 62 (1952): 243–365.

161. Georg Everard Rumpf [Rumphius], *D'Amboinische Rariteitkamer* (Amsterdam: François Halma, 1705); L. B. Holthuis, "Notes on Pre-Linnaean Carci-

nology ... of the Malay Archipelago," in de Wit, ed., *Rumphius*, pp. 66–70. Merian's name is not on the book, but she referred to it in a letter of 8 October 1702 to Johann Georg Volkamer; and Zacharias Conrad von Uffenbach, visiting her in 1711, saw her paintings for the edition (RS*Mer*, no. 7, p. 65; Uffenbach, *Reisen*, vol. 3, p. 553). They then became part of the collection acquired by her daughter Dorothea Maria for Peter the Great (now in the archives of the Academy of Sciences in Saint Petersburg, PIX, on. 8). Simon Schynvoet had a remarkable collection of shells, which he drew on for the Rumphius edition, of which he was editor for Halma (Uffenbach, *Reisen*, vol. 3, p. 670; W. C. Muller, "Eerste proeve van een Rumphius-Bibliographie," in *Rumphius Gedenkboek*, pp. 6–7).

162. On Gerard Valck (or Valk), see I. H. van Eeghen, *De Amsterdamse Boek-handel, 1680–1725*, 5 vols. (Amsterdam: Scheltema and Holkema, 1965–1978), vol. 4, pp. 278–279. Merian's engravers were Pieter Sluyter, Joseph Mulder, and Daniel Stoopendael, who signed their individual plates.

163. *Met*D and *Met*L, "To the Reader."

164. Georg Marcgraf devoted a few chapters to the insects of Brazil, with several fine studies of spiders, beetles, and butterflies. But these are brief; he gives little discussion and no representation of metamorphosis, nor does he depict the relation to plant food (*Historia Naturalis Brasiliae* [1648], Book 7, pp. 245–259; *De Indiae utriusque* (1658), Book 5, chs. 10–12). Plumier, *Plantes de l'Amerique;* McClellan, *Colonialism and Science*, p. 113; Stroup, *Company of Scientists*, p. 71. Hans Sloane's first publication about Jamaica was the *Catalogus Plantarum*, containing very brief entries about each plant and where he saw it, with references to other observations of the same plant in other naturalists' accounts. There are no pictures. Sloane's illustrated folios *Voyage to Jamaica* of 1707–1725 were to be his major work. Sloane had been elected to the Royal Society in January 1685 (de Beer, *Sloane*, p. 24), which placed him in a central position for communicating his Jamaican findings to European naturalists. On communicating New World information, see Henry Lowood, "The New World and Natural History," in Karen Ordahl Kupperman, ed., *America in European Consciousness, 1493–1750* (Chapel Hill: University of North Carolina Press, for the Institute of Early American History and Culture, 1995), pp. 295–323.

165. *Met*D and *Met*L. Habitat: no. 46, "Under this jasmine bush, many lizards, iguanas [as Marcgraf calls them; *leguaan* in Dutch], and snakes often conceal themselves; for this reason I added a beautiful and unusual snake that I found at the roots of this plant." No. 56, frogs and water scorpions in their habitat. No. 59, toads and shellfish in their habitat. "To decorate the plate": no. 4, lizard; no. 5, a snake and its eggs; no. 23, a lizard and its eggs. No. 48 depicts a bee and its larva on the "tabrouba" plant that had served as food for the larva. Merian also added a large flying beetle "to fill space on the plate," and a fan-palm worm and the adult beetle into which it metamorphosed. Merian explained that the leaves of the fan palm were too large for her to paint on a page, so she showed the

transformation here. She went on to describe the fan palm, its growth, and the location of these worms on the trunk of the palm.

166. *MetD* and *MetL*, nos. 1, 60.

167. Mary Louise Pratt, *Imperial Eyes: Travel Writing and Transculturation* (London and New York: Routledge, 1992), pp. 29, 31, 33–34.

168. British Library, Manuscripts, Sloane 3339, fols. 153–160b: James Petiver, "An Account of Madam Maria Sybila Merians History of Surinam Insects Abbreviated and Methodized with Some Remarks," ch. 1, fol. 153r–v; ch. 2, fols. 153v–157v; ch. 3, fols. 157v–160v.

169. MSM to James Petiver, 17 April 1705, RS*Mer*, no. 15, p. 72. In 1708 she wrote Petiver about having copies of the Latin edition of the *Metamorphosis* sold in England with an English title page and preface, but otherwise the same (MSM, 14 March 1708, ibid., no. 16, p. 74).

170. *MetD* and *MetL*, "To the Reader"; no. 19 against Leeuwenhoek. In no. 34 she rejects another claim by Leeuwenhoek for eyes along the sides of a caterpillar. The caterpillar has a row of tiny simple eyes (ocelli) on each side of the head. References to other naturalists also in nos. 1–2.

171. *MetD* and *MetL*, "To the Reader." MSM to Johann Georg Volkamer, 8 October 1702, RS*Mer*, no. 7, p. 65. *Rup*13, fols. A2v–A3v.

172. For debates on these matters, see Rosalie Colie, *Light and Enlightenment: A Study of the Cambridge Platonists and the Dutch Arminians* (Cambridge: Cambridge University Press, 1957). For a transformation similar to that of Merian's— from "a spiritualistic and millenarian religious sect" in the early seventeenth century to "rational religion"—see Andrew Fix, *Prophecy and Reason: The Dutch Collegiants in the Early Enlightenment* (Princeton, N.J.: Princeton University Press, 1991). The Collegiants ultimately arrived at "a secularized philosophical rationalism" (p. 3), a position more radical than that of Maria Sibylla Merian, so far as we can judge.

173. *MetD* and *MetL*, no. 57. The collection of Merian watercolors made by Hans Sloane includes a picture of two snakes fighting, a scorpion eating a frog, and other violent scenes from her Suriname trip (British Museum, Prints and Drawings, Case 198* b. 5, Bibl. Sloan 5275, vol. 1, nos. 56, 61, 71, 81).

174. *MetD* and *MetL*, no. 18. Most spiders have eight eyes, as Merian says, but some have only six, four, or two.

175. *MetD* and *MetL*, no. 18. It is interesting to compare Merian's treatment of the Suriname ants with her pastoral image of European ants in the preface to the third volume of the *Rupsen*. Ants are pictured there in a garland of leaves and flowers on the title page. It was presumably taken from a painting made around 1694, for Merian says she was given an ant nest that year and had been able to observe that ants underwent transformation like caterpillars. "In this picture I have placed on a small green leaf the King of the Ants, as she is called in the East Indies." *Rup*17, note following the preface by Dorothea Maria Hendriks.

176. *Met*D and *Met*L, no. 7: cherries could be better cultivated if the country were inhabited by more industrious and less selfish people; no. 9: pomegranates grow well, "yet they are cultivated very little by the inhabitants"; no. 13: plums grow wild and ungrafted, "for the Europeans grow nothing but sugar cane"; no. 21: the passion flower is suitable for growing in gardens, but the Dutch in Suriname make little use of it; no. 25: concerning vanilla, "It is a pity that no one in this country is interested in cultivating such things, as well as other plants which could doubtless be found in this large fertile country"; no. 33: figs "would be more prolific if people would only plant them"; no. 34: concerning grapes, it is regrettable that one cannot find anybody interested in cultivating them, for then one would not have to bring wine to Suriname but could export it from Suriname; no. 52: the caterpillar whose thread she had sent back to Holland, where people thought it very good.

177. Steven Shapin, "The Invisible Technician," *American Scientist*, 77 (November–December 1989): 554–563.

178. Plumier, *Plantes de l'Amerique*. Plumier gave local names infrequently (p. 5: "Les Caraibes la nomment Hamamaligra"; pp. 61, 71), and in the few instances where he included information on plant use, he cited Willem Piso's work more often than he suggested he had used native informants (pp. 45–46, 56–59). Jean Baptiste Labat, *Nouveau Voyage aux Isles de l'Amerique: Contenant l'Histoire naturelle de ces Pays, l'Origine, les Moeurs, la Religion et le Gouvernement des Habitans anciens et modernes*, 2 vols. (The Hague: P. Husson et al., 1724), part 4, ch. 1, vol. 2, p. 9. Sloane, *Voyage*, vol. 1, Preface, fol. A2r.

179. *Met*D and *Met*L, "To the Reader" and no. 27.

180. This English translation is written in an eighteenth-century script in the hand-colored 1719 Latin edition at the John Carter Brown Library (J719 M561d, 3-size, copy 1): *Mariae Sibillae Merian Dissertatio de Generatione et Metamorphosibus Insectorum Surinamensium* (Amsterdam: Johannes Oosterwijk, 1719), translation of nos. 27 and 36. The plant that gets dug up by her Indian slave ("ab Indo servo," no. 36; "mynen Indiaan" in *Met*D, no. 26), becomes "having caused my Indian Servant to dig one of them up by the Roots." The words "slave" and "slavery" are used in a few entries about Suriname (no. 59), but not in any entry pertaining to Merian. This cannot be another effort by James Petiver to translate Merian's work into English, for he died in 1718 and this translation is written in a book published in 1719.

181. *Met*D and *Met*L, no. 45.

182. George Warren, *An Impartial Description of Surinam upon the Continent of Guiana in America* (London: William Godbid for Nathaniel Brooke, 1667), p. 20. Charles de Rochefort, *Histoire naturelle et morale des Iles Antilles de l'Amerique: Enrichie de plusieurs belles figures . . . Avec un Vocabulaire Caraïbe* (Rotterdam: Arnould Leers, 1658), p. 332. Richard Ligon, *A True and Exact History of the Island of Barbadoes* (London: Peter Parker, 1673), pp. 44–46, 51. Sloane, *Voyage*,

vol. 1, p. xlvii: "The Negroes from some Countries think they return to their own Country when they die in Jamaica, and therefore regard death but little, imagining they shall change their condition, by that means from servile to free, and so for this reason often cut their own throats." P. liii: "The Blacks . . . from Angola run away from their Masters, and fancy on their deaths they are going Home again, which is no luciferous Experiment, for on hard usage they kill themselves." For further discussion and evidence, see Barbara Bush, *Slave Women in Caribbean Society, 1650–1838* (Kingston, Jamaica: Heinemann Publishers, 1990; Bloomington: Indiana University Press, 1990), pp. 55–56. Professor Margaret Washington of Cornell University has also written me, "In my research for my last book, I came across a place in South Carolina and one in Georgia called Ibo Landing. The story goes that in both instances a shipload of Ibo Africans, after disembarkment, walked right into the Atlantic Ocean before they could be stopped. Clearly they expected to die and return to their homeland. Ibo were not in high demand in South Carolina because of their tendency toward 'melancholy' and 'suicide' " (letter of 6 August 1990).

183. For example, the letter of Fray Pedro de Córdova to Charles V, written in the late 1520s or 1530s, speaks of women "exhausted by toil" who are unable to conceive, or who abort their children, or who kill them with their own hands so they will not have to endure "such harsh servitude" ("Carta al Rey, del Padre Fray Pedro de Córdova," *Colección de documentos inéditos del Archivio de Indias,* in *Colección de documentos inéditos, relativos al descubrimiento, conquista y organización de las antiguas posesiones españolas de America y Oceania,* 42 vols. [Madrid, 1864–1884], vol. 11, p. 219).

184. Sloane, *Voyage,* vol. 2, p. 50. Sloane describes the plant also in his *Catalogus Plantarum,* p. 149, but here gives no uses. There are two references to cases of abortion in Sloane's general introduction to *Voyage to Jamaica* (pp. 143, 147), both evidently instances in which white women tried to conceal an abortion. "If women knew how dangerous a thing it is to cause Abortion, they would never attempt it."

185. On the evidence for and controversy about low slave fertility (Is it due to uneven sex ratio? hard living conditions? African sexual customs? duration of lactation? etc.), see the balanced pages of Bush, *Slave Women,* pp. 132–150, and the well-documented investigation of fertility among the slaves of the sugar-producing Roosenburg plantation. In the period 1766 to 1788, it ranged from 11.4 births per thousand to 17.1 per thousand. (*Roosenburg en Mon Bijou,* pp. 132–135). From 1778 to 1784, the birth rate per thousand among the Sephardic Jews of Suriname was 31.2 births per thousand (Cohen, *Jews,* p. 65). A recent overview of the African diaspora in the Americas notes the contrast between low slave birth rates in the Caribbean and rates in the colonies of North America, and comments: "This resulted from disproportionate sex ratios, physical abuse, and overwork, malnutrition, and disease. Some women may have practiced contraception and

abortion but existing evidence only permits generalizations to be made. Most African cultures would not have endorsed abortion, affirming childbirth as a time of special joys and an event that strengthens ties of kith and kin." Michael L. Conniff and Thomas J. Davis, *Africans in the Americas: A History of the Black Diaspora* (New York: Saint Martin's Press, 1994), p. 80. The evidence from Merian about the use of abortion, if overstated, is precise. Ideally, one would want to compare the fertility of African populations on plantations with those in the independent maroon villages of Suriname.

186. *MetD* and *MetL*, nos. 59, 48.

187. *MetD* and *MetL*, nos. 7, 14–17, 19, 29, 33, 55; compare nos. 45, 48, 59.

188. Piso and Marcgraf, *De Indiae utriusque*, pp. 114–117. For an introduction to such description, see Daniel J. Slive, *A Harvest Gathered: Food in the New World—An Exhibition at the John Carter Brown Library, November 13, 1989–April 29, 1990* (Providence, R.I.: John Carter Brown Library, 1989).

189. *MetD* and *MetL*, no. 30. MSM to Johann Georg Volkamer, October 1702, RS*Mer*, no. 8, p. 66.

190. *MetD* and *Met L*, no. 7 on the American cherry. The fruit could be better cultivated if the country were inhabited by a more industrious and less selfish population ("door een meer arbeitzaan en minder baatzoekend Volk"). Is this the topos of the lazy male Caribs, who retired to their hammocks (so it was said) after hunting and fishing, and confined themselves to opening fields for the cassava planting? (See Labat, *Voyage*, part 4, ch. 15, vol. 2, pp. 106, 110–111). Or is this the emerging topos of the lazy European male planters? (See Stedman, *Narrative*, pp. 364–366; and Pratt, *Imperial Eyes*, p. 62.)

191. Herlein, *Beschryvinge*, ch. 6: "Aard, Natuur en Eigenschappen der Swarte Slaven." Herlein's views and those of eighteenth-century Dutch writers on Suriname are discussed in Gert Oostindie, "The Enlightenment, Christianity, and the Suriname Slave," *Journal of Caribbean History*, 26 (1992): 147–170.

192. Labat, *Voyage*, part 4, ch. 7, vol. 2, pp. 49–50 (respect for the old). Part 2, ch. 3, vol. 1, p. 32; part 4, ch. 15, vol. 2, p. 110: the obedience of "these Savage women" to their husbands "without talking back" could serve as a model for Christian families, to whom one has preached in vain since the death of Sara and probably will preach to the end of time. On black libertinage, religion, and sorcery, see part 4, ch. 7, vol. 2, pp. 43–56; part 1, ch. 21, vol. 1, pp. 163–167. Religious indifference of Caribs: part 2, ch. 2, vol. 1, p. 9.

193. Peter Kolben or Kolb was a young German serving as secretary to Baron von Krosick, privy counselor to the king of Prussia, and was sent at von Krosick's expense and with the authorization of the Dutch East India Company to the Cape of Good Hope especially to do astronomical observation. He arrived there from Amsterdam in June 1705, stayed there "many years," and then returned to Nuremberg, where he published his first description of the Cape in German in 1719. Editions followed in Dutch, French, and English. The edition used here is *The*

Present State of the Cape of Good-Hope: OR, A Particular Account of the Several Nations Of the Hottentots: Their Religion, Government, Laws, Customs, Ceremonies, and Opinions; Their Art of War, Professions, Language, Genius, etc. Together with A Short Account of the Dutch Settlement At The Cape, trans. and ed. Guido Medley (London: W. Innys, 1731). A second volume, *Containing the Natural History of the Cape*, focused on the husbandry of the European settlers and then provided a general natural history of the Cape. Kolben, *Present State*, vol. 1, pp. 37–38 and ch. 8. Pratt discusses Kolben's "dialogic" presentation of the Khoikhoi in *Imperial Eyes*, pp. 41–49. Though agreeing with Pratt that Kolben undermines important stereotypes about the "Hottentots," I think we must not overestimate the extent to which the mere use of descriptive categories such as "religion" and "government" effaces the savage/civilized border. Many Europeans, like the Jesuits, make that leap without abandoning the notion of "savage"—that is, of characteristic and often inferior customs, institutions, humors.

194. For instance, Herlein, *Beschryvinge*, ch. 6: "Aard, Natuur en Eigenschappen der Swarte Slaven"; Labat, *Voyage*, part 2, ch. 2; part 4, ch. 7.

195. Sloane, *Voyage*, vol. 1, p. lvi; "these punishments [of slaves] are sometimes merited by the Blacks, who are a very perverse Generation of People," p. lvii; vol. 1, pp. 21–24, 117, 146; vol. 2, p. 193.

196. Lukina mentions a lost watercolor by Merian of "twelve Negroes" (*Merian*, p. 197); but having examined the original source, I fear this is unlikely. Writing from Saint Petersburg to Duke Ernst Christoph von Manteuffel in 1724, Jean Le Fort urged the duke to purchase for the king of Poland "un autre livre Original" by "la fameuse Maria Sibylla Merian," then in the possession of Merian's daughter in Saint Petersburg. The letter was followed by a list in German of thirty-seven watercolors on parchment by Maria Sibylla Merian, depicting flowers, insects, crustaceans, crocodiles, and other tropical animals. Amid a list of flower paintings is the item "zwölf Africanen" (Sächsisches Hauptstaatsarchiv Dresden, Loc. 3315, vol. 3, fols. 278r–280v). I don't think we can translate "Africanen" as "Negroes" here. First, the word "Africans" was not ordinarily used at that date to refer to persons from Africa; the terms used were "blacks," "Negroes," "Hottentots," and like nouns. Second, the form that would be used to refer to people is "Africaner." Thus, this appears to be a reference not to people but to flowers from Africa, such as the African lily, brought from the Cape of Good Hope to Amsterdam in the seventeenth century. A watercolor by Merian was described in a 1730 Dutch catalogue as "Melianthus Africanus seu pimpinella fatida of Caapse honingbloem"; an 1857 sale catalogue listed a Merian watercolor as "Bouquet d'Africanus" (Graft, *Agnes Block*, pp. 135–141; Stuldreher-Nienhuis, *Merian*, pp. 164–165).

197. GAA, Notary Henrick Outgers, 3369, no. 133, pp. 1145–1149, contract of 24 and 27 February 1706. Chr. P. van Eeghen, "Dirk Valkenburg: Boekhouder, schrijver, kunstschilder voor Jonas Witsen," *Oud-Holland*, 61 (1946): 58–69; A.

van Schendel, "Een stille plantage in Suriname door Dirk Valkenburg, 1707," *Bulletin van het Rijksmuseum,* 11 (1963): 80–86. Valkenburg's drawings of Witsen's plantations (Suromombo, Simimonbo, and Palmeniribo), most of them without human figures, are in the Print Room of the Rijksmuseum in Amsterdam, 05:102–108. The Rijksmuseum has also two oil paintings of plantations, one with an Indian dwelling (Inv. A 4075), another with an Indian family visible in the foreground. Two still-lifes from Suriname are in the Musée des Beaux Arts in Quimper, Brittany. His painting of the Africans collected for dancing is in the Statens Museum for Kunst, Copenhagen, Inv. 376, and is reproduced in the illustrations here. On the slave escape from Palmeniribo Plantation around 1710, see Price, *First Time,* pp. 108–111.

198. Frans Post (1612–1680) was one of the artists taken to Brazil by Prince Johan Maurits in 1637–1644, during his years as governor there for the Dutch West Indies Company. Among the many paintings of Brazil he did in the course of his life, at least eight were remarkable depictions of sugar mills, worked by Africans. Reproductions in Joaquim de Sousa-Leao, *Frans Post, 1612–1680* (Rio de Janeiro: Livraria Kosmos Editora, 1973), nos. 33, 34, 55, 60, 64, 69, 70, 71. Post also did some scenes of everyday life, but the Africans who stroll through them, carrying baskets, talking, and in some instances dancing, are usually small figures, dominated by luminous Brazilian landscapes or cast into a middle ground by pineapples, grasshoppers, monkeys, and birds. There is an engraving of an African man and woman dancing with instruments in Jan Nieuhof, *Gedenkwaerdige Zee en Lant-Reize door de voornaemste Landschappen van West en Oost Indien,* ed. H. Nieuhof (Amsterdam: Widow of Jacob van Meurs, 1682).

199. Of the African dances described in the Caribbean and in Suriname (the *soesa,* a martial arts dance between men; the *calenda* and other dances between men and women; and the *winti* dance of possession), the dance portrayed in Valkenburg's painting seems closest to the *winti,* especially since smoking tobacco, special drinking, and the calabash (used for watering the ground in the *winti*) are present. Labat, *Voyage,* part 4, ch. 7, vol. 2, pp. 52–54; Stedman, *Narrative,* pp. 526, 537–541, 663; Melville J. Herskovits and Frances S. Herskovits, *Suriname Folk-Lore,* Columbia University Contributions to Anthropology, 27 (New York: Columbia University Press, 1936), pp. 72–82, 86–99.

200. Labat, *Voyage,* part 4, ch. 7, vol. 2, p. 52; Stedman, *Narrative,* p. 526. Official lists of the slaves owned by the Society of Suriname itself at the end of the seventeenth century place family units together: the husband's name, followed by that of the wife (when there was a wife), and then the number of children (e.g., SocSur 227, fols. 28r–29r: "Neeger Rol," 1699).

201. Sutton, *Dutch Genre Painting,* pp. xxviii, l, lvii; plates 2, 28 (David Vinckboons, *Peasant Kermis*), 33, 96; pp. 133, 237, 284–285, 351.

202. Aphra Behn, *Oroonoko, or, The Royal Slave,* with an introduction by Lore Metzger (London: William Canning, 1688; reprint New York: W. W. Norton,

1973). Parham Hill and Saint John's Hill were two of three plantations belonging to Sir Robert Harley during the period of English settlement in Suriname and can be found on either side of the Suriname River on the map by J. Thornton in 1675 and the one by J. Ottens in 1718 (reproduced in RS*Mer*, pp. 16, 24–25). Behn seems to have put the two plantations together for the purposes of her narrative. The Labadists' Providence Plantation was on the east side of the Suriname River, only a short distance downriver from Saint John's Hill and across the river from Parham Hill. On Behn's life and other evidence for her trip to Suriname, see Maureen Duffy, *The Passionate Shepherdess: Aphra Behn, 1640–89* (London: Jonathan Cape, 1977); Angeline Goreau, *Reconstructing Aphra: A Social Biography of Aphra Behn* (New York: Dial Press, 1980); and Jane Jones, "New Light on the Background and Early Life of Aphra Behn," *Notes and Queries*, 37 (September 1990): 288–293.

203. There were several maroon escapes during the English rule: Warren, *Impartial Description*, pp. 19–20; Price, *Guiana Maroons*, p. 23. Oroonoko said they would first found "a new Colony" of their own and then hope to find a ship and sail back to Africa (Behn, *Oroonoko*, p. 62). The manager of Parham Plantation, recognizing the greatness of Oroonoko, gave him "Caesar" as his slave name (p. 40). We find a "Prince" among the male slaves in Suriname in 1699 (SocSur 227, fols. 28v–29r), and Stedman lists "Caesar" among slave names there in the 1770s (*Narrative*, p. 524).

204. Laura Brown, "The Romance of Empire: *Oroonoko* and the Trade in Slaves," in Felicity Nussbaum and Laura Brown, eds., *The New Eighteenth Century* (New York: Methuen, 1987), pp. 41–61. See also Margaret Ferguson, "Juggling the Categories of Race, Class, and Gender: Aphra Behn's *Oroonoko*," in Margo Hendricks and Patricia Parker, eds., *Women, "Race," and Writing in the Early Modern Period* (London and New York: Routledge, 1994), pp. 209–224, 342–347).

205. Aphra Behn, *Lebens- und Liebes-Geschichte des königlichen Schlaven Oroonoko in West-Indien . . . Verteutscht durch M. V*** (Hamburg: Heirs of T. von Wiering, 1709).

206. The Caribs hunted varieties of wild boar, armadillos, and tapirs for food. They raised turkeys, which, according to Merian, were fed on the leaves of the *Muscos Bloem* (*Met*D and *Met*L, no. 42). But the meal would more likely have consisted of fish or other seafood. Stedman refers to the Amerindians' food as sea and land turtles, crabs, and leguana or wayamacca lizards (Stedman, *Expedition*, pp. 310–312). Twentieth-century targets of Carib hunts are deer, peccaries, akuti, and monkeys (Kloos, *Maroni River Caribs*, p. 59).

207. *Oroonoko*, pp. 2, 59, 63: "by Noon about 600 Men . . . came to assist us in the pursuit of the Fugitives"; " 'tis not impossible but some of the best in the Country was of his Council in this Flight, and depriving us of all the Slaves."

208. Brown, "The Romance of Empire."

209. According to Gerd Oostindie, the status of Suriname slaves brought to the Netherlands is not clear. Some people claimed that anyone setting foot on Dutch soil was free, whereas others claimed that slave status could be maintained (telephone conversation with Oostindie, 4 July 1992). In Suriname itself, private manumissions up to 1733 were made by notarial act (Smidt and Lee, eds., *Plakaten*, no. 350, p. 411; Rosemary Brana-Shute, "Approaching Freedom: The Manumission of Slaves in Suriname, 1760–1828," *Slavery and Abolition*, 10, no. 3 [1989]: 40–63). I searched the notarial volumes of Samuel Wijmer, the Amsterdam notary used by Merian and her daughter, and found no letter of manumission by Merian or by anyone at all in the years through 1705. No slave is mentioned in Merian's will of 1711 (GAA, Notary Samuel Wijmer 4849, no. 42, pp. 193–198).

210. Price, *First Time*, pp. 45–49.

211. Imoinda stayed at Oroonoko's side during his last stand against the governor and his soldiers and wounded several of them, including the governor himself (Behn, *Oroonoko*, pp. 64–65). But all initiative came from Oroonoko. Price, *First Time*, pp. 70–72. Ma Kaàla left Providence Plantation with her brother Pikapai, but he turned back, fought, and eventually went back to slavery.

212. SocSur 227, fols. 28v–29r (list of 17 April 1699). Other women's names are: Sieclie, Herta, Rosetta, Trorjntje, Calbassie, Iaca, Madam, Cathrina, Trees, Wora, Grietje.

213. Behn, *Oroonoko*, p. 57; Merian, *MetD* and *MetL*, no. 18 on food taboos of Peii; Stedman, *Narrative*, pp. 304, 314. Sloane, *Voyage*, vol. 1, pp. 147–149 (on ecstatic use of tobacco by "Priests and Indian Inchanters") and p. 174; W. Ahlbrinck, *Encyclopaedie der Karaïben* (Amsterdam: Uitgave van de Koninklijke Akademie van Wetenschappen, 1931), pp. 399–408; Kloos, *Maroni River Caribs*, pp. 209–218; Whitehead, *Lords of the Tiger Spirit*, pp. 62–63.

214. Ahlbrinck, *Encyclopaedie*, pp. 298–303; Kloos, *Maroni River Caribs*, pp. 218–223; Henri J. M. Stephen, *Geneeskruiden van Suriname: Hun toepassing in de volsgeneeskunde en in de magaie* (Amsterdam: Uitgeverij de Driehoek, n.d.) pp. 87–93. Toads and reptiles, depicted and discussed in the *Metamorphosis*, also had religious uses among the Arawaks. Images *(ʒemis)* of powerful and dangerous lesser spirits were made in the forms of toads, reptiles, and distorted human faces. They were kept in special houses in Arawak villages and in individual dwellings and also carried around by persons for protection (Dale Bisnauth, *A History of Religions in the Caribbean* [Kingston, Jamaica: Kingston Publishers, 1989], pp. 3–4).

215. Ahlbrinck, *Encyclopaedie*, p.323; W. Ahlbrinck, *Op Zoek naar de Indianen* (Amsterdam: n.p., 1956), pp. 26–35; Kloos, *Maroni River Caribs*, pp. 75–77; Philip Hanson Hiss, *Netherlands America: The Dutch Territories in the West* (New York: Duell, Sloan and Pearce, 1943), pp. 74–76; Jean Hurault, *Les Indiens Wayana de la Guyane française: Structure sociale et coutume familiale* (Paris: Oritom, 1968; reprint 1985), ch. 6, especially pp. 93–95, 101–102, 105 on the test by ants for

both males and females and the wasp test for males. Wasp mats from Suriname can be found in the Rijksmuseum voor Volkenkunde, Leiden (2352-80 and 5379-41); the Stichting Surinaams Museum, Paramaribo; and the University Museum of Archaeology and Anthropology, University of Pennsylvania (SA 773). The Rijksmuseum voor Volkenkunde in Leiden also has three ant mats (1817-86, 87, 88) and two ant belts (1817-89, 90). The wasp mats in the museums seem to go back no earlier than the nineteenth century, but there is no reason to believe that the initiation rite did not go back in some form to Merian's day and earlier.

216. Warren, *Impartial Description,* p. 25; Herlein, *Beschryvinge,* p. 155.

217. Stedman, *Narrative,* pp. 520, 522–523, 660 (reports the taboo foods as "one Particular kind of Animal Food, this may be eyther Fowl, fish or Quadrupede"). Herskovits and Herskovits, *Suriname Folk-Lore,* pp. 36–37, 63, 67. The word *trefu,* which was still current in the 1930s, is from the Hebrew *trefe* and goes back to the early connection of some African slaves with Jewish plantation owners. The maroons used a Bantu-derived word meaning "father-taboo" (Bisnauth, *Religions,* pp. 84–85, 96). *Met*D and *Met*L, no. 59.

218. Labat, *Voyage,* part 4, ch. 7, vol. 2, p. 50.

219. Willem Bosman, *A New and Accurate Description of the Coast of Guinea, Divided into the Gold, the Slave, and the Ivory Coasts* (London: James Knapton, 1705), p. 322 and Letter X, p. 146. Bosman served as a commercial agent on the Guinea coast for fourteen years before he published the first Dutch edition of his book in Utrecht in 1704. The importance of Anansi stories in West Africa is evident in Harold Scheub, *African Oral Narratives, Proverbs, Riddles, Poetry and Song* (Boston: G. K. Hall, 1977). The earliest known European record of an Anansi story heard in America dates from the journal of Matthew Gregory Lewis, kept during his visit to his estate in Jamaica in 1815–1816: *Journal of a West India Proprietor* (London, 1834; reprinted New York: Negro Universities Press, 1969), "Nancy stories" on pp. 253–259, 291–296, 301–308. But the spider's adventures must have been told from the earliest arrival of the Africans. Herskovits and Herskovits, *Suriname Folk-lore,* p. 138; Roger Abrahams, ed., *Afro-American Folktales: Stories from Black Traditions in the New World* (New York: Pantheon Books, 1985), p. 17; no. 59, pp. 182–183.

220. Labat, *Voyage,* part 4, ch. 7, vol. 2, p. 55; Stedman, *Narrative,* pp. 536–537, 663; Herskovits and Herskovits, *Suriname Folk-Lore,* pp. 109–111, 138–146; Abrahams, *Afro-American Folktales,* Introduction and pp. 15–20; Richard Price and Sally Price, *Two Evenings in Saramaka* (Chicago: University of Chicago Press, 1991), pp. 1–37.

221. Herskovits and Herskovits, *Suriname Folk-Lore,* pp. 198–201.

222. Herskovits and Herskovits, *Suriname Folk-Lore,* no. 65, pp. 266–269.

223. *Met*D and *Met*L, no. 41.

224. The story of Phyllis' riding Aristotle is found in Europe as early as the thirteenth century. Aristotle admonishes Alexander for his excessive attention to

Phyllis, one of his beautiful subjects in India. To get revenge, Phyllis coquettishly persuades the old philosopher to get down on all fours and, saddled and bridled, carry her through the garden before Alexander's eyes. (Natalie Zemon Davis, *Society and Culture in Early Modern France* [Stanford, Calif.: Stanford University Press, 1975], pp. 135–136).

225. The plate is copied and discussed in Johann Christoph Volkamer, *Continuation der Nürnbergischen Hesperidum* (Nuremberg: Johann Christoph Volkamer, 1713; Frankfurt and Leipzig: Heirs of Johann Andreas Enders, 1713), fols. 215v–216r, fig. 2. Volkamer was the brother of Johann Georg Volkamer, Merian's correspondent in Nuremberg. Sloan also referred to Merian's Plate 18 and her text accompanying it (*Voyage*, vol. 2, p. 222). Carl Linnaeus, *Systema Naturae per Regna Tria Naturae*, 10th ed. (Holm, Sweden: Laurentius Salvius, 1758–1759), vol. 1, p. 622, no. 26: "*Aranea avicularia*." Linnaeus cites, among references besides that of Merian, Marcgraf's contribution to *De Indiae utriusque*, p. 248 (*sic* for 284). Marcgraf here describes briefly and gives an illustration of the Great Spider, or Nhamdu-guaça, of Brazil, but says nothing about it hunting birds or about its prey (pp. 284–285).

226. Stedman, *Narrative*, p. 314; Kloos, *Maroni River Caribs*, p. 212.

227. Alexander F. Skutch, *The Life of the Hummingbird* (New York: Crown Publishers, 1973), p. 74: "Hummingbirds almost invariably lay two tiny, white eggs." If there are more than two eggs in a nest, it is because another female has dumped eggs into an existing nest; this happens most frequently with hermit hummingbirds, who have hanging nests, not nests on branches as in Merian's picture. Merian was clearly not thinking of such a case, for she said in her text to Plate 18: "They [hummingbirds] lay four eggs, like all other birds." Carlos Martinez del Rio of Princeton University, a specialist in the hummingbirds of the Central and South American rain forests, has pointed out to me that the bill on Merian's hummingbird is impossibly bifurcated. See also the hummingbirds in John Gould and A. Rutgers, *Birds of South America* (London: Eyre Methuen, 1972), pp. 162–321; the closest to Merian's is the white-tipped sicklebill (p. 186), whose bill is curved but not bifurcated.

228. Henry Walter Bates, *The Naturalist on the River Amazon*, 2 vols. (London: John Murray, 1863), vol. 1, pp. 160–161 with illustration. James Duncan, "Memoir of Maria Sibilla Merian," in Duncan, *The Natural History of British Moths, Sphinxes, etc.* (Edinburgh: W. H. Lizars, 1836), had said that Merian's account was "wholly improbable" (p. 42), and Bates noted that he was the first to find an example. I am grateful to the biologist Leslie K. Johnson for her guidance on the habits of tropical tarantulas.

229. Uffenbach, *Merkwürdige Reisen*, vol. 3, p. 552. Lukina, *Merian*, p. 146; *Stud*, pp. 44–47; *Leningrader Aquarelle*, Introduction. The second visit of Peter the Great to Amsterdam was in 1716–1717. Peter's physician, Robert Erskine, is said to have ordered more than two hundred paintings from the family the day of Merian's death, but presumably he had visited Merian in the months before.

230. *Der Rupsen Begin, Voedzel, en Wonderbaare Verandering: Waar in De Oorspront, Spys en Gestoltverwisseling: Als ook de Tyd, Plaats en Eigenschappen der Rupsen, Wormen, Kapellen, Uiltjes, Vliegen, en andere diergelyke bloedelooze Beesjes vertoond word . . . Door Maria Sibilla Merian* (Amsterdam: Printed for the author, also available from Gerard Valck, n.d. [1713?]). *Der Rupsen, Begin, Voedzel en Wonderbaare Verandering . . . Tweede Deel* (Amsterdam: Printed for the author, also available from Gerard Valck, n.d. [1714?]). Pfeiffer, *Merian*, pp. 10, 23–24.

231. Uffenbach, *Merkwürdige Reisen*, vol. 3, p. 553. The confusion about her life is suggested by the account of Michael Bernhard Valentini. In both the 1704 and 1714 editions of his *Museum Museorum*, Valentini said that not long after he had seen her in Frankfurt in the early 1680s, Merian had simply moved to the West Indies "with her family" (vol. 1, p. 512); that she was carrying on her observations in the West Indies, "where she had to go with her husband" (vol. 2, p. 170).

232. In an act of sale of 28 September 1717, she signs "Dorothea Maria Merian, weduwe van Philip Hendrix" (GAA, Notary Pieter Schabaalje 6107). She signed documents of 1702 and 1705 "Dorothea Maria Graafen" (GAA, Ondertrouw 533, p. 304, 14 October 1701; Notary S. Wijmer 4837, no. 31, 26 August 1705).

233. MSM to Johann Georg Volkamer, 8 October 1702; to James Petiver, 20 June 1703 and 29 August 1712 (RS*Mer*, nos. 7, 10, 17, pp. 64–65, 68, 75).

234. *Deerde en Laatste Deel der Rupsen Begin, Voedzel en wonderbaare Verandering . . . Door Maria Sibilla Merian, Saal*r: *Als mede een Appendix Behelsende eenige Surinaamsche Insecten, geobserveert door haar Dochter Johanna Helena Herolt, tegenwoordig noch tot Surinaame woonagtig: Alles in Print gebracht, en in 't licht gegeven door haar Jongste Dochter Dorothea Maria Henricie t'Amsterdam: Gedrukt voor de Uytgeefster Woont in de Kerkstraat tusschen de Leydsche en Spiegel straat in de Roozetak* (Amsterdam, n.d. [between Merian's death on 13 January 1717 and 2 March 1717, when a notice of the book appeared in the *Leipziger Gelehrte Zeitungen;* see Pfeiffer, *Merian*, p. 12]). Merian's observations included those dated 1683–1684 in Germany (nos. 14, 21, 22), from Friesland, and from Amsterdam as late as 1706 (no. 30).

235. An edition of all three volumes of the *Rupsen* at the Library of the Nederlandse Entomologisch Vereniging in Amsterdam has, bound in, the engraved portrait of Maria Sibylla Merian made by Jacob Houbraken. It also circulated separately, for there is a copy in the Print Room of the Kunstmuseum in Basel. The engraving was based on a drawing done by Georg Gsell, the Swiss artist who lived with the Merian family and later became Dorothea Maria's second husband (RS*Mer*, p. 60). In some sense the picture represents a family stance. An unsigned oil portrait of an unnamed young woman at the Kunstmuseum has been thought to be of Maria Sibylla Merian (reproduced ibid., p. ix), but Paul-Henri Boerlin, former curator of Old Master Painting, has recently proved that the woman it depicts is not Merian.

236. By August 1712, numerous specimens for sale had already arrived from

Johanna Helena in Suriname (MSM to James Petiver, 29 August 1712, RS*Mer*, no. 17, p. 75). The departure of Johanna Helena Graff and Jacob Hendrik Herolt may well have been in 1711, for Maria Sibylla remade her will in October of that year. Both daughters were still joint heirs, as in her 1699 will, but all Merian's clothes, linens, woolens, and other household belongings were now bequeathed to whichever daughter was living in the house with her at her death. Dorothea Maria Graff, who was then living with her first husband, Philip Hendriks, in Merian's house, was made one of her executors, but not Johanna Helena (GAA, Notary Samuel Wijmer 4849, 3 October 1711, no. 42, pp. 193–198). Jacob Hendrick Herolt is referred to as a *weesmeester en commissariss der onbeheerde boedels* in Suriname in SocSur 241, fols. 504r–505v, 451r, 457r; SocSur 23, fols 269v–270r. On the oath and duties of the *weesmesteren*, see Smidt and Lee, eds., *Plakaten*, vol. 1, pp. 147, 164–165.

237. The promised appendix by Johanna Helena is not included in any of the editions of the last volume of the *Rupsen* that I have seen (Senckenberg Collection, SUBF; Library of the Nederlandse Entomologisch Vereniging, Amsterdam; Houghton Library, Harvard University, two copies). A second printing of the book appeared later in 1717, with the reference to Johanna Helena's appendix dropped from the title page (Pfeiffer, *Merian*, p. 26; Houghton Library *Rup*17, *H732-47, announces the appendix; *Rup*17, Typ 732.13.567, does not). Conceivably some or all of the twelve engravings added to the 1719 Johannes Oosterwyk edition of the *Metamorphosis* could be Johanna Helena's work. They were said to be made from watercolors found among Merian's possessions after she died, but they do not resemble Maria Sibylla Merian's other paintings and engravings. Pfeiffer suggests that some of the plates added to the 1730 French and German editions of the European caterpillars might be by Johanna Helena (*Merian*, pp. 14–15). I have been through all the extant lists in SocSur of passengers returning on boats from Suriname to the Netherlands through 1723 and have not found Johanna Helena or Jacob Hendrik on any of them.

238. Dorothea Maria Merian, widow of Philip Hendriks, sold Merian's insect and flower books and the right to publish them to Johannes Oosterwijk for 1,200 guilders; she also sold a copy of Willem Goeree's *Jewish History* and the four volumes of Cornelis de Bruyn's *Voyage to Moscow and Persia* (GAA, Notary Pieter Schabaalje 6107, 28 September 1717). On Dorothea Maria's life, teaching, and painting in Russia until her death in 1743 and on her three children born in Russia, see Lukina, *Merian*, pp. 147–150; and Ullman et al., *Leningrader Aquarelle*, Introduction. Georg Gsell died in 1740. On the settings in which she and Gsell taught painting, see James Cracraft, *The Petrine Revolution in Russian Architecture* (Chicago: University of Chicago Press, 1988) pp. 244–245.

239. *Erucarum Ortus, Alimentum et Paradoxa Metamorphosis* (Amsterdam: Johannes Oosterwijk, n.d. [1718]). Dedicated by Oosterwijk to Theodore Huygens. Latin poem signed "Salomon de Perez, Phil. et Med. Doctor fecit." (Perez is

listed in Hindl S. Hes, *Jewish Physicians in the Netherlands, 1600–1940* [Assen, 1980], p. 200.) Frontispiece signed by Simon Schynvoet: "Schynvoet del. et fec. 1717." *Erucarum Ortus* also includes the portrait of Merian by Jacob Houbraken. *Dissertatio de Generatione et Metamorphosibus Insectorum Surinamensium* (Amsterdam: Johannes Oosterwijk, 1719). Dedicated by Oosterwijk to Balthazar Scott. Poem by Brouërius van Niedek. Frontispiece by Frederic Ottens signed "F. Ottens Inv. et fecit." (Ottens frequently designed portraits for Amsterdam books, including a portrait of Christian Huygens [Amsterdam, Rijksmuseum, Print Room, 26–466].) On Oosterwijk's publishing career, see van Eeghen, *Amsterdamse Boekhandel*, vol. 4, pp. 26–29.

240. *Horti Medici Amstelodamensis Rariorum tam Orientalis, quam Occidentalis Indiae, aliarumque Peregrinarum Plantarum . . . Auctore Joanne Commelino . . . Opus Posthumum* (Amsterdam: P. and J. Blaeu and Abraham van Someren, 1697). Among the antecedents to this picture is the frontispiece to the 1658 Rotterdam edition of Charles de Rochefort's *Histoire naturelle et morale des Iles Antilles de l'Amerique*, published by Arnout Leers. Three Amerindians, one of them kneeling, present natural objects to a queenly figure. In his dedication to a French privy councillor, Rochefort pretends that it is the "poor Americans" themselves who are offering this book "in all humility and submission" (fols. a3v–a4v).

241. The frontispiece to *D'Amboinische Rariteitkamer* is signed "Jan Goeree del. and Jacovus [*sic* for Jacobus] Delater fecit." A colored version, with the kneeling man painted brown, is among the collection of Merian's own paintings and her illustrations for the Rumphius work at the Archives of the Academy of Sciences in Saint Petersburg (PIX on. 8 wı).

242. *Erucarum Ortus . . . Metamorphosis*, Oosterwijk's "To the Reader."

Conclusion

1. I have given some archival evidence on these matters in my essay "Women in the Crafts in Sixteenth-Century Lyon," *Feminist Studies*, 8 (1982): 47–80.

2. There is a page missing from the opening of Book 2 of Glikl's autobiography (KM, p. 24), in the section where Glikl begins to talk of her parents. Since David Kaufmann had access to two manuscripts at the time of his Yiddish edition, presumably the page was missing in both copies. Could there have been something that subsequent generations did not want people to read?

3. [François Poullain de La Barre], *De l'égalité des deux sexes, discours physique et moral, où l'on voit l'importance de se defaire des préjugez* (Paris: Jean Du Puis, 1673). [Mary Astell], *A Serious Proposal to the Ladies for the Advancement of their True and Greatest Interest: By a Lover of Her Sex* (London: R. Wilkin, 1694). For background on this thought, see Ian Maclean, *Woman Triumphant: Feminism in French Literature, 1610–1652* (Oxford: Clarendon Press, 1977); Joan DeJean,

Tender Mercies: Women and the Origins of the Novel in France (New York: Columbia University Press, 1991); Erica Harth, *Cartesian Women: Versions and Subversions of Rational Discourse in the Old Regime* (Ithaca and London: Cornell University Press, 1992); Hilda Smith, *Reason's Disciples: Seventeenth-Century English Feminists* (Urbana: University of Illinois Press, 1982); Ruth Perry, *The Celebrated Mary Astell: An Early English Feminist* (Chicago: University of Chicago Press, 1986).

4. Michel Foucault, *The History of Sexuality*, trans. Robert Hurley (New York: Vintage Books, 1980–1990), vol. 1, pp. 92–93.

5. [David Nassy et al.], *Essai historique sur la colonie de Surinam*, 2 vols. (Paramaribo, 1788; facsimile reprint Amsterdam: S. Emmering, 1968), vol. 2, pp. 39, 60; Robert Cohen, *Jews in Another Environment: Surinam in the Second Half of the Eighteenth Century* (Leiden and New York: E. J. Brill, 1991), pp. 156–172. After 1754 Jewish persons of color were relegated to the status of *Congreganten*, rather than that of full members, though there continued to be marriages between full members and *Congreganten* (p. 162, p. 305, no. 39).

6. *Vie*, p. 737.

7. Copy of the *Vie* at the Thomas Fisher Rare Book Library, University of Toronto (D-10 2448): "Ce livre apartient aux R[o]sair[es] du tiers ordre . . . [Rosaires du tiers ordre crossed out] aux Carmelites de [word illegible]." Copy of the *Vie* at the John Carter Brown Library, Providence, R.I. (E677 M379v): "Ce livre est de la Communaute de Ste Ursule de Vitré." A subsequent owner: "Ex Libris McCoy." *Retraites de la venerable Mere Marie de l'Incarnation religieuse Ursuline* (Paris: Louis Billaine, 1682): "A l'usage de Sr Ste Elizabeth" (Houghton Library, Harvard Univesity, *FC6.M3376.682r).

8. Soeur Sainte-Julie, O.S.U., "Marie de l'Incarnation: Sa relation spirituelle manuscrite de l'année 1654" (Ursuline house of Trois-Rivières, 1977).

9. Jeanne-Françoise Juchereau de St-Ignace and Marie André Duplessis de Ste Hélène, *Les Annales de l'Hôtel-Dieu de Québec, 1636–1716*, ed. Albert Jamet (Québec: Hôtel-Dieu, 1939), pp. iii, xli. Albert Jamet (1883–1948) was a Benedictine of the congregation of Saint Maur, like Claude Martin himself. On Jamet's edition of the spiritual autobiography of 1654, see note 1 to "New Worlds," above.

10. *Cor*, p. 804, n. 5. The missionaries who took Marie de l'Incarnation's manuscripts were religious Oblates of the Immaculate Marie.

11. [Pierre Chaumonot], "Dictionnaire Huron," Archives du Séminaire de Québec (University of Washington Microfilm A1705, no. 62). There is also an indication of Amerindian family ownership written on another manuscript of Chaumonot's dictionary by Prosper Vincent Sawatanin (John Carter Brown Library, Providence, R.I., Codex Ind 12).

12. See notes 237 and 239 to "Metamorphoses," above, for the editions published by Johannes Oosterwijk in 1718 and 1719. Editions of the *Raupen* appeared in Dutch and in French in 1730 (Amsterdam: Jean Frédéric Bernard) and in a

combined Latin-French in 1771 (Paris: L. C. Desnos). Editions of the *Metamorphosis* appeared in Dutch in 1730 (Amsterdam: Jean Frédéric Bernard) and in a combined Latin-French version in 1726 (The Hague: Pierre Gosse) and in 1771 (Paris: L. C. Desnos).

13. Carl Linnaeus, *Systema Naturae per Regna Tria Naturae*, 10th ed. (Holm, Sweden: Laurentius Salvius, 1758–1759), vol. 1, p. 541: Phalaena *Tinea* Merianella. This species is described among several moths named for entomologists: Petiverella, Swammerdamella, Mouffetella, Goedartella, Leuenhoekella (pp. 540–541). Both the European caterpillars and the *Metamorphosis* are frequently cited in Linnaeus' notes. John Lewis Heller, *Studies in Linnaean Method and Nomenclature* (Frankfurt am Main: Verlag Peter Lang, 1983), pp. 306, 315, 240–241 (translation of Linnaeus, "On Sumptuous Books"). Carl Linnaeus to Abraham Bäck, 25 September 1754; to Carl Alexander Clerck, 6 July 1759, in Carl Linnaeus, *Bref och skrifvelser*, ed. T. M. Fries (Stockholm: Aktiebolaget Ljus, 1907–1912), vol. 1, part 4, p. 305; part 5, p. 292.

14. *Stud*, pp. 44–48.

15. Vladimir Nabokov, *Speak, Memory: An Autobiography Revisited* (New York: G. P. Putnam's Sons, 1966), pp. 121–122 and ch. 6; Brian Boyd, *Vladimir Nabokov: The Russian Years* (London: Chatto and Windus, 1990), ch. 4 and passim.

16. The two editions in the library of the Surinaams Museum are the 1705 *Metamorphosis* in Dutch (no. 1348) and the Latin-French edition of 1726 (no. 1347): *Dissertation sur la generation et les transformations des Insectes de Surinam* (The Hague: Pierre Gosse, 1726). Henna Malmberg-Guicherit, "Coup d'Etat, Revolution, and Museums in Suriname in the 1980s," Paper presented at the Colloquium on Museums and Collecting, Colonial and Post-Colonial, Shelby Cullom Davis Center for Historical Studies, Princeton University, 3–4 April 1992.

17. On Bertha Pappenheim, see Max Rosenbaum and Melvin Muroff, eds., *Anna O.: Fourteen Contemporary Reinterpretations* (New York: Free Press, 1984), especially the essays by Max Rosenbaum, "Anna O. (Bertha Pappenheim): Her History" (pp. 1–25), and Marion A. Kaplan, "Anna O. and Bertha Pappenheim: An Historical Perspective" (pp. 101–117). See also Daniel Boyarin, "Retelling the Story of O: or, Bertha Pappenheim, the Fulfillment of a Jewish Woman's Rebellion," to appear in Boyarin, *Judaism as a Gender* (Berkeley: University of California Press, forthcoming).

18. Mary Wollstonecraft, *Eine Verteidigung der Rechte der Frau mit kritischen Bemerkungen über politische und moralische Gegenstände von Mary Wollstonecraft, London 1792, mit einem Bilde der Verfasserin*, trans. P. Berthold [Bertha Pappenheim] (Dresden and Leipzig: E. Pierson's Verlag, 1899). Citing an essay by George Pollock, Rosenbaum has said that Mary Wollstonecraft herself "was aware of Gluckel von Hameln" ("Anna O.," p. 15). Pollock's article makes no such claim, but merely says that Pappenheim translated both women (George H. Pol-

lock, "Glückel von Hameln: Bertha Pappenheim's Idealized Ancestor," *American Imago*, 28 [1971]: 216–227). Nor does Pappenheim say anything about such a connection in the brief biography of Wollstonecraft included in her translation (pp. viii–xx). One can always imagine that somehow one of Glikl's descendants through her daughter Freudchen in London had met Wollstonecraft, but I have found no mention of Glikl in the *Vindication* or in the sections on Hamburg in Wollstonecraft's *Letters Written during a Short Residence in Sweden, Norway, and Denmark*.

19. The secondary literature repeats that Bertha Pappenheim was a "descendant" of Glikl, that Glikl was Pappenheim's "ancestor." But this is not what Pappenheim says or shows in the genealogies published in her translation; see PM, "Genealogische Bemerkungen," unpaginated frontmatter. Pappenheim's mother, Recha Goldschmidt, was a descendant—through her paternal grandmother Bela Braunschweig over eight generations—of Yenta bas Joseph Hamel, sister of Haim ben Joseph. On Recha Goldschmidt's family in Frankfurt am Main, see Alexander Dietz, *Stammbuch der Frankfurter Juden: Geschichtliche Mitteilungen über die Frankfurter jüdischen Familien von 1349–1849* (Frankfurt am Main: J. St. Goar, 1907), pp. 115–121. This is not the same Goldschmidt family as the one founded in Frankfurt in the early seventeenth century by Haim's brother Isaac Hamel, also known as Goldschmidt (pp. 121–126).

20. Pollock, "Pappenheim's Idealized Ancestor," p. 220.

21. The book was published in 1910 by Dr. Stefan Meyer and Dr. Wilhelm Pappenheim, and printed by the Buchdruckerei Helios. Described in the frontmatter as a "private printing," it nonetheless was produced in a considerable number of copies; the network of Goldschmidt relatives with whom Pappenheim was in touch was itself large. The Leo Baeck Institute in New York has a presentation copy to Henriette May from Bertha Pappenheim. KM, p. 271; PM, p. 257. See also "Arguing with God," note 1, above.

22. Alfred Feilchenfeld, *Denkwürdigkeiten der Glückel von Hameln* (Berlin: Jüdischer Verlag, 1913), pp. 8–10. He claims to have learned of the 1910 Pappenheim translation only after he had completed his own. This is hard to believe, since he was in touch with the editor of the Yiddish edition, David Kaufmann, who had authorized Pappenheim's translation. Among other works, Feilchenfeld had previously published *Napoleon und die Juden* (Vienna, 1899), and a book about a Jewish school in Furth (1912). On Feilchenfeld's translation see also Dorothy Bilik, "The *Memoirs of Glikl of Hameln*: The Archeology of the Text," *Yiddish*, 8, no. 2 (1992): 5–22.

23. The two stories retained for the appendix were the Bird Story and Sincere Friendship; Feilchenfeld also had a third appendix with an excerpt from Glikl's moral commentary. The young psychoanalyst Theodor Reik published a short article on Glikl's memoirs in 1915 in Freud's *Internationale Zeitschrift für ärtzliche Psychoanalyse* (3 [1915]: 235–239). He analyzed the Bird Story, referring in the

note to the version in Feilchenfeld's appendix, but he may well have known Pappenheim's translation, which had gone to readers in Berlin. Reik saw the Bird Story as expressing a wish to return to the Mother through the birth process (carrying the bird over the water) and ambivalence toward the Father. The possible ambivalence of a mother toward her own children he did not discuss. Perhaps Freud himself knew the book, and even in Pappenheim's edition, which was printed and circulating among families in his circle in Vienna. In June 1913 Freud published an essay entitled "The Three Caskets," in which he suggested a psychoanalytic meaning for the choice made among the gold, silver, and lead caskets by the suitors seeking Portia's hand in *The Merchant of Venice;* the choice of Lear among his daughters; and the story of Cinderella ("Das Motiv der Kästchenwahl," *Imago*, vol. 2, no. 3 [June 1913]: 257–266; "The Theme of the Three Caskets," trans. C. J. M. Hubback, *Collected Papers*, ed. Joan Riviere [London: Leonard and Virginia Woolf and the Institute of Psychoanalysis, 1925], vol. 4, pp. 244–256). He said the scenes from Shakespeare had got him started on his quest. But the Bird Story, of the same tale type, could have also been a spur. Marjorie Garber has suggested that in this essay Freud was choosing his third daughter, Anna (*Shakespeare's Ghost Writers* [New York: Methuen, 1987], ch. 4). Could Anna O. and her Glikl have also been part of the choice?

24. On Jewish assimilation and the scholars devoted to the Wissenschaft des Judentums, see Marion Kaplan, *The Making of the Jewish Middle Class: Women, Family, and Identity in Imperial Germany* (New York: Oxford University Press, 1991); and Dan Ben-Amos, "Jewish Studies and Jewish Folklore," Proceedings of the Tenth World Congress of Jewish Studies (Jerusalem: World Union of Jewish Studies, 1990), Division D, vol. 2, pp. 1–20.

25. The 1913 Feilchenfeld translation was reprinted in 1914, 1920, and, with illustrations, in 1923.

ACKNOWLEDGMENTS

I FIRST CAME TO KNOW the three women of this book in 1971, when I was seeking sources for a course that I gave with Jill Conway at the University of Toronto entitled "Society and the Sexes in Early Modern Europe." Maria Sibylla Merian was just then becoming a subject in the new scholarship on the history of women artists. Marie Guyart de l'Incarnation was especially appropriate in a Canada arguing about the status of Québec, French-Canadian culture, and Native American peoples. As for Glikl bas Judah Leib, I might have heard of her from my aunt Anna Landau, who to this day praises her piety. But in fact it was Rosalie Colie who told me that she had once seen a German edition of the memoirs of "Glückel von Hameln," and wondered whether an English edition existed for the students in the course.

The three women lived over the years in my lectures and in dialogue with students at Toronto, Berkeley, and Princeton. In the late 1980s, I decided I wanted to learn much more about them and their significance for early modern history. My chance came when I was invited to give the Carl Becker lectures at Cornell University in the spring of 1990. The lively response of listeners at Cornell was immensely helpful as I rethought the advantages of comparative biography and the frames I could give to these women's lives and works. And an additional bonus: Cornell's Entomology Library had many rare books from the days of Maria Sibylla Merian.

Over the past five years, I have received courteous assistance at many archives, museums, and rare-book collections. Here I want especially to acknowledge the help of Peter Freimark, formerly director of the Institut für die Geschichte der deutschen Juden at Hamburg, and the late Günter Marwedel, research specialist at the same institute; Elke Wawers of the Staats-und Universitätsbibliothek, Hamburg; Gilbert Cahen, formerly curator at the Archives départementales de la Moselle; Susan Danforth of the John Carter Brown Library in Providence, Rhode Island; Sharon Liberman Mintz of the Graphics Department at the Library of the Jewish Theological Seminary, New York; Sabine Solf of the Herzog August Bibliothek, Wolfenbüttel; Katia Guth-Dreyfus, director of the Jüdisches Museum der Schweiz, Basel; Françoise Durand-Evrard, director, and Monique Fournier of the Archives d'Indre-et-Loire; Rita Coulombe, Mother Superior of the Couvent des Ursulines de Québec; Germaine Blais, archivist, and Suzanne Dargis, assistant archivist, of the Archives des Ursulines de Trois-Rivières; Susan Campbell of the National Gallery of Canada; Susan Halpert and Jennie Rathbun of the Houghton Library, Harvard University; Bernhard Reichel, archivist at the Stadtarchiv, Frankfurt am Main; Kurt Wettengl, curator at the Historisches Museum, Frankfurt; Peter Fleischmann, archivist at the Staatsarchiv, Nuremberg; Ursula Mende of the Germanisches Nationalmuseum, Nuremberg; G. W. van der Meiden, formerly archivist at the Algemeen Rijksarchief, The Hague; S. A. C. Dudok van Heel, archivist at the Gemeentearchief, Amsterdam; Jerry Egger, director of the Surinaams Museum, Paramaribo; Olaf Koester, curator of old-master paintings and sculpture at the Statens Museum for Kunst in Copenhagen; Niels Jessen of the Rosenborg Slot, Copenhagen; Inge Schjellerup and Barbara Berlowicz of the Etnografisk Samling of the Nationalmuseet, Copenhagen; and the personnel at the archives and library of the Academy of Sciences at Saint Petersburg (still called Leningrad during my visit in the autumn of 1989).

Women on the Margins took me not only to new research sites, but also to new languages of research. Sidney Gray got me started reading the seventeenth-century Western Yiddish of Glikl bas Judah

Leib and gave me the courage to master the text myself. Mark Cohen, Sidra Ezrahi, and Chava Weissler provided patient advice as I made my final translations from Glikl into English. Leonard Blussé reviewed with me a few particularly difficult pages in seventeenth-century Dutch to make sure I'd understood them aright. Mark Cohen and Moshe Sluhovsky translated some Hebrew texts for me; Anita Norich gave me a full report on an important article in late twentieth-century Yiddish; Chandler Davis translated some essential pages from Russian.

Parts of this book were presented to audiences in North America and Europe as I continued my research and writing. Each occasion yielded questions and comments that were precious contributions to my work. In addition, there were countless discussions with scholarly friends, who gave me advice on sources, bibliography, and approaches I might employ in my research. Roger Abraham was a helpful sounding board for the ways I hoped to use stories and folktales through the entire book. Ellen Badone sent me interesting comments on my comparison of Marie de l'Incarnation and Maria Sibylla Merian in their "New World encounters," presented to the Society for the Anthropology of Europe.

Marianne Constable and Lisa Jardine gave me good ideas for strengthening my prologue. For the chapter on Glikl bas Judah Leib, Dan Ben-Amos gave me his learned reactions to my search for sources for Glikl's stories. I am immensely grateful to him. In addition, I received suggestions for this chapter from Ruth B. Bottigheimer, Daniel Boyarin, Mark Cohen, Elisheva Carlebach, Harvey Kaye, Gustav Henningsen, Judith Herrin, Peter Hulme, Yosef Kaplan, Dov-Ber Kerler, Franklin Kopitzsch, Dominick LaCapra, Jean Bernard Lang, Mary Lindemann, Frances Malino, Cyril Manco, David Ruderman, John Theibault, Chava Weissler, Yosef Yerushalmi, and Jack Zipes. Jean Fleury of the Cercle généalogique de Lorraine helped me locate Jewish marriage contracts in the Archives de la Moselle. Leslie Tuttle tracked down some much-needed information in the Princeton library.

Joan DeJean gave me excellent advice for the chapter on Marie Guyart de l'Incarnation, even faxing me reactions from Paris. Further helpful suggestions were made by Peter Brown, Raymond Fogelson, Jorgé Klor de Alva, Shepard Krech III, Toby Morantz, Réal Ouellet, Ruth Phillips, Daniel Scalberg, Chantal Théry, Bruce Trigger, and Marina Warner. Cynthia Cupples located a letter for me at the Bibliothèque Nationale; Alfred Soman kindly checked something in the Archives de la Préfecture de la Police in Paris.

For the third chapter, Christiane Andersson introduced me to the study of Maria Sibylla Merian's art in Frankfurt and continued to send me books and suggestions throughout my work. For the study of Suriname, Sally and Richard Price played the same facilitating role. I thank all three of them here warmly. I also received guidance and suggestions from Svetlana Alpers, Wayne Bodle, Rosemary Brana-Shutte, Miriam de Baar, Rudolf Dekker, Steven Feierman, Andrew Fix, David Fletcher, Gerald Geison, Michael Heyd, Graham Hodges, Leslie K. Johnson, Thomas Kaufmann, Virginia Roehrig Kaufmann, Lisbet Koerner, Nicolas Kopossov, Gloria Leurs, Heidrun Ludwig, Murdo MacLeod, Carlos Martinez del Rio, Gert Oostindie, Katharine Park, Ruth Perry, Benjamin Schmidt, Carmel Schrire, Robert Shell, Dirk J. Struik, Lotte Van de Pol, Margaret Washington, and J. B. C. Wekker. Simone Davis kindly examined some sources for me in the Bancroft Library, University of California, Berkeley.

Suggestions from Patricia Hudson and Froma Zeitlin and an excellent sharp question from Gisela Bock helped improve my conclusion. Throughout Dean Dabrowski located materials for me at libraries at Princeton and elsewhere and provided me with essential secretarial services, for which I am very grateful. At Harvard University Press, Aida Donald and Elizabeth Suttell were supportive of this project from the start. It was a joy to work with my copyeditor at the Press, Maria Ascher, who did much to assist the readability of the book.

Women on the Margins is dedicated to the memory of two dear friends, who exemplified intellectual creativity, adventure, and moral commitment. Rosalie Colie not only introduced me to Glikl bas Judah Leib, but also knew superbly the cultural world in which Maria Sibylla Merian flourished. Peripheral places, rhetorical figures, and motifs became central in her hands. Michel de Certeau transformed the many fields he touched, including the mystical explorations of the seventeenth century. Critical and generous both, loyal to the highest values even while always on the move, Michel de Certeau wrote with discernment and empathy about the native peoples of South America.

Chandler Davis wins the prize for husbandly good-sportsmanship. His Russian smoothed my way to the State Library in Moscow and the Academy of Sciences in Saint Petersburg; he trudged with me through the deep winter snows of the Ville de Québec; he strolled with me through the heat and colors of Paramaribo. His editorial eye insisted, as always, on clarity in my text. Luckier than Glikl, I have been spurred to write not by the melancholy of loneliness but by the intensity of companionship.

ILLUSTRATION CREDITS

Following page 48:

Elias Galli, *Alte Börse und Waage* (ca. 1680). Museum für Hamburgische Geschichte.

Detail of *Plan relevé et très exact de la ville de Metz* (1696). Cliché La Cour d'Or, Musées de Metz.

The piety of Jewish women. From Johannes Leusden, *Philologus Hebraeo-Mixtus* (Utrecht: Francis Halma, 1683). Princeton University Libraries.

Torah binder (1677). Braunschweigisches Landesmuseum, Inv. Nr. R 391.

Torah binder (1711). Hamburgisches Museum für Völkerkunde, Inv. Nr. 17. 6. 1.

Eruv-holder from Alsace (1770). Musée de la Ville de Strasbourg.

Signatures of Cerf Levy. Archives Départementales de la Moselle, 3E3964, no. 115.

Yizkor (memorial) notice for Glikl bas Judah Leib from "Pinkas Kehilat Mets." Library of the Jewish Theological Seminary of America, Ms. 3670, fol. 3A. Photograph by Suzanne Kaufman.

Signatures of Esther Goldschmidt and her family. Archives Départementales de la Moselle, 3E3728, no. 333.

Title page of the *Mayse Bukh* (Basel: Conrad Waldkirch, 1602). By permission of the British Library, 1954 c 42.

Title page of Jacob ben Isaac Ashkenazi, *Tse'enah u-re'enah* (Amsterdam: Immanuel Benviste, [5]408 [1647–1648]). Herzog August Bibliothek, Wolfenbüttel.

Opening page of the autobiography of Glikl bas Judah Leib, copied by her son,

Moses Hamel. Stadt- und Universitätsbibliothek, Frankfurt am Main, Ms. hebr. oct. 2, fol. 2r.

Portrait of Sabbatai Zevi. From Thomas Coenen, *Ydele Verwachtinge der Joden getoont in den persoon von Sabethai Zevi* (Amsterdam: J. van den Bergh, 1669). Library of the Jewish Theological Seminary of America. Photograph by Suzanne Kaufman.

Following page 122:

Marie de l'Incarnation at age forty. From Pierre François-Xavier de Charlevoix, *La Vie de la Mere Marie de l'Incarnation* (Paris: Louis-Antoine Thomelin, 1724). Thomas Fisher Rare Book Library, University of Toronto.

Title page of Teresa of Avila, *Le Chemin de Perfection*, trans. Elisée de Saint Bernard (Paris: Sébastien Huré, 1636). Couvent des Ursulines de Québec.

Soeur Georgina Vanfelson (attributed to) after Joseph Légaré, *Vue du premier monastère des Ursulines de Québec*, ca. 1847. National Gallery of Canada, Ottawa.

Claude Chauchetière, "Narration annuelle de la Mission du Sault depuis la fondation jusqu'à l'an 1686," no. 3: "On travaille aux champs." Archives Départmentales de la Gironde, H Jésuites.

Huron wampum belt, "Quatre Nations huronnes," seventeenth century. Musée de l'Homme, Paris, no. 78.32.61.

Huron wampum belt, Ancienne Lorette, eighteenth century. Collection: McCord Museum of Canadian History, Montréal, M20401.

Attestation of convent boundary by Marie de l'Incarnation, 1645. Archives des Ursulines de Québec, 1/1/1.1.

Letter on birchbark from Amerindian seminarians to M. Sain, receveur général des finances à Bourges, October 1676. Bibliothèque Nationale de France, nouv. acq. fr. 6561; cliché © Bibliothèque Nationale de France, Paris.

Passage from the manuscript of Marie de l'Incarnation's spiritual autobiography, by an unknown female copyist, late seventeenth century. Archives des Ursulines, Trois-Rivières, Québec.

Page from Marie de l'Incarnation and Claude Martin, *La Vie de venerable Mere Marie de l'Incarnation* (Paris: Louis Billaine, 1677). By permission of the Houghton Library, Harvard University.

Western side of the Jesuit map, *Novae Franciae Accurata Delineato*, attributed to François Bressani, 1657. National Archives of Canada, Ottawa, NMC6338.

Eastern side of the *Novae Franciae Accurata Delineatio*, 1657. Bibliothèque Nationale de France; cliché © Bibliothèque Nationale de France, Paris.

Following page 156:

Jacob Marrel, *Floral Cartouche with Insects around a View of Frankfurt,* 1651. Historisches Museum, Frankfurt am Main, Inv. Nr. B2.

Caterpillars, from Jan Jonston, *Historiae Naturalis de Insectis Libri IV* (Frankfurt am Main: Mathias Merian the Younger and Caspar Merian, 1653). By permission of the Houghton Library, Harvard University.

Caterpillar, pupa, and butterfly, from Jan Swammerdam, *Historia Insectorum Generalis, ofte Algemeene Verhandeling van de Bloedeloose Dierkens* (Utrecht: Meinardus van Dreunen, 1669). Princeton University Libraries.

Maria Sibylla Merian, *Der Raupen wunderbare Verwandelung und sonderbare Blumen-nahrung* (Nuremberg: Johann Andreas Graff, 1679), Plates 23, 26. By permission of the Houghton Library, Harvard University.

Map of Suriname by A. Maars, from J. D. Herlein, *Beschryvinge van de Volk-Plantinge Zuriname* (Leuuwarden: Meindert Injema, 1718). By permission of the Houghton Library, Harvard University.

Maria Sibylla Merian, *Metamorphosis Insectorum Surinamensium* (Amsterdam: Maria Sibylla Merian and Gerard Valck, 1705), Plates 11, 5, 60, 18. By permission of the Houghton Library, Harvard University, Typ 732.05.567PF, hand-colored edition.

Waiyana wasp mats. Collection of the Surinaams Museum; photographs courtesy of the Surinaams Museum.

Dirk Valkenburg, *Slave Play in Suriname* (ca. 1707), 58 cm. × 46.5 cm. Den kongelige Maleri- og Skulptursamling, Statens Museum for Kunst, Copenhagen, KMS inv. 376.

Frontispiece, designed by Jan Goeree and engraved by Jacob Delater, to Georg Everard Rumpf [Rumphius], *D'Amboinische Rariteitkamer* (Amsterdam: François Halma, 1705). By permission of the Houghton Library, Harvard University.

Frontispiece, designed and engraved by Frederic Ottens, to Maria Sibylla Merian, *Dissertatio de Generatione et Metamorphosibus Insectorum Surinamensium* (Amsterdam: Johannes Oosterwijk, 1719). By permission of the Houghton Library, Harvard University.

Portrait of Maria Sibylla Merian, based on a drawing by Georg Gsell and engraved by Jacob Houbraken; frontispiece to Merian, *Der Rupsen,* 1717. By permission of the Houghton Library, Harvard University.

INDEX

Abaisas, 174–175

Abatenau, Marie Madeleine, 95–96

Abduction, 135–138, 260, 293n259, 295n268

Abenakis, 86, 88, 95, 107, 283n164, 288n220, 290n232

Abraham ben Hananiah Yagel, 19

Acadie, 81, 84

Acosta, José, 119

Africans, 327n196; belief in rebirth, 186; conversion of, 188; dances of, 190–191, 199, 328n198; instruction by, 187, 197; storytelling of, 196–198; in Surinaine, 172, 174, 175, 176, 184, 211, 212

Aiguillon, Marie-Madeleine de Vignerot, duchesse d', 83, 270n69

Alexander the Great, 54, 55, 56, 59, 194, 252n184, 254n193, 331n224

Algonquins, 85, 86, 92, 96, 100, 106; as converts, 97, 98, 109–110, 114, 115, 124, 126–127, 213; and illness, 88–89; and Iroquois, 90, 91; and Jesuits, 93, 95; language of, 132, 134; as seminarians, 108; and Ursulines, 120, 121, 123, 126, 138; women of, 124, 127, 138

Allouez, Claude-Jean, 94, 118

Alsace, 18, 19

Altona, 35, 223n18; Jews in, 9, 10, 11, 14,

15, 22, 28, 33, 42, 43, 59; publications in, 19, 21

Amboinische Rariteitkamer, D' (Georg Everard Rumpf), 179

Amerindians: in Caribbean, 40, 171, 172, 173, 175, 179; Christian, 97–98, 101, 112–113, 116, 289n228; conversion of, 97, 102, 108, 109, 110, 113–114, 115, 118, 121, 139, 188, 208, 289n229, 317n130; descriptions of, 107; divinities of, 123; division of labor among, 87–88, 114; and Dutch, 175, 176, 184, 185–187; and importance of dreams, 124–126, 128, 288n220; and Labadists, 171; and Lost Tribes of Israel, 41; love of metaphor of, 121; political institutions of, 90; ritual practices of, 195–197; spirit world of, 98; storytelling of, 196–197; of Suriname, 179, 184, 185, 187, 197; and trade, 86, 89–90; and Ursulines, 120–121, 132, 134; and women, 117, 127. *See also entries for individual tribes*

Amsterdam, 10, 166, 190, 209; artists in, 143; Merian family in, 140, 141, 164, 177, 194, 198, 214, 316n127; naturalists in, 144, 156, 167; publishing in, 178, 201; Rijksmuseum in, 328n197; scientific societies in, 313n114; trading in, 12, 14, 173

Frankfurt am Main, 21, 149, 307n72; engraving and publishing in, 42, 157, 165, 207, 215; fairs at, 12; Merian family in, 141, 142, 143, 144, 145, 159, 160, 172, 212; paintings of, 298n15; schools in, 23; trading in, 14

Frederick I of Brandenburg, Prince, 36

Freud, Sigmund, 215, 216, 338n23

Freudchen bas Haim, 12, 22, 42, 62, 225n25, 259n222, 338n18

Friesland, 27, 141, 155, 157, 163, 170, 172, 308n73

Fronde, 85, 91

Fürst, Haim, 33

Fur trade, 85, 86, 89–90, 91, 92, 97, 111

Gabay, Esther, 174

Genesis, 53

Geneviève the Nipissing, 111, 123, 128

Glikl bas Judah Leib, 1, 2, 3, 4, 5–62, 64, 65, 140, 197, 203; autobiography of, 6, 7, 14, 19–62, 100, 101, 199, 207, 215–216, 220n1, 230n53, 239n97, 240n98, 335n2; and centers of learning, 210; and flexibility in work skills, 203, 204–205; on non-Jews, 35, 36; on honor, 32, 34–36, 50, 53; as Jewish woman, 205, 209; marriage of, 208; as mother, 208–209, 225n23; and political power, 209, 210, 211; pregnancies of, 207; and religion, 59–62, 101, 129, 141, 204, 205, 206; and sin, 51–53, 61; as storyteller, 53–60, 253n185; on wealth, 32, 33–34, 37, 50, 53, 56; widowhood of, 30, 31, 32, 34, 46–49, 55, 240n98, 241n101; writing of, 205

Glikl's children, 207, 251n169; Hannah, 25, 225n23; Hendele, 14, 25, 29, 225n22, 241n105; Joseph, 25, 225n25, 233n66; Mattie, 32, 52, 57, 60, 61; Mordecai, 13, 36, 62, 225n25, 226n28, 249n158; Nathan, 13, 35, 44, 49, 225n25; Zanvil, 25, 32, 225n22, 233n66, 240n98; Zipporah, 12, 25, 36, 56, 57, 225n23. See also Freudchen bas Haim; Goldschmidt, Esther; Goldschmidt, Miriam; Hamel, Leib; Hamel, Moses

Glückel of Hameln. See Glikl bas Judah Leib

Goedaert, Johannes: Natural Metamorphosis, 152–153, 156, 182

Goldschmidt, Esther, 209, 222n6, 251n169, 254n194; marriage of, 14, 225n25, 229n48, 240n98; in Metz, 12, 17, 18, 49, 50; and mother, 19, 49, 50, 61, 240n99

Goldschmidt, Haim. See Hamel, Haim

Goldschmidt, Joseph (Joseph Hamel), 11, 45–46, 248n153, 338n19

Goldschmidt, Miriam, 8, 15, 18, 19, 48, 49, 225n25, 229n45, 240n99

Gompertz, Elias (of Cleve), 33, 36, 225n25

Gompertz, Jachet/Agathe. See Jachet bas Elias

Gompertz, Kossman, 225n25

Graff, Dorothea Maria, 145, 155, 334n238; journey to Suriname, 140, 168, 170, 172, 175, 176, 177, 316n127; and Labadists, 164; marriages of, 201, 333n235, 334n236; and mother, 199–200, 208, 214, 238, 322n161, 327n196, 334n236

Graff, Johanna Helena, 155, 316n127, 334n237; birth of, 145; marriage of, 164, 166, 312n109; and mother, 170, 199–200; in Suriname, 200–201, 214, 334n236

Graff, Johann Andreas, 143, 144–145, 154, 157, 160, 207–208; death of, 178, 199; divorce from Maria Sybilla Merian, 82, 83, 141, 161, 166, 309n81; travels of, 143

Grandier, Urbain, 75

Grands Voyages (Théodore de Bry), 142, 170

Gruel, Charles, 81

Gsell, Dorothea Maria. See Graff, Dorothea Maria

Gsell, Georg, 201, 333n235, 334n238

Guinea, 172, 185, 196

Guyana, 174

Guyart, Claude, 66, 68, 71, 72, 83, 89, 134, 262n12, 293n259

Guyart, Marie. See Marie de l'Incarnation

Halevi, Asher, 21; Book of Remembrances, 19

Leipzig, 12, 13, 26, 226n31

Le Jeune, Paul (Echom), 78, 80, 95, 97, 107, 117, 118, 120, 136, 288n220

Lev Tov (Isaac ben Eliakum), 23

Levy, Hendele/Anne (Glikl's stepdaughter), 25, 62, 229n48, 251n168, 258n220

Levy, Hirsch/Cerf, 29, 38, 48, 229n45, 251n168, 258n220; bankruptcy of, 30, 31, 49–50, 50, 229n46, 240n99; marriage of, 9, 15, 16, 18, 57, 209, 241n101; and son, 36, 62

Levy, Raphaël, 17

Levy, Samuel, 18, 19, 25, 36, 62, 228n43, 229n45, 235n77, 240n99

Liebmann, Jost. *See* Berlin, Judah

Ligon, Richard, 186

Lilith, 246n141

Linnaeus, Carolus, 154, 180, 198, 213–214, 332n225, 337n13

Locke, John, 164–165

London, 12, 42, 62, 143, 247n146, 259n222

Lorraine, duchy of, 18–19, 36, 44

Lost Tribes of Israel, 41, 247n144

Loudun, Ursuline convent of, 75

Louisa Ulrika, Queen (Sweden), 214

Louise the Algonquin, 110, 126

Louis XIII, 80, 82, 266n46

Louis XIV, 16, 17, 18, 28, 44, 86, 92, 113, 130

Loyola, Ignatius, 6, 76

Lüneburg, 40

Luther, 28

Lutherans, 16, 28, 59, 157, 160

Machado, Imanuël, 174

Malpighi, Marcello, 152, 162

Marcgraf, Georg, 165, 168, 179, 315n122, 322n164, 332n225

Marcus, Moses the Elder. *See* Hamburger, Mordecai

Marcus, Moses the Younger, 62, 246n141, 258n222

Marie de l'Incarnation, 1, 2, 3, 4, 63–139, 141, 142, 159, 169, 189, 203; on Amerindian customs, 107–108, 197; and Amerindian women, 117, 191, 193, 194, 211; ancestors of, 261n6; and centers of learning, 210; and chastity, 104–105; and communication, 68, 130; compared with Jesuits, 116–121; confession of, 133, 164; death of, 212; and feminism, 209, 282n160; and flexibility in work skills, 203, 204–205; letters of, 99, 103, 191, 198, 199, 213, 279n137; marriage of, 208; and mortification, 68, 69–70, 71, 75, 102, 104, 131–132, 133, 263n19; and political power, 209–210, 211; pregnancies of, 207; reading of, 68; relations with son, 103, 128–129, 206, 208, 280n150; *Sacred History*, 99, 106; and "savage" girls, 82, 92, 93, 95, 108, 113, 116, 121, 132, 133, 274n86; on "savages," 78, 80, 81, 88, 89, 92, 98, 115–116, 117, 119; and sin, 68, 70, 76, 98, 125, 131; spiritual autobiography of, 99, 100, 102–103, 107, 129, 199, 207, 213, 259n1, 268n54; as storyteller, 134; teaching of, 98, 206, 211; and vow of chastity, 71; on women and theology, 105–106; writing of, 68, 69, 76, 77, 83, 98–107, 128, 129, 133, 139, 191, 205, 268n53, 279n137

Marie de Saint Joseph, 74, 82, 83, 95, 97, 101, 115, 120, 121, 133

Marrel, Jacob, 142, 143, 144, 145, 146, 148, 157, 204, 298n15, 307n69

Marrel, Sara, 145, 157

Marriage, 207–208; age at, 11, 207, 224n20; Amerindian, 136; Amerindian/French, 113, 114, 284n188; Christian/Christian, 115; Christian vs. Amerindian, 114–115; and dowries, 44, 49, 241n108, 265n37, 276n108; duties of, 105, 160; feigned, 81–82; Labadist, 160–161; Lutheran, 160; negotiating, 43–44

Martin, Claude (husband of Marie de l'Incarnation), 65, 66

Martin, Claude (son of Marie de l'Incarnation), 63–64, 66, 69, 76, 81, 100; additions to mother's *Vie*, 134–135, 241, 243–245, 281n153, 290n238, 291n240, 292nn247–249; biography of, 154,